West of Wichita

WEST OF

Settling the High Plains of Kansas,

WICHITA

1865–1890

Craig Miner

University Press of Kansas

*For those things from thee I have
    so loved—
For the sky, the wind, the open road
    and freedom.
And for thy native son
My father
Stanley C. Miner
The boy and the man.*

Published by the University Press of Kansas (Lawrence,
Kansas 66045), which was organized by the Kansas
Board of Regents and is operated and funded by Emporia
State University, Fort Hays State University, Kansas State
University, Pittsburg State University, the University of
Kansas, and Wichita State University

Photograph on p. 195 courtesy Wichita–Sedgwick County
Historical Museum Association. All other photographs
courtesy Kansas State Historical Society; photograph on
p. 170 used by special permission of Dorothy Dresher
Richards, Hays, Kansas
Material from the Norton family diaries used by
permission of Henry L. Norton, Wichita, Kansas

Library of Congress Cataloging in Publication Data
Miner, Craig, 1944–
    West of Wichita.
    Bibliography: P.
    Includes index.
    1. Kansas—History. 2. Frontier and pioneer life—
Kansas. I. Title.
F686.M56   1986   978.1′031   85-26013
ISBN 0-7006-0286-0
Printed in the United States of America
10   9   8   7   6   5   4

Contents

Preface

In this space, before roman numerals change to arabic and before the author begins hiding within a narrative woven from archival sources, I wish to acknowledge some personal facts about the writing of *West of Wichita.*

The initial and strongest continuing motivation for writing this book came not from the documents but from my strong sense of the High Plains of Kansas as a special and powerful region, a sense that has been part of my consciousness since childhood. It may be in my blood. My great-grandfather was among the most optimistic of the 1880s western Kansas boomers: mayor of Ness City, founder of the town of Harold in the beautiful Pawnee Valley, and a director of the Ness City and Sidney Street Railway Company. But the generation I knew best was ambivalent about the place. My grandmother told me as we sat in her Ness City house that still smelled of dust from the 1930s agricultural readjustment that she was happy Great-Grandpa hadn't gone any farther west: it was worse there. But for a year the two-year-old that was me had lived in that western country, and my father's family connections and continued interests there guaranteed my regular return, the car journeys he and I took together replete with stories of his childhood. The result was an unintentional but powerful boost in my awareness of the impact places could have on people. I sensed that the blue hills seen always on a limitless horizon to the west of Ness City had had as important an effect on my father's character and outlook as they had had on his father's or his grandfather's and that the lack of everyday proximity would not keep the blue hills from also swaying me.

What I experienced in western Kansas—and shared with many others whose lives have touched the region and been touched by it since the first settlers moved west of Salina in 1865— was what historians have described as a cultural landscape. A special combination grounded in history as well as geography sent an ever more developed and more subtle message to people about nature and about themselves.

The historical element came eventually to interest me most. My professional training in western history came first from William Unrau (now my colleague at Wichita State), who impressively combined the detailed, comprehensive primary research of James Malin, whom he admired, with the communication skills of his own mentor, Robert Athearn. Malin, Athearn, and Unrau gave me a strong sense of regional history's academic respectability and importance. Later I was an Athearn student myself, a situation that accounted initially for my method of titling chapters and encouraged my appreciation of the virtues of scholarly books with basic narrative form and attention to literary and aesthetic values. The first thing we were instructed to read in Athearn's research seminar was Walter Webb's essay "History as High Adventure."

West of Wichita tries to avoid both environmental and cultural determinism and intends to contribute to our understanding of how a person and a physical landscape interacted during a specific historical period. I learned that western Kansas in the nineteenth century existed, as it always had for me, partly as a feature of the planet and partly in the psyches of those who saw it or lived within it. To study it was to study them and, to a degree, myself. Whatever the effect of the place on individuals—and, as will be seen, it varied widely—it was inevitably deep and lasting. Therefore, it seemed to me clearly worthy of investigation.

In the search for raw materials for this volume, I contracted innumerable personal obligations, only a few of which I can acknowledge. Foremost, the Kansas State Historical Society must be mentioned as one of the real historical treasure-troves of the nation, with a staff whose skill and helpfulness match the worth of its collections. That institution began collecting diaries and letters from western Kansas pioneers and subscribing to western Kansas newspapers in the 1870s, the time of the initial thrust into the region. The society's resources for a study such as this are thus incomparably rich. My special thanks, too, to the Interlibrary Loan Service at Wichita State University and to the Kansas Heritage Center at Dodge City, both of which loaned me many western Kansas newspapers on microfilm. The Office of Research and Sponsored Programs at Wichita State University provided financial support for travel, and the university reduced my teaching load for a year to advance this work. David Rohr of Wichita took several bicycle rides through the region with me; his keen mind and interest in history gave me both ideas and encouragement. Jim Forsythe and Leo Oliva of Fort Hays State University on several occasions shared with me their expertise, and Sally Price of Wichita combined forces with my mother, Marybel, to provide loyal and understanding babysitting when I had to pretend I was on sabbatical from ordinary daily life. I would like especially to acknowledge the role of my editors at the University Press of Kansas. They have been important to the development of all aspects of the manuscript.

Most contemporary historians, myself included, would hesitate to go so far as Walter Webb in advocating as a research tool that personal experience imitate that of the historical figures being interpreted. Still, I have found days in a tent in western Kansas to be useful preparation for choosing materials, and having a family has been relevant in turning my research attention to aspects of everyday pioneer life to which I might have otherwise given short shrift. My acquaintance with numerous residents of western Kansas was among the elements that initially suggested there might be a cultural as well as a physical reason for thinking of western Kansas as a region.

Most prefaces end with a tribute to the author's spouse, and there is a reason for that. Research and writing take not only time but emotional energy in great chunks. Except in the rare case of superpeople, something else must suffer, and it is often household and family obligations. Professors' wives are justly renowned for tolerating this (some understandably leave in disgust and thus forgo the honor of being acknowledged in prefaces), and mine has been particularly sensitive and supportive throughout. I hope my thanks to her here will suffice until she is better rewarded.

Introduction

On Regional History

The history of the American West as a distinct field of study did not get under way until Frederick Jackson Turner's famous 1893 interpretive address, "The Significance of the Frontier in American History." Despite much outstanding scholarship since, it has quite recently been regarded as "decerebrate" by some academic critics. Understandably, the study of regions within the West, and particularly of subregions within a single state, has had an even more difficult time in garnering academic respectability.

There have, of course, been serious scholarly studies of both regions and subregions of the West. Turner himself wrote with subtlety for a large public about the significance of regions in American history. Walter Prescott Webb's *The Great Plains,* controversial as it remains, is accepted by most historians as a classic not only of western, but of American, history. Regional western studies by such scholars as Howard Lamar, Leonard Arrington, Duane Smith, Henry Nash Smith, Eugene Hollen, David Emmons, D. W. Meinig, Frederick Luebke, and Earl Pomeroy have commanded serious attention in the profession as well as wide interest among the reading public. There are good examples also of awareness of the importance of studying intrastate regions unified by geography, climate and historical experience. For western Kansas, an intrastate region especially definite in appearance, climate, and history, there have been outstanding fragments of serious, interpretive history over the years, written by such scholars as James Malin, George Anderson, Paul Gates, Robert Dykstra, Minnie Millbrook, Leslie Decker, James Forsythe, and Leo Oliva.

Still, these accomplishments have not been enough to do away altogether with the disparagement of state and local history. Over the years publication of thousands of quick commercial county histories, township and village studies, and autobiographies short on research and long on genealogy and uninformed local pride have left their mark. As historian Jerome Steffen aptly put it, writing about regions within western America has until recently been regarded by many scholars as a quaint retreat from the mainstream of American life, the ultimate example of "local-color" antiquarianism.

There are several reasons for this. Foremost is that it takes a large number of outstanding academic studies of a region to overcome the sense that a narrow focus can yield only parochial truths of use to the Chamber of Commerce. Some combinations of limited time and geography—medieval European provinces, colonial

New England, the American South, for example—have achieved respectability through the attention of many gifted interpreters; others have not. "One can understand," Steffen wrote, "the American tendency to assume that an agricultural history of a French province is sophisticated but that a similar study of a county in rural Kansas might be considered parochial."[1]

Second, there has been at work in the historical profession a social science paradigm that encourages the creation of models of broad application and eschews the complications that careful regional studies present. As one analyst of the historiography of regional studies recently pointed out, the idea that there may be something sufficiently unusual about a single region to merit detailed study on its own rather than as a case affronts the "cosmopolitan values" of a professional culture that generally holds geographic and social mobility in high regard and devalues attachment to place.[2]

Third, narrowing the geographic focus and limiting the time frame of academic studies tend to create an awareness of the importance of underlying patterns of everyday life as lived by ordinary people, located there and then. Fernand Braudel called it "a rich zone, like a layer covering the earth" and found that before he could write his history of the development of capitalism he needed to devote an entire volume to everyday life.[3] Interestingly, it is this volume, *The Structures of Everyday Life: The Limits of the Possible,* that has received the most attention of Braudel's three volumes. But prior to the quite recent fascination with the historical study of everyday life and the development of methodologies to deal with it in a sophisticated way, its prominence in regional studies was another difficulty in fitting this kind of research into the broader mission of academic history.

There is now considerable evidence that these roadblocks to the acceptance of regional studies of the West are disappearing and that the current increase in sophisticated examinations of regions and of everyday life within them marks the beginning of a trend. One only hopes that this increased attention from professional scholars will enrich understanding without alienating the relatively broad audience that regional history of all qualities has long enjoyed.

Careful regional accounts are able to counter the "mythological" regional images that were born in the perceptions of the pioneers themselves and have persisted precisely because professional historicans have shied away from the field. The most brilliant student of the West as myth, Henry Nash Smith, was well aware of the problem. In his prize-winning book *Virgin Land: The American West as Symbol and Myth,* Smith established the power of myths such as the passage to India, the safety valve, and the garden of the world to influence behavior. In a less-well-known article, however, entitled "The West as an Image of the American Past," Nash suggested that the pioneer stereotype was a shallow basis for a large piece of American identity. Among other things, he argued, it left senses of evil and of failure out of the American historical consciousness.[4]

It is just this shortcoming of the stereotype that detailed narrative regional history—concentrating as it can upon the experiences of individual communities, colonies, and even families—best corrects. As Gilbert Fite put it, at least as many nightmares as daydreams are to be found when analysis reaches the everyday lives of individuals. "There was a huge gulf between imagination and achievement, hope and actuality. Thousands of people helped to conquer the frontier, but thousands more were conquered by it."[5]

Who were these people? What were the conditions of their success or failure? What exactly constituted the contrast between image and reality within a certain "behavior setting," as a social scientist might put it?[6] To answer such questions adequately requires the selection of an area limited both spatially and temporally. In this process, people can be understood, with a certain set of ideas, moving into a certain area, during a time period that is sufficiently limited to show change without encompassing modifications so fundamental as to blur the specifics beyond recognition.

The history of a region must have an organization of material both specific and relevant; it is frequently quite different from the organization that would best serve a study of national trends in the same period. We tell our students that all presentations of history are, to some degree, simplifications for pedagogic purposes, but we may not sufficiently realize the extent of this. For example, the 1873 depression was a bona fide national event and did affect railroad building and cattle prices in western Kansas. The pre-Populist and Populist movements, of course, can almost be said to have put Kansas local history in the national spotlight. However, the 1874 grasshopper invasion was not a universal phenomenon, even on the Great Plains, and the 1880 drought affected eastern Kansas much less severely than western Kansas. Yet the facts require that both these events be given prominence in any presentation of the history of the western half of the state. The years from 1865 to 1877, called by historians the era of

Reconstruction nationally and emphasized because of significant changes in race relations, make little sense as an organizational unit for Kansas history. For Wichita, the years between the arrival of its first railroad in 1872 and the end of its cattle trade due to changed state quarantine regulations in 1876, mark a recognizable historical era that differs significantly from the same period in national history. Similarly, the history of western Kansas finds its natural periodization in Indian treaties, railroad decisions, natural disasters, weather patterns, and technological and industrial panaceas that are unique, at least in their timing. One cannot successfully transfer to local history organizational schemes suitable for a broad view. They must be derived, as must the explanation and interpretation, from facts about actual life—in a particular place, at a specific time.

For example, one of the most fascinating general themes of western Kansas in the years 1865 to 1890 is the recurring cycle of hope and despair that characterized the region's experimental period. But to understand the dialectic dance of panacea and disaster that dominated western Kansas during that quarter-century, one needs specialized historical periodization. The three periods that work best are 1865 to 1874, 1875 to 1880, and 1881 to 1890. Each began with the emergence of new technology and ended with disasters, usually natural. None of the periods corresponds exactly to the divisions used in textbooks to cover national events during Reconstruction and the Gilded Age.

The assumption that regional history should be somehow simpler, more easily comprehended than national and international syntheses is belied by research into the sources. Historians have increasingly found that life studied in small regions is more complicated and varied, even within a limited time and place, than any of us might imagine. Historian and geographer Andrew Clark noted that within a region as seemingly narrow as the Great Plains, "transformation of experience into images of perception gave results as diverse as the environments themselves."[7] Howard Lamar concluded there were at least three definable regions within the Dakotas, with noticeably different histories.[8] Donald Meinig, in his outstanding study of Texas, found the environment too varied and changes in the way it interacted with culture over time too great to offer conclusive statements about a single homogeneous Texas character or to talk about "the Texas experience," much less "the national experience."[9] In our present state of knowledge about the West, detailed research is, for some years, likely to focus our attention on complexities and differences before another grand western synthesis emerges. And when it does, the "big-picture" people will always be tested by the findings of regional specialists, dragging their nets deeper rather than casting them wider.

Andrew Clark has warned against the tendency to oversimplify regional history by always connecting regions with a larger whole rather than examining them occasionally on their own terms; this can distort not only the regional history but national history as well. "What is important," Clark wrote, "is that attempts to characterize the greater wholes necessarily gloss over individual peculiarities, and clearly there are attributes of those larger wholes which are not very apt in relation to many parts of the Great Plains, taken alone." Nor is that the end of it: "The most serious danger of all is that what is absorbed through the partial model into the general image often feeds back into our partial models and turns up in the creation of images where it is entirely inappropriate."[10]

To argue thus is not to claim that western regions are unique in some overriding sense: the influences of cultural baggage, outside capital, and outside technology in a place and time like western Kansas in the late nineteenth century are overwhelming. But in fleeing the danger of geographic determinism, one must not embrace an equally simplistic cultural determinism, which reproduces the illusion the settlers themselves cherished—that the natural environment was almost beside the point. That has been the tendency of historians reacting to the exaggeration of, for example, Webb. It is, however, an interpretive approach that, taken singly, is highly inappropriate to the factual content of *West of Wichita*.

This book argues that the mix of culture and geography in western Kansas was not typical: there were in the late nineteenth century significant regional differences in the effects of technology, economics, and culture on individuals and on communities, differences due largely to regional differences in topography and climate. Western Kansas was a place not amenable to manipulation, even when approached with the full panoply of the nineteenth century's "instant civilizers": railroads, forts, hybrid crops, irrigation technology, scientific method, bank loans, real-estate jobbers, sugar mills, and canned fruit.

Western Kansas was one of the most arid areas to which it was seriously contemplated that nineteenth-century agricultural civilization might be imported whole. The test was severe and the stakes of pioneering particularly clearly revealed there in the interaction of men, machines, climate, and landscape. Thanks to the emotion and respect for Western Kansas engendered in its pioneers by the region's capacity to resist their efforts, to remain its frustrating and glorious self, sources for creating this history are as dramatic as the physical place. People loved or hated it, often some of both, and when they wrote of it, often in newspaper reminiscences that were their only published compositions, the accounts came alive with familiarity, emotion, description. Whatever their opinions of having decided to leave more familiar climes for western Kansas, and however great their disappointments in having failed to achieve their economic goals, in hundreds of surviving memoirs people visualized and recalled the region as central to their lives. That was a gift of the heart. It is also the best sort of raw material for regional history.

The goal of this book is to provide a study of both fact and illusion in a limited region during a relatively short period of time. It is organized inductively, in response to primary sources, rather than deductively, according to a preconceived model. I hope that the resulting story, while no more "total history" than any attempt to reconstruct from surviving fragments, is one that the participants would recognize, because in it loom large the same issues in the same proportions that appeared in their day. At best it will respond well to the criticism of Laurence Veysey, who noted that the "cult of the consensus" has distorted our view of the importance of regional differences in the nineteenth century, "cloaking crucial distinctions between men and between decades behind a bland facade of sameness." What is needed, Veysey said, is "a line of regional distinction which, besides being neither too thick or too thin, will take its colors more from the social landscape and less from the historian's paint box."[11]

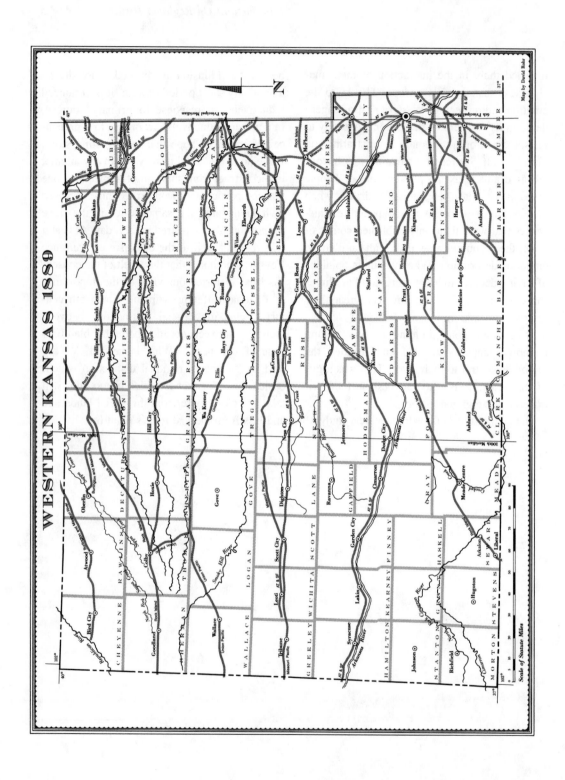

WESTERN KANSAS 1889

Map by David Rohr

Chapter One

The Blue Hills

here are two places called Kansas. One is a well-watered pastoral haven lying between forested hills and tallgrass prairie. The other is an area of extremes, the true nature of which is still mysterious after more than a century of settlement by an advanced industrial civilization. The haven, and most of the population of Kansas, is in the east; the mystery, and most of the emotion about Kansas, is, and has been, in the west.

Most people living in Kansas, and many who have driven through it from east to west, could define where western Kansas begins: at old Highway 81, a short distance west of the tallgrass Flint Hills prairie. It is marked south to north on the east by the cities of Wichita, Salina, and Concordia. The sixth principal meridian, running through west Wichita, is the point where the range numbers in the Kansas survey begin being followed by a W rather than an E, and changes in the altitude, the physical landscape, the climate, culture and perceptions, and the history of settlement at just that point confirm its appropriateness as a regional divider. It is at just that line that Kansas straddles two of the United States' five major physiographic provinces as defined by geographers: the central lowlands east of Wichita and the Great Plains to the west.[1]

This line has consistently marked the onset of climate-related emergencies, from the 1874 grasshopper devastation, to the 1880 drought, to the 1930s' dust bowl.[2] It is the line where tall grass gives way to short-grass prairie; it is where naturally occurring trees cease growing; it is the boundary between humid and subhumid to semiarid sections of Kansas; it is the point where population densities drop drastically and the size of congressional districts increases dramatically.[3] For all these reasons, it is no wonder that in a recent survey of "Popular Regions of North America," based upon "spatial entities recognized as such by the people who live in or near them," the perceptual map of Kansas was divided just where the physical and historical one would be—on a north-south line running through Wichita.[4] There is no question that west of Wichita one encounters a new kind of country.

Western Kansas so defined encompasses 61 of the state's 105 counties and about 60 percent of its 81,787 square miles. Within it are five physiographic subregions. The largest, the High Plains region, contains over half its area on the west, while the Wellington Plain region merely catches the southeast corner. Between the High Plains and the Flint Hills region to the east of Wichita lie three transitional zones—the Smoky Hills on the north, the Great Bend

Prairie in the center, and the Red Hills in Barber and Comanche counties on the south.[5]

Through the years some have complained that popular understanding about eastern and western Kansas is not logical. In 1888, a man working at a definition for the "New Western Kansas" found it absurd that the representative from Dickinson County (just east of the Wichita line) should say he was from western Kansas, or that Wichita, which barely escaped being in the eastern third of the state, should so often be called a western Kansas town. He thought it would be better to define western Kansas as the western third of the state, beginning at about the one hundredth meridian. The problem was, as he admitted, few Kansans thought of it that way.[6] To convince a Kansan that Hays, Larned, and Ellsworth are not western Kansas towns would be difficult because geographic, climatological, and historical factors combine to define true regions for only two areas: eastern and western Kansas. Central Kansas, not to mention south-central Kansas, exists mostly in the minds of map makers, census takers, and marketers of television news.

Some of the natural signs of arriving in western Kansas that struck the first settlers are no longer much in evidence. The buffalo and antelope whose herds were focused in the region have disappeared; much of the open buffalo-grass prairie has been plowed and planted to resemble at a glance similar fields to the east; and farmers and townspeople, aided by numerous government programs to standardize regions, have planted groves of trees where none existed before. The absence of running, much less navigable, rivers, is, however, more striking to us in the age of irrigation and a lowered water table than it was to the

pioneers. There appear, beginning just west of Salina, land forms that are identifiably western or southwestern: cliffs and buttes, sometimes mesas. And there are signs among the residents of the natural world. One begins, for example, to see red-winged blackbirds and magpies shortly after leaving Wichita in the direction of Colorado. Not too deep into the region yucca and cacti are glimpsed, first sometimes, then regularly. Altitude and aridity mean the heat in summer is drier, a breeze or shade more refreshing, the falling of night a greater contrast, colors at twilight more intense.

There are signals too in the human landscape. Country replaces rock and easy-listening music on the car radio; there are more pickup trucks; and in some places, where there existed the limestones treasured by settlers the six-hundred-pound fence posts that gave the stone its popular name, post rock, can yet be seen.[7] Most noticeable of these human clues is the way natural vistas break through the thinner layer of industrial intervention. This is not so noticeable along I-70, which follows the fertilizing line of the first western Kansas railroad and where the tourist notices a lack of metropolitan areas but not an obvious gap in the string of well-kept Kansas towns. But a few miles away from this strip, it becomes evident that the region possesses, as Walter Webb said of the entire Great Plains, a kind of "oasis civilization."[8] It is as though one were passing through the outer edge of a galaxy, where the stars thin and, despite familiar benchmarks, one senses the proximity of something powerful and unknown.

Urban development in current western Kansas mirrors not only the place but its early settlement history. The locations of the major towns are along east-west ribbons following river valleys that were the original immigration and rail routes into the region. Major highways were superimposed upon these traditional routes, and, as has always been the case, the north-south transportation avenues in the west are relatively poor. There is no north-south, four-lane highway, much less interstate, between I-35, running parallel to Highway 81 at the eastern boundary of western Kansas, and I-25, connecting Denver with Cheyenne. The region remains, as it had become in the 1870s, divided into transportation- and trade-route-related districts. The old Kansas Pacific region, the Santa Fe region, the Rock Island region, and the far north region (which, because of north-south spur lines and lack of an east-west railroad trunk, was and is tied as much to Nebraska as to the rest of Kansas) are still readily identifiable by their economic and social interchanges and loyalties. In the 1880s it was common for residents of Hays City to confess that they had been to Denver but never to Plainville, twenty-three miles north. The automobile and the tendency of twentieth-century western Kansans to follow their high school sports teams and farm auctions all over the region have much decreased the impact of transportation access on perception among residents. It does, however, affect intraregional trade and is as significant as ever to travelers, who still experience western Kansas as a place to cross on the way somewhere else.

Some strictly twentieth-century phenomena have affected western Kansas towns (oil exploration and feed lots come to mind), but it is striking how important the patterns of settlement history remain. Most larger towns in western Kansas are located along the Solomon and Republican Rivers in the north; the Smoky Hill and Pawnee Rivers and Walnut Creek in the center; and the Arkansas and Cimarron Rivers in the south. These are towns, not cities. The largest regional centers—Hays City, Great Bend, Dodge City, Garden City—are all on the two original rail routes, the Kansas Pacific and the Santa Fe. They range now between 15,000 and 20,000 in population. The Rock Island towns (Pratt and Liberal, for example) got a later start, too close to the crash of the 1890s, and remain smaller, with populations around 10,000. A common current size for towns that did not share in the initial nineteenth-century trunk-line building is 2,000 to 4,000, no matter what their hopes or regional fame once were. Osborne, Stockton, and Phillipsburg fall into this class, as do Ness City, Dighton, and Scott City. Some places with a railroad and great hopes found that there was no need for two regional centers. Given their nineteenth-century prominence, it is surprising to find Larned with a current population of about 5,000 and WaKeeney, Wallace, and Ellis with about half that.

The urban projectors in nineteenth-century western Kansas did not misjudge the important role of towns in developing the region, nor did they miss the appropriate locations or underestimate what the growth of the area would mean to its towns. What they did severely misinterpret was the potential extent of that regional growth. David Emmons in his study of Plains boomer literature commented on an 1883 prediction that Garden City in 1983 would have a population of one hundred thousand and be the agricultural metropolis of southwest Kansas. Though Garden City missed the population goal by a great deal, Emmons noted that the publicist was right about one thing: "The town did become the agricultural metropolis of southwestern Kansas—and northwestern as well."[9]

Any length of stay in western Kansas brings one's attention to the effects of the two dominant natural characteristics of the region: altitude and semiaridity. Mount Sunflower in Wallace County on the western border is the state's highest point at 4,039 feet, while the altitude of the Kansas River near the Missouri line is about 600 feet. The rise from east to west is a regular eight feet per mile. The increased altitude combined with transparent skies and low population density make sunsets and nights revelations to a city dweller, even one from eastern Kansas. In the country, one can see 6.5-magnitude astronomical objects with the unaided eye, view the Milky Way as a bright band resolved into faint individual stars, and notice our sister galaxy Andromeda as a glowing orb the size of the full moon. This constant intrusion of elements of the atmosphere and beyond into the cycle of residents' living must have affected the settlers' outlook, bringing about, according to their varied experiences and emotional make-up, oversized hopes or magnified fears. In any case, it was not the ideal setting for cold logic.

In all farming regions, climate is of central importance. In western Kansas the climate has several features that lead to confusion, inappropriate strategies, false starts, and painful economic cycles. The rainfall is, over the long term, marginal for commercial agriculture at the low grain prices and high machinery prices that have often prevailed over the past one hundred years; the temperature range through the year can be extreme; and, most important,

both factors vary widely intraregionally and over time.

Climate over the Great Plains is formed by a volatile interaction of polar and southern air masses. Usually the prevailing summer winds bring dry air from Mexico, but moist air from the Gulf can sometimes be blown in, over a short or a long period, making the rainfall figures look subtropical or causing flooding in the midst of a drought.[10] Rainfall can vary enough in a given year in places forty miles apart to make a good crop in one of them and a complete failure in the other. When storm clouds build, one can often see the exact extent of the rain. It is common to hear people in western Kansas say, "It rained south of town last night," meaning that the vital shower covered only a few square miles. In some years rainfall is adequate and timed well for winter wheat. Sometimes it is adequate but timed for summer crops such as corn and milo. At other times the yearly fall is barely enough to sustain yucca. Plotting actual rainfall patterns over a graph of the so-called "normal" values is something Kansas newspapers often do as a New Year's humor piece.

Temperature is affected by the same climatological patterns. On a late December day in 1984, Wichita had a high of 67 degrees, matching the all-time record for that day. Just a year earlier on the same date, the all-time date low of 9 degrees below zero was set. The settler regularly experienced summer highs of 110 degrees and found winters varying from the mild ones of the early seventies, when cattle needed no winter forage, to the blizzards of 1886, when there was snow cover for months combined with temperatures of 20 below, and forty-mile-per-hour straight winds. It was little comfort that some Great Plains locations were worse: Glendive, Montana, in 1893 had a summer high of 117 degrees and a winter low of 47 degrees below zero—a 164-degree range.[11]

Marginality, extremes, and variability all make it difficult for a civilization to thrive when it is based on commercial values that depend on predictability and planning. Settlers of the 1870s and 1880s not only did not have records of the long-term patterns of the western Kansas climate but were encouraged by wet, mild years to image that settlement itself might be changing the climate or that modern technology was sufficient to allow agricultural prosperity despite the climate. While the experience prior to 1890 covered by this book did not lay entirely to rest the idea of some kind of technological fix, it was a time of learning the real nature of the place. From 1865 to 1890, residents concluded that climate could not be ignored and would not fundamentally change and that modern civilization as they had known it farther east could not simply be superimposed on the new region.

That these seemingly simple conclusions took so long to arrive at, and that so much rich history turns exactly on the dynamics between humankind and environment in the learning, were due to the transitional nature of western Kansas, located as it was just on the border between the old and new kinds of agricultural frontier, both physically and in time of initial settlement. It was exactly in the center of the United States, neither northern nor southern, neither eastern nor western, neither predictably hot nor cold, wet nor dry. Colorado was more

obviously arid, Nebraska and the Dakotas were predictably colder in winter, Oklahoma was settled later, Texas was predictably warmer, places farther west were more consistently semiarid. It can be argued that western Kansas was *the* most frustrating representative of the general frustration of agricultural civilization in the Great Plains. "In a Desert," C. Warren Thornwaite wrote of the Great Plains, "you know what to expect of the climate and plan accordingly. The same is true of the humid regions. Men have been badly fooled by the semiarid regions."[12]

Explorers' earliest descriptions of the western Kansas region suggested that it was truly an American desert best left to the nomadic Indians. However, as confidence grew in the great rush to the West following the Civil War, descriptive accounts began to take on ambiguity that left room for hope and set up a challenge. An Atchison, Topeka & Santa Fe Railroad pamphlet published in the wake of the drought and grasshopper troubles of the mid-1870s stated that while the idea of the Great American Desert was a "geographical bugaboo," western Kansas was nevertheless an "agricultural puzzle." "We have no desire to mislead immigrants. Our only point is that the western belt may turn out better than Kansans are now disposed to think."[13]

Sometimes, perception that western Kansas was an unusual place led to descriptions marked by unbounded optimism. This was particularly true when viewers concentrated on the delights of simply living there rather than the difficulties of making a living there. Josiah Copley, surveying a railroad route across western Kansas in 1867, called it "as unique as it is stupendous."[14] A man arriving at Russell, Kansas, from Chicago in 1877 reported that "the life currents are quicker and stronger, the air lighter and clearer, the vision has greater range, thought and action get new impulse and one feels one's self the gainer of new power in the upward march toward the blue mountains." On the divide between the Smoky Hill and Saline Rivers, this visitor felt "an emotional transport" he attributed to the climate and the "glorious, bewildering landscapes."[15] Wrote L. D. Burch, who visited the region first in 1878: "The soul keeps pace with the wonderful range of vision and is touched by a sweet sense of the infinite."[16] "Old Cactus," after a trip to the wild gorges of Clark County in 1877, returned to Dodge City to say that "to describe the surface and scenery of this part of Kansas . . . so that it can be appreciated by those who have never seen a prairie country, would be probably quite impossible; and scarcely less difficult is it to describe it to one who has only seen the flat, low, swampy, ague and peculiar fever-generating prairie regions of some parts of Illinois and Indiana."[17] One man remembered strongly all his life his father's exhilaration in that western Kansas country: "The landscape of those pristine plains was a power so tremendous that no wholly well man could escape its enchantment."[18]

Alongside that breezy, bracing feeling, though, there was the sense of mystery not necessarily benign. A centennial celebration orator at Osborne in the Solomon River Valley noticed it in his 1876 address to settlers there. While confident that the appearance of the place would soon change radically, he observed that at least now it gave the onlooker a strong sense of the mysterious. Many with whom he

had spoken, he said, shared his impression of "antiquity and desertion." It was as though someone had already come and gone, as though the land was laughing softly at the new attempt. "The whole surroundings make the traveler feel that the country had been abandoned a thousand years ago, and that all traces of an inhabitation had faded away."[19] A similar note was struck by William Dixon, who crossed western Kansas by stage at the close of the Civil War. "In these uplands," Dixon concluded, "nature is lord and king. . . . The prairie is not man's home," Dixon wrote, and his best efforts there would fade into universal nature "like autumn flowers or the track of a ship at sea."[20] A member of a colony arriving in Osborne County from Iowa in the 1870s had a fear of becoming lost in a land without landmarks: "A plowed furrow looked like a great unnatural thing."[21]

One of the most mysterious features eliciting comment from early settlers was the mirage that happened regularly in the first years and then faded as the land was plowed, as though giving way to a flood of the rational. At sunrise and at sunset especially, mirages would occur, and the first to spot them would rush to share the news with others. Wild horses in the distance would suddenly seem forty feet high, ready to carry giants. A farm house miles away would shoot up to three times its normal size. "The ground would rise steeply in some places and fall away sharply in others, hills would spring up out of nothing" during the few minutes that the invaders were "granted the rare privilege of beholding this manifestation."[22]

Perhaps the real message of the mirage to its viewers was missed. Their vision was in fact far and their hopes large. C. M. Garrison of Wichita, visiting several booming though small western Kansas towns in 1886, said that Scott City looked like the Topeka of 1860 and Garden City like the Wichita of 1870.[23] He was only expressing the certainty held through twenty-five years of inconclusive struggle with nature in western Kansas that eventually things would proceed as they had at other times and in other places. A reporter in Dodge City stated during the height of the boom in 1885 that western Kansans no longer feared the desert: "Whatever man has done man may do, and the Kansas man can do lots of things that no man has ever done before."[24] It did not occur to these people that the clear air might deceive them into reaching beyond their grasp and that it was not only the wild horses and the blue hills but their own futures in this strange country that were distorted and made to appear larger than life.

Chapter Two

Savages

It was the ninth of April 1867. Mrs. Sutzer was at home on White Rock Creek with her small son. Erastus Bartlett, who boarded with them, was working along the stream splitting wood. Across the White Rock Creek were the Wards—father, mother, and adopted son. Late in the afternoon the Cheyennes rode up with so little warning the mother had to send her son to alert the Wards. The tribesmen wanted dinner.

The White Rock Creek settlement, close to the geographic center of the United States and along the state's northern border where southern and northern Indians ranged, was not an ideal place for a woman alone with a child. The Cheyennes had visited Mrs. Sutzer's neighbor, Mrs. John Marling, last spring. They had put a rope around her neck and dragged her into the timber, where thirty of them raped her. When they left, the settlement was deserted. The woman wandered about, holding her toddler by the hand, in a "dazed condition," said the returning community members, "almost like a wild animal." She did not recognize her friends until they said her name. It had been worse on the White Rock in 1862 when Indians had chased Asbury Clark, formerly of Knox County, Illinois, and cut him into little pieces. No doubt these horrors were on Mrs. Sutzer's mind as she stood at the stove that April afternoon.[1]

As the light faded, Erastus Bartlett returned for dinner, his iron splitting wedge in his hand. An Indian tomahawked him as he rounded the corner of the house, then grabbed Bartlett's small knife and buried it in his throat. Mrs. Sutzer ran for the woods but made it only thirty yards from her door. A warrior crushed her head with a rock.

The Cheyenne group enjoyed another dinner at the Wards, smoking their pipes and chatting amiably. Presently one stood up and loaded a gun. "Do you think this would kill a buffalo?" he asked. Mr. Ward responded that he thought it would. At that the Indian leveled the weapon at the white man and shot him in the chest. The house filled with smoke and noise, crying and fear. The two boys ran outside, tripping and rolling down into the stream bed with armed Indians close behind. The Sutzer boy died quickly, but Nicolas Ward survived with a bullet wound in the neck. While the Indians went about shooting these two young settlers, Mrs. Ward barricaded herself in the house. Searchers later found the door smashed. Inside were signs of the struggle that had occurred when the Indians captured her.

The Ward boy lay for a long while on the

bank of White Rock Creek, in shock and weak from loss of blood. After nightfall, he reached the house and, tripping over the body of his father in the darkness, found a blanket to warm him in the night outdoors. Soldiers in the area got a description of Mrs. Ward: tall, fair, twenty-two years old. Two months after the incident at White Rock Creek, black troopers reported they saw a tall young white woman on the prairie. When they approached, she ran.[2]

About twenty miles southeast of the White Rock settlements a spring had created what was thought to be a bottomless pool. To the western tribes, this spring, called Waconda, was a sacred place where they had for generations carried out parts of a rich ceremonial life. Perhaps it was partly for that reason that early in the 1860s, as hunters and a few settlers started to filter into the area, the Indians set a "dead line" beyond which they would not allow the white man to proceed. It ran to the Arkansas River in the south. In the north, it crossed the Solomon River at the mouth of Pipe Creek. This was a few miles northwest of Salina (where the town of Minneapolis now stands), close to the Waconda spring and almost exactly on the line dividing the western from the eastern Kansas region in so many other ways.[3]

White settlers and the soldiers who protected them ignored this dead line and also the warnings about a "sacred spring," which, it was believed, came from a people of the past, whom one Kansas soldier called "monsters" and another characterized as "a treacherous, thieving set of *villains.*"[4] The view was that these dirty, unpredictable types clung to outmoded customs and were destined to disappear before a strong thrust from those who knew the proper use of the land. To believe otherwise was to fundamentally threaten nineteenth-century ideas of progress and evolution.[5]

Eastern philanthropists talked of the nobility of the Indian way of life and hoped it could survive in some form. The Little Arkansas Treaty of 1865 and its sequel, the Medicine Lodge Treaty of 1867, both negotiated at the dead line, promised reservations in Indian Territory (now Oklahoma) and aid from the federal government to western Kansas tribes if they would confine their hunting and roaming to the unsettled area of Kansas south of the Arkansas River. The hope among officials of the Office of Indian Affairs and Quaker agents appointed under the government's new Peace Policy was that negotiation would open western Kansas to settlement without bloodshed.[6] Just in case, however, the army constructed a line of forts there. To Fort Larned, established in 1859, the military added Fort Harker (in 1864), Fort Zarah (1864), Fort Kirwin (1865), Fort Hays (1865), Fort Dodge (1865), and Fort Wallace (1865).[7] Fort Kirwin was near the attractive Solomon and Republican River settlements; Forts Harker, Hays, and Wallace lined the projected Smoky Hill route of the Union Pacific Railroad, Eastern Division. Forts Zarah and Larned were on the Arkansas River survey of the Atchison, Topeka & Santa Fe Railroad.

The Civil War was over. The negotiators were ready; the soldiers were ready; the locomotives were ready; the plows were ready. But the Indians were not ready. Just when the Cheyennes visited White Rock Creek, General Winfield S. Hancock gathered 1,400 soldiers at Fort Larned and informed Indian agents in the

Waconda, the Spirit Spring. For both Indians and early settlers, the spring, now covered by a lake, was the symbolic dividing line between eastern and western Kansas. These ladies are visiting the health spa that was established there after the Indians had gone.

area that, despite the Peace Policy, the flag needed to be shown to Indians in Kansas with force behind it. Hancock's meetings with Indian groups were heavy handed. He burned an Indian village and, in the view of most historians, further angered rather than intimidated the tribes.[8] But the military could not ignore such experiences as those of Mrs. Sutzer, Bartlett, and the Ward and Sutzer boys. A pattern of revenge began with the Sand Creek massacre of Cheyennes by Colorado militia in 1864, seizing Indians and officers in turn. The War Department argued with the Interior Department over how the Indian question should be handled, while western Kansas settlers died without much knowledge of the policy involved.

Kansas Governor Samuel Crawford was not a calming influence. He was angry enough at the delay in negotiations that he eventually gave up his official post in order to fight Indians personally.[9] Crawford wrote Senator E. G. Ross that it was time to raise a volunteer force to kill Indians and to "cut them off from all connection with Washington red tape." He reported to Ross late in June that Kiowas had attacked a wagon train between Fort Harker and Fort Larned, killing eleven teamsters, and had then moved to the Union Pacific, Eastern Division (UPED) Railroad to kill an engineer and another employee and effectively stop work by the contractors. Meanwhile, Indian agents Jesse Leavenworth for the Commanches and Kiowas and Edward Wyncoop for the Apaches, Arapahoes, and Cheyennes distributed 160,000 pounds of annuity goods "to the murderers." Crawford minced no words: "If those who believe that the Indian embodies in his nature everything that is noble and great could see their friends butchered and mangled as we of the West have seen ours, the probability is they would change their opinions." Crawford thought the Indians were "irresponsible, uncivilized, blood-thirsty fiends" and that it was time to stop allowing one hundred settlers to be scalped before any Indian should also die.[10]

Because military campaigns against Indians in 1867 were unspectacular and because the history of Indian trouble has been written with a focus on military campaigns, the hard year that settlers and railway workers experienced gets scant attention in the literature.[11] In addition to a cholera epidemic that affected towns and forts across western Kansas, the tension over Indians was constant.[12] In April "a poor Irishman" came running into the military post near Hays covered with mud and "minus everything but a pair of trousers." Soldiers could find none of the thousands of Indians he said were after him. In June came the Kiowa attacks complained of by Crawford and a battle between troops and Indians near Fort Wallace.[13] Late in July there were two nighttime assaults against black soldiers stationed west of Fort Hays.[14] One observer figured the small camps of black soldiers along the railroad right of way were stationed there "as bait for the Indians."[15] On 1 August, however, thirty Cheyennes attacked seven unarmed railroad workers on the UPED west of Russell. The Indians killed and scalped the entire group.[16]

Smaller incidents were harrowing, too. J. W. McConnell, breaking his claim in Rooks County that August, was attacked by a single Indian. It seemed to McConnell that an eternity passed before he managed to join settlers hiding from a larger Indian group. McConnell, from one hundred yards away, yelled to the leader, "Are you a Pawnee?" The answer was "No." "Otoe, Cheyenne, Arapaho?" "No." "Then," screamed McConnell, "what the hell are you?" The Indian muttered something unintelligible and the group trotted away.[17]

The enemy was equally abstract to an Ohio railroad contractor and his young wife living in a dugout along the rail line. An arrow came through a knothole in their door one night and killed the man. His wife lost her mind. She took to riding around in a black habit and became known in the Hays area as the "Wild Huntress of the Plains." She may have noticed on her rides a beautiful black pacer heading a wild herd near the fort. It was the mount of a man who had accompanied the wagon train attacked in June. When the rider was hit, he clung to the saddle for one hundred yards or more before rolling lifeless to the prairie, leaving his horse free. No one telling the story recalled his name, if any of them ever knew.[18]

In July 1867, E. S. Lane was in Ellsworth, then the terminus of the UPED Railroad, a place so rough he had no wish to linger longer than was necessary to recover from an attack of cholera. When he felt well enough, he joined a railroad surveying party ordered "to the front" in what is now Trego County. The surveyors worked under military guard, and two camps of graders, numbering several hundred, arrived in mid-August. Though all had guns, the regularly seen moccasin and pony tracks frightened the men. "If they had only been sure they could make the 40 miles in safety (to Hays), nothing could have kept them in camp."[19]

On 19 September the supervisor of one camp, Thomas Parks, went out after buffalo meat. He did not see any Indians, he said, and they could not amount to much if they did not show themselves. Parks left with his driver Charles Saffel and a young black cavalryman (Lane did not bother to record his name) who sneaked out of camp after them to provide military escort. A wood wagon left at the same time to gather timber. The morning was cloudy and misty, a rare day for that part of the world, but at noon the mist lifted, and to their surprise the men in camp saw the wood wagon less than a mile away, being hotly pursued by forty Indians. Though wounded, the wood wagon's driver reached the camp where there was a discussion about the probable situation of the buffalo hunters. At that moment another apparition appeared. Over a rise, walking very slowly, came the black and tan dog that always followed Parks' white horse. An arrow in the

News of Western Kansas. A drawing from Harper's Weekly, *7 September 1867, showing Cheyennes attacking a work party on the Union Pacific Eastern Division Railroad in August. The reaction of the man beneath the wheelbarrow was typical of railway workers' responses.*

dog's neck trailed its bloody shaft through the sod.[20]

The search party found evidence of a fight— arrows, lances, pieces of cloth. Shortly, they came upon Saffel's body, lying on its face in a ravine, bristling with arrows and minus its hair. Farther along the draw was Parks. He had put up a stiff fight from beneath a limestone outcrop, but the Indians had broken it off and pinned him. The contractor was dead but not scalped. His watch, his wedding ring, and his new Henry rifle were carefully laid out beside him and he had been covered with a blue mackinaw blanket. It was the Indians' way of honoring Parks's bravery.

The graders loaded Saffel's body onto a wagon and then used crowbars to extricate Parks. Beneath his body they found the black cavalryman yet alive, though with fifteen spear wounds suffered when the Indians poked at him through cracks in the rock. Later, while serving as a scout at Fort Wallace, Lane recognized Parks's white horse in a Cheyenne village.[21] It

all seemed an odd prelude to the Medicine Lodge peace conference, held within a month of the attack on Parks.

At Medicine Lodge, the southern Cheyennes, the Arapahoes, the Kiowas, the Commanches, and groups of Apaches promised to move to reservations and stop bothering the Kansas settlements. Yet 1868 and 1869 were not peaceful years. In fact, the August 1868 raids on the Solomon and Republican River settlements by two hundred Cheyennes, four Arapahoes, and twenty Sioux led by Black Kettle were doubtless the most destructive of the decade. The army estimated that seventy-nine western Kansas settlers were killed in August and September 1868.[22]

There was insult as well as injury, as the Indians again ate before killing. At one northern settlement the women served the warriors coffee in tin cups, only to have it thrown in their faces before a mass rape.[23] The soldiers at Fort Hays—where Black Kettle's band had stopped, professing love of their "white brothers'' only three days before the round of August killings—were enraged and bitter.[24] The settlers were desperate. ''Our situation here is past endurance,'' wrote a man living almost in the shadow of Fort Wallace. ''We are penned in [.] we can get no wood nor hay without being shot at by the fiends [.] the women & children are in constant terror.''[25] Governor Crawford telegraphed the military: ''These things must cease. . . . I cannot sit idly by and see our people butchered.''[26]

Statistics do not tell the story of the psychological effects living under siege had upon western Kansans. Historians, particularly in the twentieth century, have been so justifiably concerned with correcting the stereotype of the savage Indian and portraying Native Americans as the complex and varying human beings they really were that modern readers can almost lose sight of the legitimacy of the settlers' feelings of terror. One recent account of women's images of Plains Indians, for example, admits that the dangers of rape and kidnapping did exist but still takes pioneer women to task for having failed to view the Indians as human beings.[27] Such interpretations indicate so strong a desire to defend the reputation of the Indian that, as in the above case, the reputation of even the pioneer woman, another historical figure of great attractiveness at present, is compromised. To reemphasize the terror and the true savagery of some Indians is not to generalize about all, not does it justify white military terrorism in response. Such an emphasis explains and empathizes with some western settlers' negative attitudes toward Indians. The War Department reported fourteen women raped and four women captured (there were doubtless at least five) during the two peak

years of raiding.[28] That may not impress a student of twentieth-century terror, but it is sobering if one looks at these in context.

Thirty Indians raped Mrs. Shaw of Spillman Creek and her sister, Mrs. Foster, ''until long after they had become senseless.'' Sarah White, age eighteen, found herself on the back of an Indian pony heading south after a day that included the death of her father and the narrow escape of her little sister. Mrs. Anna Morgan, age twenty-three, married one month, heard Indians shooting her husband. She mounted a horse, grabbed a revolver, and tried to protect him. But the horse threw her and she was captured. Mrs. Clara Blinn was captured along the Santa Fe trail with her two-year-old child. Three days after her capture, Mrs. Susanna Alderdice watched the Indians kill her baby because it cried too much. Her husband came home from a trip to Salina to find her gone, his eleven-year-old boy wounded, and his other two children dead, one with five arrows in its body, another with four bullets.[29] Maria Weichell, twenty years old, recently arrived from Hanover and hardly able to speak English, had to learn to communicate with Cheyennes when they abducted her, leaving dead on the ground in northwest Kansas her husband and another man who had tried to defend her.[30] Mrs. David Bacon was raped and beaten until it was feared she would die.[31]

Some of the women were rescued, and an eye for an eye was taken at the Battle of the Washita in November 1868. These particular Cheyennes would not again raid on so large a scale.[32] But there were no happy endings. Mrs. Blinn was not rescued. She was tomahawked when troops attacked at Washita, and her child's brains were dashed out against a tree.

Custer recovered Anna Morgan and Sarah White together, both pregnant. Mrs. Alderdice was tomahawked to death by a squaw during a military attack on the Indian village where she was kept, and Mrs. Weichell, in the same village, was stabbed in the breast. Both women were pregnant by Indians at the time.[33] One of the soldiers who watched Mrs. Morgan and Miss White leave the Indian camp was not certain it was a great day. He wrote that, though they were young women, "their bodies bore the marks of more hard and cruel usage than a century of ordinary hardship entails." He could only imagine what a strain a several months' stay with the Indians had been on the women's Victorian sensibilities. The wonder to him was that "these tender plants of the American home" had survived at all.[34]

Mrs. Morgan bore her child, but it died at the age of two, much to the disappointment of her brother who had planned to train it to kill Indians.[35] David S. Bacon submitted a claim to the state in 1872, saying that the Indian raids had ruined his life. His wife, four months pregnant at the time of her rape, later divorced him, and his property was destroyed by Indians. "I have been cursed & hunted," he wrote, "all because I would settle in this country & my family broken up in consequence in a very bitter way, as wife's folks blamed me for settling out here. Who will pay me for their curses? Who will give me back my wife & babies?"[36]

As the impact of the terror was heightened by the gulf between Victorian moral concepts and Indian behavior, so was the response to suffering crippled by nineteenth-century ideas about the proper role of government. If ever there was a disaster area, western Kansas in the late

1860s was it, and one might have expected massive federal and state aid to be forthcoming. It was not. In fact, as was true with reverses in the region throughout the rest of the century, the settlers' suffering was viewed by many as an embarrassment that might discourage immigration. Besides, the first significant experiment with federal aid to individuals—the help given free blacks in the South during Reconstruction—was then barely under way and was extremely controversial.

The caution of the bureaucrats was broken by an individual. All sources agree that the quick action of Mary A. Bickerdyke, a widow who ran a railroad hotel in Salina, was critical. Mrs. Bickerdyke, already known as Mother Bickerdyke, had gained a national reputation among soldiers as a Civil War nurse and then as a locating agent for soldiers wishing to come to Kansas. With a $10,000 loan secured by her own note, she helped more than three hundred Kansas families get settled during this period and was not about to see them return east because of an Indian attack.[37]

Mrs. Bickerdyke contacted General Sherman about the settlers' situation, and Sherman in November 1868 ordered rations for 1,000 people for four weeks. Not satisfied, Mrs. Bickerdyke went to Washington and, with the help of letters from Kansas Senator S. C. Pomeroy, convinced the Department of War to order government rations for 500 people for ten months until crops could be harvested. General O. O. Howard, in charge of the Freedmen's Bureau to aid blacks, gave Mrs. Bickerdyke 500 blankets to take to Kansas, and in New York City she acquired 500 Bibles for the settlers' spiritual nourishment.[38]

Still, there was criticism in Kansas, particularly from the town of Salina, which depended for its economic growth on the continued attractiveness of the country to the west. Early in 1869 the *Salina Herald* alleged that the suffering was being exaggerated. This led General Alfred Sully of Fort Harker to send an officer to investigate the situation in the settlements. Sully did not know whether to issue further rations and wrote that he surely had "no wish to injure the prosperity of the state by so doing." He was careful, however, that the person he picked to report was not interested in land speculation.[39] N. H. Davis returned from a visit to the Solomon and Saline River settlements in late February. He told Sully that, in addition to the Indian trouble, many there had had crop failures for two years running. Without food, clothing, and seed wheat, most would have to abandon their claims, "and the section of the country will again be occupied by the Indian and buffalo."[40] Another visitor in June estimated at $30,000 the loss from Indians in the area up to fifteen miles west of Salina. In that month even the city of Salina began raising money for the settlers.[41] But official reluctance remained. One army officer wrote that he had no authority to issue rations and that only those actually driven out by Indians had any right to them. "It is absurd to suppose that the Gov't can give rations to all persons who have lost their crops by Drouth, Grasshoppers &c."[42]

With the notable exception of the Dull Knife raid of 1878, Indian troubles in western Kansas diminished slowly through the 1870s. But they did not disappear. R. G. Kshenka, a Bohemian who worked for a law firm in Milwaukee before coming with others of his nationality to the Solomon River, wrote Governor James Harvey in the spring of 1870 that he and his hunting party were besieged by Indians and had lost three men.[43] A spokesman for a Scandinavian colony in Republic County wrote about the same time that, being "greenhorns here in a New Country," they wished the state would tell them if they were to be protected so they could act accordingly.[44] The new town of Great Bend on the Santa Fe Railroad route was visited in 1871 by 400 Indians.[45] Also that year Governor Harvey protested strongly when the Interior Department gave some "peaceful" Sioux Indians permission to hunt south of the Platte River.[46] Indians killed twenty-seven Kansans in 1874, and the military fought Cheyennes along Sappa Creek in 1875.[47] Militia companies were organized and armed in Norton County in 1876.[48] Dr. William Tichenor was wounded by Sioux Indians while on a hunting trip in Ness County in 1877.[49]

Three western Kansas events of the early 1870s had impact beyond numbers killed and were immediately elevated to the stature of massacres. There is no overstressing the importance to frontier psychology of the Jordan massacre of 1872 and the Lone Tree and German massacres two years later. All possessed the drama and pathos from which western myth has risen.

Richard Jordan, a twenty-five-year-old buffalo hunter, lived in 1872 with his wife Mary at Parks' Fort (now WaKeeney), a place named after the contractor who had died there in 1867. In July 1872 Mary, in low spirits because of the recent loss of a child, decided to accompany her husband on a hunting trip. Her mother in Ellis tried to dissuade her, but Mary said the Indians were on reservations and Richard knew what he was doing. They left in August, accompanied by Richard's brother George, a hired man named Fred Nelson, and a Newfoundland dog. Three weeks later the dog appeared at Jordan's parents' farm at Ellis. Richard and Mary had said not to worry about them for six weeks; perhaps the dog had been in the way. Late in September a hunter spotted an abandoned wagon along the Walnut just west of the present Lane County line. A search turned up the bodies of the men, riddled with arrows having a blue band around the notched end, probably Kiowa. Mary's description went out over the frontier: five feet tall, dark hair, dark complexion, dark gray eyes, a slight limp. However, when a search party left Ellis to look for her a week after the funeral of the others, they were turned back by soldiers who told them they could not carry arms into Indian Territory. This so enraged Mary's younger brother that he was taken in irons to Fort Dodge. There was thought of a ransom for the woman, but General Sherman said that would only encourage raids. "After having her husband and friends murdered," the general wrote, "and her own person subjected to the fearful bestiality of perhaps the whole tribe, it is mock humanity to secure what is left of her for the consideration of five ponies." Nothing more was ever heard of Mary Jordan.[50]

The Lone Tree massacre, named after the Meade County site where the victims were first buried, resulted from a series of contracts let in 1874 to finish the survey of southwestern Kansas. An expedition of twenty-two left Dodge City in August but divided to do field work in different regions. The ill-fated group that set out for a week's survey on 24 August included Oliver Short, his son Daniel (fourteen years old), James Shaw and his son Allen (age eighteen), and two other young men, Harry Jones

and John Keuchler. Two days later, friends found their wagon. The oxen stood dead in their yokes, their hind quarters cut off. The camp dog lay stiff beside its master. Short, his son, and Harry Jones were scalped, their heads mashed. The pockets of all were turned inside out, and there were twenty-eight bullet holes in the wagon. Mrs. Short, mother of six, filed a $10,000 claim against the government. After much debate, she and Mrs. Shaw were eventually paid $5,000 each for the losses.[51]

The German family massacre in September 1874 was perhaps the most heartrending. John German, his wife Lydia, his son Stephen, and daughters Rebecca, Catherine, Joanna, Sophia, Julia, and Adelaide were on their way to Colorado in a covered wagon when, in present Wallace County, their doom overtook them. Cheyennes led by Medicine Water killed the father, tomahawked the mother (an axe was found in Lydia's head), and killed the oldest daughter. Shortly they also killed Joanna because they thought her long hair would make a good scalp. They considered killing one of the other daughters for crying but eventually took the remaining four with them. Julia and Adelaide were abandoned for several days on the prairie when the Indians were temporarily frightened by some cowboys. The captivity of these girls became a national *cause célèbre,* and within a year all four were recovered by the military, though in emaciated condition.[52]

These events struck deeply at the sensibilities of westerners, who had a tenuous hold on civilization as they burrowed homes into the ground but who had brought with them high hopes that their culture would distinguish them from the natural environmental features, among which they classed Indians. The brutal excesses

Sophia German. Pictures of the German girls, distributed nationwide, created special loathing for their captors.

of some Indians reminded westerners of their own vulnerability. Not to respond vigorously was to fail to defend an idea of human progress that was not yet secure enough, particularly in this place, to ignore challenges.

The people of Elgin, Kansas, near Russell, where the Germans had resided for a year before leaving for Colorado, passed a resolution calling upon the governor of Kansas "to see that every brutal wretch who assisted, aided or abetted, in the murder and capture of the Germain [*sic*] family, expiates his crime upon the gallows" and that the surviving girls be

cared for and educated out of the appropriations for the subsistence of the Cheyennes.[53] Mrs. Short, widow of the deceased surveyor, pleaded with Kansas Governor Thomas Osborn to see that the Indians responsible for the German killings, as well as those of her own husband and son, be punished. She made the request, she wrote, "as a Christian duty; as I cherish the memory of a loving husband and a darling son" and despite the fact that "my crushed spirit has no desire for retaliation." It should be done as an example "of teaching civilization."[54] Similarly moved was buffalo hunter S. S. Van Sickel, who often passed the temporary grave at Lone Tree on his journey into southwest Kansas. Van Sickel could not understand the "loss of a very bright, youthful and innocent boy, who had to suffer death at the hands of the heartless, merciless savage." It changed his mind about Indians, with whom he had formerly had some sympathy, and led him to conclude that they were not human beings but "only human in form."[55]

The *New York Times* in 1868 was willing to speculate that Kansans, trying so hard so quickly to get rid of the Indians and get busy farming, might be partly responsible for their own troubles, but few Kansans agreed.[56] Governor Osborn expressed a common view when he wrote in 1875 that "while the people of Kansas are far from believing that the wild Indian tribes upon our frontiers have no claims upon the justice and humanity of the white race, they do believe that there are no interests of such transcendent importance associated with the future of these tribes as to justify the arrest of civilization by locat[ing] them permanently in its pathway." Merely removing them to Indian Territory "will not change the nature of

Lone Tree. This tree in Meade County for sixty-four years marked the site of the 1874 massacre of the O. F. Short surveying party.

the savage and treacherous tribes whose barbarities have disfigured almost every page of our history.'' Osborn estimated that the state had spent more than $300,000 since 1861 to defend its western section against Indians, and he reported that claims for the loss of more than $350,000 worth of property had been verified.[57] The *New York Times* had to admit that ''settlers and soldiers do not regard the Indian in the poetic and philanthropic light of peace societies.'' Upon reflection, the reporter decided there might be justification for this. ''It is

so easy to rejoice over the tomahawking of somebody else's kith and kin, the disemboweling of somebody else's babies, with your own safe and happy a thousand miles away.''[58]

It mattered then, as it matters to people reading histories now, from what perspective western Kansas events of the 1860s were viewed. From the perspective of the relatives of the victims, there could be only one interpretation. The editor of the *Osborne County Farmer,* serving the Solomon River settlements, felt Indian actions could have ''no apology, no justification'' and recommended total extermination of the warrior class as thieves, ravishers, and murderers. As long as the waters of the Solomon flowed, he mused, the settlers there could never see ''the wild Indians who raided here with a spirit of sickly sentimentalism which pervades so many of the American people who know nothing of the treachery of Indian character. The NOBLE Indian is a myth.''[59] A Dodge City editor believed Indian policy was based on illusion: ''The noble red man comes into camp says: 'I killed your wife; I harmed your daughter; I burned your baby; I find no buffalo to eat—I surrender. Give me rum and pork and tobacco for peace.' The voice of the Quaker responds: 'O, how my heart bleeds for the poor Indian.' ''[60] Mrs. M. A. Smith of Ellis, mother of the Mary who died with Richard Jordan, spoke at Hays in 1876 on the Indian question. She recommended that settlers be allowed to deal with the Indian themselves and thought that thus ''many of the murdered ones would be avenged.'' She herself had lost a son-in-law, and there was no clue to the fate of her daughter. ''How many more sorrowing mothers could tell the same tale.''[61]

History seldom justifies. Its purpose is empathy, to provide means of understanding people long buried who in their time saw the present passing in pieces and experienced in enlarged form that part of history directed at them. If one's experience with the race of Indians was all murder, rape, and pillage; if one had seen them in their lust, in their greed, and in their cowardly glee, could enlightened views result?

Historians have not ignored the brutalities of the Indian wars. However, recent literature tends to concentrate attention elsewhere and to shy away from details of individual atrocities that created unique horror. The purpose here is not to conclude that westerners' views of Indians contained no sympathy for them but rather to reemphasize, in light of recent literature concentrating on redeeming the Indians' reputation, that Indian terror was a real and important factor in settlers' lives. Sandra Myres, for example, has recently concluded that frontier women's fear of Indians was largely a male invention. "For most Midwestern frontier women," she writes, "Indians were a sometimes bothersome, but not a particularly frightening part of the landscape." Myres mentions the case of an Indian agent's daughter who, having been raped by Indians, managed to differentiate among individuals and not indiscriminately apply her rage to all Indians.[62] Western Kansas sources strongly indicate that such benign conclusions were not reached by the majority of western Kansans.

Evidence minimizing western fear of Indians as a Victorian stereotype has drawn extensively on travel accounts. It was a different experience to watch Indians from the safety of a wagon train in the midst of an armed group or from a railroad car than from an isolated farmstead about to be attacked. Fear of Indians may not have been universal on the early Kansas agricultural frontier, and it is easy to show that the scattered raids were statistically not a logical cause of mass panic. Yet there were terrible incidents, widely advertised in grisly detail to those in the region or thinking of moving there. There was more danger in the 1860s or 1870s that Indians would attack a family in Kansas than one in Iowa or Massachusetts. In such a situation the farmer did not, as the scholar may, calculate the odds and adjust his attitude accordingly. As danger increased, so did fear. As fear increased, so did intolerance and stereotyping. So it was with western Kansans and Indians.

Chapter Three

The Steel Nile

John Stilgoe in his thoughtful study *Metropolitan Corridor* argued that the "built environment" of railroads changed the way Americans perceived their surroundings. By 1880, the railroad line, its stations, its machinery, and the subculture that existed aboard its cars represented a world apart. That world was largely the world of urban civilization, and it was one that travelers by rail did not leave no matter how primitive or unusual the area through which the express passed. Regionalism was crippled by mimicry, and life styles were influenced by the "organized haste" of railroad life, metropolitan life, and, finally, American life. By the time toy electric trains were available to children, the psychological effect of the corridor was overwhelming. "They fell asleep," Stilgoe wrote, "after looking at the lighted locomotives and cars circling and circling in darkened rooms, recreating in miniature the landscape and the vehicle of American traveling romance."[1]

It had long been customary for Americans to view the West through a "cultural screen" or "secondary environment" such as the one Stilgoe suggests was created by railroads. Students of western history have noticed that the strikingly unusual environment was described, even drawn, differently by persons who brought along varying attitudes.[2] As the previous chapter suggested, western Kansans of the 1860s and 1870s viewed Indians through this kind of cultural (ethnocentric) lens. Indians were in the way of something whose time had come. That something was nothing less than civilization as defined by *homo Americanus*, subspecies Gilded Age. And, no question about it, civilization so defined was symbolized to western Kansans of the 1860s and 1870s by just the kind of metropolitan, civilized railroad corridor Stilgoe described.

In fact, the aptness of Stilgoe's thesis there is striking because the contrast between the elegance of the Pullman palace cars shooting passengers toward Denver or Santa Fe and the real wilderness of early western Kansas was more extreme than in the East. Also, because the civilization—and even the civilizability—of western Kansas was in doubt, the railroad was not only a symbol but a daily weapon in a struggle with raw nature.

General Winfield S. Hancock described the viewpoint well in a talk he gave excursionists on the Union Pacific, Eastern Division (later Kansas Pacific) Railroad in June 1867. Hancock was ready to leave on his sweep through the Indian tribes, and the carnage of Indian raiding was ahead. Yet he thought the mere presence of the railroad made all the difference and would transform the wilderness immediately, like waving a magic wand. When the cars arrived at Fort Harker, the buffalo ran away. Hancock said they might never return. Only a few days earlier, a "careless soldier" had been scalped. "This will never occur again," Hancock asserted. And why not? "This great railroad brings civilization with it, so that when the Rocky Mountains are reached, the wild Indian and the buffalo will have passed away."[3]

Historians have been divided not only on the extent of the economic and social effects of railroad building in nineteenth-century America but on where to look for evidence of those effects. The American studies school emphasizes rhetorical and psychological factors, while the quantitative school that cut its teeth on the western railroad issue argues that the test is profitability, hard economic return for private and federal investment.[4]

While these approaches lead scholars to different conclusions about the desirability of the massive government land grants given to western railroads, including those crossing western Kansas, most scholars agree that to some extent rail building in the West in the 1870s and 1880s was "premature," that is, developmental. In places like pre-railroad western Kansas, a kind of catch-22 situation prevailed: there could be no market to pay, through traffic, for a railroad's construction costs unless there was a railroad, and there could be no railroad unless a market was already in place. Government intervened by giving railroads a part of the public domain, thus with the same action providing "social overhead capital" making settlement possible and tying the interest of powerful corporations to encouraging that settlement. There would be, it was felt at the time, not only a quantifiable economic return, but social and political returns as well. The settlement and exploitation of the West were seen as desirable goals. In such situations, the government was not likely to be overcareful about determining precisely what was required and how much aid was too much aid. The aid given was the aid that imprecise politicians and an eager public thought was needed. And it should be remembered, as the example of western Kansas shows, that these groups considerably overestimated the likely direct economic returns that western regions would provide individuals and the nation.

At the outset the prospect of railroads penetrating the western Kansas wilderness seemed such a positive development that few would have balked at any social price. The railroad corridor in early western Kansas, creating towns and pockets of settlement along the steel-girded lines of the Smoky Hill and Arkansas River Valleys, was a kind of Nile. It attracted population, distributed wealth, and promised long-range growth, automatic and independent of the place or time. It could hardly be expected that the promoters of the 1870s, confident in their successes, would recognize as they laid rail past Fort Harker and toward Hays City that they were joining a struggle of uncertain outcome between powers that were and powers that always had been.

When Congress, by the Pacific Railroad Acts of 1862 and 1864, created the Union Pacific, Eastern Division Railroad and its federal land and bond aid package, it did not envision that the railroad would run through western Kansas at all. Rather, it was to join the main line at the 100th meridian via the Republican River Valley and to serve eastern Kansas. However, powerful backers acquired by the UPED in 1865 sponsored a survey to Denver and reminded Washington of the road's ambition. In 1866 Congress authorized the former branch to construct an independent line up the Smoky Hill River Valley and to collect lands from the government all the way to Denver. Congress did specify, however, that the railroad would definitely join with the UP north of Denver.[5]

At the time of the route change, few people lived in western Kansas. In the spring of 1866, the railroad found only seventy-nine preemption filings and twenty-five homestead filings within the area of its proposed land grant west of the sixth principal meridian. Fewer than ten thousand of about four million Kansas acres available to the railroad were then occupied.[6]

Some wanted to keep it that way. Wagon freighters, for instance, did not look forward to rail competition and protested.[7] Also, a group of businessmen criticized the route on behalf of the Ellsworth & Pacific Railroad. In November 1867, a representative of the E&P wrote from beautiful Ellsworth, then enjoying seventy-five-degree winter weather, that paradise ended there. Beyond, on the proposed Smoky Hill route, was "a veritable desert," visited by continuous dry winds and covered with "hard baked loam." Maybe the UPED should turn south toward Santa Fe.[8] Despite this kind of special-interest carping, however, Kansans generally recognized that federal aid to a rail line to the Colorado mining camps and timber supplies was vital to settlement of the western half of the state. Wrote one supporter: "We are now in the world and belong to the 'rest of mankind.'"[9]

Construction into western Kansas beyond Salina began in the spring of 1867 and was finished in Kansas by the fall of 1868. For a time the fifty-six-pound-per-yard rail went down across the prairie at a rate of two miles per day. Horses pushed a car loaded with rail to the end of the track, and when it was offloaded it went into a ditch to make room for another loaded car.[10] It was a marvel of coordination of men, machinery, and movable towns, an industrial pageant ambling with a complex gait over the wilderness. Not everything, however, went as expected.

For one thing, the Indians did not stand aside. Speaking to an appreciative crowd in St. Louis in June 1867, a railroad officer boasted that funds were available, iron was on the ground, and progress should be rapid "unless the men get frightened away by Indians."[11] He was confident that the military would prevent that, but even such an aggressive commander as George Custer, who patrolled the Smoky Hill Valley that year, could not throttle the Indians. In May, surveyors fought a four-and-one-half-hour battle in present Logan County. In June, five railroad men were killed and scalped in two separate attacks within twenty miles of Fort Harker, and two men died at Bunker Hill. Workmen were entirely driven off twenty miles of line. There was a lull when fifteen hundred rifles and fifty thousand rounds of ammunition arrived for use by rail workers. But in October, Indians fired on a construction train and killed a contractor. The next spring they tried stopping a locomotive by stringing telegraph wire across the track.[12]

The little crew of section men living at Fossil Station (later Russell) in the spring of 1869 thought they had relatively elegant arrangements. John Cook, a Lutheran from Central Germany, pumped water for locomotives that stopped, and his wife cooked for the section men. Cook made $75 a month, plus $6 a week per man for the meals. The workers lived in a large dugout with a fireplace supplied through the winter with wood thrown from locomotive tenders by sympathetic firemen. There was even a dugout housing chickens, and at breakfast everyone had fresh eggs. During working hours, the men traveled up and down the track for several miles in a handcar, inspecting the line without the least thought of danger. That changed on 28 May 1869.[13]

That day the men pumped the handcar back to the dugouts to save their very lives. Indians killed two and wounded four. They did not attack the dugouts once the men were inside and armed but did tear up about two miles of railroad track, lighting several fires, burning the ties, and then bending the light rail. They hovered all afternoon, mostly east of the station. After dark, unnoticed by rail employees, they crept away toward the Saline Valley where two days later they killed eleven people.[14]

What about the westbound express, due at midnight? It was Cook's duty to flag it, but he did not wish to try evading the Indians who presumably waited in the darkness. He did the reasonable thing. When he saw the headlight of the locomotive, he lit a hay bale on the track. The engineer misunderstood the signal. The train derailed and rolled over in the ditch, giving the sleeping-car passengers a rude awakening.[15]

The passengers were angry. This was not the ride they had paid for. Promoters of the town of Russell were embarrassed when a few years later excavators uncovered the section men's shallow graves.[16] Management was outraged. Wrote UPED President C. D. Perry: "Un-armed men cannot be expected to expose themselves to these savages."[17] Even the state historical society did not know just what to do with the piece of Indian pony tail and single arrow it received in 1877 as a memento of the event.[18] Why should Indians not cooperate with the railroad like everyone else? Could they not be content to lend a touch of the exotic to the route, as did the group of Cheyennes who were docile enough in August 1868 to be teased by giggling ladies from Topeka about whether "they would like some scalps of foreign hair" when an excursion train stood for a few hours at Hays City?[19] Apparently not.

Indians were not the only difficulty. The railroad lacked adequate traffic. In March 1869 the UPED changed its named to Kansas Pacific, thus trumpeting independent status and transcontinental aspirations. However, a serious lobbying campaign the year before to get federal aid for a second true transcontinental route had already failed.[20] This left the KP as a feeder line for the UP which, like modern railroads, was not interested in "short hauling" itself by transferring to the Kansas line traffic that it could carry to Missouri River towns itself. The question of whether the KP could thrive serving only settlers in western Kansas and eastern Colorado was open to speculation. Also, the company was being, as the UP had been, thoroughly milked by its original promoters, leaving it a financial shell unprepared for capital challenges.[21] Few were shocked when in March 1880 the Kansas Pacific changed its name again, to Union Pacific, Kansas Division.[22]

Because securities manipulation and collection of maximum aid from the federal government were the roads to profit and because these

Tools of Civilization. A construction train on the UPED Railroad two miles west of Yocemento, Ellis County, 1867.

returns resulted from speed, not quality, of construction, the KP was built shoddily and at inflated prices. Estimates of the cost of the Kansas line run as high as $60,000 a mile, twice what it would have cost to replace it in 1887.[23] Yet the track was light and the engineering hasty. An editor riding the railroad in 1867 noticed that even short trains had to reach maximum speed on the downgrade to make it up the next hill. "It is said by some—we did not examine for ourselves—that if one will take a position on the track and look after a train, that the locomotive will sink out of sight about twice in two or three miles."[24] What western Kansas had was more a speculative device, or the remains of one, than a railroad.

Although the Atchison, Topeka & Santa Fe received a land grant for its Arkansas River route through western Kansas in 1863, construction was not completed until 1872. This was close to the limit allowed by the land grant and so, as on the KP, crews were in a hurry. The road reached Newton, just north of Wichita, in the spring of 1872. It stretched to

Hutchinson by June, Larned in August, Dodge City in September, and to the western border of the state in late December, having constructed 271 miles of railroad in 222 days. Ties were cut in Colorado and floated down the Arkansas River, where they were collected in 200,000-tie groups by a boom at Great Bend. The Irish construction crews once built three miles, four hundred feet of track in a single day, a record for railroad building at that time.[25]

There were promises of more railroads in the region. The northwestern tier of counties seemed particularly promising, as it was along the Republican and Saline Rivers that some of the densest early settlement and most successful agricultural experiments occurred. Surveyors for the Junction City, Solomon Valley & Denver Railroad called the area "magnificent" in 1869.[26] In 1870 Senator Samuel Pomeroy took a ten-day trip through the area on behalf of the Union Pacific Central Branch (formerly Atchison & Pikes Peak). Pomeroy thought it was fortunate that the Indians had kept settlers out so that a railroad could select the best lands.

The people seemed eager for a railroad. At Clyde in Cloud County, Pomeroy spoke to a crowd about railroads and politics, a "sort of hash," he said, "which they seemed to relish—having good appetites to relish anything." He had buffalo meat and wild turkey at Jewell City, visited the famous spirit springs at Waconda, and reported with jubilation that the streams marked on the map were really all there. Waconda, a tall cone with a perfect circular pool at the top, could be a key resort on the new line, "another Saratoga."[27] A year later the Kansas Central narrow-gauge railway made a study of the same area, searched for bond aid from the same communities, and promised track.[28] Like so many other rail promises in the years following the initial breach by the two lines, nothing came of these plans. Western Kansas did not have another east-west trunk line until the completion of the Chicago, Rock Island & Pacific in 1887. Adequate north-south communication had to wait for the pickup truck.

The Kansas Pacific and the Santa Fe Railroads formed corridors in ways that went far beyond psychology. Trade and familiarity with

End of the Line. An AT&SF train just west of Larned in 1872. Notice the shadow of the photographer with his bulky equipment.

other towns of western Kansas in the nineteenth century revolved greatly around the physical layout of railroads. So did patterns of agricultural settlement and town building. There was a sharp division in style and prosperity, recognized at the time, between railroad and nonrailroad districts. Both railroad and public-land selections in the early seventies hugged the railroads and timber-rich tributaries of rivers along which the railroads ran.[29] An extensive study of Ellis County by historian James Forsythe showed that all government and railroad lands acquired by individuals before 1875, with the exception of two and one half sections, were within a mile and a half of the railroad or the streams.[30] The two railroads had a vested interest in the shape of the settlement grid, holding as they did several million acres in two long strips. They did not, however, encourage the modest, nonlinear growth statistics that became the rule for western Kansas in the early 1870s.

The Kansas Pacific started vigorously by organizing the National Land Company and appointing W. E. Webb of Hays City as its Kansas agent.[31] The railroad gave reduced rates to settlers buying from the National Land Company, offered five-year terms with 6 percent interest on deferred payments, and advertised 200,000 acres that flyers said had been "personally inspected by experienced farmers." The National Land Company had offices in all principal cities of the United States and had agents in England and Scotland. It published a quarterly newspaper called "The Star of Empire" that circulated to 80,000 readers, and the company claimed to have settled 18,000 people in western Kansas in 1869.[32] In fact the KP sold almost 400,000 acres of its land grant that year

at an average price of three dollars per acre. Thereafter, however, KP land sales declined each year until 1877 and never again reached the level of the first year following completion of the line. Sales in the national financial panic of 1873 were 25,423 acres and in the grasshopper year of 1874, 35,393 acres. By the end of the decade the KP had sold 1,515,059 acres in Kansas, about half its grant there, but less than 50 percent of this was then patented and placed on tax rolls to aid local communities.[33]

Ellis County, were Hays City was located, provides one example of buyer hesitancy about farming the KP corridor. The first sale the railroad made in the county in 1867 was for the location of Hays City—confirmation indeed that the establishment of towns preceded development of the agricultural hinterland. The next sale, in 1871, was five sections to the Western Kansas Agricultural Association, a group that had a contract with the railroad to experiment with the growing of crops and trees. The third sale, influenced by the failure of those experiments, was a tract of more than 25,000 acres purchased in 1872 by George Grant of London as stock ranches for young Englishmen. No large-scale agricultural settlement on public lands in Ellis County occurred until 1876, and this was by German-Russian colonists especially courted by railroad agents.[34]

The Santa Fe, with its more effective advertising department and its more attractive lands in central western Kansas, charged a higher price (five to six dollars an acre) through the 1870s. Its sales statistics, however, are also unspectacular. Of its grant of about three million acres, the company sold 71,801 in 1871 and only 45,328 in the year the Santa Fe was completed.[35] In March 1872 there was thought

Along the Corridor. A Santa Fe engine at the sparsely settled town of Dodge City, 1879. The dugouts along the right-of-way were typical of housing for rail crews as well as for the earliest settlers in western Kansas.

of stopping construction at Larned because a few company officials said the land grant beyond that would not return expenses. Santa Fe Land Commissioner D. L. Lakin assured company President Thomas Nickerson that the lands west of Larned would bring $3,385,000 —"not even would any ordinary drouth, revolution, or rebellion reduce it below that"—and probably more like $4.5 million. If the climate changed, it could be nearly $7 million.[36]

As with the KP, sales were erratic and reflected the current state of hope for farming the region. From 200,459 acres in 1874, sales dropped to 75,415 acres the next year. In the wet year of 1878, sales were 267,122 acres. One can then watch sales plummet as the drought developed: 104,744 acres in 1879,

78,241 in 1880; and 50,033 in 1881.[37] Of 2,475,221 acres patented to the Santa Fe by 1878, 1,833,491 remained unsold, most of these in western Kansas. In Sedgwick and Reno Counties that year, the railroad reported twice to three times as much land sold as unsold, but the western statistics were different. In Barton County, 70,606 acres were sold, 245,677 unsold; in Edwards County, 23,473 sold, 120,645 unsold; and in Ford County, 2,640 sold, 59,263 unsold.[38]

The railroad would have liked to sell some of its acreage quickly and in large blocks to speculators, as it was to do in the 1880s. However, although a few buyers purchased more than one 160-acre tract in the 1870s, sales of larger parcels were rare. Of 1,200 transactions recorded in Santa Fe land contracts in the period between 28 December 1878 and 17 April 1880, only nineteen were for parcels exceeding 160 acres. These records also indicate how specific were the targets for railroad land excursions. Of 892 transactions involving 122,201 acres in 1876 (a 137-acre average), 432 buyers were from Kansas and 125 from Illinois. Though the size of the sales was to change dramatically in the 1880s, the concentration of buyers in a few states would not.[39]

Railroad statistics are important to a history of the region for several reasons. They indicate the tentative nature of the movement to railroad lands in western Kansas during the 1870s; they show the importance of weather patterns to variations in total sales; and they reveal localized interest induced specifically by railroads in selected audiences. We may conclude that these railroads were "premature" in the sense that they had to develop their own traffic, and we may conclude that their efforts were fundamental in boosting settlement of western Kansas beyond its natural pace. It is also clear that no amount of inducing would deliver a child instantly nor much modify the new creation's ultimate potential.

In fact, looking beyond raw statistics for western Kansas growth to an examination of the composition of that growth reveals even more clearly the experimental nature of the first settlement there. It may be said that western Kansas in the early 1870s was urban, male dominated, and railroad dependent and that its survival was due to economic situations that were not only temporary but often counted on the continued delay of the creation of a lasting agricultural economy.

The building of the railroads themselves— along with their shops, roundhouses, and housing and entertainment facilities for employees— was obviously one of these transient situations. A number of the booming villages of the period were in fact "air towns" that existed only as supply points for construction crews. The 1870 federal census described the population of Buffalo Station in Wallace County, Kansas, as nine laborers, all born in Ireland, and one washerwoman: not a propitious start for a stable, longterm existence. The same was true of Monument Station, Pond City, and Phil Sheridan, though the last mentioned had some carpenters and dressmakers.[40] Phil Sheridan, the terminus of the Kansas Pacific for one year before the Colorado extension began, once had a population of close to 2,000.[41] In 1870 its population was 80: 64 men and 16 women.[42] By 1873 a dozen remained, and, as in the town of Coyote before it, "thousands of oyster and fruit cans alone marked the spot where vice had lately rioted."[43]

A second temporary feature was the presence of the military. Historians have long been aware that western town building was so strongly related to the early markets provided by the military that dangers were exaggerated to keep soldiers around as customers.[44] This was especially true in western Kansas. Ellsworth, Ellis, and Wallace Counties on the KP line and Ford and Pawnee Counties on the Santa Fe had significant military populations in 1870. Fort Hays had 180 male and 140 female residents, while Hays City had 215 men and 105 women. Also in Ellis County was the camp of the 7th Cavalry (80 men) on the Saline River and Camp Sturgis with 181 men and 131 women. The military population of 720 was over half the total county population of 1,336. A third of

A Certain Elegance. The Wallace station and railway hotel in the 1870s. Residents were proud that things were this up to date 400 miles west of the Missouri River.

Ellsworth County's population of 1,185 was at Fort Harker. Fort Wallace housed 238 men and 158 women, while the total population of Wallace County was only 538. The populations of Pawnee and Ford Counties consisted entirely of the military at Fort Larned (179 people) and Fort Dodge (427 people). Oddly, too, populations of the forts were more balanced than those of the towns. At Forts Hays, Harker, and Larned there were almost as many women as men, and there were more than 100 women at Fort Dodge. By contrast, a county without forts had a very different gender ratio. Russell County in 1870 had 149 men and 7 women; Trego County, 156 men and 10 women. Forts also contributed nearly the entire number of blacks residing in western counties at this

time.[45] The presence of the army meant business for the freighters and the railroads. The UP and the KP between June 1867 and September 1868 transported 36,347 tons of munitions and 13,810 persons for the War Department, charging the government $1,601,931.[46] Understandably, the abandonment of western Kansas forts in the late 1870s and early 1880s was a blow to the regional economy.

A third fleeting factor was the Texas cattle trade. So much has been written about this that there is no need to describe it in detail here.[47] But the cattle trade did dramatically increase the summer and fall transient populations of Wichita, Ellsworth, and Dodge City while shipping centered there. Their business boomed in boots, shirts, and all forms of vice; railroad

and stockyard receipts skyrocketed; city services were supported without local taxation; and
much free, if not always desirable, advertising
resulted in the eastern press. Unfortunately for
farmers, the cattle-trading business depended
on sparse population and used capital that might
otherwise have been available at lower interest
for farm loans.[48] Its inevitable end at about the
same time the forts were abandoned was another shock. The Kansas prohibition amendment of 1880 made western towns wonder how
they could survive without sin.[49] The departure
of the cowboys raised questions of how the
towns could survive at all.

It was an interesting cast of characters:
railroadmen, soldiers, cowboys, some hunters,
some freighters. But one group was not much in
evidence: farmers. Ellsworth County had 2,476
acres of improved land in 1870, acres that
yielded 2,175 bushels of spring wheat, 1,456
bushels of barley, and 12,167 bushels of corn.
However, other western counties along the KP
are conspicuously absent from census agricultural statistics.[50] In 1872, acres in cultivation in Ellsworth County had risen to 5,723, but
Russell County had only 711 and Ellis, Ford,
Pawnee, and Rooks Counties none. By comparison, Dickinson County, just east of the
sixth principal meridian, had 30,707 acres in
cultivation that year, Jewell County in the near
northwest was cultivating 16,319 acres, and
Osborne County, on the Solomon River at the
eastern edge of the arid region, but with no
railroad, was cultivating 9,000 acres.[51] In 1875
Pawnee County had about 3,000 acres in corn
and 748 in winter wheat; Edwards had 855 in
corn and 202 in winter wheat; Ellis, 422 in corn
and 93 in winter wheat; Ford, 41 acres in corn

and one-half acre in winter wheat.[52] None of
these figures indicates impressive agricultural
development for counties of 800 to 1,000
square miles, most lying along major railroads.

The first three United States land offices
truly in western Kansas were not established
until mid-decade—in Larned and Hays City in
1874, Kirwin in 1875.[53] Even then there was a
marked preference for lands along the Arkansas
River where it was thought irrigation might be
possible. For the year ending 20 June 1877,
only 31,895 acres in homestead entries were
recorded at the Hays City office, while the
Larned office showed 145,878 acres.[54] The
railroad corridors remained corridors in the
early 1870s, enlivened by industries tied to the
region's frontier status and populated by men
who, as a Larned resident put it, "came only
for a temporary purpose and, too, for the worst
of purposes."[55] A passenger got on a Santa Fe
train in the 1870s in far western Kansas. Asked
where he was going, he replied, "Hell." The
conductor said, "That's 65 cents and get off at
Dodge."[56]

It was not enough that the region's reputation
was exciting and its image exotic. To carry out
the promises that it could be civilized, it had to
be perceived as more malleable than threatening, more standard than odd, truly part of the
everyday world. In the early 1870s, even with
two railroads and their long Nile of American
culture stretching over the High Plains, the
state's western region was not viewed that way.
J. H. Tice, who rode a KP passenger train to
Denver in 1871, was typical. As night fell, Tice
looked out over western Kansas from his window and found that his principal feeling was
fright:

The loneliness of the landscape, the sombre appearance of the sky, shut out by the thick haze, seemed to grow oppressive and to excite a vague, indefinite feeling of anxiety, akin to fear. I looked out, the pall of darkness had settled on the plain. In front was our engine, like a monster, breathing smoke and flame, giving a lurid tint to the thick haze, but all else was impenetrable gloom and darkness. I felt as though we had left the coasts of light, and Milton's description of the arch fiend's flight through the domains of Chaos vividly recurred to me:

> On he fares, through a dark illimitable
>   ocean, without bound
> Without dimension; a vast vacuity, where
> Length, breadth, hight [*sic*], time and
>   place are lost.[57]

If the goals of promoters were to be realized, it would be necessary for such images of the western Kansas prairie ocean to change greatly.

Chapter Four

"This Ocean of Bloom"

To understand the initial impressions of the climate and prospects of western Kansas, it should be remembered that Coronado had someone strangle the guide who led him there.

This attitude prevailed for a long time. Dendrochronologists know that 1806, when Zebulon Pike passed through the region, was a dry year. Little wonder that he regarded the Kansas High Plains as a desert. The Stephen Long expedition of 1820 agreed, and until about 1870, maps in school textbooks marked the area "Great American Desert." It was throught to be flat and monotonous, like the ocean.[1]

Responses were little different in the 1860s when soldiers, hunters, cowboys, and freighters began spending considerable time in the region. Will Mitchell wrote his sister from Fort Larned in 1864: "This is the poorest country I ever saw. The land we passed over this side of Saline is not worth one cent an acre."[2] Seth Dorsey, there at the same time, would have bid higher but remembered he would not "have given $1 an acre for all of Kansas when I first saw its short grass after coming from a land of timothy and clover."[3] A third Larned soldier recalled that in 1866 if he had been offered all the country twenty-five to thirty miles from the fort at twenty-five cents an acre, he would have preferred investing in a bottle of beer at the sutler's store.

That horizon then was as barren of life as "the fig tree" in the parable except when great herds of buffalo were on the uplands grazing or frequented the Arkansas and Pawnee Fork for water; or when a band of Indians came into sight with a suddenness that recalled the mythological story of him who sowed dragon teeth which immediately grew a crop of warriors armed *cap-a-pie;* or when the far extending view was broken by some slow creeping government train from Ft. Hooker [Harker] or an occasional ambulance full of officers from Ft. Dodge coming to break the monotony of our existence and break the tedium of their own.

He could not understand why the soldiers were going to so much trouble to wrest the country from the Indians, "as we thought it only fit for the Indian."[4]

John Morrill wrote in a similar vein to his wife and children from Fort Ellsworth (later Fort Harker) on the Smoky Fork during 1865. "You would laugh to see the Ft.," he said, as it was nothing but a series of dugouts in a river bank and a few log shanties for the "aristocracy." He told his children they would think it a "strange country" where there were no trees for miles and "you can look away & see nuthing but high stony hills & valleys." On the plains Morrill saw a flat surface with short grass, where the soldiers had to pick up buffalo chips to use as fuel for boiling their coffee. He thought it might be a healthy area in cool weather, but "the vegitation [is] dead & dried up so it would not be worth much for stock." Morrill concluded that at Fort Ellsworth he was quite "out of Sivilization" and in a true desert. "This country should be left to the Indians & Wild beasts & such is pretty much the case."[5]

Potential settlers were not more cheery about it than those residing there on a tour of duty. John B. Edwards set out from Salina in the fall of 1866 to help found the town of Ellsworth on ground forty miles to the west. Looking at Salina, then a town of fewer than 200 persons, he had some doubts. His trepidation became more severe when the stage driver became lost, and Edwards passed the time by looking at such improvements as there were in the region. The few houses "seemed as if the people had been in the act of moving and had been caught by the winter, and were only waiting until spring opened up to move on." At Fort Harker the party stayed at the Picket Hotel, where sleeping accommodations were the dirt floor, and went in a borrowed ambulance to their proposed townsite. "If I had been already discouraged from the desolate and barren appearance of the country through which I had passed, I confess that I was now completely so; for a more discouraging prospect never greeted mortal eye." In all directions there were "black hills" and plains. The buffalo grass was "sere and yellow" from the action of the frost and gave the country a "dead" look. "I thought that if this was to be the future scene of my labor that it would take but a short time to make my report." It looked impossible. "All appeared but one broad limitless expanse of desert."[6]

Over a decade later, railroad promoters were still struggling with the impression that western Kansas was a desert. Stump speakers praised the "brilliant azure" of the western Kansas skies.[7] The High Plains were healthy. It was true, as a Kansas Pacific handbook put it in 1870, that "the weather and condition of roads enable you to do more work here than elsewhere." The bottom lands might not be, as claimed, "superior to those of the Nile, Amazon and Shenandoah," but the soil was rich. Unquestionably the region was "free of swamps."[8] But there was no proof it could be successfully farmed.

An 1868 traveler reacted typically when he complained of the western Kansas wind and described "dreary reaches of level sand where there are no hills, no water! not a tree, nor a bush nor a blade of grass; not a green herb, not a living thing, not any trace of any one of the multifarious forms of life with which God has filled the Earth appears to break the unending monotony of the dreary expanse." It led him to think of the biblical idea of God as "the shadow of a great rock in a weary land."[9] At about the same time William Bell crossed the divide between the Smoky Hill and Arkansas River Valleys. He wrote that the area was "not only practically a desert, but by no means a good desert for railway purposes."[10] Francis Richardson, having ridden the KP from Kansas City to Denver, wrote his wife in July 1872 that the Smoky Hill valley was the only good land he had seen and that it was only a hundred miles

An Agricultural Puzzle. Wilson, Kansas, in its natural—and bleak—setting in the 1870s.

long and a mile wide. With that exception "the whole route is a barren waste[.] from Ellis out there is not a tree or shrub growing and nothing but buffalo grass one or two inches long."[11] J. H. Tice, a KP passenger the same year, became bored with looking out his window at the "jackass" rabbit, the burrowing owl, and the prairie dog. He jotted down station names: Walker, Hays, Ellis, Ogallah, Parks' Fort, Sheridan, Wallace, Eagle Trail, Monotony.[12]

Agricultural advisers in Kansas recognized early that farming there would not only be different from that in other states but that the proper crops and techniques would vary within the state itself, particularly between its eastern and western sections. "Our soil and climate," wrote a correspondent in eastern Kansas in the mid-1860s, "are somewhat peculiar, and hence we must learn from experience rather than from observation." Although the editor of the *Kansas Farmer,* which was founded in that period, advised his readers to subscribe also to eastern agricultural papers, the primary justification for the existence of a regional sheet was that various areas of Kansas contained combinations of soil, rainfall, temperature, and wind that were not reproduced anywhere else. James Malin's study of Kansas agricultural history maps six identifiable farming regions in Kansas, two of them in western Kansas, each with its special combination of traits and requirements for crops and husbandry.[13] To a farmer whose livelihood depended upon raising a crop precisely where he lived, getting the general idea about conditions in, say, the Great Plains or the West would not suffice.

Despite this discouraging publicity, there were experiments with agriculture in western Kansas. In 1860 two men from New York, one from New Hampshire, one from Michigan, a German, and a Mexican tried planting corn at the later site of Ellsworth. It came up but was destroyed by grasshoppers. There was drought even in eastern Kansas at that time, and the winter was severe, with snow two feet deep. However, two of the men, Joseph Lehman and P. H. Page, broke about twenty acres that next spring and harvested a crop. Some farming was done also by a second group in the area, consisting of men from Kentucky and Ohio led by S. D. Walker of Wisconsin. However, there was almost no rain during the growing seasons of 1862 and 1863, and the crops at the settlement were a total failure. Shortly thereafter, Walker was killed by Indians and the entire group moved back to Salina.[14]

W. E. Webb and Martin Allen were active in agricultural experimentation at Hays City. In 1867 or 1868 Webb enclosed twenty-five acres with a board fence, ruined a number of plows trying to break five acres of it, and had so little prospect of a harvest that the gardener who was to share the proceeds with him joined a wagon train without waiting for the results.[15] Louis Agassiz of Harvard rode out to Hays on the KP, looking at the soil, and declared it "eminently adapted to the culture of wheat." The scientist predicted that the region would eventually become a world leader in wheat production. This encouraged Allen, who was of a more scientific bent than was Webb. In 1873 and 1874, Allen planted a variety of trees forwarded to him from a nursery in Illinois. Drought and

grasshoppers killed all of them. The surface of the ground was hard, Allen wrote, "and would shed rain nearly equal to a shingle roof." Allen kept trying and in the early 1880s was to be instrumental in establishing an agricultural experiment station at Hays. However, before the mid-1870s he had only speculation, not results. All he could do was to observe that the natural prairie had abundant plant life, a variety of trees—cottonwood, black walnut, white elm, red elm, ash leaf maple—and many shrubs: wild plum, wild rose, Indian currants, sumac, gooseberry, and wild grape among them. If the prairie could support these, surely it could support wheat and corn.[16]

There were other attempts. Henry Schultz of Hanover, Germany, for example, planted six acres of sod corn and two of oats in Barton County in 1870. He broke and planted ninety acres by 1873.[17] More important, though located just at the eastern edge of the western Kansas region, were the extensive experiments in large commercial farming by T. C. Henry of Abilene. Henry broke 500 acres of KP land in 1873 and by 1875 had a 1,200-acre farm planted mainly in wheat. He was *the* pioneer in Kansas in using size, hybrid crop varieties, and what would later be called dry-land farming techniques to adapt agricultural methods to the regional environment. In his writings, Henry called for "a greater attention to the advantages that peculiarly belong to our section and locality, so that a system of agriculture—distinct and apart—as our necessities are distinct and apart, may be created, and which shall secure to our farmers a success commensurate with their unrivalled . . . opportunities."[18] Henry contended that the more exactly the method fit the place, the greater would be the success. Therefore, he would have been the first to admit that the trials most relevant to western Kansas were the Kansas Pacific–sponsored farms located in several climatological subdistricts of western Kansas and operated by Richard Elliott and Dr. Louis Watson. No agricultural experiments in western Kansas prior to the grasshopper disaster of 1874 rank with these in scale and scientific approach.

R. S. Elliott published a pamphlet in March 1870 entitled *Climate of the Plains.* In it he advanced some of his optimistic theories about increasing rainfall and agricultural possibilities in the area. Partly as a result of this, he soon began an association with the Kansas Pacific Railroad and became industrial agent for the company in September 1870. One of his duties was to prove that farming was possible on the company's lands.[19]

Elliott oversaw the establishment of three experimental farms in three distinct western Kansas ecological zones. Wilson, just northwest of Ellsworth, was 240 miles west of Kansas City with an altitude of 1,586 feet; Ellis was 302 miles west and 2,019 feet; Pond Creek was 422 miles from Kansas City, close to the west line of the state, and had an altitude of 3,075 feet. Elliott made a try at plowing on the Wilson tract in the late summer of 1870, using a hired ox team and a large prairie plow. Like Webb, he broke his plow instead of the ground. The buffalo looked on languidly, Elliott wrote, "as if his ancestral acres were in no immediate danger from our operations." The practical-minded rail workers were no more encouraging and told the agent that his work was all "(blank) nonsense." Elliott overheard them as they worked: "I don't reckon that old chap

believes anything will grow out here, but like enough he has a nice berth, anyway."[20]

The Kansas Pacific finished its line to Denver on 1 September. Elliott then requested mules and heavy equipment of the type used by construction crews. When these arrived with two Irish laborers at his tract at Pond Creek, he attacked the soil again in earnest. On 28 September, Elliott and his men sowed wheat, rye, and barley at Pond Creek. On 20 October, they did the same at Ellis, and on 11 November at Wilson. Some grass seeds and trees went in also. Wrote Elliott, "The work of redeeming the domain of the buffalo was begun."[21]

Until the KP stopped supporting these farms in 1873, they produced mostly rhetoric. Elliott searched quack literature for evidence that rain followed the plow or the railroad or the telegraph.[22] He averred that "were it possible, by some magic process, to break up the entire surface of western Kansas to a depth of two feet, we should thereby begin to make a new climate." Plowing, he thought, would mean taller herbage; less reflection of the sun's heat; more humidity in the atmosphere; more constancy in springs, pools, and streams; "fewer violent storms; more frequent showers; and less caprice and fury in the winds."[23]

The trouble was that Elliott's practical tests did not work. The editor of the *Junction City Union* was a guest in the fall of 1870 on a KP excursion to show off Elliott's prairie gardens to the press. At Salina the train was greeted by a crowd with a banner reading, "Welcome to the American Desert." As the excursion pushed on west the next day, Elliott himself was on board the press car and made a speech "giving his theory for what he called the 'redemption of the

The Enthusiast. "Rain Follows the Plow" publicist Richard Smith Elliott, who encouraged the first experimental farming on the Kansas High Plains.

plains.' '' During the talk, the editor looked out the window at the landscape passing at twenty miles per hour. "The utter barrenness and desolate appearance of the country seemed to mock his words and stamp him as a crack brained enthusiast." That impression was con-

firmed when the group got off at Wilson station to look at results. The cabbages were about the size of apples and "his corn was inferior to ordinary resin-weed in eastern Kansas." Even in this carefully nursed plot, "everything was stunted and unpromising," and the editor concluded that Elliott "was visionary, and that the plains were beyond hope of salvation or redemption."[24] J. H. Tice visited the farms the next spring and found much of the crop destroyed. At Ellis, everything had been mowed by hail, and the plants elsewhere were not robust. Railroad employees, whom Tice thought had probably never set a tree before, had planted maples, elms, chestnuts, ailanthus, oaks, and walnuts. While it was true that "incontestable facts prove that of all agencies within the control of man for the amelioration of climate, that of covering the earth with forests was most effective," it was questionable if this little stand of puny trees bending in the prairie wind was what was meant.[25]

Our knowledge of early Kansas Pacific farming operations might be limited to Elliott's grandiloquent prose and a few impressions of visitors had it not been for the Ellis experimental farm of Dr. Louis Watson. Watson's farm was operated by a private corporation rather than by the railroad company directly, but it was subsidized considerably by the railroad as an advertising device. In fact, though Watson's farm does seem to have been separate from Elliott's tract at Ellis, there is no question that Watson's five railroad sections, surrounding the Ellis station on all sides, would have been more prominent to any visitor than the official railroad experiments there. Watson wrote regular letters to his mother, from which comes much about the trials of the day-to-day operation of a High Plains experimental farm.[26]

The Kansas Pacific Railroad agreed to sell Watson one to five sections of land (the sale was eventually five sections) between Hays and Sheridan for fifty cents an acre. For every $3,000 the doctor expended on the farm, the railway company would give him one section of its lands east of Fort Harker (just in case the desert was real). The railroad would furnish four freight cars and transportation for twelve men, as well as two passes lasting two years for Watson and his assistant. Watson agreed to break by July 1871 at least twenty acres of every section he purchased and to test the capability of the lands "for agricultural purposes, for tree and fruit growing and grape culture."[27]

This contract was negotiated before June 1870, but Watson, then living in Quincy, Illinois, took some time to round up backers who would finance the purchase and buy tools for the venture. Finally he was able to gather fourteen investors. The largest was J. B. Cahill, collector of internal revenue for the fourth district of Illinois. Watson sold these men stock in a $25,000 corporation he had already established, called the Western Kansas Agricultural Association. The company then employed Watson as general manager to supervise the farms at Ellis. What is surprising is that not only was the desert to be farmed at this early date, but it was to be farmed for profit, in a 3,200-acre block, and by a corporation.[28]

The corporate prospectus shows what was envisioned. If irrigation were needed, the association would dam Big Creek or build windmills. It would market products to the "large number of nonproducers" living at Fort Hays, Wallace, Lyons, and Camp Supply or working on the railroad. It would collect the state bounty of $2 per acre on lands planted to forest trees and the $2 the state paid for every forty rods of hedging or stone fencing. Then there were the lands the company would gain eighty-four miles east of Ellis in a proven agricultural zone through its contract with the railroad. These could be sold. Last, employees of the association were to be given a special option to colonize company lands, which could be purchased through investment in Western Kansas Agricultural Association stock. Watson would provide such colonists free transportation from Kansas City.[29]

Watson's first annual report to his Illinois directors was optimistic. He had arrived in Ellis on 1 April 1871 (a portentous date), having contracted with Thomas Arrowsmith of Quincy, Illinois, to attend to details in Ellis when Watson might be away raising funds. By June, 120 acres were broken and 100 acres planted with corn and sorghum. In September, 20 acres were cross-plowed and sowed to wheat, rye, and barley. In November a small plot was plowed repeatedly; into it went currants, blackberries, raspberries, young peach and cherry trees, acorns, hickory nuts, pecans, and six barrels of black walnuts. Watson and Arrowsmith planned to put in various kinds of grass seed and to plant Osage orange hedge. Arrowsmith was interested in the company stock "and may be willing to do this at a trifling more than the payment of necessary travelling expenses."[30]

Watson's letter to his mother in July had a different tone. Arrowsmith had gone back to Illinois for a visit, and Ellis was hot and lonesome. Although the farm looked "pretty well, better than I expected in some respects," there were problems. "The potato bugs have nearly destroyed the potatoes which otherwise would have turned out well, and the grasshoppers have eaten some of the other things." There had been rains, but the dry air and wind still shriveled crops, which were then attacked by insects. Arrowsmith was to bring some turkeys and chickens to eat the six-legged creatures that seemed to thrive in the area—"I saw *ten thousand million* flying by a day or two ago." Meanwhile, Watson would try to survive the danger, not of Indians, but of "lightning or being blown away in some hurricane."[31]

The drawbacks could not be entirely hidden from the investors. Watson pled with his directors in January 1872 to pay the debts the company owed or risk losing the ground and failing to benefit from the development of the townsite of Ellis.[32] That month he became so uncomfortable in the severe winter at Ellis that he retreated to Topeka, where he slept in the office of an insurance agent. He wrote his mother that he had tried to get more aid in Illinois, "but the Chicago fire burnt out all my hopes." His directors would allow him to expend no funds unless he raised them by selling stock in the company. "I wanted to have things go on nice & smooth next summer, have a comfortable room for myself & a horse to ride and I could enjoy myself amazingly in botanizing & collecting specimens in all branches of Natural History, besides exploring the country generally."[33]

It was not to be. Instead, Watson had to fall back on his medical training, making calls in Ellis to earn enough income to maintain himself on the company farm. The Western Kansas Agricultural Association folded that winter.

Watson's December 1871 accounting showed farming expenses of $5,295.49 and total expenses, including miscellaneous items and Watson's $1,166.66 salary, of $6,462.15. No income offset these expenses. J. B. Cahill, the major investor, wrote Watson on 19 December to stop all expenses as he could not stand any more assessments.[34]

Watson put in crops for at least the next three years, but the marginal first season was his best. "It is a curious 'desert,'" he wrote in June 1873, "where animal and insect life is so abundant—Things grow on the farm very well, but some insect, bug, grasshopper or worm or gopher, ground squirrels or rabbits play the deuce with whole crops—Gophers have eaten off underground the roots of even oak trees and destroyed whole nurseries." Local residents did not support his work any more generously than had the stockbrokers from Illinois. "The skinning propensities of Kansas people—their dishonesty & corruption disgusts one with human nature such as it appears to be becoming all the country over. . . . I wonder whence I obtained all my *hope*!"[35] In 1874 the weather was dry and hot. Watson recorded no measurable rain at Ellis from 14 June to 2 August, and the temperature was over 100 degrees day after day, sometimes as high as 115 on the north side of a house. That summer an immense invasion of grasshoppers destroyed the withered stalks that remained.[36] The doctor was still hopeful, writing his mother in 1875 that "I firmly believe that *within a few years here* 300 miles west of the Missouri River, many agricultural products will be bountifully produced."[37] But he had to be honest about his own efforts: "I shan't have much of a forest for some time."[38]

The Santa Fe Railroad was interested also in

proving either that the western Kansas desert was not so bad or that, if it were, it would change. The company sent John Bonnell in January 1872 to examine a particularly desertlike section of its land grant, the Sand Hills south of Larned. Bonnell found little valleys there with buffalo and bluestem grass. The soil was not bad, and beyond was good country. "The sand hills from Larned present a bleak and barren appearance," Bonnell wrote, "but in and through them is splendid grazing, and when once past (and they are barely 4 miles wide) the beautiful valley above described opens to view and is all open to settlement."[39]

The Santa Fe farms concentrated on trees more exclusively than had the Kansas Pacific experiments. Tree planting had for some time been thought a panacea that would both prove the adaptability of the Plains climate and make contributions to changing it. They were also rumored to contribute to health, and certainly it was felt that any truly civilized region required trees to surround fine homes and to grace courthouse squares. In 1873, the very year the Santa Fe established its first western Kansas tree farm, Congress passed the Timber Culture Act, marking the height of a tree-planting movement in the West in its fad phase.[40]

By the end of the decade, the Santa Fe company had extensive plots at Hutchinson, Ellinwood, Garfield, and Spearville. These sites were spread along the line to a point just east of Dodge City, where Santa Fe land sales were concentrated in the 1870s, and were successful. The largest plot at Garfield, ten miles southwest of Larned, was eighteen and a half acres. In 1879 it had 5,700 cottonwood trees, 6,000 ailanthus, and 2,500 ash. At Ellinwood, just east of Great Bend, an eighteen-acre

tree farm was enclosed by a panel fence. There in 1879 grew 100 six-year-old silver maples eighteen feet high, 500 honey locusts, 350 catalpas, 300 box elders, 2,000 Osage orange trees, 1,000 green ash trees, 400 black walnuts, over 1,000 cottonwoods up to twenty-two feet high, and a few willows, hackberries, and elms. There were sixteen acres at Hutchinson, and even the westernmost farm, Spearville, had six acres of trees by 1879, including 2,000 box elders twelve feet high.[41] Unquestionably these efforts were important to the Santa Fe's colonization efforts, peaking as they did just as the memory of the grasshoppers faded and a few wet years seemed to justify claims that trees changed climate.

Indeed, the initial hope, and one that can be identified as a second major illusion about the western Kansas region (after the magic influence of the railroads), was that civilizing the area and farming it would permanently change its climate. Josiah Copley in 1867 thought he saw signs of that process: "No part of the earth's surface has ever passed so suddenly from the condition of a vast, trackless, desolate abode of wild beasts and roving savages to one of complete and beautiful Christian civilization as this; and probably no other could have been so quickly transformed." Looking at the prairie flowers in bloom, Copley commented, "God's own hand has planted a garden here, and all that is required of man is that he shall go in and occupy and dress it, and keep it."[42] The Kansas Pacific *Hand Book* of 1870 had a similar focus. It was not a desert fit only for "savage beasts and more savage men," the pamphlet said of western Kansas, but a "vision of beauty" which "the planting of shade trees, the digging of wells, and the cultivation of the soil" would

Hardly a Forest. The Kansas Pacific Railroad's experimental tree farm at Wilson, Kansas, in the mid-1870s.

redeem from the "curse of sterility and cause the desert to blossom as the rose." It was necessary, KP advertising said, to see the region *"in posse"* rather than *"in esse."*[43] One analyst in 1884 was certain that overall weather records indicated a change. "Here certainly, if human agency could anywhere affect climate, would such an effect be produced."[44]

Fundamental to theories of climate change was the idea that rainfall was increasing as settlement progressed.[45] For a time during the 1870s there was evidence of this, and the idea, damaged as it was by the severe drought of 1880, did not fall into entire disrepute before the extended dry spell of the early 1890s. Although Louis Watson kept a careful and discouraging record of the rainfall at the Ellis experimental farm from 1871 on, widespread

scientific data on rainfall in the region were not available to the newspaper-reading public until about 1875. Between then and 1880, the trend was for rainfall to increase.

A Hays City newspaper reported in 1877 that since 1870 it had rained 210.75 inches, according to the unofficial (and, I believe, optimistic) collectors there, an average of 28.75 inches per year. In the first three of these years, the average was 21.52 inches, but for the latter three it was 35.20 inches, an increase of 13.77. "Still," commented the *Hays Sentinel,* "there are skeptics who say it never rains in Kansas."[46] At Ellinwood and Great Bend, where records were kept by a sober-enough local science buff named B. B. Smyth, the trend also looked definite for a time. In 1874 he reported a total of 24.92 inches; in 1875, 25.06; in 1876,

35.32; and in 1877, 40.07. It was troublesome that these dropped to 28.68 in 1878 and 20.43 in 1879, but perhaps these were temporary aberrations.[47] Dodge City showed a similar pattern. In 1875 rainfall was only 10.99 inches, but it increased to 15.40 in 1876 and 27.89 in 1877. Late in the decade the statistics wobbled there too: 17.36 in 1878; 15.42 in 1879; 18.12 in 1880.[48] Breakdowns by month indicate that even in years when averages were high, rains did not always come when needed for crops. Also, rainfall varied widely in a single year within the region, and there was slight to moderate upward exaggeration in press reports when compared with the figures printed by the state board of agriculture.[49] But science for a time could be bent to the dreams of the true believer.

Related to wishful thinking about rainfall was the belief that vegetation changed as settlers moved in. The buffalo grass seemed to be giving way to big and little bluestem; the impression was that the High Plains would someday look like the Flint Hills. The editor of the *Osborne County Farmer* wrote in 1876 that it took five to ten years from the date of settlement for buffalo grass to change to bluegrass.[50] Colonel Thomas Murphy, former head of the Central Superintendency of the Office of Indian Affairs, returned to western Kansas in 1878 after an absence of twelve years and said he did not recognize it. "The buffalo grass and cactus had disappeared, and in their stead tall, rank prairie grass, five to six feet high, was waving in the breeze; the soil even seemed to have undergone a transformation, losing its dry, sandy appearance, taking on a darker hue, and filled with moisture."[51] Kansas Pacific publicists advised passengers that seeds carried by

the railroad cars germinated instantly along the right of way until the railroad corridor was covered with "plant-waifs."[52] C. C. Hutchinson, in his 1871 guide *Resources of Kansas,* pointed out that the vast herds of buffalo and antelope would not return to a real desert. Surely their presence indicated possibilities for profits from grazing, if not from farming, in western Kansas.[53] A writer for the *Dodge City Times* thought in 1879 that the bluestem and grama grass already in the buffalo wallows would soon spread over everything and would "solve the rain problem, by equalizing, increasing and extending the process of evaporation." Thus would the desert be conquered. "Two years more, we will hardly realize that we once stood on the barren, cheerless plain, over which hot southern winds swept with scorching fury, burning the scanty and sparsely growing herbage."[54]

The evidence for climate change was thin, and many remained unconvinced. The Hays City editor thought exaggeration was as dangerous as underrating and that it was "abominably mean" to lie to strangers.[55] More telling in its documentation was a response to talk of changing climate written by Henry Inman of the *Larned Chronoscope* in 1878. Inman studied rainfall records of Fort Larned extending back to 1861 and found the pattern in the 1860s as erratic and inconclusive as that of the 1870s. For the 1860s, beginning in 1861, he gave the following rainfall figures: 17.99, 17.21, 22.85, 29.81, 36.30 (no record for 1866), 18.35, 24.70, 9.41. Beginning in 1870 at Larned: 37.39, 13.64, 12.97, 18.23, 21.78, 17.80, 18.27, 30.29, 14.13. Long-time resident Inman said the idea that in the old days there was no dew was absurd. If statistics were studied over a long period of time, it could be demonstrated that the climate was highly variable (9.41 inches of rain in 1869, for example, and 37.39 the next year) but showed no consistent trend. It was as it always had been—"mild, healthy and genial" but not wet and not predictable.[56]

A similar view was expressed in 1879 by Edgar Guild, who lived at Monument along the western Kansas line of the KP Railroad. Perhaps western Kansas was not a desert, Guild wrote, but in mid-July it "certainly comes nearer to being a Sahara than an Egypt, and, to make it the earthly paradise that enthusiasts predict, will certainly require a thorough understanding of its atmospheric peculiarities." Average rainfall statistics were meaningless, Guild thought, because drought resulted not from lack of rain so much as from imperfect distribution and excessive, wind-aided evaporation. He believed that the area might support agriculture but that it was better adapted to raising stock. The breaking of a few thousand acres of sod would not be enough to bring about a change of climate and would only better absorb the rain that did fall. This greater absorption would not, as some theorists had it, bring more rain. "Like may attract like, but it is hardly an axiom." Guild decried the "unwonted enthusiasm" that had "made western Kansas a fertile and prolific region—on paper."[57]

The very first agricultural experiments in western Kansas yielded abundant evidence of the true nature of the region and of some of the adaptations it would ultimately force upon agriculture. For one thing, an unbiased observer might have noticed that western Kansas was not the best place to pursue successfully subsistence farming on the 160-acre plots the govern-

ment was offering through the Homestead and Timber Culture Acts. Ironically, because of the timing of settlement and the railroad land-grant patterns, it was to be just in this region that homesteads and timber-culture claims had their greatest importance in Kansas as means of gaining land. It might also have been noticed that the region rewarded large-scale operations and that meeting its special problems required not only cooperation in exchange of information but capital beyond the means of individual settlers. As scholars have noticed about other Plains regions (Howard Lamar's studies of the Dakotas are a good example), these needs for organized study and capital expenditure created a good opportunity for government action.[58] The same needs—for capital, for large-scale vision, and for organized distribution of information on experiments—favored corporations. Watson's Western Kansas Agricultural Association is a small but telling example. More obvious were the railroads, which went far beyond mere transport in contributing to the region. Their effectiveness in establishing and promoting experimental farms to foster confidence was only an initial example of direct aid to the region before 1890, aid that, however self-interested, was demonstrably vast. The settler was not eager to recognize this. It offended his values and denied him a "soulless" scapegoat to blame in place of the environment or his own illusions. Nor did he care to see T. C. Henry with his large farm, his heavy investment in machinery, and his talk about hybrid grains and dry-land farming techniques, developed perhaps in cooperation with government, as the wave of the future. But waves of the future are not respecters of images, even deeply cherished ones.

However great may have been differences about methods of attack, it is important to reemphasize that there was broad consensus about the idea that attack—exploitation and modification—was in general the appropriate means of dealing with the new country. Perhaps as much as Coronado had to accept western Kansas as a place without the gold he had expected, and Pike and Long had to view it as a desert, the progressive late-nineteenth-century pioneer was bound to see it as a wild garden waiting to be changed to a tame one.[59] The editor of the *Wichita Eagle* wrote that the goal had been "to add to the prairies what the prairies had not, trees where there were no trees, water where there was no water, cereal where there was only grass, fuel where there were no hills, roads and steel rails where there were no navigable rivers, manufacturers where there was no raw material."[60] A Kansas governor could boast in 1983 that the state had more shoreline than Minnesota and, if one left out the qualifier "natural," be nearly right. The spectacle of pioneer farmers attempting to train buffalo to pull plows or trying to domesticate prairie chickens was just one sign of a manipulative attitude toward the environment.[61] Ultimately, they would not even try to adapt but to import a life style whole. One hundred years after the initial assault, many western Kansans retreat to air-conditioned houses on hot summer nights and gather around television sets attached by cables to the real world, while outside the night breezes blow and the galaxies whirl.

Probably, as John Madson speculates in *Where the Sky Began,* his masterly look at the tallgrass prairie's past and present, women were better able than men to see what great beauty and scope for the spirit were being lost in the assault on the "desert."[62] Children, unconscious as they were of needing to use the land for anything other than delight, adapted to the new country most quickly of all and loved it all their lives.

What they saw was a kind of richness, spiritual as well as physical, that escaped progressives who, while they might see the necessity for adapting agricultural methods, never considered the more fundamental adaptation of abandoning agriculture and developing economic and social life styles more perfectly suited to the country as they found it. What was there and was quickly lost was a virgin mature prairie, an ecosystem that Madson estimates would take more than three hundred years to recreate. Breaking the sod and running the trains meant destroying a floral and wildlife treasure. In May 1879 B. B. Smyth listed the flowers and birds he saw near Great Bend. There were red-winged blackbirds, skylarks, yellow-headed blackbirds, bitterns, kingbirds. Flowers were abundant: the plums bloomed on the first of May, buffalo peas on the third, box elder on the seventh, garden cherry on the tenth, wild onions on the fourteenth, Solomon's seal on the eighteenth, wild cherry on the nineteenth, pink sorrel on the twenty-fifth, and white mallow on the twenty-eighth.[63] In July he spotted yellow sorrel, flat-stem bluegrass, trailing verbena, crimson mallow, wild grape, white pentstemon, scarlet mallow, sweet gaura, false gromwell, ground cherry, bush primrose, Virginia creeper, indigo, larkspur, yarrow, spider lily, wax-leaf pentstemon, leatherroot, dwarf pink, showy milkweed, flowered evening primrose, red pincushion cactus, large-flowered evening primrose, salt grass, sensitive brier, dogwood, graceful stickseed, dwarf morning glory, wild rose, dogbane, cane flower, horsemint, little sunflower, buffalo thistle, squirrel-tail grass, and long-leaf milkweed.[64] The names were a symphony of sound. The reality was a miracle only a few saw and lived in before it was largely gone.

"The pleasantest recollection I have of pioneer days in Western Kansas," recalled an old lady who had been a girl in Lane County in the 1880s, "is the memory of the prairie in springtime with green grass as far as one could see dotted here and there with millions of beautiful wild flowers."[65] Many others who knew it as children, particularly little girls who played

house with buffalo bones down in the grass where the breeze was cool, looked back with equal fondness on the unimproved desert.[66] Their aesthetic vision was of course ignored, though in its innocence it contained a certain humble wisdom that only the passage of a good deal more time with the American industrial system would reveal. Wrote a pamphleteer in 1878: "The great God swept away the ancient forests, and in their stead, planted an illimitable garden of waving grasses and wild flowers. The children of the pioneer have reveled in the fragrance and beauty of this ocean of bloom, while he turned the furrow and planted the corn."[67]

Chapter Five

The Ravaging Hopper

The summer of 1874 was hot and dry. The corn withered, and families hid within the thick sod walls of their houses. Suddenly, late in July, the grasshoppers arrived. "They came gradually," wrote Percy Ebbutt, "like a fall of snow. We saw first a glittering cloud high in the sky, and all sparkling in the sun, from which they fell one or two at a time."[1]

Melanopolus spretus was not an impressive-looking insect. From its head to the tip of its closed wing, it measured about one and a third inches. Colors varied, but commonly its underbody was white; it was glaucous or cabbage blue across the breast and mouth parts; pale blue to purple on the sides of the head, thorax, and the front of the face; and had yellowish front and middle legs. Its shanks were coral red with black spines, its antennae pale yellow, and its powerful bent back legs striped with reddish marks. When it died these colors rapidly faded, and, picked up along the margin of a corn field, the Rocky Mountain locust appeared to be a most ordinary tiny grasshopper.[2]

Louis Watson watched the blizzard from Ellis. "I don't know how better to describe it," he wrote his mother in Quincy, "than to compare them to a snowstorm." They covered fences and houses at Ellis and formed a moving current on the ground "as thick as swarming bees."[3] "I never saw such a sight before," wrote a settler in Edwards County. "This morning as we looked up toward the sun we could see millions in the air. They looked like snowflakes."[4] Mary Northway along the Solomon River compared the fall to a hailstorm. "When we started home we could hardly walk for them. They would fly up in our faces and nearly blind us."[5] Marsh Murdock in Wichita saw them coming "in untold millions, in clouds upon clouds, until their fluttering wings looked like a sweeping snow storm in the heavens,— until their dark bodies covered everything green upon the earth."[6] "Onward they came," wrote a Kinsley poet, "a dark continuous cloud / Of congregated myriads numberless, / The rushing of whose wings was as the sound / Of a broad river, headlong in its course, / Plunged from a mountain summit, or the roar / Of a wild ocean in the autumn storm, / Shattering its billows on the shore of rocks!"[7]

The chickens cleaned up "the beastly things" for a time, but when they started to fall in numbers they were impossible to control. The ground was several inches thick with them, and it was difficult to keep them brushed off one's hands and face. An apple in the orchard might have twenty insects on it. "Presently it would fall to the ground, and amongst the struggling mass there it soon totally disap-

Terror from on High. An illustration from Harper's Weekly, *3 July 1875, showing an attempt to clear a Kansas field of grasshoppers. All activities for the settlers, pleasant or unpleasant, were family affairs.*

peared."[8] The hoppers ate holes in girls' dresses, ate all the crops, and then stripped the leaves from the trees.[9] Within days of their visit the countryside looked like a wasteland, just as if the strange snow had been real and winter had arrived. The insects particularly loved onions and left large holes in the ground where the plants had been. They disliked tomatoes but eventually ate those too, vines and all. A girl remembered with horror that the ground seemed to be in motion and that a person walking could hear not only the crunching of bodies underfoot but the working of millions of

tiny jaws.[10] When vegetable food ran out, the host ate other things: house plants, curtains, screens, twigs, and finally each other. They did so in a swath 250 miles wide and 20 miles deep from vanguard to rear, moving eventually across several states and covering 5,000 square miles of farmland at a sitting.[11] Locomotives lost traction from grasshopper bodies on the tracks and came into stations varnished brown with gore.[12] "Their numbers," one man confessed, "were awful to contemplate."[13]

Settlers' immediate response was to search their hearts for the grievous secret sin that had caused such a plague to be loosed upon them. Immigrants looked to legends about the evil that dwelt below and sprang from the north, while settlers from other areas of the United States searched no further than the Book of Exodus and the eighth plague of Egypt.[14] "It was as though the land were directly smitten by the Almighty," a Wichita man wrote. "The disaster came as comes an earthquake, which fulfills its destructive mission at once, without delay and without warning: against which there is no defense; which prostrates the staunchest, unnerves the boldest, and gives to all an indescribable feeling of hopeless helplessness."[15] A father at Bull City (now Alton) in Osborne County became so distraught at the grasshopper invasion that he killed his child, tried to kill his wife, and then killed himself.[16] A family heading for the same town that dreary summer met hundreds of wagons heading east. "Everyone advised us to turn and go back to *God's country* or we would sure starve to death."[17]

The hoppers were the "scourge of all scourges," the ultimate counterattack from nature.[18] Men who had held up through two years of drought and short rations put their heads in their hands and cried. Women leafed through the Bible for the verse in Ecclesiastes that seemed so exactly to apply: "Also when they shall be afraid of that which is high, and fears shall be in the way . . . and the grasshopper shall be a burden, and desire shall fail."[19] Cyrus Holliday, first president of the Santa Fe Railroad, wrote his son Charlie from Topeka in September 1874 and described a grim statewide scene. People were filled with anxiety about the future, and though the Indians had for the moment quit scalping, the grasshopper had flown, and starvation did not seem an immedi-

ate problem, life in western Kansas was being lived on a ragged edge. "We can only hope," wrote Holliday, that Providence "who tempers the wind to the shorn lamb" would ensure a mild winter and lift up again in forgiveness the westering families it had so rudely pummeled.[20] "This is the varmint," said a man examining the dead body of a tiny insect, "the ravishing hopper, / Ain't he a whopper."[21]

The grasshopper plague was not visited only on Kansas, though sometimes the national publicity almost made it seem so. Nor was 1874 the only Plains invasion, though it was one of the most widespread and, because of the lack of defenses of the new settlers, one of the most devastating and well known. Grasshoppers had threatened Vermont agriculture in 1797–1798, eaten the crops of the California missions in 1746, 1753, 1754, 1765–1767. They invaded Minnesota and Missouri in 1818–1819 and were a greater or smaller problem to the Mormons in Utah nearly every year from 1848 to 1880.[22] Swarms had visited Kansas in 1820, in 1848, in 1850, in 1860, in 1864–1866, and in 1868.[23] The combination of drought and grasshoppers in the 1860s had seriously affected farmers in eastern Kansas and necessitated a state relief program.[24] The 1874 trouble was one of the most widespread, caused perhaps by a large hatch in northwestern breeding grounds and insufficient local food.[25] It affected the Dakotas, Colorado, Nebraska, Missouri, Iowa, and Kansas severely enough that year to require public relief.

One would assume, then, that the grasshopper invasions of 1874 were a great unifying factor for the Plains as a region. But that was only partly true. One of the earliest governors' conferences for the Plains resulted, and there was some cooperation in the appeal most of the states needed to make for federal aid. But grasshopper problems, like droughts, do not have the same effect on all areas at a given time. For example, Utah, which had experienced nearly constant grasshopper troubles, had none at all in 1874.[26] Also, while there are some similarities in how different states approached the grasshopper relief question, the major one being early reluctance to seek federal aid, there were, as will be seen, significant differences. The Kansas legislature, for instance, merely gave permission for counties to issue relief bonds and authorized a private committee, in contrast to Minnesota, which made substantial and immediate direct appropriations for food, medical aid, and seeds.[27] The extent and nature of the devastation varied across the region, as did the philosophy and means of those assigned to carry out the relief function. In Kansas, one might even examine the political relationship of the developed eastern section, whence tax money derived, and the pioneer western section, where the bulk of the damage was done and to which relief funds were directed. In short, a study of the grasshopper invasion *in toto,* such as the one now being undertaken by University of Southern California historian Thomas C. Cox,[28] is likely to reveal as much variation as unity in the response to this natural disaster.

One could see the human parameters of the problem anywhere it struck, and it struck western Kansas hard. Barton County reported that five hundred to a thousand persons needed aid. It requested 2,000 bushels of potatoes, 450 bushels of flour, 200 bushels of corn meal, 1,100 bushels of onions, 100 barrels of pickles, 50 barrels of vinegar, 50 barrels of sugar, 300 pounds of tea, 600 pounds of coffee, 75 bushels of white beans, 25 barrels of dried apples, 25. boxes of concentrated milk, and 1,000 pounds of butter.[29] James Walker wrote from Edwards County that twenty-five or thirty families there were wholly destitute. One family living in a twelve-by-sixteen dugout existed on flour and tea, another on wheat, another on parched corn ground in a coffee mill and wet with water. According to Walker's survey, twenty-two children lacked proper underclothing and shoes.[30] An aid committee in Smith County estimated that two thousand people there would need help as a result of the hoppers and that not more than 10 percent of county residents had supplies enough for even bare subsistence.[31] Some in Rush County got scurvy before the winter ended.[32]

There was no shortage of editorials on the theme "How the Sympathies of the Credulous Are Abused" suggesting that the hopper problem was exaggerated for selfish ends. The *Chicago Tribune,* for example, chuckled that aid solicitors made statements "which would go to show that the fertile plains of Kansas were in danger of becoming one vast charnel house; no great stretch of the imagination has been required to see skeletons glistening in the sunlight on every hill, and grim death stalking over every plain." But, the urban editor concluded, actually the suffering was limited to a few sparsely settled western counties, and the rest of the state was well off. "The entire state will suffer more during the next five years," he concluded, "from the vague rumors of widespread suffering than from a dozen grasshopper raids. The fair name and future prosperity of the state are being recklessly endangered and her matchless climate and superior soil in future years will tempt the settler in vain, unless the grasshopper phantom is narrowed down to reasonable proportions."[33]

The truth lay between the extremes. The figures collected in a survey conducted by Alfred Gray for the State Board of Agriculture in December 1874 showed twenty-six counties (most of the occupied western group) in need of aid. The compilation gave the total population of the county first and the number needing aid second: Barber (608; 200), Barton (860; 300), Ellis and unorganized Ness and Rush (1,325; 400), Ellsworth (3,275; 200), Edwards (500; 100), Decatur (300; 189), Ford (333; 150), Harvey (3,600; 300), Jewell (7,674; 1,000), Lincoln (2,220; 450), McPherson (4,837; 600), Mitchell (5,473; 600), Norton (844; 600), Osborne (3,890; 1,000), Ottawa (4,990; 400), Pawnee (710; 150), Phillips (2,409; 100), Pratt (300; 100), Reno (6,467; 1,000), Republic (8,020; 300), Rice (2,366; 100), Rooks (900; 600), Russell (815; 300), and Smith (4,460; 1,500). Some returns for Trego, Hodgeman, and Kingman Counties were too indefinite to be counted, and surely the totals, used as they were as a basis for solicitation by a state that did not want to solicit, were conservative. Still, the total (out of a western population of 66,104) was 12,089 people needing food and an estimated 18,134 needing at least clothing and bedding.[34]

While the state debated the type of aid to give, appeals for help went directly east from Kansas. Some counties with substantial need printed circulars. From Smith County in October 1874 came this plea: "Forced by the illiberal and narrow spirit of the Legislature to look outside the State for that assistance we had reason to expect would be afforded by our own citizens, [we] make this appeal to all benevolent persons, who may learn of our distress." A little "from your abundance," the circular claimed, would "enable us to retain our homes, for which we have tempted the dangers and endured the trials of the last two years."[35] Printed circulars were sometimes issued by church groups, such as the one by the American Home Missionary Society on behalf of Rice, Barton, Pawnee, and Edwards Counties. In these cases the address given was a church that took responsibility for distribution—here the Congregational church at Peace in Rice County.[36]

Letters often came to easterners from individual families. J. G. Sampson wrote from El Paso (now Derby), Kansas, to his brother in Sedalia, Missouri, asking for aid; the letter was printed in the Sedalia paper. "This is humiliating," the editor commented, "but absolutely true, as they have no money, nothing to sell and no credit."[37] Surely more difficult to write were letters to complete strangers. Judge B. F. Hartshorn of Mason City, Iowa, received a note in December 1874 from Thomas Byrne of Great Bend, a man unknown to the judge but whose embarrassment receded in the face of his family's plight. There were eight of them, the eldest twenty-two and the youngest five "We have toiled hard—all of us—and have struggled to ride the waves—but the storm has beat too hard for us—Any kind of food—no matter what—or old cast-off clothes—boots or shoes—as all our family are barefoot—and destitute of all kinds of clothing." The applicant admitted there was no special reason why someone in Mason City should help him: "I have no other earthly claim on you than a family on the verge of starvation can have on any one—and nothing

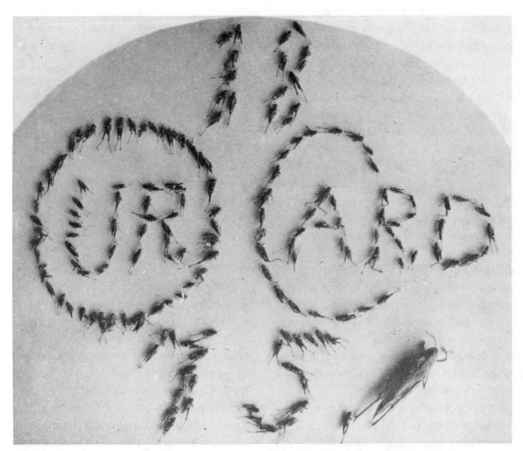

Greetings from Kansas. An attempt at humor in sending to friends in the east a calling card made of the invading grasshoppers. Notice the standard-size grasshopper in the lower right-hand corner, included to illustrate how small individuals of the terrible host really were.

but the cries of helpless destitute children for 'something to eat—Father' could force me to make this disconnected appeal.''[38]

Sometimes a generous person in the East would read a circular or a newspaper appeal, respond to the appropriate address, and only later learn just how desperate individuals had been for the smallest amount of help. E. C. Redington of Vermont probably never imagined the response he would get for sending $50 to the Reverend E. B. Foster to distribute to the needy of Osborne County. Foster gave $10 to a minister in Smith Center and then gave $5 each to eight local families. Redington received not only a several-page report from Foster but personal letters of thanks from each family aided. R. S. Osborn, the local Methodist minister, had not had butter or milk in his house for three weeks and had tried to bring his fifteen-year-old daughter Estelle back to health on borrowed flour.[39] He wrote Redington that the $5 "came as a Christmas present, like an oasis in the desert, bridging over a present necessity that *could not otherwise have been met.*"[40] Louisa Seaver, a widow with a daughter, wrote: "I regard the gift as coming from God. I thank you from my hart [*sic*] for your opportune gift."[41] Isaac Irey could not write but had his crippled son, who had been ill for six months with a stomach ailment, compose a letter thanking Redington for making it possible to buy medicine for the boy.[42] This may seem like Dickensian sentiment to some modern readers, but Redington was genuinely moved. He saved the little packet of letters from grasshopper country all his life, and when his son found it in the desk drawer in 1925 he forwarded it to the Kansas State Historical Society to remain as a record of a gift well directed.[43]

But the problem was too large for the E. C. Redingtons alone. Central coordination of aid was needed to prevent fraud, and public aid had to supplement private giving. A special session of the state legislature convened in September 1874 to consider the question of relief. However, the expense of holding the session— $16,000—was about all the thrifty lawmakers felt they could spare for this emergency. After much debate, it was decided to establish the Kansas Central Relief Committee and authorize it to act as a clearing house for private aid.[44] This was necessary not only to encourage gifts but because the state's railroads, which had offered to haul cars of relief goods free, wanted to protect themselves against exploitation.[45]

However, although many bills for an appropriation of direct aid were introduced during the next several months, the only monetary assistance the state granted was in the form of a loan. A bill passed authorizing needy counties to issue relief bonds, which the state would then buy at ninety-five cents on the dollar, using its own bonds to acquire the funds.[46]

The response of other Plains states ranged from slightly to greatly more generous. The legislature of adjoining Nebraska authorized the issuance of $50,000 in state bonds to buy seed and grain, though not food and clothing.[47] Even in remote Dakota Territory, the legislature earmarked $25,000 in bond aid.[48] Farther east, there was more generosity by local government. Minnesota, which had recently carried out a major state relief effort in response to hail and prairie fire in 1871, appropriated more than $100,000 in direct relief funds during the grasshopper troubles there in 1873 and 1874. Iowa granted $50,000 outright to destitute settlers to be used at their discretion and distributed nearly $40,000 worth of wheat, corn, oats, potatoes, and garden seed to 1,750 families.[49] Kansas, it appeared, had relief needs greater than most and a legislative response smaller than any. Therefore, the situation of its settlers was seen at the time as especially difficult.

Western Kansans were more than annoyed at the minimal state action and fired the initial salvos in a battle with Topeka that was to lead several times to calls for the secession of the state's western section. County bond issues required a two-thirds majority, and in the new regions of western Kansas, where the tax base was small and the future unknown, those were not forthcoming.[50] Also, the state's fiscal agents reported that there would be a weak market for state bonds issued to back the county bonds. The country was in the midst of a financial reverse in the wake of the Panic of 1873.[51] A Smith County man thought that issuing county bonds was a case of "taxing the beggar to support the pauper."[52] Wrote another from the same region: "We have received from the State mockery and insult in the sacred name of charity; we asked for bread, and they have given a stone."[53] Most galling to western Kansans was a statement made by legislators and repeated by Lieutenant Governor E. S. Stover, head of the new Kansas Central Relief Committee. The destitution was not general, state officials claimed, but limited to frontier counties and recent immigrants with crops on sod. "Strictly speaking, they are not citizens of Kansas at all."[54]

As bill after bill was debated in Topeka, subjected to criticism on constitutional and legal grounds, and rejected, bitterness mounted. The *Russell County Record* noted in February that a bill had passed changing the name of the Grasshopper River. The editor said it was well that the legislature attended to *"important* bills with promptness and dispatch."[55] In April, one legislator explained that something might have been done had the western counties not demanded relief rather than politely asked for it. "Its Royal Highness the senate," wrote the Russell editor, "was offended because that insignificant element, the people, rose up and demanded relief when an uncontrollable calamity had fallen upon the state." He suggested that the entire Kansas Senate be sent to the upcoming Centennial Exhibition as a display of demagoguery.[56] John Edwards wrote Governor Thomas Osborn from Ellis that "the legislature by a series of bun-

combe resolutions have undertaken to show that the state is abundantly able to provide for her own poor, and have for the last 30 days been endeavoring to prove the assertion, and have only succeeded in having introduced a large number of bills showing upon their face such impossibilities, as about to make the whole thing a huge farce."[57] Robert Wright of Dodge City suggested that the following resolution could probably pass the strict state legislature: "Resolved: That 100,000 copies of the constitution be printed in pamphlet form for distribution among destitute people of western Kansas to enable them to get through the winter and to furnish seed wheat for planting . . . and in order that no expenditure be made for expressage and freight on the same, each member is expected to carry home in his carpet sack the quota belonging to his county."[58]

The relief committee was optimistic. "Our people have not lost faith in themselves," its initial publication claimed, "or in the resources and prospects of the State in which they live, nor in Him without whom not a sparrow falls to the ground."[59] However, the direct role of the state was small, consisting mostly of licensing agents and sending elaborate forms to the counties to assure donors and railroads through statistics that the need was real. How many children are in the community, the state form asked? How many bushels of wheat are on hand? How many hogs do you have? How many milk cows? How much money? How many acres of land are under cultivation? Have you any potatoes? How many children are without shoes? Stockings? How soon will you need aid and what will you need first? The committee wanted the form notarized by the local justice of the peace.[60]

The victims of the grasshopper invasion had a good deal more to worry about than filling out forms asking for information they often did not have, and the forms left an impression that the state bureaucracy was short on trust for the hardy, honest settlers about whom it boasted in the press. Critics thought that the state's role in relief could hinder collections. Some charged that the state committee was dominated by land speculators who wished to minimize the crisis and that the private Nebraska Relief and Aid Association was doing a better job of attracting funds and goods for settlers to the north.[61]

There was doubt, too, whether the Kansas Central Relief Committee, with little funding and a volunteer staff of prominent Kansans, could adequately carry out even its administrative functions. One member of the committee, newspaper editor Marshall Murdock of Wichita, did not seem to think so when he penned an anguished letter to Lieutenant Governor Stover in December 1874. Murdock said that the Alfred Gray report sponsored by the State Board of Agriculture had seriously underestimated the destitution west of Wichita and that consequently he was besieged by requests he could not honor. Murdock had seen one hundred men in the previous twenty-four hours and had received three delegations while trying to compose his letter. "The risks I have run and the responsibilities I have assumed are fearful to contemplate." He thought the state should not worry too much about the type of people approved as agents but get as many as possible headed east to collect aid as soon as possible. "It will set me crazy. Send me circulars, instructions, anything you got. You see, the proportions of this relief elephant are growing to be something immense."[62]

The key was the enterprise of private agents, who varied from wonderful to fraudulent. The good ones were very good. Mother Mary Bickerdyke made ten trips from Salina to Illinois during the winter and was able to shepherd two hundred carloads of relief goods back to Kansas.[63] Mrs. Bickerdyke personally supplied not only settlers around her home at Salina but as far afield as Great Bend and Dodge City.[64] She met the cars at Galesburg, Illinois, and rode with them into the Plains, becoming as familiar to the grasshopper sufferers as she had been to the victims of the Indians five years earlier.[65] Other agents organized aid in other regions. William Whitney from Mitchell County stopped in St. Louis, Buffalo, and Cincinnati. In December he described his pragmatic methods to the relief committee: "Where we effect an organization in larger cities it is not practicable to work for a county that seems too small: we say for the State and send to you and then trust to your sense of Justice and right to deal justly by us; we think that if goods are raised through our efforts we should have the benefit."[66] H. C. St. Clair of Atlanta, Illinois, reported the same month that he had organized four Kansas aid societies in two counties and would organize six more in another week. Bankers, ministers, and merchants were good targets, but he had been especially successful with "charitable Christian ladies."[67] In January 1875, Stover received a check for $64.47 from the Ladies Temperance League of Elgeria, Ohio, "contributed for the benefit, of the sufferers, by the grasshoppers, in Kansas, and now forwarded, to you, to be used, as you *deem* best, for their comfort."[68] Their hearts, if not their commas, were in the right place.

The bad agents were very bad. C. C. Hutchinson of Hutchinson, who had a reputation for fraud in his former role as Indian agent for the Ottawas, complained mightily about the relief committee's restrictions on the number of agents who could go east from any county and about the general feeling that Reno County was not one of the hardest hit. "You have organized a com[mittee] & are doing an excellent work," he wrote, "but is it just the thing to telegraph & advertise that all *responsible* agents will have your endorsement—& then refuse to endorse good men whose labor we need?"[69] Even greater protests, however, came from licensed agents and from donors of aid concerning the number of bogus collectors in the field. A donor wrote in December, "I find it very hard to convince the people that a proper use will be made of what is collected." He and his friends had sent $1,000 to a private enterprise in Nebraska and later found it had been loaned out on one-year notes.[70] "People are afraid of being humbuged," wrote another.[71] Said a third: "We wish not to be imposed on as *many persons* are solisiting ade that in all probability was never in *Kansas*."[72] Regular agents were supported by their counties, but the bogus types begged money for their own expenses as well as for the grasshopper sufferers and then often stayed in first-class hotels.[73] A man in Illinois said "hundreds" of these charlatans were traveling his region, "gambling and drinking."[74] No sooner "is the talismanic word 'Aid' sounded through the land," said a Wichitan, "than every mouth, as if acted upon simultaneously by all the mechanical powers, flies wide open with the expectation of swallowing a grub, every man becomes suddenly poor, every pocketbook lean, every stomach empty."[75] The existence of the relief committee at least re-strained some of the worst excesses of that type.

No matter how private aid was organized, however, it was not enough. Almost certainly there would have been widespread suffering in Kansas during the winter of 1874–1875 had not the private giving been substantially supplemented by federal aid in the form of appropriations, legislative relief letting homesteaders vacate their claims for a time without penalty, and distribution of military supplies.[76]

Philosophical opposition to government intervention was a stumbling block for Kansans. Kansas representative Stephen Cobb told the U.S. House of Representatives that introducing a measure to appropriate federal money for the relief of Kansas was "to the last degree offensive to my pride as one of the Representatives of this afflicted section of the country." He said he felt compelled to do so to save people in Kansas from "the horrors of death by starvation and exposure" but emphasized that he and Kansas were reluctant petitioners. "The act of God alone could reduce us to this extremity."[77] Still, *in extremis* Kansas was and ask Washington it did.

Army action began in November 1874 when the secretary of war informed President Ulysses Grant that the Quartermaster's Department at Jeffersonville, Indiana, had several thousand forage caps, sack coats, jackets, boots, and greatcoats that could be issued to settlers in Kansas and Nebraska.[78] Grant gave the authority to distribute these, and in December 3,596 wool blankets along with large numbers of shoes and overcoats went to Kansas.[79] That winter the army distributed, primarily in western Kansas and Nebraska, 10,004 heavy infantry coats, 6,285 other coats, 20,664 pairs of boots and shoes, and 8,454 woolen blankets. On 10 February 1875 Congress approved a bill authorizing the army to offer food. Between February and May 1875, 1,957,108 rations were given to 107,535 people in the grasshopper regions.[80] There were forms to be filled out by the township trustees; there was another set of agents to recognize for receiving and distributing goods funneled through Kansas forts; and sometimes the shoes did not fit.[81] Still, it was a blessing, a lifesaver for many.

Many army officers contributed more than was required during the emergency. One, James G. Brisbin of Omaha, Nebraska, turned down an offer from the Kansas Central Relief Committee to pay his traveling expenses for the time he spent arranging hopper relief. Brisbin wrote that he would have done more if he had recognized the true situation earlier and that he kept no account of his expenses. "I don't like to do charitable work for money even if it is in return for money laid out," Brisbin commented. "I have been kept miserably poor this last winter by this grasshopper business and the Madam says she is the worst *sufferer* in Kansas or Nebraska." Brisbin forbade the Kansas committee to publicize his generosity, as he said he hated notoriety.[82] Those at Topeka wished such an attitude had been universal.

Instead, confusion was the rule and dishonesty not unknown in the distribution. Russell County residents complained that the goods were distributed among its townships according to political influence rather than by population or need. The county got from Fort Hays 5 pairs of pants, 5 shirts, 75 overcoats, 200 blankets, and 150 pairs of shoes. "It was kind in our government officers in giving us just a pair of pants to each township, thus avoiding the neces-

sity of a subdivision."[83] Goods were forwarded to Russell County for shipment elsewhere and lay on the ground. "Everybody helps themselves and much is wasted."[84] Railroads complained about charges on freight cars detained at various distribution sites without explanation.[85] Many shipments were misdirected and ended up where there was no need.[86] Shipping bills got mixed up, and requests that the relief committee forward goods to the county whose agent solicited them usually were lost in the shuffle.[87] Competing relief societies divided county efforts in the interest of potential county-seat towns.[88] Regular railroad rates increased as though "the free transportation of relief goods was only the miserable little worm which the railroad company threw away in order to catch the fish."[89] Favoritism in railroad rates was shown to certain towns.[90] "The Central Committee should either regulate this entire thing," wrote a Russell man, "or cut entirely loose from it."[91]

Kansas did not need bad weather just then. But a severe winter was what came next. On 9 January 1875 it was twenty-six degrees below zero in Osborne County, and the winter months all over western Kansas were unusually cold.[92] During January there were no trains at Dodge City for fourteen days due to the snow blockade on the Santa Fe.[93] The Kansas Pacific managed to break its trains out a little more often but only through the use of mammoth snowplows pushed by multiple engines. Even so, KP passengers were marooned for a number of days on several occasions, sometimes at towns and sometimes in the cars, half buried in a cut.[94] Henry White of Russell froze to death near Dodge during a January blizzard and S. S. Van Sickel lost three hunting companions and his own fingers and toes to a storm that month.[95] Wrote Van Sickel: "I have been in some of the terrible battles of the late war, where I have heard the continual roar of musketry and cannon, and seen my comrades falling all around, but never experienced anything so truely terrible as the storm I have . . . attempted to describe."[96] The heavy snows and low temperatures interrupted rail shipments of relief supplies, and the condition of the roads made wagon deliveries impossible. The meager committee budget for the hire and shelter of teams was quickly exhausted due to the unusual weather, leaving women and children on the frontier to cope a little longer with the cold in their summer dresses and bare feet.[97]

When, despite the delays, the politics, and the weather, the relief cars did arrive, settlers were delighted. "The cars came all right," wrote a Solomon Valley agent to Topeka. "General Grant could not have had a greater ovation. There was much crying for joy."[98] G. A. Atwood of Ellsworth wished there had been more shirts and drawers in his consignment from Fort Hays, but there were enough blankets and overcoats for 175 families. "We are thankful for what we have received."[99] W. H. Odell of Great Bend appreciated the 90 greatcoats, 5 sack coats, 7 pairs of pants, 200 blankets, and 200 pairs of boots he got from Fort Larned and noted that beggars could not expect to choose.[100] R. B. Foster at Osborne late in December distributed 1,975 pounds of corn meal, 1,500 pounds of flour, 3 barrels of rice, 3 barrels of beans, 2 barrels of beef, 250 pounds of shoulders, 125 pounds of hominy and rice, 200 pounds of dried fruit, 68 pounds of salt, and 8 boxes and 14 barrels of clothing.[101]

The total work of the relief committee was more impressive than was the impact of the state bonds that were the official legislative solution to the crisis. The special session of the legislature had authorized the state to borrow $73,000 to be distributed as a loan to the counties in return for their bonds at 10 percent interest. "When people came to make calculations of the amount coming to each county," wrote a man from Cawker City, "they found out there wouldn't be more than enough to buy each one of the destitute a pair of shoes; so we thought if we had to starve, we would do it barefooted and without bonds."[102] Only $7,500 worth of these relief bonds were issued statewide.[103] The private relief committee, however, managed to raise $73,863.47 in cash from private sources with no strings attached. Twenty thousand dollars in cash came from California, almost $10,000 from New York, and a similar amount from Pennsylvania. More important, states nearer Kansas contributed food and clothing directly in amounts far greater than the state loan would have provided. The relief committee by June 1875 had distributed 319 full railroad cars of relief goods plus 48,000 individual barrels and boxes. Railroads contributed free transportation worth $100,000, and the federal government gave $20,000 worth of clothing and $75,000 in rations to Kansas. The relief committee kept its administrative overhead low and so was able to spend much of the cash for relief goods and for crop and garden seeds for the spring. The state legislature was asked for an appropriation for seeds, but no money was forthcoming. Therefore, the relief committee bought $20,000 in seed from dealers in Iowa, Illinois, and Missouri.[104]

The committee's methods were neither elegant nor particularly efficient, but it did act and no one starved or froze in Kansas because of the grasshopper. Committee members reminded the governor in February that western Kansas settlers had faith that their state would help them somehow in an emergency that involved "the lives of a multitude of hardy men and patient women and innocent children." The committee thought that "every consideration of policy, every sentiment of honor and humanity and religion, demands that their cry shall not be disregarded."[105]

Western Kansas survived the grasshopper invasion of 1874, but barely. It was sobering to the confident and chilling to the meek. For years afterward, a cloud of high-flying birds or wind-borne seed pods, looking like a snowstorm in summer, could cause panic. Kansans kept their "hopperdozers" and various other devices designed to vacuum, burn, or crush insects ready in their sheds so they might at least put up the appearance of a defense.[106] Wits made binoculars of soda-pop bottles to give the gullible a better look and laughed when they tried to adjust the focus.[107] There were clever suggestions that machine oil might be made from the hoppers if they returned, to "stop the squeaking of machine politicians."[108] But to most who had been through the raid it was not funny at all. They watched carefully for a return in 1875 and were relieved when a late frost killed the newborn hoppers. They attributed this not to science but to the grace of God. It was an answer to prayers offered on innumerable local prayer days that God might "stay the expected ravages of the grasshoppers this coming spring."[109]

Mr. G. Hopper's Presumed Defeat, 1875. This cartoon is typical of attempts to anthropomorphize the robotic insects, perhaps to arouse hopes that they could be stopped.

The drought that surrounded the grasshopper invasion (and was perhaps one of its causes), unfavorable publicity about the invasion itself, and the effects of the national panic that began in 1873 combined to reduce the pace of settlement for the next few years. In 1874, 16,018, claims were filed in Minnesota, Nebraska, Dakota Territory, and Kansas. In 1875 there were 8,284 for the same region and in 1877 just 7,236.[110] Nature had struck hard and had humiliated nineteenth-century man with the tiniest of her creatures.

The possibility of a return of the insects

forced upon officials the necessity not only for federal aid but interregional cooperation. Governor Thomas Osborn of Kansas met with representatives from Missouri, Illinois, Iowa, Nebraska, Minnesota, and Dakota Territory in October 1876 at the Grand Central Hotel in Omaha to study how to deal with possible future infestations of the Rocky Mountain locust. Bounties for eggs and active insects were suggested, and entomologists thought that control might come from careful analysis of the insects' breeding habits. The problem was that "the sudden and fitful movements of the locusts, the limitless field of their operations and the mysterious and predatory nature of their inroads" made them too large a problem for one state to handle. Yet Congress did not believe in the danger. "Congress," said the report of the conference, "regarded anything with the name of 'bug' attached to it as something to be laughed at."[111] An entomological commission was funded in the spring of 1877. Its scientists said in their report the next year that, given the slight interest in the topic nationwide, it was lucky that *Melanopolus spretus* had decided to disappear on its own, almost as though it had risen in such numbers only for a special purpose.[112]

"In the realm of social results," writes an early student of the Plains hopper invasions, "the outstanding fact was that the farmer alone could not meet the emergency."[113] Seeking any kind of relief, however, offended the Gilded Age mentality, steeped as it was in the myths of social mobility and the self-made man. The onus of begging was only intensified when the provider was a state or federal government that might exact a permanent price in loss of individual independence. While, as Robert Manley puts it, "the 'booming facet' of the frontier personality was momentarily subverted by a realization of the dreadful impact of the insects," there was great embarrassment about the necessity.[114] It will be recalled that a representative from Kansas, speaking in February 1875 on behalf of an army appropriations bill for grasshopper relief, had concluded his remarks by expressing a pain that was widely felt. He regretted, he had said, having to bring such a measure before the Congress: "It is in the last degree offensive to my pride as one of the Representatives of this afflicted section of the country. . . . The act of God alone could reduce us to this extremity.[115] In fact, as Manley's study of Nebraska relief perceptively points out, settlers sometimes conveniently forgot this aspect of regional history when writing memoirs. "These sturdy, early settlers," wrote one Nebraska man, "that have succeeded and made this broad prairie blossom as a rose . . . did not 'holler' for the government to help make the grass grow, abolish snakes, or even rid them of the bugs and grasshoppers."[116] Perhaps Kansas wished to think that the private relief committee could have done it alone or that such groups could meet any future emergency.

People living on prairie farms struggled for an interpretation that was hopeful. Maybe it was a winnowing, some kind of trial to separate the worthy from the unworthy. "Does the Lord chastise those whom he loveth not?" wrote Farmer Doolittle in Sedgwick County.[117] It could be imagined that the strong remained to reap the rewards of a new day while the "shiftless element" returned east to see their wives' relations.[118] It did not occur to many that such a disaster might also have given settlers a more realistic understanding of the natural environment. They could recognize the limits of their manipulation and comprehend while reading their Bibles that nature was not really theirs to modify.

To strike some balance between a proper humility and the continued confidence necessary to carry on the work of civilization in western Kansas was the goal of a harvest festival address Abraham Essick gave to a group of thankful settlers at Fort Harker in October 1875. We have learned, Essick said, to be less wasteful and to look ahead to emergencies. "We 'lords of creation' have been made the sport of fortune—or, to speak from a Christian standpoint, we have been made to feel out dependence upon divine Providence." Individually, the grasshoppers had been tiny and insignificant, "but as an army of myriads, who can stand before them?" Surely not the United States and its settlers, who had dealt with buffalo, Indians, and rattlesnakes but were no match for this force. "An army of grasshoppers will fly over us and crawl over us—eat up our substance and devastate the land, while we are powerless to resist or expel the intruder."[119]

Still, it was a harvest festival, not a wake. People had come to farm, not to meditate, and needed with the catalog of lessons to be learned some reinforcement of battered pride. The speaker gave it. "We are not cast down for all that," he cried. "The mission of the race is to replenish the earth and subdue it, and bravely we are doing it. Mind is achieving victories over matter—intellect is advancing to control the elements of nature." It was not going to be easy in western Kansas, for it was a special place. "When it blows it storms, and when it rains it pours. When crops yield they are enormous, and when they fail the failure is complete." Yet how rewarding it would be for the strong and the pure in heart eventually to gain victory over such formidable odds. Were these western Kansans who had just survived a plague in the wilderness not more the chosen of God? Would not God gird their loins especially for the struggles of the future?[120]

Finally, Essick quoted to the assembled families standing in the Indian-summer sun a psalm to remember as they returned to the plow. It was Psalm 24. "The earth is the Lord's," it began, "and the fullness thereof; the world, and the fullness thereof; the world, and they that dwell therein." The world and all its parts were made for man, and people could stand in its holy places if they had "clean hands, and a pure heart" and were not vain or dishonest. The harvest had been good. Ellsworth County wheat in 1875 averaged eighteen bushels per acre and corn thirty-nine bushels per acre.[121] So perhaps these settlers, purified as they were by suffering, could stand on the High Plains and hope, even be confident, that if they plowed and planted, if they read their Bibles and built churches, no scourge would visit them again. It was another illusion.

Chapter Six

Colonists

ho were the settlers—the pioneers? They are ourselves, we think, or rather, ourselves idealized. As Henry Nash Smith brilliantly demonstrated, western settlers have provided "an image of the American past" to the exclusion in some minds of nearly everything else about it.[1] Who faced the western Kansas wilderness, fought the Indians, survived the grasshoppers, began wheat culture, and founded towns? Quintessential Americans, surely—white, Protestant, male, alone, unselfish, English speaking, competent, and unafraid. So have the sod house and the High Plains settler grown to mythic proportions, obscuring a truth that is more complex and less immediately satisfying but embraces, as the stereotype does not, all of what it means to be human.

In 1870s western Kansas few shared all the characteristics of the nostalgic ideal type, and many did not come close to fitting the mold. "The typical Kansan," wrote Senator John Ingalls, "has not yet appeared."[2] Blacks fought dust and wind along with whites; women "manned" the homesteads while their husbands worked in distant towns; Catholics built cathedrals and Orthodox Jews broke prairie sod; sheepskin coats, embroidered boots, and samovars were as much part of western Kansas as Levi overalls and sunbonnets. The prospect of a new start appealed to socialists and capitalists, corporations and individuals. Charlatans migrated with honest people, agnostics with Christians, and little rain fell on any of them.

One thing they had in common is unexpected: many of the 1870s settlers arrived and lived in groups, as colonists. There were, for example, at least twenty-four organized colonies in Ellis County in the decade. An initial group in 1867 was followed in the early 1870s by two colonies from Ohio and one each from Illinois, Ireland, Pennsylvania, New York, and England. In 1875 and 1876, waves of Germans arrived from Russia. Later there were groups of Bohemians from Chicago, a black colony from Kentucky, a party of French from Château-Thierry, a colony of Austrian Lutherans, and one of Danish socialists. That is not to mention a stream of colonists in groups from places such as Alliance, Ohio; Ripon, Wisconsin; Brooklyn, New York; York, Pennsylvania; Medaryville, Indiana; and Turkville, Tennessee.[3] The *Hays Sentinel* noted in 1878 that the rate of settlement in colonies, which often bought land in blocks from railroads, made it difficult to estimate growth from statistics on the standard homestead and timber-culture claims.[4]

Because German-Russians from the valley of the Volga concentrated there, Ellis County had a higher proportion of foreign born than did surrounding counties (1,945 foreign born compared with 4,234 native born in 1880), but its pattern of heavy 1870s colonization was typical throughout western Kansas.[5] Without knowing that the first residents of Edwards County were the Massachusetts Colony of 1873, one could surmise it by noting in the 1875 census that 119 of 144 county residents hailed from Massachusetts. Similarly, the highest number of people from a single state in Russell County in 1875 was from Wisconsin. That year 159 people from Wisconsin were counted there, while nearby Pawnee County, which also had a total population of about 1,000, had only 13 Wisconsin settlers. The difference was due to the Northwestern Colony from Ripon and Fond du Lac, Wisconsin; it arrived at Fossil Station on the Kansas Pacific early in 1871.[6] It was no accident that McPherson County in 1880 had 2,115 Swedes of a total population of 12,270, that one-eighth of Graham County's residents were black, that 1,245 of Osborne County's 11,478 native-born residents were from Pennsylvania, that one-quarter of Trego County residents were from Illinois, or that New England was unusually well represented in Edwards County.[7] Distribution by point of origin in 1870s western Kansas had been carefully planned.

Some reasons for settlement in colonies are clear. Railroads encouraged it. They reduced travel rates for groups with baggage, discounted railroad lands sold in significant quantities to a single organization, ran excursion trains filled with people from one location where railroad agents had been proselytizing,

and combed Europe and Russia for groups that might want to come to the United States. Mutual defense was a consideration. Racial and ethnic groups found colonization on the frontier as desirable initially as voluntary ghettoization in cities had been. Common interests created colonies: religious groups, utopian experiments, and veterans' organizations all were active colonizers. Greed also spawned colonies. Real-estate speculators formed colonization companies to provide basic amenities and thus increase the value of the lands they held. Other colonies had political ambitions. A colony gave a chance to populate a new area quickly with people of like mind, to create a county, county political machinery, a county-seat town, and a bond issue—all controlled by those who had organized the venture.

Most important, however, was the need for camaraderie in facing the unknown. "The attachment to home and the strength of old friendships have a strong hold on most people," wrote a pamphleteer, "and it is not at all surprising that the immigrant should wish to make settlement in a new country by the side of his old friends and neighbors." Women particularly were "more dependent upon social relations for personal enjoyment," but all favored colonies because of a feeling that the settler would find in his new home "strange and perhaps peculiar people, wholly unlike himself in social, mental and moral characteristics and he must need have his old friends about him in order to preserve the identity and completeness of the life he has lived in his early surroundings."[8] An editor concluded that most people did not come west to escape society but rather to recreate a society from which they had been somehow forced. "Their business has gone wrong and they have had losses; their social connections have in some way become unpleasant; they have committed some fault and fled from a damaged reputation."

Whatever the reason, they yearned for connection with the old, not adaptation to the new, and they lived double lives, part of them always pining for scenes of childhood and sight of old friends and relations. "We are like trees pulled up in middle age, never getting fully and exclusively rooted in the new soil."[9] The impetus to association was even greater for foreigners for whom the change of environment was more extreme. Francis Swehla, who began colonizing Bohemians in Ellsworth County, noted that "customs and habit were second nature" to his people and solitude frightened them. "An American farmer in a well-settled country seemed to them a poor human lost in a wilderness. How then would a pioneer miles from his nearest and also lonesome neighbor, look thirty to sixty miles from the nearest little station? Horrible! Unbearable! Buried alive!"[10] Colonies gave a sense of community, security, and familiarity that pioneer settlers needed as much as anyone else.

Contemporary writers observing the phenomenon of colonies in western Kansas did not like the idea. Romanticization of the frontier experience and the elevation of its people as models of American character had begun before the frontier experience itself ended. "The colony plan," wrote one observer, "is a provincialism and is wholly antagonistic to the American idea." The average American, he thought, was "a restless, speculative, adventuresome character" with "neither the patience, love of locality, or the grace of humility to submit himself to the community plan."[11]

The editor of the *Kinsley Graphic* said in 1878 that when a group arrived there claiming to represent thirty to forty families from a distant state, "we welcome the train that bears them away." He preferred individual entrepreneurs "who will buy lots of land and will soon have a wheat field two miles square" and thought Americans would stay in colonies only during emergencies. "You may with some degree of success colonize the unsocial, 'unmixable' Mennonite, or Digger Indian, but the American never, and the German only with great difficulty."[12]

That was only rhetoric. There is no evidence that a railroad or a town ever failed to provide the broadest welcome for representatives of colonies, or that American pioneers shied away from colonies, or that colonies were failures, even though the rapid filling of western Kansas made many colonies short-lived. Until settlers could expect to find society already in place in the new land, they liked to bring society with them.

The experience of the Pennsylvania Colony, which founded the town of Osborne in 1871, was typical of colonies of Americans without a particular religious or reform purpose. As was usual with these enterprises, the potential colonists held meetings in their home cities for some months to plan and recruit. Representatives asked Kansas officials for circulars, maps, and sometimes geological and botanical specimens.[13] Mrs. Alice Young of Downs, Kansas, remembered one of these representatives having visited her school in Pennsylvania and at recess having shown the children a map of an unorganized, unnamed Kansas county with a circle around the township where his colony planned to settle. "I have a pretty good notion," the man told the children, "that there is a good place for a poor man to get a home."[14] More direct appeals came at mass meetings during the winter of 1871 in the Pennsylvania towns of Lancaster and Reading. W. L. Bear of Lancaster, Major H. D. Markley of Reading, and a group of others who had originated the scheme addressed these gatherings. A colony, they said, would make the trip easier. The executive committee would put the group's transportation out for bids and choose the best service at the lowest price. Going as a group would also ease individual anxiety about making property arrangements once in the West. If the colony were large enough, its members could organize a county and a county-seat town "and thus become happy and prosperous if not wealthy."[15] According to Mrs. Young, that hope was the most realistic of those advertised. "Among the first crops which yielded well," she wrote, "were politicians. They seemed like sunflowers—to be of spontaneous growth, and unfailing."[16]

The Pennsylvania Railroad was the low bidder. It furnished the colony a first-class car to itself and allowed 100 pounds of supplies for each person. Settlers could carry guns aboard the cars, and a Pennsylvania Railroad agent was assigned to them as far as St. Louis. The agent was to save the party a delay at Pittsburgh by telegraphing ahead for permission to attach their car to another train[17]—a relief, for another Pennsylvania colonist reported that the stopover was "not half comfortable."[18] Arrangements made, at eleven at night on 10 April 1871, sixty people from two Pennsylvania counties paid their $17 fare, boarded the car at Lancaster, and turned their thoughts westward.[19]

The journey was more eventful than had been expected. For one thing, as the colony developed, "our numbers and great wealth apparently increased until at last we amounted to a full regiment and every man armed with a musket; and the money we carried with us was something enormous." The rumors drew crowds to every station to peer at the adventurers—150 people at one place. A town in Missouri offered each colonist a good farm if they would stop there. However, after a short wait in Atchison, they journeyed on to Waterville, Kansas, the northern supply terminus for persons settling in the Solomon and Saline River Valleys. As they reached the prairie, men fired their guns out the window. "The appearance of a jack rabbit or a pair of prairie chickens created unbounded enthusiasm." They stayed overnight in Waterville and the next day proceeded to a campsite west of the village on the banks of the Little Blue River. There they argued.[20]

The surviving minutes of the colony indicate both the promise and the difficulty of cooperative settlement. During their week's camp at Waterville, the colonists met and debated every night. Several (six immediately and five later) decided to return east.[21] These "deserters" thought a repayment of $30 for the $40 they had paid in would be fair. There was a counteroffer of a pair of mules. Finally, those departing "reluctantly agreed" to $25 and a share of the proceeds when the stock of the colony was sold. Those remaining were assessed $10 each in order to pay for $1,407.75 in stock and equipment and $202.10 in provisions purchased at Concordia.[22] The small party that had been sent out to search for an exact location encountered a sand storm that cut their faces, a flood

Arriving at the West. The neat Russell depot, seen here in 1873, was a familiar sight to travelers along the Kansas Pacific corridor.

that nearly swept away their camp, and prices at frontier stores that were astonishing. However, with much effort and the help of a probate judge from Concordia who advised them in exchange for meals, the locating committee decided on a site in Osborne County. When all individual claims were taken, the land not chosen for farms became the townsite, dubbed Osborne City, later shortened to Osborne.[23]

Amid the dissent and confusion there was evidence also of group cooperation and democratic procedure. When some came to prefer the Osborne County location over the initial goal of Rooks County, the group did not split.

There was debate and a close vote, with the losers abiding by the decision of the majority.[24] Because some felt that families and relatives would like not only to be in the same area but adjacent to one another, the colony decided by vote that groups of four families should file claims on individual sections and then divide the property by drawing lots. Timber and building stone on all lands taken by colonists were by agreement used in common by the Pennsylvanians for the one year it would take to construct basic improvements. They dug a common well and began to build a stockade to contain their tents, even going so far as to specify how far the tents should be from the walls and from each other. A colonist made a motion in May to buy eight plows for breaking ground. An examination of the treasury led to an amendment to buy six and then a second amendment to buy four. These obviously had to be shared. For a time the executive committee purchased all supplies from the common fund and issued rations to individual families. The colony paid the salary of a guard to watch the group's cattle. Only when there was a motion that the committee be allowed to regulate the hours and value of each colonist's work were there objections about regimentation.[25]

The Pennsylvania Colony's cooperation climaxed when Osborne City became the temporary county seat. The colonists kept quiet about their new city until the time for the election arrived, and then one of them rose at a public meeting to suggest that Osborne City be the county seat. Where is Osborne City, someone asked? The colony president stood up and presented a city seal complete with the signature of the secretary of state of Kansas. There was a motion to delay. The colonists voted it down, and Osborne became the temporary and later the permanent county seat.[26]

Because after that "the necessity of remaining together as one family no longer existed," the colony organization converted itself into a town company.[27] Early in July 1871 all remaining common property was sold at auction. However, minutes were kept by the executive committee until early in 1872 when there was a fund drive for a courthouse.[28] Residents continued to feel that the experience of coming as a colony gave the town of Osborne a special unity and that its early experience with adjusting differences at meetings aided it for years.[29]

Counties farther west than Osborne often depended more heavily on colonies for early population and official organization. Edwards County, for example, was established because two competitive colonies, the Chicago Workingmen's Colony and the Massachusetts Colony, both arriving in 1873 in what was then Pawnee County, created rival townsites; by confusing Pawnee County elections, they dictated the creation of Edwards County the next year. The Massachusetts people got the new county seat, thanks partly to money from E. W. Kinsley of Boston, after whom their town was named, and to funds coming through Boston's Homestead and Colonization Bureau from others who liked the financial promise of the West but did not want to go there themselves. With this money from organized friends, the Kinsley people established necessary economic institutions for the town, though these did not include the orange groves originally envisioned by Boston planners. A colony of Germans arrived in 1874; a colony from Henry County, Illinois, founded Offerle in 1876; John Fitch and a group from Hyde Park, Illinois, came to Fitchburg (later Nettleton) the same year and introduced gas lights and a wind-powered mill; and in 1877 Edwards County got a utopian colony on the cooperative plan with the arrival of Professor J. R. Wentz. Wentz built a twenty-four-by-forty-foot colony house for cooperative living and advertised plans to farm with a steam plow to be purchased with contributions from the colonists.[30]

James C. Malin, one of the premier students of western demography, was the son of an Edwards County pioneer and studied the settlement pattern there in detail. He concluded that settlement in colonies was predominant, almost universal, until the year 1877, when, coincident with a general boom in western Kansas, more independent settlers began arriving. In 1877, assessments of railroad property accounted for 86 percent of Edwards County's tax base.[31] In a place with so little social-overhead capital, real self-sufficiency was required, and that was not available to an isolated individual.

There were many colonies with tighter organization than these examples and with specific goals that went beyond, although they seldom excluded, surviving the first year and establishing a county-seat town.

Dr. Samuel Grant Rodgers mixed social philosophy in the plan for his Chicago Workingmen's Colony, which he tried to locate first in Pawnee County and second in the entirely empty and unorganized Ness County in 1872 and 1873. Rodgers later lost his legislative seat from Ness County on the grounds that the colonists' organization of it was fraudulent, but unlike county schemes for profit at the same time in Harper, Comanche, and Barber Counties, Rodgers did bring people, selected for their varied skills, to his colonies. By contrast, a state investigator camping at the county-seat town of Comanche County in 1874 amid magnificent desolation, reported that, despite bonds issued for a $29,000 courthouse and a $20,000 bridge, the town "has no inhabitants and never had."[32] Ness County issued only $5,000 in bonds, compared with a $40,000 issue for Harper County, $72,000 for Comanche, and $141,300 for Barber. It is likely that bond speculation in this case was only an adjunct to the colony plan.[33] When Rodgers in September 1873 moved away from colony crowding in Pawnee County to a site on Walnut Creek in Ness County called Smallwood City, he be-

lieved that being first to a rich farming region would make him and a group of Chicago workingpeople wealthy.

While Rodgers spent most of his time during the brief active life of the colony in the East trying to sell bonds, in Topeka defending his legislative seat, and, for a brief period, in jail, he did not leave the forty settlers at Smallwood City without hope or supervision. Colonists reported that Rodgers promised to furnish them groceries, pay their transportation costs, provide farm equipment and seeds, and employ them in building the town at a wage of $30 a month. That would have looked attractive to unemployed immigrant workingpeople (two-thirds of the colonists were Irish) at the meetings Rodgers held in Chicago. The only sure evidence of cost to them was that Rodgers charged $30 ($10 down) for lots in what quickly became the temporary county seat of Ness County.[34] He had an assistant on the scene named C. A. Smallwood, who acted as combination groceryman, work supervisor, and advertising agent for the colony. The town was named after this man, not after Secretary of State W. H. Smallwood, as has been almost universally assumed.[35] The steam plow, the brick machine, and the artesian well Rodgers talked about never materialized, but the craftsmen did find work constructing a dugout town with a large central community building and unusual red stone fireplaces and Dutch ovens in most homes.[36]

A large block of land could be homesteaded in Ness County because there was no railroad and therefore no railroad lands there, but the four-day walk to Smallwood City from Hays City began convincing some that this was a haven, but not a heaven, for the poor. They circulated a petition for organization, took their fradulent census listing 643 residents, and held an election. However, farming did not go well during the drought, the people were not skilled hunters, and Rodgers, who was already in debt on a hotel he had built in Pawnee County, had no funds to advance them. People began to drift, then rush, away. A local cattleman not friendly to colonies of working-class farmers swore to a state investigating committee that only forty-eight votes were cast in the November election at Smallwood City. When troops from Fort Hays checked on the enterprise on 20 December 1873, they found only two families, the Henry Maguires and the John Shannons, "shirtless, shoeless and nearly destitute of clothing, their appearance cadaverous and very emaciated apparently from hunger." The soldiers issued the six men, six women, and nine children rations for twelve days and, when at the end of that period Rodgers had not come with help, removed them to Fort Hays. Ness County was never officially disorganized, and Smallwood City remained the county seat until the 1880 reorganization. It was listed as the distribution point for Ness County for grasshopper relief in 1874. But it was a shell—an empty workers' paradise and the political capital of an empire of fewer than one hundred people.[37]

The area near Smallwood gained a fair population, though no railroad, by the late 1870s, which led Ness County workmen's colonies to locate in that period along Pawnee Creek ten miles south. A workers' colony from Pittsburgh, Pennsylvania, settled next to a similar enterprise from Brooklyn, New York, and in 1878 founded the town of Riverside. The vista was genuinely beautiful there, though the set-

tlers learned that few of their homesteads faced the river, as a clever Larned land agent with a modified map had promised they would. Wrote J. C. Lohnes, a German-born member of the Pittsburgh colony: "A chance on Uncle Sam's unoccupied fertile acres appeared as magic on the horizon and loomed as large as the Promised Land must have loomed to the Hebrews in Bible times."[38] Like the Smallwood colonists, the Riverside people had the idea that "to secure a quarter of land was to transform a poor mechanic into a wealthy prince."[39] Unfortunately, they were no more experienced in farming or in surviving in the country than their predecessors had been.

The Pittsburgh Colony was well prepared. At one time before emigration it had 300 members; these people supported not only extensive trips west to scout for locations but lobbying in Washington in favor of bills to give financial support in beginning western farming to workmen fleeing the effects of the Panic of 1873 and subsequent depression. Like the colony that went to Osborne, it negotiated favorable accommodations and railroad rates and left for Ness County in March 1878 with fifty of its most adventurous types joined in lusty song.[40]

Disappointment was almost immediate. The bills in Congress to provide $500 for each homesteader to buy livestock and tools failed to pass. And there was some question whether tools would have helped much. Lohnes remembered that they had three coal miners, one peddler, one carpenter, a saw grinder, a plasterer, and the rest unskilled day laborers. Lohnes had raised a garden one year in a Pittsburgh suburb, so he became the agricultural adviser in a group without a single farmer. The first winter most of the men went to Larned, forty-five miles away, to search for work, leaving their wives and children alone. There was not enough rain to sprout a crop in 1879, the cattlemen thought farmers were ruining the grazing, and three people were killed trying to dig a community well. The first good crop at Riverside was in 1884, by which time only four members of the Pittsburgh Colony remained.[41]

Some colonies went beyond the workers' havens in utopian goals. The York Colony, operated by the Southwestern Agricultural and Migration Company of York, Pennsylvania, bought 20,000 acres in the southwest corner of Ellis County and the northwest corner of Rush County in 1878. Supposedly there were a thousand people waiting to move west, and the leaders said there would be one excursion a week until five hundred people were on the site. Each colonist wore a "colony badge," and people at Hays City thought this group had "the advantage of nearly every other body of settlers that has located in western Kansas." However, the railline the colony proposed to construct from their town to Hays City was never begun, and there was no chance to determine whether the colony's cooperative scheme of working the ground, building houses, and sharing the harvest together under the direction of a general superintendent would have worked. A little over a month after the first colonists arrived in May, a judgment was filed against what property remained to the colony after a round of internal theft and embezzlement. The superintendent in his meditation on long-range goals had neglected to pay the colony's initial supply bills at Hays City.[42]

The first settlement of Meade County took place the next year by colonies from Zanesville, Ohio; Rochester, New York; and the state of Indiana.[43] The Zanesville people founded the town of Sunshine and operated on the mutual-aid system, holding fairs in Ohio to raise the money to buy transportation for all and a team of horses for every fourth family. Hotel prices at Dodge City on the trip out consumed their financial reserves, however, and the dry winds along Crooked Creek, where they lived for the next year, finished what remained of the good feeling among them. "The disintegration was as much psychological as physical," wrote the best modern student of this venture. Heat and boredom "eroded the concepts of brotherly cooperation and mutual aid."[44]

A similar fate befell the colony established by the expatriate Danish socialist leader Louis Pio near Hays in 1877. Pio wanted a test of the theories he had espoused for years, and he quickly got one. The colony lasted six weeks before it was abandoned because of petty jealousies. The women debated rather than cooked, while the men criticized Pio's fancy clothes instead of farming. The colonists ate their cows and horses, then divided the remaining assets and left. A disappointed Pio took a job as a printer in Chicago.[45]

A female colony proposed by young women from Pennsylvania and a temperance colony outlined by Francis Murphy, whose name the famous temperance pledge bore, never got past the talking stage.[46] Even monks found a test of faith in the empty landscape of counties far from the railroad. When the Benedictine monastery at Atchison had financial difficulties in 1876, the prior sent two brothers to Clark County to found a less expensive western retreat. They did build a dugout with an altar,

Corporate Settlement. The Kansas Pacific depot at WaKeeney, constructed by the rail company in 1879 by special arrangement with land developers Albert Warren and James Keeney. It was the centerpiece of the promotion of the town and the rapid sale of the railroad lands of Trego County.

which they called Monte Cassino or, in jest, "Bueffel Au," but were glad after some months at the site to hear that the administration on the Missouri River had recovered.[47]

If extremes were to be pursued in western Kansas colonies, the record shows that those organized purely as profit-making ventures were more stable than those depending entirely upon religious feeling or social philosophy. One of the most ambitious of these business undertakings, and probably the most successful, was the rapid development of Trego County and the

town of WaKeeney by the colonial efforts of Warren Keeney and Company in 1879.

James Franklin Keeney was a Chicago real-estate developer, thirty-three years old at the time of the founding of WaKeeney in 1878 but a graduate of the University of Rochester with the promotion of the Chicago suburbs of Ravenswood and South Evanston to his credit.[48] Keeney visited the Centennial Exposition in Philadelphia in 1876 and was attracted to the Kansas exhibit. The next year, he and his friend Albert Warren, having formed a partnership, went to Trego County, Kansas, and managed to acquire control of 340,000 acres of Kansas Pacific Railroad land in that largely vacant region. Part of the deal was that the railroad build an impressive depot, for which Warren and Keeney provided a Chicago architect, and the two promoters laid out eighty-foot-wide streets as pleasant and well planned as those in their Chicago suburbs.[49] By the beginning of 1878, WaKeeney had everything but people.

Warren and Keeney were master promoters. In November 1877 they brought thirteen Chicagoans interested in colonization to the new town and showed them that lumber was on the ground, a temporary hotel already up, and stone being quarried for a larger one. Warren took the opportunity to visit editors of area newspapers and explain the settlement plans of the partners' subsidiary, the Chicago Colonization Company. In December the same editors, along with their colleagues all over the nation, received from Warren and Keeney a well-printed sixteen-page pamphlet.[50] The best investment in the world, the pamphlet said, was land "which can neither break, burn up, or be stolen," and the best bargain in land was the "dark, chocolate-colored loam" of Trego County. There was lumber, the rainfall seemed to be increasing, and Warren and Keeney could get land close to the railroad for individual settlers, for colonies wishing a township or more, or for nonresident investors looking for an asset whose value would appreciate. Excursions left Chicago on the second and fourth Tuesdays of the month and reached WaKeeney via the Rock Island Railroad's connection with the KP at Leavenworth.[51] Warren and Keeney placed more than $5,000 worth of advertising in eastern newspapers and employed publicists

to write "news" articles about the colony for editors with space to fill.[52]

Consequently, by December 1878 the local press claimed that 40,000 acres had been deeded to colonists at from $2.50 to $6 an acre; the land ten miles in any direction from WaKeeney was entirely taken; and there was little government land left anywhere in the county. "What most of the western counties have gained through a process which dragged its length through years," wrote the editor of the *Hays Sentinel,* "Trego gains at a single bound."[53] It was really just a matter of organization and money. One of Warren Keeney and Company's publicists claimed to be reporting simple fact when in May 1879 he wrote that WaKeeney was "among the wonders of modern times."[54]

Warren and Keeney's efforts were the most unequivocal success of all the 1870s colonies. J. F. Keeney lobbied hard in 1879 and got the U.S. Land Office—embracing sales for Ellis, Rush, Trego, Ness, Gove, St. John, Wallace, Scott, Wichita, part of Lane, Rooks, Graham, Sheridan, Thomas, and Sherman Counties—moved from Hays City to an already bustling WaKeeney.[55] There was a steam-powered flour mill, and Governor John St. John picked the WaKeeney picnic as the site for his Fourth of July patriotic address.[56] The two promoters were awash in money and certain enough of their ground to evaluate their enterprise purely upon its profits. "We despise shams of all kinds," said these hard-headed colonists, "especially *sham philanthropy,* as a cloak under which to serve personal interests, and make no pretense that ours is a purely benevolent work."[57]

Yet the WaKeeney Colony could also easily

be analyzed as a failure, as more evidence that Americans were not amenable to group enterprise. For it lost population quickly as the drought of 1879 and 1880 struck and people returned to their old homes. In the summer of 1879, Trego County claimed a population of over 3,500. The 1880 census taker found 2,535, and the population the next year was 1,500.[58]

Such an analysis, however, misses the point that it was not because of the colonies but despite them that initial assaults on many western Kansas counties failed. In 1880 the optimistic people of Trego County, put in place so rapidly by the Warren Keeney machine and enjoying every advantage an up-to-date town and a modern railroad could give them, planted 5,428 acres in wheat and harvested 16,284 bushels, an average yield of about three bushels per acre. Corn averaged twelve bushels and rye five bushels to the acre.[59] It helped that they had fellow Illinoisans around them; it helped that there was a mill and a market; it helped that they could get farm machinery. But it did not help enough. The Indians did not fade as quickly as had been expected in the face of the railroad, rain did not follow the plow, and the faithful were not spared the plagues of the damned. Nor would the environment fold before organization and efficiency. That was sim-

An Instant City. A WaKeeney street in 1880, less than a year after the town's founding. A town could be built and provided with the amenities of civilization at "railroad speed."

ply another illusion. Americans with ties to each other ranging from loose to only fairly strong, and with eyes over their shoulders for a place of retreat, needed colonies because they were uncertain and because the environment was harsh. But groups like the Pittsburgh colonists could not thrive forever in places like the Pawnee River Valley if others did not join them and railroads did not reach them. Theirs was a stop-gap effort. Because the environment was harsh and the next stage of development not shortly forthcoming, such colonies failed.

It is important to recognize that most colonies (religious, ethnic, and utopian ones excluded) were designed from the outset as specialized responses to a temporary situation, created to pass out of existence when, as the Pennsylvania Colony people put it, "the necessity for remaining together as one family no longer existed." The Pennsylvania Colony and the Warren Keeney Colony are two examples of the many such ventures that did not disappear totally, but instead became towns. These towns took over the functions for which the colony had been organized and often perpetuated the colony structure in their early political leadership. As time passed and the western Kansas population increased, there was less need for cooperation for defense, and the existence of towns and railroads made it no longer necessary for private cooperation to provide capital for basic economic services. The railroad lands purchased by colonies increased in price in the 1880s, and the railroads during the boom of those years began to see the greatest profit in sales of the land itself, for which nonresident speculators would pay more than colonists, rather than viewing land sales as a means to generate traffic by settling the country. For all these reasons there were more towns and fewer colonies, though, as shall be seen, the demographics of migration into these towns for the next decade suggest that they were often only slightly less homogeneous in population origin than had been the colonies.

The religious and utopian colonies were special cases, but they too became less common in the 1880s for many of the same reasons. When loyalty to the colony is no longer an economic necessity, motivation to overcome self-interest must be stronger than it was for the people at Pearlette or in Pio's socialist colony. Historians of colonial New England, who have seen seventeenth-century New England towns as experiments in utopian communitarianism, have explained their decline as such by noting that early unity was partly due to lack of alternatives.[60] Because the nineteenth century quickly caught up with frontierspeople, the time for incubation and development of loyalties before the pressure mounted was much shorter than it had been in the seventeenth century.

But the continued presence of another kind of colonist in western Kansas in those years depended neither upon commitment to an ideal nor on the weather. Racial and religious minorities and immigrants all differed significantly from the majority of the surrounding population and were not tempted to break from their colonies as the country filled. More important, they *had* to adapt. The step they took to western Kansas was a very long one, spiritually and physically, and for them there was no turning back.

Chapter Seven

Sheepskin and Teakettles

Carl Bernhardt Schmidt of Topeka, Kansas, son of the architect to the king of Saxony, graduate of Dresden Commercial College, and lately commissioner of immigration for the Atchison, Topeka & Santa Fe Railroad, was aboard a train averaging ten miles per hour through the heavy snows of Russia in late March 1875. After a rough, thirteen-day sea passage in February aboard the Inman line's *City of London,* he had visited the wealthy Mennonite settlements in West Prussia where he was received by some as a Moses. Russia, his next destination, was a more risky proposition because the tsar, who had recently withdrawn the one-hundred-year-old military exemptions for German farmers settled in Russia, was not eager to lose them to America. At Prussian settlements near Danzig and Marienburg, Schmidt had hidden letters of introduction from Mennonites in Marion County, Kansas, by taping them around his body under his clothes. He crossed the Russian border at an obscure point, but was still frightened. "On the platform . . . a dozen or more tall frontier gens d'armes loomed up threateningly through the driving snow-storm in their long gray coats, spiked helmets, and guns with fixed bayonets over their shoulders." They had not found the letters and so Schmidt was spending a week on a Russian train.[1]

He enjoyed the first-class accommodations and the lavish food but wrote his superior, Land Commissioner A. S. Johnson, that he felt homesick. When finally he came to Alexandrovsk he was met by Mennonites and taken on a day-long sleigh ride under a blanket and behind four steaming horses to Alexanderwohl, the nearest of the Russian Mennonite settlements, where he spent a month recruiting.

He was a long way from Germany, not to mention Topeka.[2]

But his mission was one his employer thought fundamental. Not only were the Mennonites in Germany and Russia experienced farmers with religious reasons for wanting to escape military conscription, but they were accustomed to living in colonies in regions more isolated and harsh than western Kansas. Schmidt had started working with the Mennonites in 1873 when he took Nicholas Jansen on a week-long tour of the railroad company's Kansas lands. At that time he established contacts with the Bernhard Warkentin family, some of whose members were in Russia and some in Newton, Kansas, at the time of Schmidt's 1875 visit. In 1874 a group of 400 Mennonite families—1,900 people—came to Kansas, largely from the Tauride province of South Russia. They brought with them $2.25 million in gold with which they purchased 60,000 acres of

The Escort. Carl B. Schmidt, colonization agent for the Santa Fe railroad. Schmidt's many journeys to Russia were important in creating the ethnic mix of early western Kansas.

Santa Fe Railroad land in Marion, McPherson, Harvey, and Reno Counties (all along the east line of western Kansas) and the equipment to farm it. The railroad, as it was later to do with many other Russian groups, allowed the visitors to stay for some time at the old King Bridge Shops in Topeka, just then being converted to railroad use, while their leaders sought good lands. They visited the governor at the capitol in full costume and were a great source of entertainment for Topekans.[3]

The contribution these Russian Mennonites made toward introducing hard winter wheat to Kansas has been exaggerated. The trend toward winter wheat was already clear, and Mennonites did not regularly grow it in Russia, nor could they have brought much in their baggage. But the importance of these and other arrivals of foreigners in creating confidence in western Kansas as a farming region cannot be overestimated. The Mennonites themselves probably added about $1 million to a depressed Kansas economy in 1874, and the $332,509.72 they spent with the Santa Fe land department before 1877 may have saved that company from bankruptcy.[4] "They arrived simultaneously with the grasshoppers," Schmidt noted, "but outstayed them."[5]

The prospect for the 1875 group was even better. Kansas in 1874 had passed an act exempting religious dissenters from military service if they simply declared their faith at the county clerk's office. Schmidt was able to spread this news rapidly because, though the Russian colonies he visited in 1875 were remote, more than twenty thousand of the seventy-five thousand Mennonites in all Russia lived there. To add to their discontent with the Russian draft, they were experiencing internal theological disputes and economic hardship from declining grain prices. There was, however, wealth. Some families owned as many as 250,000 acres and were worried that if they did not sell and move, as was allowed by the new Russian conscription law, complaints to the tsar about land monopoly would result in confiscation of some of their holdings.[6] Schmidt talked with one man who had a half-million sheep and employed three thousand shepherds. The agent estimated that most Mennonites would bring at least $10,000 with them and some would bring $50,000 to $100,000—enough to buy large tracts of the best Santa Fe lands. One religious leader gave Schmidt a draft on a bank in Hamburg for 80,000 rubles (about $56,000) to invest in Santa Fe land-grant bonds, which were selling at 65 percent of par but could be exchanged at par for company lands.[7] "The Kansas people," Schmidt wrote, "will open their eyes when *they* [the Mennonites] come."[8]

"They" did well indeed. A month after Schmidt's visit to the Russian colonies, a Red Star Line steamer departed from the Ukraine port of Berdyansk with the goods of 400 Mennonite families headed for Newton, Kansas, and carried at the expense of the Santa Fe Railroad.[9] In 1877 Schmidt reported that eight thousand Mennonites and other Germans from Russia were living on Santa Fe lands, some Mennonites settling as far west as Olmitz near Great Bend and a settlement with plastered cabins in Rush County. Schmidt wrote his superiors in June 1877 that forty thousand German colonists remained in Russia, many of whom would have to leave before 1879 to avoid conscription. Though the Kansas Pacific Railroad was competing successfully for the Volga Germans, the Santa Fe had a good foothold in

Pathfinders. A drawing of Mennonite settlers from Leslie's Illustrated Newspaper,
20 March 1875.

Moravia and Bohemia and had already planted a colony of Austrians in Barton County. Since the creation of Schmidt's immigration branch of the Santa Fe land department in 1873, he had sold more than 116,000 acres to people of foreign birth living in the United States and Canada, Germans accounting for 105,000 of these acres. To foreigners direct from Europe he had sold nearly 100,000 acres—87,000 to Germans from Russia.[10] By 1883 there were fifteen thousand Mennonites on Santa Fe lands, and eventually, thanks partly to thirty-seven career transatlantic trips by Schmidt, more than sixty thousand settled in western Kansas.[11] The editor at Hays City, observing the arrival of some Mennonites in 1876, commented that they were "strong, healthy-looking animals, and seem capable of any work, especially the women."[12] After watching them for a month he expanded his analysis: "The Mennonites are avaricious for lands, cattle, dogs, cats, and pigs and go for them for either love or money."[13]

Noble Prentis, a well-known Kansas writer and editor who had done much to help attract the Mennonites, visited the new colonies in 1875 and found the people adjusting well to Kansas. He stopped near Newton and watched them cultivate watermelons at the edge of the former desert. There were frame houses and flower gardens, brightly painted wagons, fine clocks, and in every kitchen the omnipresent Russian teakettle, made of copper and lined with tin. Prentis ate good black rye bread with butter and concluded that "the Mennonite is 'fixed'; he is a good liver."[14]

Things had changed markedly since John Swenson wrote Governor Sam Crawford in 1865 that few of the forty thousand who emigrated yearly from Europe were coming to Kansas because they had heard it was "the unhealthiest, dryest and poorest State in the Union, full of wild Indians and grasshoppers."[15] Instead, western Kansas in the 1870s became the particular destination of numerous and varied foreign groups, as well as colonies of blacks and Jews. The region's difficulties guaranteed tolerance of any who could survive there; shared language, customs, and geographic origins of the immigrant and minority groups ideally suited them for the colony life that was early most effective as a means of settlement; and the area's isolation presented an opportunity not available in places where the social and economic patterns were already set by tradition.

They saw the region with new eyes and called its elements by other names. A dugout was a "simlinka," and its occupants could drive their "jemtshick" over the "steppe" to the "ambor," singing happily perhaps: "Wie schoen is das ländliche Leben! Kein Koenig kann glücklicher sein."[16] A story was current in central western Kansas in my father's boyhood that a German from Russia had gotten off the boat in New York and, looking around, said, "My word! If this is New York, what must Olmitz [Kansas] be?"

Some American colonists in Kansas may have seemed more foreign than some of the actual foreigners. For example, blacks who left the South beginning with the withdrawal of Union troops and the end of Reconstruction in 1877 and peaking with the great 1879 "Exodus" to Kansas—hence the term "Exoduster"—were, as minorities with no place to return, more like the Volga Germans than they were like the polo-playing Englishmen at the Kansas colonies of Wakefield, Victoria, or Runnymede. The chief black colony of western Kansas, Nicodemus in Graham County, was a genuine cultural outpost for many years after its founding in 1877.[17]

As Robert Athearn emphasized in his book on the Exoduster movement, the early black colonists, scattered in a half-dozen places in western Kansas, were not the poverty-stricken field hands typical of the 1879 migration but had some money and definite plans. The earlier black colonists in fact seem to have felt that the later refugee movement ruined their own colonial enterprises and created, by its size, prejudices that their small and well-controlled inroads into western Kansas agriculture had not.[18] The black colonists were not the Mennonites, and they did need help along with many of their white neighbors in the drought of 1880. But like many foreign groups, they were persistent and hard working. A. J. Hoisington of the *Great Bend Register* wrote, "We have been so long aiding white people coming here that certainly no one would think of refusing the freedom of the state to a few hundred colored people seeking liberty and a home. Treat the colored people exactly the same as if they were white people in like circumstances."[19]

Historians have focused on Nicodemus and the black exodus almost as if they agreed with a contemporary observer who thought that "if

Nicodemus failed, it would darken the whole future of the colored race in this country."[20] Actually, people at Nicodemus saw no such portent in the experiment, and it was one of several black colonies in western Kansas. A reporter from the *Topeka Commonwealth* visited a colony of blacks from Kentucky in 1879 who had settled in Hodgeman County two years earlier. He found the people there poor but optimistic. Lafayette Green said that he trusted God would see him through and that it could not be that he should "loose from his grasp the broad, free home that had been given him." Green was digging a well as he spoke—hard work, but work that he said would free him and his children from the dependence and uncertainties that had always beset his people. Mrs. Perry expressed similar sentiments, saying, "It seemed as if God had prepared [western Kansas] for the colored people, that they might come out from a land of trouble and live and enjoy it forever."[21] Two small children had died in the colony, far from medical care, but no one thought of going back.[22]

As will be seen, considering the time and place, blacks were well accepted in western Kansas towns. But it is not surprising to find prejudice and fear as well. While 1870s western Kansans could not afford the provincialism that led to a story circulated in several towns there in the early twentieth century that no black had ever spent a night in that town or ever would be allowed to do so, the Hays City paper was able to comment in March 1878 that a colony of 205 Kentucky blacks en route to Nicodemus "consists of brawny young darkeys, old and decrepit men, women and pickeninnies."[23] There were charges that W. R. Hill of Hill City and his Topeka associates, who

promoted the townsite, "care[d] no more for the colored man or his welfare than they do for the smallest insect that crawls" and that the white people in Graham County were at least "perturbed in spirit" when they saw the blacks on the way.[24]

Such negative feelings became stronger as the numbers of blacks heading west increased late in the decade. The *Ford County Globe* then explained that race was not the problem; the blacks were usually old and poor, unlike the Russians who were able bodied and had money. The *Hays Sentinel* did not think western Kansas should be forced to take part in the philanthropy of eastern Kansas, which was welcoming blacks to Topeka, then forwarding them west along the Kansas Pacific and the Santa Fe.[25] Capital was needed to develop the prairie, and "to send the indigent negro out upon the Government lands of Kansas, would be an outrage only equalled by the treatment he is fleeing from."[26] W. H. Smith, president of the Nicodemus Colony, could only respond that his people were not bound to Hill but glad that he had explained the land laws to them before they came. They were not all poor and had contributed as much to the trade of nearby towns as had any other class of colonists. The colony, however primitive, had been to the benefit "of my family and my almost ruined race." To that, the *Sentinel* responded that surely Hill, the white land speculator, not Smith, the black settler, had written that eloquent letter.[27]

By contrast, Victoria Colony, a genuine foreign enclave near Hays City, seemed an enterprise more like WaKeeney than like the semicommunal Volga German colonies that soon replaced it. Here the place of Warren and Keeney was occupied by a Scotsman named

George Grant, and the attempts at the hunt, introduction of blooded stock, and boating on Big Creek by the English colonists were more colorful than anything in Trego County. Still, the technique of an individual buying a large block of railroad land for subdevelopment was the same, as was the businesslike attitude of the colonists who inhabited the ranches around Victoria. Grant, like Warren and Keeney later, even got his settlement started by making a deal with the Kansas Pacific for the erection of a large depot at the center of his empire.[28]

There were and are many regional legends about Grant as a fabulous dreamer ensconced in a baronial mansion studying the genealogies of bulls. He had bought all of Ellis County— 576,900 acres—reported the editor of the *Wilson County Citizen,* and he had a thoroughbred stallion worth $25,000.[29] A Santa Fe Railroad pamphlet published in 1876 stated that Grant had purchased 250 square miles of land, probably the largest holding in America, and would show profits of $2 million on his sheep alone within ten years.[30] The historical marker at Victoria says he owned 69,000 acres, and various works talk about a "vision" that moved Grant to a utopian undertaking.[31]

Detailed research by James Forsythe of Fort Hays State University demonstrates that Grant's "dream" was a calculated business risk; his estate is better described as ambitious than princely. Grant made his initial deal with the Kansas Pacific late in 1872, when he promised to buy land and bring twenty-five hundred colonists to western Kansas in return for the railroad's constructing stock pens and a depot. His warranty deed dated 4 June 1873 was for 25,244.99 acres, for which Grant paid two dollars an acre. His personal holdings, which amounted to 31,165 acres in 1877, he called the Victoria Stock Farm. The rest, Victoria Estates, was offered to Englishmen with the promise that through owning a section they could graze livestock over the unsettled open range for miles. Grant's vision was not limited to Kansas (he had a similar operation in Colorado), and his personal wealth, estimated by a Chicago paper at $700,000, was at his death sufficient to leave only about $35,000 to relatives.[32]

Grant and his Englishmen did bring blooded sheep and cattle to western Kansas—the earliest extensive experiments with many breeds. They did experiment with the farming of feed grains and enjoyed modest success. But profits from selling wool were not as expected, beavers damned Big Creek the year of their arrival and reduced it to a trickle, and increasing settlement broke up the expanse of buffalo grass.[33] Most important to the colony's brief life, however, was that Grant died in 1878, and his colonists, not having motivations stronger than economic interest, found in the dry weather of the late decade compelling reasons to seek greener pastures.

Somewhere between the extremes in commitment represented by blacks and Englishmen fell immigrant groups like the Bohemians. Francis Swehla brought some Bohemians south into Kansas from Nebraska in 1874, but after watching the "grab game" played at northern Kansas land offices and feeling a little of the hot dry south wind, all but Swehla himself turned back. He went on in a wagon bearing the legend "Ceska Osada," or "Bohemian Settlement," and stopped at Bosland station (eventually Wilson, Kansas) on the KP. For two years Swehla wrote letters to Bohemian newspapers and farm clubs in Chicago and other eastern cities emphasizing his good well and eighteen acres of plowed ground and passing quickly over the inroads of the "konici" (little horsemen), as he called the grasshoppers. In 1875 several of his countrymen arrived from New York City, and the next year a large contingent came from Chicago organized by Jan Oliverius, the editor of the Bohemian-American weekly *Vestuik*. Soon there was a large hall for social gatherings, and Swehla was elected county surveyor for Ellsworth County.[34] Smaller groups of Bohemians inhabited other regions. Among the settlers of Decatur County, for example, were Joseph Cilek, born in 1832 in Sobeslav and a veteran of the Austrian army, Frank Tacha, Charles Votapka, and Vaclav Janousek.[35] In Republic County there were largely Bohemian towns with names such as Cuba, Munden, Narka, and Agenda.[36]

More highly organized were the Swedes. The initial meeting of the First Swedish Agricultural Company at Chicago in April 1868 began with the reminder from the New Testament book of 1 Corinthians that Christian love "beareth all things, believeth all things, hopeth all things, endureth all things"—fit advice for western Kansas colonists. Using funds contributed by the colonists, the company purchased from the Kansas Pacific Railroad 13,160 acres near the sixth principal meridian. Pastor Olof Olsson brought the major party in June 1869, and that fall the largely Swedish town of Lindsborg was laid out. Though the land was auctioned from company to individual ownership as settlers arrived, the agricultural company remained active until its dissolution in 1877. Early on it purchased arms for the community for defense against Indians, then

encourged the creation of a store, promoted a railroad, and advanced the interests of Lindsborg by giving away lots on condition that recipients plant trees or build homes.[37] In a tragic incident in 1879, the inability of a Swedish man and his son to speak English led to the boy's being killed by a local marshal who mistook the pair for criminals, but for the most part western Kansans understood Swedish organization and drive as well as they had understood similar qualities in the Mennonites.[38] Assimilation of Swedish settlers was therefore rapid.

There is no question which western Kansas foreign colonies received the most attention and still appeal most powerfully to the imaginations of Kansans and visitors to Kansas. What one sees from I-70 at Victoria is not George Grant's house but the "Cathedral of the Plains." That cathedral was not built by Episcopalian Englishmen but by German-Russians from the Volga region. Their town, Herzog, was attached to Victoria and quickly dominated it. A trip of a few miles reveals other enormous and elaborate cathedrals in small, sometimes almost nonexistent towns: Catherine, Schoenchen, Munjor, Pfeifer, and Liebenthal. The German-Russians started coming in 1875 (eventually there would be about four thousand of them), they brought their families, they minded their own business, and they farmed as successfully as any and with more determination than most.

Soon after the military law affecting Germans in Russia passed in January 1874, German Catholics in the Volga region, like Mennonites in the Russian colonies, began organizing. About three thousand people from the towns of Katherinenstadt, Boregard, Obermonjour, Zug, Luzern, Schoenchen, Solothurn, Rohleder, Graf, Herzog, Liebenthal, and several others met at Herzog, Russia, that year to discuss emigration.[39] Balthasar Brungardt, the secretary of Herzog, brought out maps and spoke of the possibility of going to Brazil or Nebraska. Nebraska was better, the group thought, because the climate more closely approximated what they were used to. Five delegates were selected from five Russian communities to visit the New World, financed by their individual towns, and to report on the prospects. They came to the United States that grasshopper year and traveled by way of Buffalo, Chicago, and Omaha to Sulton in Clay County, Nebraska, where they stayed ten days gathering literature and samples of the soil and grass. Toward the end of December, two other German-Russians, Joseph Exner of Obermonjour and Jacob Bissing of Katherinenstadt, came to Topeka and accompanied C. B. Schmidt to inspect Santa Fe lands near Larned. Their report was unfavorable. Other scouts went to Arkansas, but it was dismissed because too much land had already been taken, precluding the establishment of the village-colony these people had in mind.[40]

In November and December of 1874, young men began to be drafted in Herzog and Katherinenstadt; shortly the Volga Germans began applying to town authorities and then to the governor for passes to leave the country. The first left Katherinenstadt in October 1875 for Berlin, where they arranged passage on ships of the North German Lloyd line bound for the United States. Others quickly followed. After a twenty-one-day voyage aboard the ship *Ohio,* a group landed in Baltimore on 23 November 1875. They were met there by Nicolas Schamme, one of the 1874 scouts, and

No Turning Back. Volga German settlers in Ellis County.

C. B. Schmidt of the Santa Fe. Apparently Schmidt's enthusiasm was enough to overcome the unfavorable scouting reports about Kansas. On 28 November their arrival in Topeka created a sensation.[41]

Like the Mennonites before them, these Catholic Russians stayed at the vacant King Bridge building, where newspaper reporters outdid themselves trying to describe the exotic scene. The mustached men wore large sheepskin coats, the upper part fitting tightly to their bodies with the lower part spreading out like a skirt. Their trousers were tucked into tall boots, often decorated with embroidered flowers, and their long hair flowed out of high elliptical winter hats. The women and girls never wore hats or bonnets but covered their heads with black shawls, also often decorated with flowers embroidered in colored silk. Heavy hand-knit stockings and mittens and the constant presence of black iron teakettles completed the picture.[42] Noble Prentis, describing them for the *Topeka Commonwealth,* observed that they went "heavy on sheepskin" and that the high coat collars, extending to the upper edges of the ears, when combined with a hat "shaped like a sausage," made the Russians seem quite out of this world. "Arrayed in such a costume," he wrote, "our Russian friends might move unharmed through the midst of an Irish row—the flying brickbats rebounding without effect from their sheepskin armor." At night they brewed tea and sang melodies with a "strangely plaintive character." Prentis thought they would become Americans bit by bit, though probably their teakettles would be the last thing to go.[43]

Railroad land agents visited the bridge company building early and often. Schmidt, having gone to such trouble to recruit the Russians, had the first chance at settling them. He took some of the men to Great Bend and Larned and showed them Santa Fe lands. But the price, around $5 an acre, was too high, and there did not seem to be a good spot for the formation of the several colonies further immigration would require. Therefore, Adam Roedelheimer of the Kansas Pacific began taking expeditions of Russians farther west. The first land he showed them was so poor that there was discussion of returning to Russia, but when they saw the

country along the Smoky Hill River in Ellis County, where vast tracts were available for $2–$2.50 an acre, they were encouraged.[44] The land scouts talked in Hays City with Martin Allen, who showed them his agricultural plots and gave them his usual confident spiel about the region's potential as agricultural country.[45] That sold them. On 21 February 1876, fourteen families came to Hays City and the next day started work on the colony of Liebenthal (Valley of Love) in Rush County. On 1 March, families from Katherinenstadt arrived, rented Kreuger's store at Hays City, and lived there for a month while they built the town of Katherinenstadt (later Catherine). In April, Herzog was begun, Munjor and Pfeifer were organized in the summer, and Schoenchen in the spring of 1877 after an argument at Liebenthal.[46] Noble Prentis said the Russians "moved, like the children of Israel, rather more by faith than by sight."[47]

The creation of a kind of Russia Minor in Ellis County was a surprise to the colonists from American cities already in place, and they were uncertain how well the experiment would work.[48] "They are here; they are there," wrote the editor at Hays City when one group arrived in August, "and at every corner they may be seen gathered, jabbering about this and that and no one knows what." What he noticed was not so much the sheepskin as the odor that being so clothed generated in the winter sunshine of Ellis County. "Even now our olfactories are protesting; and to our knowledge there isn't a Russian within twenty rods of us." There were other unattractive features, including the group being, according to the editor, "filthy" in person, talk, and dress. "We seriously object to having our streets turned into manure heaps [*sic*] and a depository of filth of all kinds." In fact, he concluded, "the Russians nearer approach the aborigines, in the mode of life, than any other class of people we have chanced to fall in with."[49] They seldom changed clothes, they ate with their fingers, shared common pasture lands, farmed in strips with shared tools, baked bread in odd-looking ovens, brewed a lot of tea, and would be seen in winter wrapped in sheepskin but barefoot.[50] Still, even the critical editor confessed that the new settlers seemed industrious and honest and therefore he was glad they had come. They "will soon be Americanized," he thought.[51]

Surely their manner of living differed from that of the usual western Kansas pioneer. At Catherine, for example, the colony bought school lands, set aside fifty acres for the village and common grazing, and divided the rest. Each head of family got one or more shares, and five acres of land gave one a lot in the village and a lot in the cemetery. In Munjor, government was by mayor and legislative body as in Europe until the settlers learned that that form had no legal status and changed to township government. At Herzog the land was divided into strips, and families got one or more depending upon how much they had contributed to the purchase of the colony section. At Pfeifer four men bought the entire site, and individual families purchased from them. All cooperated in building sod houses plastered with mud, straw, and dried prairie grass, which the women held in their aprons while troweling it on. They made whitewash from burned gypsum and used for fuel an artificial peat of manure and straw tramped into a compact mass by horses and cut into squares. This they called mistholz, or manure wood, and it was no more

loathsome than the buffalo chips used by their neighbors. They roasted watermelon and sunflower seeds and ate these "Russian peanuts" as snacks while they worked.[52]

They spent a large part of their incomes for churches and schools. They had elaborate, colorful weddings, with brides bedecked in ribbons and men riding decorated horses. Their cemeteries were filled with little buildings, and graves were marked with hand-wrought iron crosses decorated with painted porcelain. They played odd games with names like Durack, Kopfbauer, and Solo. And on Christmas, Santa did not come to Munjor and Herzog. Rather, there arrived a lady with a girdle of blue and a veiled face, heralding the "Christkindlein." She tinkled a bell, entered the low door of the sod house, and said, "Gelobt sei Jesus Christus." She then called for the youngest child, had it say a prayer, and distributed presents to families a very long way from home.[53]

What concerned other Ellis County residents was not the unusual customs but the possible political influence of so large a group of foreigners, many of whom could not speak English and had no experience with democratic procedures. At the local Republican primary in the fall of 1876, the Hays City *Sentinel* charged that a candidate named George Miller had registered large numbers of Russians, who had to have been in the state only six months to vote, and then handed them ballots they could not even read. When interviewed after voting, several said they had voted for "Miller and Moltz" but did not know for what office and could not say whether a king or a president ruled in the United States.[54] The editor, F. C. Montgomery, charged that Miller would have

Texas cattle vote if he could benefit from it. Miller's response was to circulate a pamphlet among the Russians charging that Montgomery had compared them to cattle and sheep and called them ignorant and open to bribery.[55] The Democrats were apparently not inactive either, as there were charges that their candidates had bribed votes out of the Herzog Russians by promising to raise a thousand dollars to build a church there.[56]

Local fears and superstitions about the Russians surfaced in the argument over their possible political influence. These were often incorporated into the nineteenth-century equivalent of mid-twentieth-century Polish jokes. Hays City people chuckled at the so-called "Russo-Turkish Watermelon War," when in 1877 Liebenthal residents attacked a threshing-machine crew moving across their watermelon patches.[57] "Probably there is not a man in all this bright sunny land of ours," went a newspaper filler in 1879, "but thinks the Russian wears his sheepskin coat solely to be laughed at."[58] Or: "The reason the Russians never whistle is this: they can't do it with a pipestem between their lips and they never remove the pipestem."[59] Then there was poetry: "If a Russian meet a Russian, / On the way to Hays; / Need a Russian tell a Russian, / Of the Greenback craze? / If all the Russians in a body, / Voted as they're told, / Those betters on a greenback man / Would be most completely, everylast- / ingly, majestically sold."[60]

Some of this matter found its way to the editorial page. The *Sentinel* in 1877 referred to the "benighted foreigner, bowed down with the weight of superstition and retrogressive ideas acquired by a life-long residence in a semi civilized land." His impact might not be so much felt in eastern Kansas, "but in the west where whole tribes of Russians and other aliens have settled down upon the country like a swarm of locusts, there, we say, there the bad effect is manifest."[61] Russians, it was sometimes said, ought to serve simply as the brute force of the pioneering process because at that they were unquestionably efficient. Then perhaps the public schools would eventually change them into Americans.[62] "So long as they exert no influence on politics," the Hays City editor wrote, "they are a spendid institution."[63]

Theoretically, foreign colonists were no more attractive to Americans as a means of settling the Kansas High Plains than were native-born colonists. Practically, in the environment of western Kansas in the 1870s, both were absolute necessities.[64]

In both cases it seemed that the less theory was connected with the form of the colony and the more limited were the actual options of the settlers, the better it was for their battle there. For example, the colony of Beersheba in old Garfield County, formed in the early 1880s by the Hebrew Union Agricultural Society for the benefit of Russian Jewish refugees, found that the abstract desire of its eastern sponsors to prove that Jews could be successful farmers was a disadvantage in adjusting to the location of the colony astride a cattle trail. When the colonists tried to survive by leasing part of their holdings to a cattle syndicate, their supporters withdrew all aid and the enterprise folded.[65] Utopian undertakings fell to quarreling, and groups formed expressly to reap political or economic advantages found that their motivation could divide them when there was not enough power or wealth to go around.

The most culturally stable early residents of western Kansas were therefore probably the foreign born who had as unifying factors their distance from home, their natural cultural isolation, their common religious beliefs, and their almost complete lack of options. In fact, Frederick Luebke, a careful student of Great Plains historical ethnicity, has concluded that the Plains' rural environment might actually have strengthened the immigrants' imported culture. Critical to this, Luebke thinks, is the degree of concentration of a certain ethnic group in a certain place. In 1890, ethnic concentration reached its all-time peak for Kansas, Nebraska, and the Dakotas, and in areas like Ellis County the concentration certainy met Luebke's standard.[66]

No foreign enclave, however, no utopian commune, could escape the pervasive influence of the developing towns, which brought with them, almost as effectively as had the railroads, concentrated metropolitan civilization, nineteenth-century style.

Chapter Eight

At the Front

Western Kansas towns in the nineteenth century were anything but sleepy villages maintaining a size and serving a function to which residents had long been accustomed. Because the region they served was in flux, growing and shrinking in great spurts as weather and promoters came and went, so the towns were characterized by the sometimes desperate aggressiveness and exaggerated rhetoric that distinguished cities on the make and in a boom.

As has been seen, many western Kansas towns began as the kind of "covenanted communities" urban historian Page Smith describes in creating a major historical category for "colonized towns." Yet their subsequent history shows unquestioned dominance by what Smith assumes to be the exclusive category of "cumulative communities." The example of western Kansas indicates that town type may vary over time according to the perceived kind and extent of opportunity. Cooperation, a rudimentary plan, and common rules characterized the response to a threatening environment and were designed as survival mechanisms. When survival itself appeared no longer at issue and growth and wealth were possibilities, the "cumulative community," that is, "one that, without plan, or with no more than a townsite

plot, grew by the gradual accretion of individuals, or, sometimes by rapid but disorderly accumulations of fortune seekers," quickly became the dominant model.[1] *Ad hoc* adaptiveness took the place of logic when in the 1870s and 1880s the possibilities changed too rapidly to analyze. James Bryce, the British social commentator, visited Bismarck, North Dakota, during the great Dakota boom of the early 1880s and concluded that the rapid development of such western regions encouraged everyone to become a speculator and that American town life at the time was like that of a squirrel in a revolving cage: never calm no matter how little difference his struggles might make. Wrote Bryce: "To a stranger who asked in a small Far Western town how such a city could keep up four newspapers, it was well answered that it took four newspapers to keep up such a city."[2]

Despite their much smaller sizes, western Kansas towns of the 1870s and 1880s shared many of the characteristics described by Roger Lochtin in his study of early San Francisco or by Gunther Barth in his stimulating *Instant Cities: Urbanization and the Rise of San Francisco and Denver.* Like the larger cities, western Kansas towns grew rapidly enough during certain years of the nineteenth century to outrun their municipal services and form of govern-

All the Comforts. Great Bend in 1879. Street improvements were rudimentary, but there were already some fine structures and evidence of the importation of the most modern farm machinery.

ment. They also shared the "instant-city" characteristics of an early transient population (cowboys, railroad workers, and lot speculators paralleled miners and suppliers) whose long-term loyalty to the city was in question: small enough to operate a face-to-face contact, "street-corner society"; high vulnerability to physical change through fire; fluctuating demand for labor; difficulty controlling crime and creating a stable social life (Dodge City was world famous for being unable to enforce civility, much less create civilization); a classless culture; and, most fundamental, "a hectic pace of living" that caused settlers to favor "abrupt solutions to their problems over solutions produced by steady attention to everyday tasks." Through all, a sense of drama and adventure was stimulated through newspaper rhetoric that Barth notes "heightened the magic and unreality of the scene."[3]

Hays City, Garden City, Dighton, and Ravanna differed in degree and in significant detail but not in kind on such issues as, for example, the better integration of minority groups because of the needs of a small place. Unfortunately, however, the region did not respond as readily to the wave of the magic wand as had Denver and San Francisco, and economic reverses came quickly and painfully. The story of a rapid rise and fall in towns that had fewer accomplishments to buttress their dreams is in many ways more revealing of the psychology of that dreaming than are the success stories of places like San Francisco and Denver. As Lewis Atherton put it in his study of the midwestern town, "The influence of this boom-and-bust philosophy, this constant starting over, this eternal looking to the future, this concern with material accomplishments is most

clearly revealed in terms of individual families and individual towns, even though the process affected no two towns or families in exactly the same way."[4]

The early period of western Kansas urban history can be divided into two parts, the 1870s and the 1880s, based not only on the difference in size of the booms of those periods but on a perspective on growth possibilities and a sense of humor about wilder imaginings characteristic of the 1870s town publicist but not of his dazzled counterpart of the mid-1880s. Towns in the 1870s were dots on a vast prairie, and their populations were obviously only prototypes of what would be required for thriving, permanent cities. City building in 1870s western Kansas was an experiment, and residents, for all their trying to change that situation, were unable, from their position "at the front," to avoid constant reminders of its tentativeness. However unrestrained their rhetoric, the investments and actions of 1870s town promoters in western Kansas were cautious compared with those of the next decade.

"The West is necessarily a fast country," wrote a Russell man in 1875. "Everything is rushed along at lightning-express speed, and we have often wondered why our boys don't become of age at fifteen instead of waiting until they are twenty-one years old; but it does seem that in some ways, the people of the West carry on a very large business on an exceedingly small capital." Western Kansas towns were like that. "Insignificant towns have and speak of their boards of trade; and as soon as a town is staked off on the raw prairie the citizens proceed to inaugurate a 'city government,' by electing a mayor and 'city council'; and the local newspaper scarcely ever fails to speak of it as 'our thriving young city,' and tell the people that John Smith, drayman, will transfer goods from one part of the 'city' to another at reasonable rates, and that Tom Brown & Co., grocers, will deliver goods at any place within the 'city limits.' "[5] "Ellsworth has organized a board of trade," reported the Hays City paper in 1880, "and when one of the old country dames brings in a mess of butter and eggs, the distinguished body assembles in owl-like wisdom to consider the fluctuations of the market."[6]

In western Kansas, where few towns before the mid-1880s exceeded 1,000 in population and where none could show growth without reverses, such intimations of urbanity were pretentious. But it was also typical of the western booster attitude, which historian Walter Prescott Webb thought arose from the defensiveness of desert dwellers seeking psychological magic to transform bleak reality.[7] "Kansas towns have no natural advantages," wrote the editor at Kinsley. "They are all alike, and really all have equal advantages. They all make an even start, with a proportionate share of prairie grass and sunshine, and it is the first fellows who settle in a Kansas town who make or break it."[8]

As long as they were dreaming, western Kansas towns dreamed big. "Ellis is a city," wrote a correspondent in 1876. "She has all the hopes and aspirations of Chicago; the enterprise of St. Louis; the prosperity of Kansas City, and the trifle of cussedness Hays hasn't got."[9] The masthead of A. J. Hoisington's *Great Bend Register* read, "The World—Our Field; Kansas—Our Garden; Great Bend—Our Residence."[10] A newspaper writer at Kinsley in 1877 saw the possibilities for the future as potentially grand: "When the daylight lightning express ten years hence, comes thundering up the rising grade of the great Arkansas Valley, bound westward, bearing the Pacific mails destined for the Golden Gate and China, as the iron horse halts for a moment at our depot shall the through passenger carelessly turn for a moment to glance at the few scattered buildings and lifeless streets, and enquire, 'What station's this?' or shall he rush to the platform and fascinated with the view, looking down our tree-line crowded avenues exclaim, 'This is the live town of Kinsley!' "[11] It may have been disappointing that President Ulysses Grant's special train passed through Kinsley in 1880 at 1:30 A.M. while the hero was asleep.[12] The young people on the way home from a dance saw only a glimpse of a fast train on the way somewhere else.

An unbiased observer would have found little there to substantiate grand hopes. Western Kansas towns said they were "at once a city and a family," but the family aspects were in the 1870s buried by the Wild West characteristics of these towns' means of support.[13] Also, lack of a steady permanent population and a dependable tax base meant that the appearance and healthfulness of these places were as the accidents of self-interest would have them.

Dodge City suffered particularly from publicity that was as unfavorable to attracting a permanent sober population as it was voluminous. "The Beautiful Bibulous Babylon of the Frontier" was pictured as a place where citizens were "walking howitzers" and religion had no chance.[14] New arrivals were surprised to find there "men as peaceful and women as ladylike as any" because they had been prepared by "yellow-covered novels and

Border Haven. Wallace in the early 1880s. The Wild West looks fairly orderly here.

continued stories in the ledger'' to expect at Dodge "a land of booted and whiskered desperadoes, armed to the teeth with bowies and six-shooters, the murderous savages, where beautiful maidens are captured by out-law bands and regained by adventurous lovers."[15] A Hays City reporter wrote in 1877 that Dodge was a "hard, bad town" whose newspapers were filled with reports of crime. "Every other item is description of how some drunken rowdy nearly beat the life out of his mistress, or somebody else's mistress; the police court report often fills columns, and even the decent portion of the community have become so accustomed to the fearful state of affairs that they regard a good stand-up fight . . . a joke rather than a disgrace."[16] As late as 1883, when Dodge City newspapers insisted that state

prohibition had calmed the town, others did not think so. The *Medicine Lodge Cresset* reported that the last preacher had left Dodge City and that "after the last distributor of the gospel flees with his family and household goods to the mountains, a blizzard or a storm of hailstones and coals of fire will annihilate the town."[17]

Dodge City admitted that its cattle business did bring some "unsettled types" who, "though not worse of heart than the average, in many instances lack the external polish of a denser population, with its well-established schools, churches, literary societies, and other means of mental and moral culture."[18] But it insisted that in this regard it was no different from several other towns in the region. Great Bend in the late 1870s had its share of "drunken sprees and knockdowns," without even a city marshal to control them.[19] Elections at Kingman were accompanied by so much drinking that editor P. J. Conklin saw fourteen drunken men lying on the street after an 1878 election. "A few stragglers who could not find lodgings in Ball's hotel, and who were not yet quite drunk enough to lie down with their brethren in the street, were still staggering about, shooting off their mouths and their guns at the same time." Kingman residents dealt with a suspected horse thief that year by shooting him without benefit of a trial.[20]

Nor did sexual demeanor always correspond to the Victorian ideal. The *Hays Sentinel* had to report in 1876 a "disgraceful row" between a prostitute named "Long Jenny" and two soldiers. "A nice sort of an affair, wasn't it? to be taking place in a town where at least *some* of the citizens have arrived at a partial state of civilization."[21] Two years later a woman traveler at Hays in need of money was convinced by a resident to earn it by sleeping with him.[22] In one two-week period in 1880, there were three attempted rapes in the sleepy town of Osborne.[23] In 1878 Mary Nicholson and Joseph Leighty were tried in Larned for "adulterous cohabitation," and Ellis residents in 1881 were treated to the story of the mail clerk and the married lady "who did not follow the virtuous example of biblical Ruth and biblical Boaz in connubial constancy."[24] Western towns were active in every way.

As regularly as reports of crime and vice came descriptions of the damage done to the wooden main streets by "the Fire Fiend." Kinsley burned down so often that fire must be considered to have been a major factor in its development. In April 1879, two-thirds of its business section burned, with losses estimated at $100,000, only $11,000 of which was covered by insurance.[25] It happened again in June 1880.[26] Yet the Kinsley city council, strapped for funds due to the decline in saloon-license revenues brought about by state prohibition, was able to appropriate only $700 for primitive pumps, relying still for the most part on volunteer bucket brigades.[27] A good part of the downtowns of Larned and WaKeeney were destroyed in 1880, the latter fire gutting the land office for which WaKeeney had lobbied so hard and damaging many records.[28] In 1883, just as it had gotten well under way, much of Garden City burned.[29]

Towns that could not afford fire and police protection understandably did little about public health, not to mention the eyesores and odor created by what industry there was. Kinsley residents thought they deserved something better than a "hide" park where twisted trees grew out of refuse.[30] Some felt that city government should be able to do something about the 120 tons of buffalo bones and garbage that smelled up the center of town in 1878 within a few feet of the office of the *Kinsley Graphic*.[31] Also it seemed reasonable that a railroad town might have a cemetery of some sort.[32] And it was just possible that a general cleanup and some regulation of outhouses draining into sluggish Coon Creek could slow the spread of the typhus that visited Kinsley constantly in warm weather.[33] The stench in some sections of town was "enough to turn the stomach of a well man," and the aesthetics of the place were not uplifting: "Dead cats, dogs, chickens, and offal of almost every kind, is scattered over town; rotten potatoes and beef hides are left to dry up and scent the air with foul odors."[34]

Yet as much feeling as there was that towns

needed help, most towns in the 1870s felt they could not yet afford the obvious methods of correcting their ills—organized city government and taxation. Almost immediately after Great Bend acquired a formal city government in 1876, residents started suggesting it might be better to go back to a township form of government. "The existence of our city government," wrote one man, "is more of a luxury than a business advantage."[35] City government in Great Bend lost further ground in 1879 when the wealthy there refused to pay a city tax, arguing that city authority had technical flaws. Some who had paid received rebates and others did not, leading directly to suspicion in the extreme.[36] Similarly, Kinsley residents became dissatisfied with the town's third-class-city status in 1879 as population began to leave during the drought. It was simply too much when city officers granted themselves a salary of a dollar apiece per meeting and then started meeting more often.[37] There were petitions in Dodge City in 1880 to dissolve city government, which was costing $5,000 a year to operate.[38] Russell saved its city government only by imposing a tax on dogs.[39] Hays City waited until 1885 to incorporate at all.[40] Where, said the editor at Hays, is there a city that is not expensive? It did not bother people there that the plat of the town, drawn in 1878, was a little askew, with streets striking off "on their own hook in every conceivable direction." It avoided a planning bureaucracy.[41] "We cannot conceive of a more useless piece of furniture for a village of four hundred inhabitants than city government."[42]

Even the prospect of being able to provide schools, which would have done so much to give western communities respectability and culture, was not motivation enough. There was some activity in establishing normal schools for teacher training, thanks partly to a state grant to counties. Great Bend, Hays City, and Russell all had these by 1880.[43] But tax-supported public schools were a different matter. A settler in Barton County suggested in 1877 that families pitch in and build their own schools rather than depend on counties or cities to do so. "We have seen too many good sturdy settlers and too many thousands of dollars of capital pass through this county and locate west of here by reason of the bonds that we have out already to wish to increase the dose."[44] G. G. Sampson, principal of Great Bend schools in 1877, complained that there was yet no adequate division of grades, though he had 157 pupils in his system. Townspeople were not interested in schools, he said, and seemed to think schools could operate with neither supervision nor money.[45] The same was true in Kinsley. When the tax collector called in Edwards County, he was likely to hear that a sod house was good enough for schooling and that in fact privation in school facilities would raise up "sturdy men and women." If the district in question happened to have a nice school building with a playground, the tax collector heard what a "pile" it had cost "and all for the benefit of other people's children."[46]

Although 100 votes could elect a mayor in most western Kansas towns in the 1870s, politics was prominent.[47] While true local issues, such as the building of waterworks, streetcar lines, or sewers, did not arise until the boom of the mid-1880s, towns were where people voted for state and national officers, and on their streets and in their newspapers took place heated debates about the issues of the day.

Local candidates therefore commonly identified themselves with state and national issues in a way that lent their campaigns exaggerated importance. A Hays City editor jested in 1883 that there would be fielded in local elections that year a "double back action, anti-monopoly, anti-Greenback, anti-Republican, anti-democrat and any thing to 'get there Eli' ticket."[48] Dodge had four tickets in the field in 1884, which a Larned observer thought could be best distinguished by labeling them "Straight Bourbon," "Mixed Drinks," "Lemon and Soda Pop," and "Holy Water."[49] Nor was careful analysis of the vote, however small, absent. It was reported that one defeated local candidate in Barton County in 1876 had said that "the d____d dutch and niggers had gone back on him and [he] cussed the Mennonites thoroughly."[50]

Partly because any political decision affecting the region could be critical to a town's survival and partly because big politics was viewed as symbolic of a big place, local rings and combinations and alleged chicanery in the state legislature got as much coverage in the local press as did national scandals. Overtaxation and the creation of too much county bond debt were the most common complaints, but close behind were the underrepresentation of western Kansas in the state legislature, lack of adequate laws regulating railroad rates, attempts by railroads to avoid a fair share of taxation, insufficient progress on currency reform to help debtors, and the effects of a state prohibition amendment.

These issues gave local figures practice in the high rhetoric they would use later to promote their booming towns. "Western Kansas has been bulldozed, gerrymandered, counted out,

unrepresented for years," wrote a Larned man, "and the beneficiaries of the fraud laugh at our calamity and sit in secure places and mock when our fear cometh."[51] The so-called Granger Laws passed in the upper Midwest to regulate railways and warehouses would come to Kansas, an editor in Great Bend predicted, unless corporations heeded the power of voters in the smallest towns. They should "harken to the 'still small voice' of those who have the power to drop little ballots, singly as light as the snowflake, but collectively like the mountain avalanche, for such men for the Legislature as will enact a law compelling them to listen."[52] Opposition to state prohibition, passed in 1880, was more difficult because economic interests were arrayed against morality and the stated desire of the towns to regulate their rowdy elements. The *New York Times* cheered the measure, noting that people on the High Plains could not afford the stimulation of strong drink and that the passage of prohibition in Kansas was merely "a measure of self-defense."[53] Robert M. Wright of Dodge City responded with gentle humor. Western Kansas, he said in a talk before the legislature, would secede from the state if a change were not made to exempt from the temperance bill the area west of the 100th meridian. The problem was snakes. Now, if a western Kansas man were bitten by a snake, the snake died. If the alcohol level in the blood of the residents there were to decline, however, the region might become positively dangerous.[54]

Temporary economic benefits such as cattle drives, construction of railroads, support of the frontier military, and serving as a supply center for opening regions farther west kept the towns in business in the 1870s and supported the publication of newspapers filled with small-time political drivel. Western Kansans, however, were keenly aware that their regional centers could not continue to thrive as primitive, male-dominated, glorified campsites. The *Russell County Record* in 1876 promised to give more balanced coverage of the kind of ordinary goings-on in town that would perhaps make it a trade center serving solid farm families. "As we live in a Christian community," the editor wrote, "it is not an easy matter to fill two or three columns of solid brevier with accounts of duels, lynchings, cold-blooded fiendish murders, suicides, prize fights, etc., etc., and we are obliged to content ourselves with the tamer sort of accidents, incidents, anecdotes and peccadilloes which fall to our lot."[55] Too many newspapers were dominated by politicians or political cliques, where "politicians seek to intimidate the printer, and egotistical asses demolish editors."[56] Consequently, there was an air of unreality and bias about the local news. The *Larned Chronoscope,* hearing of a newspaper to be started in Walnut City, Rush County, suggested it be named the *Rush County Fabricator* or the *Walnut City Fable.*[57] "The greatest curse that is visited upon the newly settled portions of the Great West," wrote the Russell editor, "is not the locust, nor the drouth, nor the Indians, though these are terrible enough sometimes, but the frontier politician."[58]

Therefore, in the late 1870s, attention in western Kansas towns turned temporarily away from the "plug-hatted, white-shirted, diamond-pinned, gold-chained class of men" and toward the plainer types who promised surer, though less spectacular, gains.[59] Settlers arriving at Great Bend were met in 1876 by an omnibus of the Great Bend Transfer Company bearing the motto "Excelsior."[60] Kinsley newspapers in 1877 and 1878 began not only reporting in detail upon the make-up of the Santa Fe excursion trains running into town with more than two hundred potential settlers each but published hotel lists demonstrating the points of origin of the land seekers in town that week.[61] Even in the slack year of 1880, the two Larned hotels entertained nearly five thousand guests.[62] When there were large excursions, like the four-hundred person extravaganza of January 1878, and Kinsley's hotels overflowed, private homes were opened and special entertainments provided for the excursionists.[63] That there were still sometimes parties who had to stay in a livery barn or on boxcars only encouraged the towns to expand.[64] Competition for immigrants' attention was fierce, and towns maneuvered to get either their literature or their agents aboard the train or to have literature and agents banned altogether.[65] When travelers did stop, there was no limit to the pressures applied. One Kinsley land agent always turned back to town after starting out with a party to get his rubber overcoat and umbrella, just in case of one of those downpours the strangers were to assume were common.[66] Wrote a Kinsley publicist: "We invite the serious attention of those who, crowded in the midst of an almost effete civilization in the East, are looking anxiously beyond the Mississippi for new homes."[67]

Competition for population led also to at least temporary tolerance for minority groups in western Kansas towns that was remarkable in contrast to the general national tone. It was part of a push for unity, an aspect of hard surroundings where one took help from wherever it came, but, however short lived and induced, such cross-cultural, interracial empathy was a secret gift of time and place.

In 1879 "Uncle" John White, a black man who had lived in Hays City since 1868, was visiting a friend aboard a train. Stepping off as it departed, he fell, was dragged twenty yards, and then run over and cut to pieces. He had been a barber and restaurant owner; his "good-humored countenance was a familiar object in Hays—everybody knew and liked him," and his death was "like the passing of a land-mark." Born a slave in Tennessee in 1815, White had gained his freedom in 1863 and come west with his wife. It was not unusual that the local paper should write up the lurid details of a grisly incident, but the recognition of a black man's central place in the life of a community, an understanding of his personal history, and an extension of the "heart-felt sympathy of our community" to his widow by name were hardly common in 1870s America.[68]

Similar identification of a black man as an individual, not just a member of a race, came in Kinsley in 1879 when Jerry Saunders, pro-prietor of a local cleaning and repair shop, crushed the skull of another black man in a quarrel.[69] In Wichita, the newspaper would be likely to have reported the wielding of razors but say it did not get the name of either party. But most people in Kinsley knew Saunders well, and his plight could not be easily ignored on account of his race. His name appeared regularly in the society columns, before and after the murder: when he fell skating on the ice and the girls giggled, or when he played base-ball on the local nine where there was "no distinction of color shown."[70] It was news in

Kinsley when the "young men's social club (colored)" gave a party, or when blacks organ-ized the Pioneer Mutual Agricultural Associa-tion, or even when a black carpenter built an especially nice addition onto his "neat and cozy residence" in town.[71] Therefore, the black murderer was for the community its friend Jerry Saunders, and the *Kinsley Graphic* editor was relieved when, after Saunders gave himself up, the county attorney reduced the charge to fourth-degree manslaughter and the court im-posed the minimum sentence. "Jerry Saunders is a hard-working colored man and has the facility of attention to his own business which has made him popular in the community, who, without an exception as far as we know, are glad that he escaped with a light sentence."[72]

Evidence pointing in the same direction can be found for other towns. When a Great Bend reporter learned in 1879 that a "colored lady of culture" from North Carolina was enrolled at the new normal institute in town, he suggested that the board of education enlist her as a teacher, especially because there were thirty black children in Great Bend schools. Some politicians would oppose it, the reporter thought, but the majority of the community would see the practicality of such a move.[73] The same paper reported on a convention of the black citizens of Barton, Pawnee, Edwards, Ford, and Hodgeman Counties held in Kinsley on 4 July 1878 to elect delegates to the Business and Industrial Convention to be held in Kansas City and suggested that Barton County blacks elect an extra delegate on their own.[74] In Larned, a black man, Jerome Johnson, was on the staff of the *Larned Chronoscope* in the early 1880s and kept newspaper readers informed of everyday goings-on among local blacks.[75]

Spearheads of the Frontier. New arrivals unloading from Santa Fe cars near the pottery at Larned in the 1880s. The towns were always the first stop, and the place to organize.

Their picnics, their weddings, their entertainments, their politics, and their dreams of a home in the West were chronicled in all the towns along with those of whites.

Not that it is difficult to find racist comments in the western Kansas press. Russian jokes have been mentioned. In both Hays and Kinsley, there was without question some tension about Germans and German-Russians that was tied directly to their voting power and business competitiveness. When the *Hays City Advocate* made some fun of an Irish girl, the *Stockton News* responded: "Say, Dutchy, if you will try and pull the sauerkraut out of your ears, keep your nose clean and wash your feet once in a while it will be a great deal better than making fun of a poor, half-starved Irish girl that is trying to make an honest living."[76] Derogatory language was also employed when the *Chronoscope* reported in 1884 that a couple of "heathen Chinee" had started a wash house in Larned. "An opium den will be the next thing to follow, for the rat-eating sons of Confucius can no more live without opium than a bourbon Democrat can live without whisky, or a cowboy can exist without a broad-brimmed hat."[77]

The important point, however, is that the prejudice was often directed at an individual German, black, or Chinese rather than against the race as a whole and was tied to town loyalty. The actions of Gustave Flohr, whom the editor of the *Graphic* thought did not, as a powerful merchant, lend enough support to the general aspirations of the town, were the source of much of that sheet's anti-German comment.[78] The same was true in Hays City, where Henry Krueger owned the main hall and was charged with "lacking that spirit of enterprise and accommodation necessary to make his Hall or himself popular as to public support."[79] And while the *Larned Chronoscope* made a negative comment about the Chinese wash house, shortly thereafter it reported favorably on the aspirations of Chin Kee, one of the town's Chinese citizens, whom it said "wants to do right" and who presented the local church with a flower basket from China valued at $5.[80] The *Kinsley Graphic* in 1882 came out against the Chinese exclusion bill, the start of U.S. immigration restriction, arguing that many Chinese were "industrious, energetic, honest, inoffensive and peaceable" and would be assets to places like Kinsley.[81] Prejudice ebbed and flowed as the needs of the community changed, but the special needs of western Kansas towns kept it in restraint.

While racial tolerance was desirable in attracting good families to the region, the development of moral recreations was essential. People might enjoy reading at a distance about the Wild West, but few would bring their families there. Therefore, instead of playing up their lurid reputations, western Kansas cattle towns downplayed them in hope of promoting stable growth. "Our population is made up of intelligent, well-bred people, from all parts of the world," claimed an Ellsworth resident in the 1870s, "those who have seen much of life, and are accustomed to the refinements and courtesies of cultivated society." Just west of Wichita there was no excuse for barbarism: "Within easy range of large cities, we have easy access to the advantages they possess in the way of lectures and amusements, and there is no need of our being out of date in the least."[82]

Literary societies were most prominent among the town institutions designed to ameliorate the intellectual monotony of farm life.

Often the impetus for their formation came from enjoyment of a traveling troupe of players or a lecturer (often a temperance lecturer) and the realization that such events would be few unless local people provided programs. In arguing for a literary society in 1878, the editor of the *Larned Chronoscope* said that more attention to reading and discussion, even after a hard day of farm work, was essential unless western Kansas was willing to leave the direction of public opinion to such "artful demagogues and skillful word-patchers, to inventors of slang phrases, and contrivers of by-words" as could influence simple farmers.[83] The Elam Bartholomew family in the late 1870s often walked several miles to visit the evening activities the Bow Creek Literary Society held for the extremely isolated settlers in northern Rooks County. Like church, it was a central part of their lives, and like church, it kept them from feeling like savages fighting the weather and digging in the ground. On 26 December 1879, Bartholomew recorded that he spent the day helping his wife Rachel clean the house so they could go together in the evening to the literary society, where settlers were debating the question: "Resolved, that the reading of fictitious literature is injurious." On a subsequent evening, as the drought deepened, the debate was "that poverty tends more to develop the character than riches."[84]

WaKeeney started a literary society immediately upon the town's founding. At the February 1879 meeting, there was a reading of Mark Twain's "Siamese Twins" by Mrs. C. P. Keeney, a history of Trego County (necessarily brief) by George Pinkham, an essay on old and new Edinburgh musical solos, and a debate.[85] When Dodge City organized a literary society in 1882, it was not only "a departure in Dodge City social ethics" but was viewed as a transforming departure, which would "soften or embellish the uncouth mind" and "marks our entry into the intellectual world."[86] Some women objected the next year to the Dodge literary meeting on Monday night because Monday was their washing day and they were too tired to enjoy it, but neither could they imagine missing it.[87] Even advertising made literary allusions. An ad in the *Hays Sentinel* in 1878 went: "Lives there a man with soul so dead, / Who never to his wife has said, / This night, before I go to bed, / I'll call at Wilson's cheap cash store."[88] Culture might not have been sophisticated, but western Kansas towns appreciated, as much as any group of businesspeople sitting on an arts council in a twentieth-century metropolis, the importance of culture to economic growth.

The literary society was a fixture of nearly every place that merited a post office. In the larger towns, variety in entertainment and edification was greater. Kinsley had an "As You Like It" dramatic club, formed after an 1878 visit by a Shakespeare company. The local talent could not manage the bard but did perform "Ten Nights in a Bar Room" before an appreciative local temperance audience. Receipts were $75, expenses nil.[89] Kinsley celebrated the opening of a public hall known as the "Gem of the Valley" in 1878 with a sit-down supper for 104 people followed by socializing that went on until three o'clock in the morning.[90] Churches held socials every other week in Kinsley—25 cents for adults, 15 cents for children—and the town boasted two dance clubs in the late 1870s: the Kinsley Quadrille Club and the Gem City Social Club.[91] Great

Bend in 1879 supported a Joseph Henry scientific society, whose activites were kicked off with an address by Henry Inman of Larned on "The Magnitude of Space."[92] The Ellis Library Association in 1876 boasted one hundred volumes.[93] In 1879 Hays City put on a concert complete with curtains in an American-flag design. Response was restrained to a vocal duet called "Fly Away Birdling" by Miss Kate Cass and Miss Emma Miller, but a Liszt piano piece and a Hummel concerto brought enthusiastic applause. Receipts of $33.40 and eighty-four one-pound packages were forwarded to the Home for the Friendless.[94]

It was not everywhere that you could join a combination lawn-tennis, croquet, and archery club, play chess in a continuous tournament, and test your skill with an air pistol for a bet of a nickel cigar, as you could at Hays by 1882.[95] But the tiniest towns showed the same drive for association and community activity. There were foot races and wolf hunts, fishing in stocked streams and ponds, sheep-sheering contests, clog dancing, kissing games, and billiards.[96] Street preachers provided entertainment and sometimes culture, and there were suggestions that even the Sunday worship had become more "sport and pleasure" than discipline for frontier people.[97] But for cheap fun, nothing beat a brass band. The little town of Bazine in Ness County waited eagerly in 1880 for someone with musical talent and then ordered instruments from Slater's Music House in New York City. Because no one could play, instruments were assigned based on personality, and soon the Bazine band not only played recognizable versions of "After the Ball" and "Only a Pansy Blossom" but drew a crowd in Ness City at thirty-five-cents admission. They got blue

A Stop along the Way. Dining room of the Larned House Hotel in Larned, 1880s. Notice the formal table settings, linens, and china. People did not expect to dine in a hovel because they were in the West.

uniforms with a spread eagle on the hats and braid on the overcoats, and as they traveled to neighboring towns in a large farm wagon, they played mightily just to show folks at McCracken, Rush Center, and Jetmore that you didn't have to be Hays City to have a brass band.[98]

At the turn of the decade, the towns of western Kansas were not in a fundamentally different situation relative to each other or to the outside world than they had been six or seven years earlier. The location of the largest of them was still determined by the route of the region's two initial railroad trunk lines, a situation that the projection of hundreds of companies and the building of several new lines in the 1880s would dramatically change. All still had an equal chance, as there were no cases of a success so impressive as to be inimitable or a failure so dismal as to be irreparable. The region had shown both its sides, but it was not clear which would dominate over time nor to what degree dealing with natural threats might itself become business for the towns. The future still looked as if it could create not only towns and cities but metropolitan regions.

There was reason for increased optimism, too, about actual accomplishment because cautious moves had had some observable results. Kinsley had a public bath with hot and cold running water.[99] Hays, with a population of 949, had 89 business houses, 184 marriageable ladies, 113 bachelors, and 182 children in school.[100] At the eastern edge of western Kansas, Wichita had a population of nearly 5,000 and Salina more than 3,000. Hutchinson had 1,528, Larned 1,066, Great Bend 1,071, Ellsworth 929, Dodge City 996, Russell 861, Kinsley 457, Osborne 719, Ellis 689, Hays City 850, and WaKeeney 418.[101] The grasshoppers had not returned in numbers, domestic and foreign colonies had force-fed population into the rural areas, nature had blessed the region with a few wet years, and amenities were sufficient to attract a class other than the most desperate. Although western counties were 75 to 90 percent rural in population in the 1870s, their towns were both gateways and links and their health a barometer of the strength of the conquest.

As usual, however, appearances could be deceptive. Town dwellers of 1870s western Kansas wanted almost as much as social scientists of the 1980s to learn something about a process of urban growth that could be reproduced anywhere. And, like modern analysts, they believed that differences in the quality of urban leadership, based on more or less subtle understanding of these factors of growth, could give some towns advantages over others and could control to a degree the accidents of climate and economic decision making from the outside.[102] However, there seems to be little correlation historically between the kind of cleverness in town-building techniques an intellectual admires and eventual success in becoming a dominant town. Regional history leads one to conclude that things as they happen are not fair and that settlers did not make rational decisions based on a careful study of the advantages of individual towns but went where railroad excursions took them, settled where land in their price range was available, and traded in the town that had, by hook or crook, attracted the land office. Early advantages, however small, were vital because later patterns were much affected by momentum, habit, and inertia.

Nor could towns themselves, individually or in tandem, create instant modernization and automatic growth in western Kansas any more than had any of the other weapons nineteenth-century civilization had been able to wield. Imported culture and lively talk about the political issues of the day, available to families shopping in Hays, Kinsley, or WaKeeney, helped pass the time but did not much ease the struggle against the elements when these families returned to their homesteads. Even amid the good years were signs of ancient wrath, and the bad years were never long in returning. Perhaps immigrants in the late 1870s could not have guessed that the Indian problem was yet unsolved in the western Kansas region. They might better have imagined that rain did not follow the plow and very dry years would return. Whether they had expected these problems and were not able to bear them or whether they had hoped against hope the problems would not arise, the people who constituted the populations of High Plains cities and counties continued to leave almost as fast as they came. Town populations in the region for 1880 showed only modest increases, sometimes declines, over 1878, and the figures for 1883 were almost the same as for 1880.[103] The gentle boom of the post-grasshopper years and the confidence of the growing towns foundered, as had similar western Kansas upturns before them, under the weight of a series of disasters.

Chapter Nine

Dull Knife

The Dull Knife and Little Wolf bands of Northern Cheyenne crossed the southern border of Kansas on 14 September 1878. Behind the 353 Indians was a year of failed experiment with reservation life in the sultry Indian Territory; before them, the long chance of a return to their cool Montana home.

They knew they probably would not make it, but to die trying was preferable to living out their days with shorn hair and white man's clothes, doing women's work digging in the soil, and watching their children be whipped in agency schools. That had been the fate of their brothers, the Southern Cheyenne; those once-feared raiders of the Kansas frontier seemed to have forgotten how to dance and to dream—perhaps they had seen too much of dying to recall how a warrior should live. In the ten years since they had struck the Solomon River settlements and were in turn decimated by Custer, they had changed, and their northern kin pitied them. "We were sickly and dying there," a Northern Cheyenne said later of the tribe's brief experience in Indian Territory, "and no one will speak our names when we are gone." Better to go north and to die in battle so that "our names will be remembered and cherished by all our people."[1]

Western Kansans were, surprisingly, initially sympathetic. Most of the region's population in 1878 had no experience with Indian raids; the last concentrated attacks on Kansas settlements had been in 1868 and 1869. In the interim, a great deal of sympathetic literature had appeared, portraying Indians as a "dying race," relatively helpless and hounded in defeat by corrupt politicians and thieving agents. Western Kansans had read of the scheming involved in removing the Northern Cheyenne to Indian Territory in 1877; and the reformist press had kept them informed since about shortfalls in subsistence goods the government had promised the Indians and about the callous disregard of their religion and cultural ways by bureaucrats whose inflexible behavior was well known to western whites.[2] Who could believe that these suffering people could be a threat or that their trek through Kansas that September was any more than a flight in panic from intolerable conditions? "There is not one particle of cause for alarm," said the *Dodge City Times* on the day the Indians entered Kansas. The "wild Cheyennes" had been treated poorly and wanted to return home. "The only probable scalps they would take on these marches would be the scalp of a Texas steer."[3]

Before the Indians left the state early in October—having killed forty-one settlers, raped twenty-five females from age eight up, and destroyed $100,000 worth of western Kansas property—the *Times* changed its tune.[4] On 21 September, there was still some tolerance left, despite Dodge City's being an armed camp whose citizens, led by Wyatt Earp, went to suspected attack sites on a protected locomotive. "We do not believe it to be their willful purpose to murder, but in committing theft they may deem it necessary to destroy the innocent protectors of the stock."[5] On the twenty-eighth the editor said that the "starving and imbecile policy of Indian Agents and the Government" was responsible for the Cheyenne action.[6] But by October, there was no explaining it away. "It is no boy's play," the editor commented, "no holiday journey they have entered upon."[7]

Reflecting on the events made them seem all the worse. Early in November, the Dodge City editor called the Cheyenne "inhuman" when speaking of how they raped women, "then beat and mangled the unfortunate victims of their brutal lust. . . . Yet every day or two we read accounts of how some philanthropic . . . ass in Boston or New York dishes up a lot of slush concerning the nobility of the savages."[8] Yes, they were more pitiful than ever. When several Dull Knife stragglers came through Dodge City with other Indians being taken to the Cheyenne and Arapaho reservation late in November, they stank, looked "haggard and sickly" and were "thinly and poorly clothed."[9] The few from the main band who survived the bloodbath at Fort Robinson, Nebraska, in January would look even worse. But their bloody deeds, unnecessary to their avowed purpose, placed their flight, to western Kansas minds, in the category of terrorism, not defensive strategy. Wrote the editor: "It is about time that the border states and territories took a contract for missionary work, in which a few companies of frontiersmen should civilize or exterminate these Government pets."[10]

This harsh western mind set, so offensive to eastern reformers, was created step by step as grisly news reached the local press and fear was transformed into aggression. As in 1868–1869, it was not so much abstract statistics that shocked as the haunting details of individual incidents and the possibility that one's own family might be the next visited.

The Indians ranged at will over southwestern Kansas in their first days after crossing the border; only one tentative skirmish on 22 September with troops and citizens delayed them.[11] On Sunday the fifteenth, just after crossing the Indian Territory line, they had come across a ranch operated by Fred Clarke and Reuben Bristow. Meeting the two proprietors on the road about eight miles from their house, the Indians killed them both, dumped their bodies into a wagon where they were found four days later, and stole their horses. Fred Clarke was twenty-four, recently from Virginia. Bristow was twenty-two and had come to Kansas from Kentucky.[12] Two days later some braves, armed only with hunting knives, approached cowboys sitting around a campfire toward evening in southeastern Comanche County. They asked for food and tobacco, and when they were refused, one Indian grabbed a gun from the nearest man and shot down Frank Dow and John Evans.[13]

On the Salt Fork of the Cimarron River, the tribesmen (and women and children) visited Wiley Payne's ranch. Indian men walked up to Payne, offered to shake hands, and, when his hand was engaged, shot him in the neck. His wife was wounded in the thigh and her baby through the breast before Mrs. Payne was able to scare the Indians away by discharging a shotgun the family had hidden in the house. The Paynes recovered from only their physical wounds.[14] In Meade County, Washington O'Conner met the Indians while driving a wagon loaded with construction equipment. They seemed friendly, but suddenly a brave grabbed O'Conner by the hair and slashed his throat from ear to ear.[15] Similar tactics prevailed at the tiny town (a population of eight or ten in 1878) of Meade City. There one resident spoke to a group of Indians who requested food. Several said: "Me good Indian; me no hurt you." To that quote, the reporter added parenthetically, "The bloody devils" because as they left, the Indians shot a man on his way into town.[16] Moving north into Ford County, the Cheyenne killed a black man cooking for a cattle crew, stole $2,000 worth of jewelry and clothing belonging to the Fowler family, recently arrived from California, and chased off or killed a large amount of stock.[17]

Some historians, trying to justify and sometimes even romanticize Cheyenne motives and actions, have argued that Chief Dull Knife attempted to control violence, failing only when the bands reached the northern Kansas settlements, where they could not resist avenging the deaths of Southern Cheyenne at the hands of United States troops at the Battle of Sappa Creek in 1875. Reading Mari Sandoz's *Cheyenne Autumn,* for example, one can hardly tell that any settlers or stock were killed or any women raped at all.[18] The facts strongly support the position that these Cheyenne did have reason to flee what amounted to captivity in Indian Territory. But it also appears that they made no attempt to restrain random violence,

and there is no good reason to believe that this group of Northern Cheyenne was interested in specifically avenging earlier actions against Southern Cheyenne.

Instead, as the most careful student of the raid, Ramon Powers, interprets it, the violence sprang from anger at whites generally. It began the moment the Indians crossed the southern border into Kansas and became more damaging in the north only because the population was more dense there. In western Kansas south of Dodge City, the Dull Knife and Little Wolf bands killed ten people, wounded five, and drove off or killed 640 head of cattle.[19] Some of the cattle were needed for Indian subsistence, and the braves might even be excused for occasionally killing a rancher who declined to provide supplies to Indians. But the killing of stock and people went far beyond explicable needs. In southwestern Kansas, the Indians rode into a flock of sheep and killed 250 with arrows, apparently as a lark. The mutton from only one carcass was taken. Little wonder that the military in the south, cautious partly out of sympathy with the Indians and partly "haunted by the ghost of Custer," stiffened its resistance as the group approached Dodge City.[20]

People in the towns of Kinsley and Dodge City were panic-stricken. "As we write," the *Kinsley Graphic* reported on 21 September, "the bloodthirsty fiends are roaming at will, almost in sight of Kinsley, butchering the honest, unsuspecting pioneer, whose reeking scalp is thronged to the belt of these satanic fiends who are armed today better than any army in Europe."[21] At Dodge City, the engine bell at the firehouse began ringing regularly on the seventeenth to call the population to arms. On that day a party from Dodge had an hour-long skirmish with some Indians, and the next day Mayor J. H. Kelly telegraphed the governor to send arms: "The country is filled with Indians." At the time there were only nineteen men at Fort Dodge, and the townspeople, not knowing the habits of Indian raiders, feared a direct attack on the town. When on Friday, 20 September, the adjutant general arrived with the first shipment of what was to amount to 600 carbines and 20,000 cartridges, his train was met by a mob of citizens and the Dodge City Silver Cornet Band. Said the local editor: "The scene at the depot . . . reminded us of rebellion times."[22] Hope for safety through negotiations faded as more blood flowed. Said a Kinsley man: "The only treaty that will bring peace to our frontier is the Winchester or 'forty-four.' "[23]

For allowing the Cheyenne to come so far, and, some charged, for "using precautions to prevent the track from becoming too fresh," Captain Joseph Rendlebrock was relieved of his command of troops tailing the Indians and was later court-martialed.[24] His replacement, West Point graduate Colonel William H. Lewis of Fort Dodge, had better support from his superiors, who were finally convinced that this was a genuine, if latter-day, Indian raid. However, when Lewis assumed command on 25 September, the Indians had slipped past Dodge City, crossed the Santa Fe Railroad, and were approaching the Kansas Pacific Railroad and the Smoky Hill River. Lewis determined to stop them there and set out from Dodge City at a fast pace.[25]

Lewis' troops found the Indians—or rather, the Indians found them—on the afternoon of Friday, 27 September, while the soldiers prepared camp on Famished Woman's Creek, a tributary of the Smoky Hill north of present Scott City.[26] Lewis had about two hundred men; the Indians numbered between sixty and one hundred twenty-five. The engagement was largely a rifle duel in a box canyon, and there was unanimity among witnesses that Lewis conducted himself bravely. His horse was killed, but he continued to direct the battle until hit in the leg in a way that severed the femoral artery and started extensive bleeding. His adjutant put a belt above the wound and used a revolver to form a tourniquet. Soon a doctor and ambulance arrived to carry Lewis away, but he said, "Doctor, I have my death wound. Do not expose yourself so; remember your wife and children; you can do nothing for me." Veterans of many Indian campaigns wept at the sad scene, and Lewis, weak from a recent attack of dysentery, died on the rough road to Fort Wallace, an authentic hero.[27] When Lewis failed, but failed so nobly, the battle became almost immediately a legend, and hatred for the alien intruders responsible for the death of such a hero increased.

The battle was dramatic but ineffective. In fact, the confusion in command following Lewis's death allowed the Indians to cross the KP Railroad, an obvious place to stop them, and by fast marches to reach centers of settlement on Beaver and Sappa Creeks in present Rawlins and Decatur Counties. There, at the northwest corner of Kansas, were numbers of settlers in almost the same situation as those on the Solomon and Saline Rivers and White Rock Creek one hundred miles to the east had been ten years earlier. The guests this time were Northern, not Southern, Cheyenne, but there were no ethnologists to make the distinction. The news preceding them had been of the same terrifying type as in 1868, and the cry of "Indians!" that went up made no distinction of tribe or purpose. Whatever the time or reason, dying violently on the prairie was much the same. And as Dull Knife, Little Wolf, and friends left Kansas, the dying rose to unforgettable, many said unforgivable, levels.[28]

On the morning of 30 September, William Laing, his fifteen-year-old son Freeman, and two neighbor girls named Eve and Lou Van Cleave started out from Decatur County to Kirwin, where they intended to prove up a claim at the land office. When they had gone about eight miles, twelve Indians rode up at a gallop, surrounded the wagon, and began to salute with the usual "How." Two of them grasped the hands of the father and son warmly while two others fired from behind, killing both. The father fell back into the lap of one of the girls, and the boy sank on his knees in the wagon. The girls then were asked to hold the horses while the Indians partook of the provisions. They then went to the creek where others of the tribe were camped, and as many as a dozen Indians raped the girls. Afterward, they were released naked and told to go to the Jacob Keiffer house a half-mile away. For a time they would not go; they thought if they turned their backs the Indians would shoot them. Finally the girls stumbled off amid general laughter.[29]

The Indians were not finished with the Laing family. At about sundown the same day, Laing's two oldest sons, William and John, saw Indians while returning home from the field. They were in a wagon with their sisters, ages twelve, nine, and seven, who had walked out to meet them and ride home. The Indians shook hands and invited themselves to dinner. But after riding alongside the wagon for a short

distance, one tribesman yelled, "Look here," and when the boys turned their heads, the Indians shot them. The girls drove ahead to the house to warn their mother, but they were too late. Five Indians raped the mother, four raped the twelve-year-old, and three raped the nine-year-old. They then placed all three girls between the feather ticks of the bed, kindled fires in different parts of the room, and threw into the flames everything they did not carry away with them. Mrs. Laing stood, beaten, abused, and without any clothes, wringing her hands and pleading for all their lives.[30]

The Laing women were lucky. A chief, who may have been Dull Knife himself, ordered their release, and the four walked eight miles to spend the night at the Keiffer house with the similarly distraught Van Cleave girls. The Indians had not burned them, and someone had drawn the line at raping a seven-year-old.[31]

John Fuller was also among the many in Decatur County who had hard experiences. Two of Fuller's friends met the Indians further south; both were wounded but escaped to warn their friends along Prairie Dog Creek (near present Jennings). Like the people at Oberlin, who had been similarly warned that Sunday, 29 September, few prepared to defend themselves, but Fuller felt the impact of the invasion before he saw a single Indian. He sat with Lucy Peck at the Peck post office and watched the slow death of a man the Indians had shot. "Even now," he wrote years later, "I recall the pathos of the evening, as we sat beside the dying man, only about twenty-one years old, pleading to see his parents."[32]

The incident enraged Fuller, who the next day volunteered to join fourteen others led by scout Sol Reese to follow to their source the trail of teakettles, buckets, cooking utensils, and chairs the Indians were dropping. The group discovered a dead man lying on his back, his arms above his head fastened by a quirt. Fuller took the quirt and kept it until his house burned in a prairie fire in 1887.[33]

Eventually the little party caught up to the stragglers and cornered an "old Indian buck," as Fuller put it, a woman, and a fourteen-year-old boy in a plum thicket. The three had killed a steer and were trying to cut the meat off. Reese started to shoot the old man, but his gun misfired. Getting another, he hit him in the shoulder. Then, growing more angry and frustrated, the white scout decided to scalp the Indian alive and did so on the spot. "I can clearly recall," Fuller wrote, "the expression on the Indian's face as he was being scalped, an indescribable look of hatred and revenge." The young Indian boy escaped, though wounded and unable to walk. The next spring a family of settlers found him thirty miles from the site. He looked as threatening as a boy could who has crawled for several months; but the children called for their father, who shot the boy dead. When the man approached the body, he was sorry. The boy had made a poultice of herbs for his wounded hip, and the gun the children had said he was brandishing was only a bone. But he was one of the Dull Knife raiders, and no one on either side had forgotten or forgiven.[34]

Incidents in neighboring Rawlins County to the west were no more pleasant. Indians visited the Anton Stenner homestead on 1 October. One took his horse, said "Nice team," then shot Stenner in the head and heart. Stenner's wife and children hid in the canyons for three days before daring to return to the house. The Reverend George Fenburgh, a fellow German who was the United Brethren minister, went to the Stenner house to help but found only Indians, who killed him as he crossed the threshold. Fred Hamper and Pat Rathburn were looking for mules when twenty-five Indians rode up. There was no sign of hostility, just friendly "How how." But as the two turned to go, Rathburn heard the click of gunlocks and dropped to his horse's neck. Hamper, thirty-five, was killed instantly, but the twenty-one-year-old Rathburn fled and survived, though while hiding in a ravine, he recalled, "the grass all around me seemed alive with bullets." George Harrison, a disabled nineteen-year-old, was killed bringing horses home from pasture. A boy died at Hundred Head Draw; his body was left for coyotes. The Indians drove Mrs. Paul Janousek out of her house after raping her, forcing her to leave her baby behind. Her relatives Egnac and Peter Janousek were killed, and Egnac's infant son Charlie, whom he was holding in his arms, was scarred for life.[35]

The Northern Cheyenne did not reach home. Shortly after leaving Kansas, they split into two groups under Dull Knife and Little Wolf. The army found Dull Knife's band in late October and forced it into captivity at Fort Robinson, Nebraska. There sixty-four Indians died in a January escape attempt. Little Wolf's band was captured in Montana in March.[36] The warriors had vowed to get out of Indian Territory or die: most of them died.

Surely that was punishment enough. However, western Kansans felt strongly that it was not punishment of the right kind to prevent such happenings in the future. "It is a fact, no less humiliating than true," said Governor John St.

John early in 1879, that Indians were loose in the state for twenty-five days—killing, raping, and plundering with impunity.[37] The military was ineffective in stopping such a lightning raid once it had started, and there seemed no way to check abuses in the policy of Indian assimilation that may have contributed to the outbreak of violence in the first place. Even had these methods worked better, Kansans believed them unfair to Indians not involved in the raiding and unsatisfactory psychologically to the settlers who had lost loved ones. Wrote a Hays City man: "The bold warrior of our national army slaughters the merciless savage even as he has slaughtered the defenceless settler, and then comes trooping back to the station, his breast swelling with the proud consciousness of having killed his score of braves and inflicted full and sweeping revenge." But would that revenge "silence the moans of widowed mothers and orphaned children? Would revenge hush the cry of the baby for its ravished and murdered mother?"[38]

What was needed, it was felt, was not revenge taken by soldiers in Kansas or at Fort Robinson on Indians at random, but justice delivered specifically to those Indians guilty of crimes against humanity. Until Indian murderers were tried and punished under civil law, wrote U.S. Indian inspector J. H. Hammond in advising the Kansas governor and the U.S. attorney, "they will regard such outrages as acts of war & be proud of them rather than fear the results." Also, Hammond thought, until Indians were brought to reasoned, ritualized civil justice, "bitterness will exist between the settler and all Indians—but I believe that if the individual Indian offender is punished, hatred

of the race will cease."[39]

Legal proceedings by the state of Kansas against the Northern Cheyenne began in November, shortly after the capture of the Dull Knife band. The precedent was a case in which Chiefs Big Tree and Satanta had been turned over to Texas civil courts in 1872 and imprisoned there.[40] In mid-January 1879, a case was filed before Ford County, Kansas, Justice of the Peace R. G. Cook: *The State of Kansas, Plaintiff,* versus *Dull Knife and One Hundred and Fifty Cheyenne Male Indians, commonly known as Warriors, whose names are each unknown.*[41] The numbers had to be reduced after the killings at Fort Robinson because only seven of the Dull Knife warriors had survived that outbreak, several of them wounded. But these "seven bucks," as the Kansas papers called them, were to face trial in Dodge City and represent for the settlers the responsible parties now dead.

The *Dodge City Times* in February called the Indians "incarnate fiends" and stated that "to accord the Indian the same privilege—a fair and impartial trial—as a white murderer, is certainly as much sympathy as could be asked for." It was not cruelty on the part of whites to do so, western Kansans said, only necessity:

> We do not enter into the discussion of the wrongs to which the Indian has been subjected. We are dealing with our own wrongs. . . . The raid last September is too fresh to admit of any palliation. The cowboy, whose unmarked grave on the desolate plain has neither flower nor tear, the grief-stricken mother who yet suffers the shame and disgrace of the Indian brute, and the

love of her innocent babes, and the dead father, whose body has fed the worms and whose bones lie bleaching, cry out for vengeance, a swift, a determined and speedy retribution.

As we value the honor, the glory, the purpose of our lives, as we cherish the memory of departed ones, as we sympathize with heart-stricken mothers, as we honor virtue, as we pride our own courage, let us be people who are generous to faults, forgiving, kind and loving, but who have the ability, the courage and the determination to condemn and punish crime whether it be done by the brutal white or the savage red man.[42]

On 11 February, W. B. "Bat" Masterson of the Dodge City police force and several witnesses who had seen the raiders and lived left for Leavenworth to transport the surviving Indians to Dodge City for a civil murder trial.[43]

The seven Indians—Crow, Wild Hog, Tall Man, Old Man, Run Fast, Young Man, and Frizzle Head—arrived at Dodge City from Leavenworth by train on 17 February.[44] The transfer, however, was not routine. Authorities feared that the large crowds gathered in Leavenworth to gawk at the remnants of the Dull Knife group would take matters into their own hands and lynch the seven. "I believe them to be the very worst tribe on our continent," wrote a member of the Kansas House to Governor St. John, "but do hope they will be tried and hung if they are found guilty, but an execution by a mob, would in my opinion seriously injure the good name of the State."[45] Masterson felt confident of his ability to handle mobs, having done so regularly in Dodge City,

but even he was frightened by the size of the Leavenworth crowds.[46] At every station a crowd of "hoodlums" assembled and cried so vigorously to see the Indians that Masterson "was compelled to use physical means in preventing his pets being trampled upon."[47] Luckily, their arrival did not provoke major activity in Dodge City. The Indians got off the train there and limped toward the jail, one having to be carried in a wheelbarrow. "They sit in a row upon the damp floor of the dim dungeon," a reporter noticed several days later, "with sorrow and despair deeply engraven upon their countenances."[48]

The first disappointment for the people of Dodge City was the granting of a change of venue for the murder trial, now renamed *The State of Kansas* v. *Wild Hog, et al.,* to Lawrence. The second was when Mike W. Sutton, who represented Ford County's interests in the case, failed to line up his witnesses and appear before the judge at the proper moments, leading to the case's dismissal on 13 October 1879. Sutton may have been distracted by his impending marriage. He may have been intimidated by the defense for the Indians being prepared by Salina attorney J. G. Mohler.[49] Most likely, much as Kansans wanted formal justice in this case, the kind of evidence necessary to convict these particular survivors simply did not exist. Dodge Citians admitted that it was "a doubtful game of chance" whether enough evidence could have been collected even had the trial remained in Dodge City, but they felt that the change of venue guaranteed eventual acquittal.[50]

The proceedings of the commission appointed by the state to investigate damage claims were more satisfactory to settlers than

Retribution. Captured members of Dull Knife's band on the steps of the Dodge City Court House. Left to right: Frizzly Hair, Wild Hog, Left Hand, George Reynolds (interpreter), Old Crow, Old Man, White Antelope, Blacksmith.

the murder trial. The three-man commission traveled 230 miles hearing testimony at Dodge City, Hays City, and Norton Center, then returned to Topeka to prepare a report released in July.[51] Of 116 claims, the commission allowed all but 26, and allowed $101,766.83 in damages of $182,646.13 asked.[52] The only classes of claims regularly disallowed were those for deaths and rapes, psychological suffering, and time lost while fleeing a homestead.[53] It was decided that those were not quantifiable.

In the fifty-eight page report detailing each claim, the randomness of the Indian activities could be seen. Harrison Beery, Ford County: house burned, furniture and beds burned,

chickens lost, crops destroyed, grain burned, provisions burned, tools taken. H. R. Fowler: surgical instruments taken, dental instruments taken, microscope and medical books taken. George Kious, Sheridan County: 25 pounds of bacon taken, 30 pounds of sugar, 200 pounds of flour.[54] Were the Cheyenne intent on survival, on revenge, or on scientific experimentation? The records suggest that any single explanation, other than Powers's conclusion that they were simply angry, would be historically risky.

Money was all that western Kansas settlers got. Much of that went to large cattle operations that had lost stock; little went to families who had lost mother or father, to little girls who had been raped and left to wander on the prairie. The bitterness was greater perhaps because the assault was so late, so unexpected, such a barbaric intrusion into hopeful, wet, civilized years. We treated the Indians in Dodge City better than white men would have been treated, wrote a columnist for the *Kansas Monthly.* We would probably have lynched whites charged with such a crime, but the Indians went to the circus in Lawrence during their confinement there. Did they have justification? Did starvation force them "to kill thousands of sheep and cattle and leave their carcasses for the birds and coyotes"? Did their feelings of wrongs endured force them "to murder defenceless women and children and glory in the act"? White people got hungry, especially settlers in western Kansas. Whites endured wrongs, but they were not excused for crimes. Western people had been greatly annoyed when the killers of the German family were brought to Wichita some years after that event and entertained at the Occidental Hotel. They were irritated now when Wild Hog and his friends were released. "If Indians are human," said one man speaking for many, "they are accountable for their acts. If they are not, there is no further argument. There never has been any question in regard to the dispositions of animals that prey upon the human family."[55]

Western Kansans of the late 1870s were not unaware of the sad plight of the Northern Cheyenne, and they might read modern accounts of the raid sympathetic to the tribe with more empathy than most of us would imagine they might. But alongside an understanding of the Indian, there also should be a historical understanding of the situation of the settler who suffered in 1878. Hardly had western Kansans learned to sleep at night without hearing Indian whoops in nightmares than it stopped raining again and the relentless sun seared crops and blasted spirits. Many faced these things alone, having been suddenly and violently deprived of their helpmates. One such, Margaret Smith of Decatur County, wrote to Governor St. John in 1881: "For I think it is pirty hard that I was brot out in a strange cuntry and my husband kiled and taking my teem a way from me and left with a large family of children and nothing to seport them with it is hard for me to git a long now with out some help for I hav lost what little crop I had this year on the account of the drouth. . . . I neede something and I live in a place that everybody has all that they can do to take car of them self."[56]

It must be appreciated also that the Dull Knife raid was a shock to western Kansas progressivism. The "cumulative communities" there were threatened in their sense of cumulativeness as well as directly by the intrusion of something that, ten years after the last major Kansas Indian raids, seemed, in a fast-changing time, positively antique. There was no question that much remained to be done to bring metropolitan civilization fully to the western Kansas country, but most felt that at least the Indian threat, a feature of the most primitive stage of the almost Turnerian frontier process the settlers had imagined, had passed away. To be forced by Dull Knife to face that early terror again must have been profoundly discouraging.

Chapter Ten

The Weak Shall Flee

The *Philadelphia Record* in 1877 advised its readers against swallowing optimistic projections about western Kansas. Temperatures ranged from over 100 degrees in the summer to 35 or 40 below in winter. It was far from markets and produced marginal crops. "Its best people are Puritanic and the rest Satanic—the one class being as disagreeable as the other is dangerous." The moral tone of society there was "as low as its winds are high and its winters cold."[1]

The editor of the *Hays Sentinel* responded vigorously, averring that the Pennsylvania man "knows no more about Kansas than a hog does of metaphysics." But calling a critic "a consummate fool . . . a mud-eater, a grubworm, a howling ignoramus, and a pre-meditated, exaggerated ass," as the Hays paper did, did not change the persuasive evidence of the late 1870s and early 1880s that a germ of truth lurked in such warnings.[2]

The hard times inaugurated by the Indian raid of the autumn of 1878 were more trying still than earlier disasters had been. More people were affected than had been in 1874; settlers were less prepared for extreme weather conditions; they were not surrounded by supportive colonies; prolonged drought could not be as easily explained away as a freak occurrence as could a grasshopper invasion; and the regional economy in 1880 depended more on farmers' families than it had early in the decade. There was uncertainty about crop choice and no experience with moisture preservation through dry-land farming. Underlying all these problems was the psychological blow delivered by the contrast with the pleasant times and high hopes that had immediately preceded Dull Knife and the great drought.

It did not take much to encourage potential settlers who wanted to be encouraged—only the slightest sign that western Kansas was a place where a farm family could survive. That sign came in 1877, which was not only unusually wet but a year when rain was well distributed through the growing months for both winter wheat and corn. At the weather station at Fort Hays, monthly rainfalls from March through October 1877 were recorded at 0.98, 2.94, 3.86, 3.20, 6.86, 4.94, 1.50, and 3.82 inches, with a total of 33.92 inches for the year ending in October.[3]

There was even reason in 1877 to believe that western Kansas could be wetter than areas further east. While the reporting stations at Lawrence, Leavenworth, Manhattan, and Independence all recorded well over 40 inches for the year, Salina, on the sixth principal meridian, had only 11 inches of rain and Smith

Center 19. Actually, this only reflected the general unevenness of rainfall in the region. Larned, for example, had 8.16 inches in May to Hays City's 3.86, but in July Larned had 0.59 compared with Hays City's 6.86. The two towns were about sixty miles apart. More remarkable, McPherson, thirty-five miles south of Salina, received 47 inches of rain in 1877 compared to Salina's 11.[4] Ness County residents complained in July that they had had no rain for weeks, "and the most singular fact about it is that all around us, rain in bounteous supply has fallen, while here, as though we were a race of ungodly people, all is parched and arid."[5] Newspaper publicists, however, did not take local and temporal variability into account but instead claimed that 1877 proved a trend. Dodge City crowed that its 27.89 inches in 1877, compared with 15.40 in 1876 and 10.69 in 1875, were scientific evidence of a change.[6] The *Hays Sentinel* emphasized that Hays's rainfall that year was greater than Fort Riley's and suggested that "we have furnished a text; will our readers preach the sermon."[7]

The weather in 1878 was not as favorable but not entirely discouraging either. Mean rainfall for the so-called Middle Belt, extending from the sixth principal meridian to the west line of Ellis County, was down from 30.04 inches in 1877 to 27.89 inches, while in the Western Belt, the decline was from 25.63 to 21.73 inches.[8] Although Dodge City rainfall dropped to 17.96 inches, Hays City still got 31.85 inches and Great Bend 30 inches.[9] Great Bend received over 11 inches of rain in June alone, including a 3.75-inch downpour on the nineteenth, the heaviest shower ever recorded there.[10]

Good rain meant good crops and a trend toward specialization. Ellis County wheat averaged twenty bushels per acre in 1877, and some thirty-two-bushel-per-acre wheat was harvested there.[11] In Ellis County that year 1,321 acres were planted in wheat, compared with 1,310 for corn, and harvest hands using the Eclipse thresher were making two dollars a day.[12] Yields in 1878 in the developed western counties averaged over twenty bushels per acre for winter wheat. That corn averages in several counties were no better than wheat averages and never over about thirty-five bushels per acre helped to hasten the trend toward wheat growing. So did the more developed markets, the availability of machinery, and the lack of the need for planting sod corn on newly broken land. Ellis County in 1878 had 4,037 acres of wheat and 3,226 acres of corn. In Pawnee County the wheat-corn ratio was 19,207 acres to 9,157 acres, compared to 8,968 to 5,678 a year earlier. In Russell County, corn and wheat had each been occupying about 4,700 acres; in 1878 more than 9,000 acres were planted in wheat and fewer than 7,000 in corn. Wheat acreage exceeded corn acreage in most western counties by 1878 or 1879, though average acreages for the state as a whole gave corn a two-to-one advantage.[13]

Specialization in wheat seemed to be the way to profit in the West. The *Hays Sentinel* estimated the cost of breaking land at $2.50 an acre; of seeding, harvesting, and threshing the crop at about $8.50; and the cost of the land itself at $10.00 an acre. That was a total expense of $21.00 per acre, while a twenty-bushel wheat crop would return $30.00, or a profit of $9.00 per acre above expenses, including buying expensive railroad land, in the first year. "The man with credit—if there be any such—can get off the cars in Hays City, without a team, without land, without friends, without a dollar, and by the use of honeyed words purchase two hundred acres of land on a year's time, have it broken on a year's time, purchase his seed on a year's time, and when his bills come due he will have the wherewithal to meet them, two hundred acres of land and eighteen hundred dollars.''[14]

Good crops meant more land sales and more prairie broken for farms. Homestead entries at the land office at Hays City were 31,395 acres in the fiscal year 1876–1877, 145,977 in 1877–1878, and 327,008 in 1878–1879. At Larned the equivalent figures were 145,878 acres, 246,377, and 247,108. Timber-culture entries in fiscal years 1877–1878 and 1878–1879 were also significant: 127,584 and 312,137 for Hays City and 169,122 and 207,222 for Larned.[15]

The figures for the drought years provide a striking contrast. From June 1879 to June 1880, the Hays City/WaKeeney land office plummeted from a total of 534,230 acres of homestead and timber-culture entries to 224,433 as people began to understand the drought. Larned fell off more, from 454,310 to 185,949 acres.[16] The next year WaKeeney reported 65,732.40 acres of homestead entries and 51,675.74 in timber-culture entries, while the Larned figures were 59,430.64 and 37,007.77—only one-fourth the volume of two years earlier.[17] These land offices did not equal their 1877, 1878, and 1879 sales figures again until 1885. Acreage broken and crops planted in the western counties continued to increase rapidly through 1880, reflecting the efforts of settlers who had bought land. Even the momentum here, however, eventually fell off, and increases slowed dramatically.[18] As late as 1883, a few western counties actually had fewer acres planted in all crops than they had had in 1880, though the trend toward wheat specialization continued.[19] There is no question that the good crop years of 1877 and 1878 created a boom lasting through the poor year of 1879 and quashed only by a second dry year in 1880.

Western Kansans were proud of the upturn in immigration and thought this surge was at last permanent. Hays residents crowed when W. E. Beach of Connecticut bought eight sections of railroad land for a cattle operation in the spring of 1877.[20] They took note of every excursion train brought from Iowa by Jacob Augustine, who, it was claimed, made $400 a month just by selling Kansas Pacific lands on a 5 percent commission.[21] Kinsley remarked on the arrival of a party of New York capitalists looking over lands in Edwards County in 1877 and the next year reported the plans of Colonel Charles Sellers of Philadelphia to create a large model wheat farm to consist eventually of 2,000 acres of waving grain.[22] There was more machinery around: four self-binders were available in Kinsley, as well as drills, reapers, mowers, and a dozen models of riding plows.[23] Record days at the land office were prime news. Once in March 1878, the Larned office reported fifty-one entries on Monday and fifty-eight on Tuesday for total sales of 17,049 acres in two days.[24] On a single day in April, 81,735.53 acres were filed on in western Kansas.[25] And there was constant reference to the way in which even remote places like Sheridan, Decatur, Rawlins, and Thomas Counties were filling up.[26] Hays City had only yesterday been on the edge of civilization, but, said its newspaper in 1878, people were beginning to think of it as "in the east." "The great tide of emigration flowed in constant stream until the great basin of Rush County was filled to overflowing, and then it burst over Ness a perfect flood, and even now the spray of that mighty wave is dashing into Lane county.''[27] The word was that potential settlers should hurry west if they expected to snatch up any good land.

However lush the landscape and crops were temporarily, the promotional prose was even more lush. Probably the most amazing piece was L. D. Burch's enthusiastic *Kansas As It Is,* published in Chicago in 1878. Although he admitted that ''we are yet in doubt of agriculture there,'' Burch asserted that man was placed in western Kansas ''to crown the work of nature with the embellishment of art.'' On the prairie was a combination of ''the sternest realism and the most delicate poetic sense,'' which set up its residents in such a way that ''conventional words have been passed from their vocabulary and conventional deeds from their lives.'' Western Kansas was ''a paradise for the lungs,'' where ''respiration has the ease and freedom to make life a lasting joy.'' ''One feels like business in this rare, radiant atmosphere. Nothing drags here. Everybody feels fresh, and youthful and self-commanding.'' There were no sloughs or marshes ''to break the furrow of the happy plowman,'' and Burch claimed he was sorry to finish his writing assignment there: ''What a grand, grand country.''[28]

A good deal of such exuberant prose was produced locally also in these fine years. In October 1879, for instance, Larned made a grand effort to transform its county fair into a forum for boosting western Kansas. Several politicians accepted invitations to appear— then-Governor St. John, General William T. Sherman, and, finally, President Rutherford B. Hayes himself.[29]

The fair day was perfect. ''The soft amber haze wrapped the distant hills in that subdued mellow tint which characterizes the delightful Indian summer of the Central Plains.'' As dignitaries alighted from special trains, the Hutchinson band played the national anthem and there followed a long round of speechmaking in the best Gilded-Age tradition. Captain Henry Booth of Larned welcomed the visitors:

> What you see here to-day is the result of five years battling of civilization against primitive nature. . . . The war-whoop of the savage has been supplanted by the shrill whistle of the locomotive, and in place of the buffalo we have the Alderney, the Devon, the Durham and the Texas steer. Here, midway between the two oceans, and under the shadow of the greatest mountain range, every true Kansan expects to build up a civilization that shall at once be the surprise and wonder of the nineteenth century.

President Hayes was driven to the grandstand through lines of schoolchildren waving flags as the national anthem rang out again, this time from the Great Bend band. Hayes spoke of his parents' pioneering in Ohio and said he believed God blessed the enterprise of settlers. ''If all new settlements in the world were built upon the same corner-stone that you build the structure of your society upon, the future of those settlements would be far more hopeful and far more prosperous than many of them.'' That drew loud cheers. General Sherman ventured that it seemed the Indians had at last ceased to be a problem in western Kansas. "I am very glad to see they are gone now, and I don't care where they are gone to."[30]

The fair at Larned in 1879 was a marvel. Few in attendance would have believed, had they the foresight to know, that it would not be held at all the next year.[31] Still, there were signs enough by the autumn of 1879 that the weather had turned sour for farmers and that ground moisture was insufficient without substantial precipitation during the winter to promise any wheat crop at all for 1880. The *Great Bend Register* noted in May 1879 that "since the earliest settlement of this country this is the ugliest, windiest spring of all." With the exception of a very wet April, it had been dry there all season, colder than usual, and windy. The April rain was accompanied by damaging hail, and in May there was even a slight earthquake.[32] Typical were months like March, when Great Bend got 0.05 inches of rain, 2.36 inches below the average March rainfall for the previous five years. "It was the dryest month on our record," wrote B. B. Smyth, able to record only two or three sprinkles and two or three dust storms during the period. "This latter article [dust storms]," he wrote laconically, "is hardly as desirable or as useful for the growth of plants as is rain."[33] The Dodge City weather station recorded moisture of 0.87 inches in January, 0.08 in February, 0.17 in March, 0.40 in April, and 0.90 in May. The 4.40 inches coming in June, 3.90 in July, and 3.75 in August (of a year total of 15.43) did not much help crops there because 4,379 acres were planted in winter wheat and only 999 in corn.[34]

Less scientific observations echoed the same theme. The Kinsley papers said that the 1879

The Weather Station. U.S. Signal Service Building at Dodge City. Here weather statistics were kept and the full unpredictability of western Kansas weather documented. During the blizzard of 1886 the gauge on the tower was destroyed by high winds.

wheat crop there was the worst since the grasshopper year of 1874. Early in August, handbills distributed in Kinsley advertised a mass meeting to devise means to procure aid for the settlers of Edwards County.[35] The *Sentinel* at Hays reported in June that the cattle drive to the Ellis County range along the Kansas Pacific Railroad had almost ceased because of the lack of both grass and water.[36] In

Meade County, there was a period of thirty-two months, beginning in October 1877 and ending in July 1880, when there were no soaking rains. Settlers who came there in February 1878 remembered the next years well. "Then were the times when the winds came from the south like the breath of a furnace—when vegetation was shriveled up as though scorched and burned in a fire. Dry! Well, we think it was, slightly so—and hope never to see such times again. But some of us remained and lived through it, how is still a mystery to those who left."[37]

Sometimes in the wetter boom years that followed, when population and crop land were again on a rapid rise, the severity of the drought of 1879 and 1880 was retrospectively exaggerated by those intent on focusing on the improvements civilization had wrought. The *Dodge City Times* in 1885 had to respond to a man who had been telling newcomers that in 1879 and 1880 it had not rained in Dodge for twenty months and that since then there had not been thirty days without a shower; the paper pointed out that there was more rainfall in Dodge in 1880 (18.12 inches) than in 1879 (15.43 inches) and that total rainfall in those years was not drastically below averages over a long period.[38]

The reasons for widespread suffering in these years were more complicated than rainfall totals. The first problem was one that western Kansans should have recognized by then as almost normal: the extreme subregional variability of rainfall. A second was the increasing specialization in wheat, which made early spring rain and winter moisture particularly crucial. A third, closey related to the second,

was the concentration of rainfall for 1879 and 1880 in the summer months.

If there can be said to be a typical precipitation pattern in western Kansas, it is dry summers and autumns (the latter the famous Indian summer) with annual moisture concentrated in the spring and to a lesser extent in winter. The drought years were slightly atypical in this regard. Spring rains came later and were lighter, and summers were unusually wet. July 1879, for example, was extremely wet. There were 6.79 inches of rain at Great Bend, 7.04 inches at Dodge City, and 7.01 inches at Fort Wallace. These were considerably higher amounts than reported that month by eastern Kansas stations and represented a high proportion of the total annual rainfall, about 40 percent in the case of Fort Wallace. A similar pattern of dry spring and relatively wet summer prevailed in 1880. The State Board of Agriculture reported that 1880 had a warmer January and a colder November than any previous year on record, a higher wind velocity than in any other year, and both an earlier spring and winter. Maples were blossoming on 11 February, and the nearly complete lack of moisture in the early spring caused frightening dust storms. The largest, on 27 March, "filled the air to great height with an almost impalpable dust and obscured the sun during the entire day after 10 A.M."[39]

The weather change was not enormous. It was nothing like the 1890s, when areas in central western Kansas would not get eight inches of total annual rainfall. It was more like the 1930s, when several years of rainfall in the fifteen-inch range eliminated subsoil moisture and spawned dust and destitution.[40] Eighteen seventy-nine and 1880 were unexpected and strange years; their adverse effects fell hardest on new settlers who were inexperienced with the West, underfinanced, and lacked savings from an initial crop to see them through.

In 1879, the attitude throughout most of western Kansas was that the drought was a survivable reverse. The editor of the *Kinsley Graphic* wrote late in 1878 that the dry weather might or might not ruin the crop. Newcomers were depressed about it, and those who had been around a few years felt that the look of the country might unduly discourage new farmers, whereas older hands had seen crops grow before in seemingly impossible conditions.[41] At WaKeeney, soil scientists were quoted to the effect that the hardpan of clay two feet down still held moisture that capillary action would send back to the surface at the first good rain.[42]

Most farmers, it was thought, could get by if they would not go too much into debt, overinvest in machinery, or lose hope. There was contempt for those who grumbled about the hot winds and drought, especially if they did so in letters to friends back east, and there was a feeling that any who left the country were weaklings the region could do without.[43] Wrote a Great Bend man: "Occasionally a man whom we suppose has more brains than 'sand,' 'gets sick' and sells out and goes back, and as a rule he has nothing to go back to, yet he is willing to sacrifice a good home here for a good deal of emptiness in Ohio or Indiana. Such men had better remain with their mothers a while longer."[44] Rather than going back "to visit their wives' relations," as the most common taunt went, settlers should be patient, trusting that the few real emergencies could be taken

care of by local communities through relief work at bone picking, watermelon selling, ground breaking, or day work.[45] The Kansas motto, after all, suggested not only rewards but difficulties, and pioneering history proved the end was sure: "The great expectancy of milk and honey is reduced when in contact with the rigors of the first year out on the plains. . . . Reducing a wild waste to a higher state of civilization is not the result of one year's labor. The process is slow, but it is sure. We must await our new development and growth with Christian fortitude. The life of new countries is but a repetition."[46]

When the same weather pattern prevailed again in 1880, however, there could be no hopeful talk about subsoil moisture and capillary action. Confidence that the relief problem would remain small enough for towns to handle alone disappeared as the skies remained blue for months on end; many who had laughed at the weak fleeing east to friends and family joined them. Pawnee County's population went from 6,114 in 1878 to 5,396 in 1880 to 4,260 in 1881 before beginning a slow recovery. Ellis County, with over 6,000 people in 1880, went to 5,519 in 1881 and 4,666 in 1882. Ellsworth County's population dropped 1,000 in a year; Ford lost one-third of its population between 1880 and 1882; and half of Edwards County settlers left between 1880 and 1881.[47] These were not statistics to place in promotional broadsides.

The first widespread suffering and the first organized drought relief were in Ness County. There was no weather station there, but, given the known variability of local rainfall, there is possibly truth to Ness County residents' claim that their region had little rain during years that were relatively wet elsewhere and so in 1879 was facing a second or third year of drought. Despite rumors of silver mines near Bazine, newspapers did not think the Ness region was a good place to go.[48] When the Larned editor learned in January 1879 of a plan to create a new county out of parts of Hodgeman, Ness, and Pawnee Counties, he commented that "it is seriously contemplated to float that portion of the county taken from Ness and Hodgeman to the Gulf of Mexico, where it will be anchored and used by the U.S. Government as an Insane Asylum. The projectors of the 'New County' will be received gratis."[49]

The *Topeka Commonwealth,* under the headline "The Folly of the Settlers Who Went to Western Counties," published in July 1879 a report from Dr. D. G. Brown from Ness County claiming that Pawnee, Rush, Hodgeman, Ness, Buffalo, and Lane Counties were destitute because of the drought and that 4,560 people were in need of basic aid.[50] Late that month Brown held a public meeting with representatives from these counties and organized an appeal for aid and seed wheat.[51] In November, Ness County residents organized vigilance committees to maintain law and order and protect property as people left their claims in attempts to earn money in the towns.[52]

Criticism of Ness County from places not yet pressed to the wall was loud and constant. The *Kansas Farmer,* reporting in July on Brown's aid meetings, stated that there were only a few poor people in western Kansas, "and the few there are should be starved out to make room for the more deserving ones." Farmers should leave their families and get work, returning in the spring feeling better "in the consciousness

of independent manhood," rather than being dependent on aid from "some old FRAUD." Agents would rake off so much money that aid would get "extremely thin, so thin it would not protect one poor child in a dozen from the average Musquito, to say nothing of the 'Wolf' these self constituted committees are barking at so long before he has selected his victims; or even his place of operations."[53] The *Kinsley Leader* wrote of the "white trash" that attended Brown's meetings: "Paupers, mendicants, a thriftless set of beggars; too lazy to work, and too mean to live."[54]

As in the grasshopper year, a major theme of this early criticism was relief fraud. People at Hays were informed that Ness County cattleman John Farnsworth, a member of the aid committee, was building a large stone barn. A poor Ness County family on aid bought a croquet set in WaKeeney; another bought a dollar's worth of prunes with aid funds.[55] The Osborne City *Truth Teller* reported in December that a Mr. Barker, collecting for Ness County, seemed responsible and that local millers were making flour at no charge from donated corn and wheat. But the *Brookville Times* noticed that three Ness agents visiting there drank four straight shots of whiskey in the saloon and paid in cash. "We think Ness County must be ahead, for we know of no one here than can afford such extravagance, unless they have access to some relief association."[56]

The town of WaKeeney, just north of the Ness County line and just getting started, was understandably the most upset of all. Its press said that Ness County was the principal source of "this starvation yawp" and that there was plenty of employment in WaKeeney for any ambitious Ness County residents who needed money. "The self-made paupers who are thus engaged in deadbeating their living out of the benevolent people of the State, and at the same time ruining the reputation of this section, number about sixty," the WaKeeney press asserted; they represented "the driftwood of immigration" who had never tried to get work. These sixty had an organ printed on brown wrapping paper called the *Ness County Pioneer,* which "vaunts their trumped-up poverty with all the slobbering pride of a mendicant showing his sores."[57]

Ness County could only respond that the suffering was real and that there was no practical alternative to aid from elsewhere. Men with no money were forced to sell what they had, often at great loss. The work available exploited them. A poor man who took his starving team to break sod at $1.50 an acre paid twenty-five cents for sharpening his plow, sixty cents for feed, and fifty cents for provisions, leaving fifteen cents to spend at the store, which made a five-cent profit on the sale. It was the storekeepers and the men hiring at such wages who were critical of aid, and their criticism arose out of pure self-interest.[58] Yes, the *Pioneer* was printed on colored paper, but at least, Ness Countians said, the articles were not written by land sharks as were the papers in WaKeeney. As for employment at WaKeeney, it was available only at rates that yielded 100 to 500 percent profit to the employer and no benefit over expenses to the worker.[59]

As the months passed with no rain, however, Ness County was joined by most of the rest of western Kansas in the aid business. At almost the same moment that the WaKeeney papers were taking the Ness County aid committees to task in January 1880, J. F. Keeney wrote Governor St. John asking for state help for the suffering region.[60] St. John in turn contacted railroad magnate Jay Gould, who advised that the governor could draw $5,000 for relief along the Kansas Pacific. St. John immediately sent two carloads of flour and meal and a large amount of bacon to settlers in Gove, Sheridan, and Wallace Counties, who were said to be among the worst off.[61] In April, Congressman Thomas Ryan introduced a bill to allow western Kansas settlers who had lost crops to leave their claims until 1 October 1880 without penalty. The bill passed in May, and the western response was that "in the midst of hard times, which must be protracted, such action as this on the part of our worthy congressmen seems much like the handwriting of God on the walls of our homes."[62]

Railroads participated in aid also, both through loaning seed wheat to farmers, donating packaging and transportation costs, and by offering maintenance jobs to persons unable for the moment to make a living on their farms.[63] Settlers complained that the companies limited aid to people near their lines and charged 7 percent interest on the loans. "This wheat and aid matter is only a business investment for the railroad," a Hays man alleged, "and, so far from being prompted by feelings of humanity, its motive was sordid enough."[64] Still, they appreciated it. The Kansas Pacific by October 1880 had furnished 55,000 bushels of winter seed wheat to western Kansas settlers at a total cost for wheat and hauling of about $40,000. It was estimated that the Santa Fe had distributed a similar amount in the Arkansas Valley.[65]

As in 1874, private contributions were channeled through a central committee in Topeka, this time called the Kansas State Aid Committee, organized on 31 May.[66] The experience of the grasshopper year had apparently been instructive because there were relatively few complaints in 1880 about inefficiency, lost shipments, or fraud. Late in June, Ness County got 5,000 pounds of meal and 2,000 of flour from the committee, Graham County received 13,000 pounds of meal and flour, and Stafford County 1,100 pounds of flour, all shipped free by the railroads.[67] Regular substantial shipments, balanced among staples and distributed by strict rules relating to family size and specific need, continued to go west through the summer and fall to the sixteen thousand people the aid committee estimated needed help. In the hardest-hit counties, fully half the remaining population got aid, and to have one-fourth of the settlers on relief was common in western counties. Kansans took pride in the fact that, unlike in 1874, little aid was required from outside Kansas to take care of the state's western region.[68]

Perhaps most surprising, however, to those who had been in Kansas during the 1860 or 1874 emergencies was that when the private aid committee disbanded in February 1881, the state legislature took up the slack.[69] On 18 February, the legislature appropriated $25,000 for the relief of western Kansas settlers still affected by continued drought.[70] That spring I. N. Holloway, the commissioner appointed by Governor St. John to administer the aid, purchased 91,400 pounds of flour, 173,000 pounds of corn meal, and lesser amounts of other supplies for distribution. In June, when it seemed the crisis was over (Dodge City was to get 33.17 inches of rain that year), the commissioner was able to turn back more than $9,000

of their appropriation, glad for once that the state had overestimated relief needs.[71]

There is no question that this generosity was due partly to the influence of Governor St. John, in many ways a humanitarian. The governor appeared in January at a charity ball where sacks of flour were auctioned off to raise money for western farmers.[72] The generosity also, however, doubtless represented a realization by state legislators that these crises in western Kansas were neither flukes nor events to be taken lightly.

In 1880 even town boosters who could overlook almost anything negative had to admit the drought situation was serious. The *WaKeeney World* in May commented that while the Ryan bill was not a good way of building up the country quickly, it was necessary because "our people who are here now need protecting, while . . . those who are not here can probably live elsewhere."[73] When what small harvest there was came in, farmers at Great Bend were in a similarly "contemplative mood" and asked themselves seriously whether the country was a failure: "Has nature performed some strange freak and left us a rusty link in the otherwise bright and continuous chain?"[74] The press was full of suggestions about reducing reliance on wheat, leaving more country unbroken for grazing, practicing more scientific husbandry, erecting dams to catch moisture, and simply remembering that all pioneering regions had to suffer.[75] Still, it appeared that only mortgages were yielding well, and the time was long past when there was any advantage for "shallow-brained and preposterous little nincompoops" interested in booming the region to deny that reality.[76] "We have seen many blue days," a settler from Iuka in Pratt County wrote in May, "but none so utterly discouraging as those we are now passing through."[77]

James Malin has demonstrated the impossibility of showing patterns over time in Kansas farm family persistence based on a single factor such as rainfall. His studies of Kansas divided by rainfall belts show no significant difference in the percentage of farmers who stayed in a region over a number of years based on this factor alone, and differences within a rainfall belt were as wide as those between belts.[78] Yet it is possible to isolate specific, if temporary, negative effects on population of events such as the drought of 1880. More important, one can document, though not quantify, the impact of such trying times on individual settlers.

The drought of 1880 demonstrates the importance of regional studies that focus on small intrastate areas. Average rainfall figures for Kansas as a whole or even for western Kansas during 1879–1880 do not reveal the drought's severity. It is necessary to examine rainfall amounts, the timing of rainfall, and crop patterns at specific places and times and to compare these with population change. The dynamics can vary in ways important to settlers from county to county.

Also, it must be recognized that however important the drought of 1880 was for western Kansas—and its importance was immense—that event does not exist at all in the general historical literature on the West because its effect was so localized. Nebraska did not suffer as severely as did Kansas.[79] W. Eugene Hollen's history of the Southwest explains heavy immigration into that region in the years 1880–1886 by noting that these were years of heavier than average rainfall there.[80] The years 1879–1885 were, according to several studies, uniformly wet years for the Dakotas, and that area enjoyed its greatest boom at just the time drought was tremendously slowing movement to western Kansas.[81] There may even be some relationship between troubles in western Kansas and prosperity in the Dakotas, as the latter area was a logical alternative for settlers who might otherwise have gone to Kansas. In both the Dakotas and the Southwest, there was a drought from 1886 to 1889, while in western Kansas the years 1886 and 1887 were unusually wet.[82] As will be seen, western Kansas in 1886 and 1887 had the kind of boom the Dakotas had experienced earlier, perhaps partly due to the same shortsightedness and subregional variation. Only in the 1890s did there come a drought widespread enough to enter the general literature (albeit so far in only a rudimentary way) as a regional event. Those who suffered the earlier disasters would surely have been surprised to discover that their experience was overlooked by history.

In western Kansas, however, the human cost of the drought was great. From 1879 to 1882, western Kansans endured countless heavy, hot, dust-laden winds and often tornadoes. Clarinda and Sidney, both of which had recently been candidates for the Ness County seat, were literally blown away during this period; Dighton in Lane County was broken to splinters and Kinsley severely damaged by relentless wind.[83] A little girl on the way to Ness City with her family blew out of the wagon—"Mother never expected to see me again."[84] Dodge City on 21 September 1882, waiting for autumn, experienced a heavy scorching wind when a temperature of 105 degrees combined with a humidity so low that an ice pitcher would have had to have been cooled 76 degrees below the air temperature to get condensation.[85] The Henry Tilley family at Scoharie in Ness County hung on through the worst, trying to keep cool in their lovely stone Victorian home, but by July 1881 they were ready to sell the farm to a man from Orange County, New York. "He said he would come and let us know what he would give us in a day or two," wrote Henry, "but it got so terrible Hot just at the time, he concluded to go back to New York again."[86] Wrote a man in nearby Nevada, Kansas, in January 1880: "The weather is dry and cold. Wheat looks dead and old batches the same way."[87]

One of the most poignant human records from the 1880 drought is a letter to Governor John St. John from Mrs. Lucena Mercier. She wrote the governor in June from Trego County, where she and her five children were living in a sod-claim house. Only two families remained in the entire township and Mrs. Mercier was alone, her husband having gone to New Mexico to find work. He had sold their horse for $30 before he left to give her a little cash, but the man who had bought it returned it, saying that everyone in the county had cheap horses for sale. She and her children were living on corn meal mixed with water, supplemented by a little salt. The older children were ill and the mother trembled so badly she could hardly write. But she felt she must beg help from someone.[88]

Mrs. Mercier had been told to seek employment in WaKeeney but reported that many others had the same idea. "In a land teeming with people anxious for employment, how could I hope to procure employment when retarded by the care of five children, the youngest twins just one year old. . . . I realize deeply what it must be to you to be thus annoyed by other people's troubles. I realize also what it is to myself to be compelled to annoy you, but more deeply than all do I realize what it will be to my children to be deprived of food."[89]

Think, she asked the governor, not of columns of statistics, but of people:

> To-night as you sit at your table laden with all of life's necessities, and probably many luxuries, think of the little children out here on the lonely prairie that are not assured of even corn meal to keep from starving. Think of the little babes only one year old obliged to live thus, and as you love your own little children, if you have any, or for the sake of the love your mother bore you when you were, yourself, as small and helpless as my babes, I beg you to help me some way, that my little ones may not have worse privations to endure than they have already endured. I ask of you in the name of all you hold most dear, not to throw this aside and forget it, for no one can realize the terrors of such a situation until placed as I am here.[90]

For over ten years, railroads had been in place in western Kansas and towns had welcomed farmers. Wichita was planning a streetcar line. Yet nature was still so dominant on the Kansas High Plains that every advance of civilization could be reduced in a season to a mother pleading for someone to save her infants from the landscape's bite.

Illusions would return with the rain. Nothing

could be more clear from historical study than the truth in the statement made in Thomas Saarinen's classic sociological study of Great Plains drought perception that ''failure to accurately perceive the drought hazard has been the focal problem on the Great Plains since farmers from humid areas first settled there in the late nineteenth century.'' Much attention had been paid since to technological fixes, Saarinen noted, ''but very little attention has been paid to the way in which the central character in the adaptation process views the central problem with which he is faced.''[91] That challenge faces sociologists and historians alike.

For the time being western Kansas was once again a place of strong, stubborn people eking out a living. If the railroads and the towns and the colonies and the scientists could not bring immediate glory, perhaps these rugged individual families could hope at least to survive. Even in the greatest adversity, there remained the chance of miracles. ''We come to the conclusion,'' wrote the editor of the little *Ness County Pioneer,* ''that the experience of Ness county, is but a repetition of what has been from the east line of the state. As far as we can learn, it has been a war with Indians, grasshoppers, bugs, worms and dry weather; and many, even the majority, have come poorly prepared to fight these.''[92] The weak, however, had fled.

Chapter Eleven

Heaven of Brass,

Earth of Iron

Even without a drought, or an Indian raid, the challenge of filing claim on lands in western Kansas and carrying out a successful farming operation there is not to be underestimated. Land historian Roy Robbins has noted an irony in the combination of federal decisions and accidents of timing that left the High Plains country west of the 100th meridian as the major "safety valve" for families seeking to achieve wealth and independence—because of all the western frontiers, this was the most difficult for those who hoped to establish a family farm. "In truth," Robbins wrote, "some of the region beyond the hundredth meridian was good farm land, but, all in all, one may doubt whether it should have been opened to wholesale appropriation by the homesteader. Here was pioneering at its worst—with almost insuperable difficulties in selecting land, building a home, finding fuel, drilling for water, fighting fierce winds, prairie fires, bedbugs, fleas, mosquitoes, and grasshoppers."[1] Gilbert Fite agreed. Though the High Plains were loved by some, he wrote, they "repelled equally as many thousands; at times men swore and

women wept at the punishment the region handed out to its inhabitants."[2] Literary observers agreed with scholars. Wrote Edna Fergusson during the 1950s drought: "The arid Southwest has always been too strong, too indomitable for most people. Those who can stand it have had to learn that man does not modify this country; it transforms him, deeply."[3]

For all the importance of analyzing grand patterns—of railroad policy, industrial development, town building, weather cycles, Indian troubles—it is equally vital to examine the experience of settling western Kansas from the limited, but to them encompassing, perspective of the individual settlers themselves. For them, the struggle with the environment narrowed, at least initially, to a single family, its land, its crops, its well, its animals, and its sod house: such a small, almost pitiful presence; a knot on a vast prairie expanse that the sun could sear without intermediaries, the tough grass could resist, and the wind and the storm could aim for miles to lay low. Yet the economic future of western Kansas ultimately depended on the ability of these individuals to deal with everyday difficulties, more frustrating than dramatic. For at base, the settlers *were* the future.

A reporter for *Scribners Monthly,* in Kansas in 1879 to report on "Picturesque Features of Kansas Farming," marveled at the contrast in scale. There was the landscape: "The eye wanders over gracefully swerving and un-monotonous lines to what seems the very limit of things; you dare not conjecture where the earth ends and the sky begins." The vision could be compared to the sea, "and then the bluish curves would be waves, and that square of newly plowed furrows a shoal of fish." But the air was sharp and dry, not foggy, and the settlers' squat homes were not tall ships coming and going but pedestrian barges, buoys, even islands that were there to take root. They looked isolated and forlorn. "They seem to belong to a condition of things which it is difficult to reconcile with so much of grass, and wild lark's songs, and clear blue sky."[4]

However modest the homes—even when they were for the moment nothing but a canvas or wagon cover on poles—the people settling the western part of the state seemed determined to prevail. "The Kansans have a phenomenal genius for homes," observed the *Scribners* reporter. "They reverse the old order of pioneering, and make the home the foundation, instead of the outcome, of their struggle with nature." It was Birnam Wood come to Dunsinane to see brightly painted machinery set in newly planted fields in such a place: "With their glare of paint and burnished steel and their overwhelming 'reels' [they] have a kind of Homeric character." And in action the machines and the men and the families and the household economies, all present in slowly growing numbers, held some promise that

some more superficially impressive approaches had lacked: "Everywhere is eagerness, energy, urgent action, for time is precious and foul weather may intervene; but how methodical it all is nevertheless, and how small is the measure of wasted power! Each stroke counts; each step is a triumph. The fields change like shiftings of scenery in a pantomime. There are unexpected lights and shades; boundary lines are abundantly transposed and confused; the landscape is momently [*sic*] made alien."[5]

There has been study of the psychological effects of a group's sudden departure from the familiar followed by a long journey under primitive conditions and arrival in utterly new circumstances. Black slaves, taken by night from African villages, suffering the long and wearing middle passage by ship, and then being deposited on plantations cut off from contact with the outside world, are one example.[6] That the journey of the settlers was voluntary made a significant difference, but their similarities to other groups in the psychological mechanics of their transition to a new life probably created in them some similar changes. Among these would be heightened sensitivity to initial impressions of the new land (a trait noticed in hundreds of pioneer memoirs) and an unusual flexibility in adapting their lives and culture to the situation in which they found themselves. Settlers of modest means who were found in western Kansas during the hard years of the early 1880s were people who had taken a more or less final leave of everything else.

No matter how much the members of the family wanted to go, or some members of the family wanted to go, or thought they did, leaving accustomed places and community supports was difficult. A girl on her way to

Hodgeman County watched her mother taking leave of her family. The mother and her own mother "stood there in a long embrace and wept," and the child saw her family's sadness for the whole trip west over leaving the old family forever.[7] Little Ann Collins was helping pack to accompany her family to Clark County, Kansas. "If you go to Kansas," her grandmother told her, "you will have to eat grasshopper soup." The older woman went on to inform the girl about droughts in that state and their accompanying insect host. Ann thought a moment, then said: "If Daddy can eat grasshopper soup, I can too." But it worried her during the entire journey. Upon arrival in Kansas in 1885, Ann was secretly overjoyed not to find grasshoppers all over the ground. The first thing she did at their homestead was to search out a grasshopper. "Whew!" she called. "A grasshopper! Well, grasshopper, I think we will have to make legs and all, if we have enough to make grasshopper soup out of you."[8]

Elam and Rachel Bartholomew left Fairmount, Illinois, where the parents of both lived, in the summer of 1876. They were going to Bow Creek in northern Rooks County, Kansas, and were not sure when or whether they would return. The young couple one evening about a month before they left walked over to Elam's parents' house and after a short visit there strolled in the woods "to revisit some of the old familiar haunts of by-gone days." They looked and talked for a "sadly pleasant hour" there, "thinking that perhaps never again in this life would we enjoy the sweet privilege of being permitted to revisit the dear old spots we may soon be leaving behind us forever!" Later they visited all their young friends in a big wagon and attended a singing social with some of them. "The night being clear," Elam wrote in his diary, "and the moon so near to full we all enjoyed ourselves to the full and came home at 12:30 o'clock." That they were tired from packing all that day for their long trip did not shorten the ritual of saying goodby.[9]

The journey west was an adventure unparalleled in the lives of most settlers and therefore indelibly engraved in the memories of the children, who as old people often decided to write about it. Ama Sharp remembered the molasses cookies Grandma Sharp had sent along getting dry and almost solid as their wagon made its way across flooded Missouri toward Osborne County in 1878. They stopped at farmhouses to buy milk and eggs and hay for the horses and were not hungry but continued to eat those stale cookies, as though clinging to some last symbol of their old home. On Sundays there was nowhere to go to church, but the family camped all day anyway that day, reproducing after a fashion the civilized routine it was used to.[10]

A similar mobile domestication characterized the Fitzgerald family's trip to Kill Deer Creek in the same region the next year. Their horses ate from a feedbox attached to the back of the wagon. Father made hooks for the cooking utensils and attached to the wagon a chicken coop with a rooster and a hen in it. Fitzgerald, who, his daughter Nellie remembered, had only nine dollars in cash when they started, sat with his wife on the spring seat, while the two girls, seven and four years old, rode in a secret space behind the seat or took naps in the wagon bed during the day.[11] The Snyder family, bound for Ness County the same year, ate on the father's tool chest throughout their journey and learned to depend upon his ingenuity. Once the wind came up at a campsite and the wagon, with the women and children asleep in it, began to roll down a hill toward a lake. Snyder was a light sleeper and saved it, adding another story to be repeated through the years on the farm and through the generations as the heirs of his fortitude scattered.[12]

Camping and traveling together, each member having a specific and important job, knit families together just as life outdoors put them in contact with the fundamentals of the universe. Nellie Fitzgerald remembered every detail of the evening's camp. At about 4 P.M. the wagon stopped. Mother and children looked for fuel and cooked dinner.

> After the horses were cared for, father would go back and set the chicken coop on the ground, usually under the wagon, open the door and out would come the chickens looking for bugs and worms until the sun began to get low in the western sky, when they sought the shelter of their coop again, and were soon asleep, while the family would sit by the campfire. We children would cuddle up to mother and dad as the shadows deepened and the noises of the night became more pronounced. It would not be long before we became sleepy and must retire to our little bed so close to father that he would put his big, gentle hand on us when fear seized our little hearts. How often along the journey of life I have longed for the refuge of his arms and the touch of his hand. It only makes me understand God's care for me better.[13]

Family closeness intensified when their wagon bumped onto the western Kansas High Plains where they were to make their home. There the tension they had felt so long met its source, and almost an overload of sensory impressions combined with alternating feelings of homesickness, hope, fear, anger, and depression.

"I will never forget that trip from Russell to Ness City," wrote a woman who in 1879 had been a girl coming from Ohio. "The road was a mere trail, and we were in an open wagon and were burned brown as a penny." The family camped in a strawstack their first night near Ness City within sight of a herd of antelope but did not sleep much for fear of snakes and anxiety that a cowboy might steal their croquet set.[14] D. E. Bradstreet and his brother Jake entered Lane County the same year after a trip from Butler County, Pennsylvania. They found the road there marked with two-foot mounds of buffalo-grass sod, visible for about two miles on the level plain, all the way from Ness City to Dighton.[15] J. S. Winget walked to Ness City from Great Bend, unable to afford $2.50 to ride with the mail carrier.[16] The Snyder family pushed on to their homestead in Ness County after dark, following the north star, and was surprised in the morning to "hear the yip-yip of prairie dogs and see the antelope running around."[17] It was clear to most, as an 1879 Pawnee County arrival put it, that the settlers were "strangers in a strange land."[18]

Often the initial contact was pleasant. Elam and Rachel Bartholomew stopped at the town of Stockton on 9 September 1876 for lunch and arrived at Bow Creek about three in the afternoon. They were excited all evening, and the next morning Elam took his wife on a two-mile walk to their claim "so that she might see her future home in the far west." That afternoon

Going Forth. Settlers crossing the Arkansas River at Great Bend in 1872. Notice the amount of water flowing in the river before massive diversions.

they went to church and on 14 October moved into their own home. "On this day," Bartholomew wrote, "we established the family altar in the home on which to offer, morning and evening, the sacrifice of prayer as long as the household shall stand!" In subsequent diary entries he expressed his delight at visiting his neighbors and in "finishing and fixing" things around the house where he at last was independent.[19] Henry and Rosie Ise were also ecstatic when they came to the same region in 1873. Although the houses they saw were usually sod dugouts, Rosie was delighted to see wild flowers growing on some of the roofs: verbena, prickly pear, portulacas. Henry rhap-

sodized about the black soil on their first day there, and Rosie noticed that the western meadowlark sang a different, longer song than its eastern cousin. "Longer and finer in every way," her husband amended, assuring her that she would love this "fine country."[20]

However, if one chooses accounts from areas farther west and looks at the initial impressions of women rather than of ambitious men or delighted children, the tone is likely to be more negative. Dee Posey and her mother arrived at Larned by train on 12 April 1879. As was common, Dee's father had gone ahead to file the land-claim papers and to build a house. It happened that the claim was about fifteen miles south of Larned, and to get there the two had to pass through the sand hills of Pawnee County. They were not pleased:

I shall never forget my first day in Kansas. We had come from southern Ohio—right on the Ohio river. It is a beautiful country of wooded hills and fruitful valleys. The Ohio valley . . . as I remember it would seem a veritable Garden of Eden to a homesick eastern girl sojourning in Kansas, and when we drove through the sand hills south of Larned, in my brother in law's wagon, I began to wonder what kind of country we had come to live in anyway. That day the wind blew a gale. Mother and I held our hats, and from the high seat on the farm wagon gazed over miles of hilly land covered with red bunch grass. As it waved in the wind we could not help contrasting the Kansas bunch grass with the blue grass in the meadows of Ohio. Before that fifteen-mile ride was ended mother and I were homesick. There were no roads then, nor trees, nor houses south of Larned. We followed the trail across the prairie and at last stopped before a good sized house made of rough pine boards. . . . When mother and I learned that this rustic building was to be our home we were more homesick than ever.

The two made a pact never to let their father and husband, proud of his handiwork and busily moving things in from the wagon, know of their disappointment.[21]

The man of the house was indeed busy in those initial months of prairie residence. The seemingly simplest thing—arranging to acquire title to a 160-acre homestead or timber-culture claim—could be a frustrating duty. The Homestead Act of 1862 promised 160 acres free to those who would pay a small filing fee and reside on and cultivate their land for five years. The Timber Culture Act of 1873 allowed the homesteader an additional 160 acres if within four years he planted one-fourth of it in trees. Strong statistical evidence shows that prior to the mid-1880s boom, western Kansas land was taken mostly by those intending to live in the region and work these 160-acre family-sized farms. It is also clear that buyers in the late 1870s and early 1880s more often saw their claims through to final titles than did the speculative non-resident investors of later years.[22] Nine-tenths of the homesteads entered in Kansas were west of the ninety-seventh meridian.[23] There was very little tenancy, either for fixed-cash rent or a share of the crop, almost all the acreage being farmed by the owner and family.[24] Ten years later, after a considerable boom and bust, the number of farms in western Kansas would actually be down by about 30 percent compared to 1880, but tenancy would be up 25 percent.[25] Comparing both Santa Fe and Kansas Pacific sales to individuals for the 1870s and early 1880s with the late 1880s leads to similar conclusions: that early farm size was smaller and owner perseverance on railroad lands was greater.[26] But myriad complications with the land-office bureaucracy's application of laws created legal challenges for frontier families as formidable in their way as the drought.[27]

Locating suitable land for a homestead or timber-culture entry was a family head's first problem, and he often had to do it on a trip west alone. A major difficulty was the situation that land historian Paul Gates has called the "incongruous" land system of the American West. The federal government used land to promote railroads as well as to aid farmers, so that much of the land near enough to towns to be practical was inside primary or secondary railroad land grants and not available for ordinary homestead or timber-culture filings. Also, some land in western Kansas (notably, the western end of the Osage reserve) was former Indian land and therefore had to be preempted at $1.25 an acre to pay the Indians.[28] Some settlers, especially within the portions of the KP land grant that were in contention, were tempted to take a chance that the land would eventually be released, but it meant that "you hung around on the 'ragged edge'" for years, while all the cheap land around was taken.[29]

A second difficulty was dealing with the land-office bureaucracy. George Anderson, who has made the most extensive study of the administration of land law in western Kansas, estimates that fraud was involved in about 40 percent of the homestead entries there. This was due partly to land-office staffs too small to protect the honest settler from claim-jumpers, partly to settlers willing to take advantage of loopholes, and partly due to settlers' ignorance of the labyrinthine rules connected with the taking of land, residence and cultivation, tree planting, and the completion at all stages of many forms. In two-thirds of the suspended entries, the reason given for abandonment was ignorance of the law.[30]

Most settlers were annoyed at these complications. In fact, Anderson argues that the opportunities for fraud and spying on each other that land-office rules created were a major source of insecurity and instability in western Kansas communities.[31] Legal witnesses to accompany a homesteader to the land office at various times were hard to find and charged high rates.[32] And the "snooping" was awful. The editor of the *Rooks County Record* wrote in 1886:

A government is in a big business when it tries to find out what kind of a crib the baby sleeps in, whether the farmer and his wife recline on wire-woven springs or antediluvian bed cords, or whether the woman of the house bakes her beans in a stone jar or brass kettle. [Land Commissioner W. A. J.] Sparks is a thousand times more particular about a homesteader's exact compliance with each infinitesimal iota of the law than he is with a railroad grant or a stock ranch of an English syndicate.[33]

Others, however, noticed that settlers were not above cheating. Many lived in towns but proved up homestead claims by sleeping in a rudimentary claim house one night every six months and then joining Old Settlers Associations to protect their property.[34] Perhaps some government snooping was justified in enforcing modest residence and improvement requirements for the free land. The editor at Hays in 1881 thought settler complaints were selfish. "Before long they will want the government to stock each quarter-section with a Steinway piano, a Polled Angus bull, and a fishpond filled with German carp."[35]

Complications in determining just who were claim-jumpers did not, however, inhibit univer-

Checking In. A land agent's office at Ashland, Clark County, in 1886. Settlers were dependent on such agents to help them deal with the official bureaucracy and find available claims.

sal indignation at them. Land entries were subject to contest at any time, even at the moment of the final proof, and few claims escaped one. Frontier newspapers survived on revenues from printing notices of contested claims, while settlers lived in fear that some oversight would take from them the product of five years of struggle. "How contemptibly mean it is on the part of these 'Carpet-baggers,' to become a worse enemy to their fellow men than the grasshoppers," wrote a Russell resident in 1874, "by jumping the claims of those who happen to be away from them; little do they know, and care less, for the hard struggle and privations they have passed through to improve their lands for a future home."[36] Professional locators, land agents, and attor-

neys were sometimes difficult to distinguish from claim-jumpers. Wrote Anderson: "They made a practice of buying and selling relinquishments; of hiring men to make entries to prevent legal entrymen from initiating claims to choice tracts, of loaning money to prove up, and in some cases of preventing by violence the entering of *bona fide* settlers."[37] Pressure could be a service. "If you want to find a homestead or timber claim south of the Walnut that can be contested," went an 1885 ad in the *Ness City Times,* "call upon J. B. Spidle at Sidney, Kansas."[38] C. L. Hubbs of Kinsley, indicted by a federal grand jury in 1877 for filing false certificates and affidavits at the Larned land office on behalf of clients, was only an early example of numerous western

Kansas land attorneys and agents who were disbarred or fined for illegal land-office activity.[39]

Claim-jumpers without legal educations were sometimes dealt with more directly. Friends of R. W. Knox, a Sunday school superintendent who held a claim near Cawker City, sent the following anonymous note to Henry Kuchell, who had built a dugout on the unoccupied Knox homestead and filed a contest:

> I have an interest not as to dollars and cents, but as a friend to common justice and human decency. I have been watching your nefarious, barefaced, shameless, thieving course against Mr. Knox, who for years has been a true friend to me. I want you and all others interested to understand that there is not a man in existence who can prosecute that damnable outrage against my friend, and your further connection with it will sever your connection with the affairs of this earth. I will give you a brief time to realize your situation and decide between the alternatives. You are an unprincipled dog, and as such I shall watch and mete out to you your deserts. . . . Better men than you have been shot and left the world better.

This letter was signed "NO MORE WORDS"; another was from "ONE OF TEN." After two years of these threats, the vigilantes in 1881 dropped explosives down the stovepipe of Kuchell's ten-by-twelve-foot bachelor dugout while he was sleeping. When the man staggered out, they shot him with a shotgun, and when he continued toward the road, they stabbed him

and crushed his head with a gun butt. So involved was the community in the round of fear and suspicion that more than two hundred people had to be examined before a jury could be chosen to try Knox, his son, and another man suspected of being in the murder party. At the trial in Beloit, the senior Knox was sentenced to twenty-five years in prison, his son Charlie to fifteen, and L. M. Souls to three years. Ironically, just five weeks after the sentence was passed, word came from Washington favoring Knox in the contest case.[40]

Even if there had been no special problems in gaining title to a homestead for a $14 filing fee, that victory was far from all that was required to survive. The settler had to break hard prairie ground and plant and harvest crops yielding a commercial return sufficient to maintain a family. Though there was no shortage of promises from the western Kansas press that it was possible to make $1,000 a year over expenses, few farmers achieved that kind of bounty.[41]

Financial planning was made difficult for new families by lack of experience and the absence of traditions in the region. There was no community consensus on what crops would prosper, the best methods of tilling them, the tools needed, or even what sort of house, outbuildings, and fencing were required.[42] The settlers at Riverside in Ness County tried to grow tobacco, and people on timber-culture claims tried, with the encouragement of the land commissioner in Washington, to grow every kind of tree except the native cottonwood.[43] In addition to the ubiquitous winter wheat and corn, there were in 1880 substantial western Kansas acreages of spring wheat, rye, broom corn, barley, and millet.[44] The newspapers were full of arguments about deep ver-

Education in Isolation. Thomas County School District #60. The library was small, and there was no playground equipment. There was special education for all, but not in a modern sense.

sus shallow plowing, hedge fences versus board fences versus no fences at all, and a herd law.[45] In Russell, it was said that if wisdom came in a multitude of councils, western Kansans should be wise: "One tells them to plow deep, another says plow shallow; one says 'plow in' your grain, another says 'don't you do it'; one says sow your winter wheat in August, another says wait until just before it freezes up, and so on until we are forcibly reminded of the blind leading the blind and we are all in a ditch."[46]

But while returns were uncertain, costs were immediately apparent. Promotional pamphlets tried to minimize these, as of course did the political rhetoric about "free homes in the West" serving as a kind of safety valve for the urban poor. L. D. Burch in 1878 advised prospective settlers that it was unnecessary to bring much along because everything was available in western Kansas at reasonable prices. A breaking plow was $16 and could be pulled by a yoke of oxen costing $80 to $100. A new wagon with a double-box whiffletree and spring seat was $75, a fair team of work horses $175 to $200, mules $250 to $350, milch cows $16 to $30, building lumber $18 to $35 a thousand feet depending on grade, and pine shingles $3 to $4 a thousand. True, these costs could mount up, especially if one bought much of the farm machinery that was as cheap in Kansas as in Illinois or New York, but the pamphleteers held that fancy machinery was not necessary, nor was an expensive house. "Hundreds of settlers in the new homestead counties start with very little expense by building a house of the firm tough sod, on the plan of sun-dried bricks. They are made very neat and comfortable by cutting the inner walls smooth and whitewashing or papering."[47]

Some had sound balance sheets, especially able-bodied bachelors willing to live in dugouts and work for wages for other community members to supplement their crop income. Howard Ruede, who lived along Kill Creek in Osborne County, managed well in the late 1870s thanks partly to relatively high crop prices ($1.25 a bushel for wheat) encouraged by the Russo-Turkish War in 1877 and thanks partly to hard work combined with a simple life style. His own farming operation was small, consisting in 1879 of only eleven acres of broken land planted with sod corn, potatoes, winter wheat, and rye. But he did a great deal of work for others, not only breaking land, building houses, and helping with the harvest but working as a printer in the office of the *Osborne County Farmer*. Like everyone else, at least among those who kept diaries, Ruede maintained careful accounts of his expenses. His provisions costs for August through December 1878 were $4.75, $4.44, $3.12, $2.70, and $7.07. The total cost of his operation from 19 August to 30 November 1877 was $60.04. Ruede regularly went without meat unless he could hunt; he wrote that for many, the ten-cents-a-pound

bacon at the Osborne store insured "that we are often vegetarians perforce." Sometimes he was paid for his work in goods, and it appears that in the community around Osborne a fairly sophisticated barter system had developed.[48]

People with larger families living through harder times found it more difficult to break even. Elam Bartholomew, living just one county west of Ruede, with a family eventually to consist of ten children, kept far more extensive records over a longer period. In fact, Bartholomew's diary is an unequaled record because he made nineteen thousand consecutive daily entries in it.[49]

The diary gives a detailed picture of income and expenses on a homestead. Bartholomew marketed his crops throughout the year, waiting for the best price, and, like Ruede, supplemented his income both by doing farm work for others and pursuing a profession—in Bartholomew's case a combination of school-teaching and various county offices and appointments. In 1879, when crops were sparse, Bartholomew sold wheat in September for 65 and 55 cents a bushel. Although he was able to get 95 cents for it in January and 90 cents in March, he sold only 11 bushels at those prices compared with 41 bushels sold in September when he doubtless needed the money to pay debts. It was a problem that was to lead to a generation of political agitation by farmers for some sort of loan program to allow them to market their crops better.

Bartholomew tried to compensate by diversifying. He grew rice corn also, which gave him something to sell at other times of the year, and he marketed garden produce to the local settlers. In 1880, he sold 160 bushels of wheat at an average of 76 cents, for an income of

$122.00 from that source. The fact that he had some of his own wheat milled for family use that year indicates how uncommercial that price was. In 1881 he sold only 90 bushels of wheat for $84.45, and, despite making $53.75 for his outside labor, selling eggs, butter, and garden produce as well as some of his livestock, had to borrow $577.00 to meet family expenses totaling $746.70 for the year. Wheat prices for 1882 averaged 59 cents a bushel, and his total income was $134.30. In that year among his expenses were $57.20 for interest on his loans and $83.95 in expenses for filing on and planting trees to a timber-culture claim. He borrowed $130.00 in 1883 to remain solvent. In 1884 Bartholomew recorded no wheat crop at all, and the family income from other crops and such sources as 182 dozen eggs sold for $17.90 was $193.10. Bartholomew that year had to pay $158.45 for labor and received only $77.35 for his own outside work. With expenses of $1,306.45 for a growing family, he had to borrow $677.00 and sell his timber claim in order to stay on. An excellent wheat crop in 1885 was offset by a price of 40 cents a bushel. The next year it was 36 cents.[50]

The deficit spending Bartholomew was forced into was not due to extravagance. Although he liked books and in 1883 bought Andreas's Kansas history for $12.50, his children shared clothing and shoes. Expenditures for toys for Bartholomew's large family were modest indeed. In 1883, the total was 65 cents—a cup for Lizzie, 25 cents; a china doll, 35 cents; and marbles, 2 cents. Never in ten years did the toys account exceed the $2.45 recorded in 1885. Entertainment expenses were limited to nuts and candy, sometimes a box of cigars, once in a while popcorn.[51]

Bartholomew had few expenses for the purchase of machinery, but this raised his costs for custom work and was apparently not the route taken by a good many settlers, who were drawn by both independence and pride to having the latest gadgets on their farms. The Curtis Norton family, living near Larned, in the 1880s recorded the purchase of a number of machines, which the boys delighted in working with and repairing. In 1885, for example, Norton bought a Steele mowing machine and a Thomas Imperial self-dumping horse rake. These were brought out to Larned in pieces, and seventeen-year-old Henry Wylie Norton recorded their names and assembly procedures in his diary.[52] Edwards County in 1877 was introduced to the McCormick self-binder harvester, which wealthy John Fitch of Fitchburg purchased and allowed his fifteen-year-old son to drive.[53] The Chicago screw harrow was much admired by the late 1870s throughout the region and even spawned a copy manufactured in Russell, Kansas.[54] The first wheat shipped out of Ford County was threshed by a threshing machine, and by the 1880s steam traction engines were common in western Kansas fields.[55]

Given such doubtful economic prospects, it can be asked why homesteaders thought they needed fairly sophisticated machinery rather than broadcasting by hand and harvesting by scythe. Admittedly, of all the western Kansas settlers' expenses, those for machinery were least justifiable purely on the basis of survival. Machinery was their one concession to their own psychological well-being, a single escape from near-slavery to the land and the climate, and a symbol of nineteenth-century civilization through mechanical control.

"The kind agencies of the inventor and the

manufacturer provided the necessities for our use," reported a Great Bend man watching the harvest of 1882. "The king of motors—steam—has been utilized successfully until now in every direction may be seen the ascending columns of coal smoke until our vast farming region has more the appearance of an enormous manufacturing center than a quiet, unobtrusive, unparalleled grain raising community." Eighteen J. I. Case "Agitator" threshing machines were working in Barton County that year pulled by Case steam engines—enough to give the look and feel of big industry, just as the arrival of custom cutting crews in the region has served to do every summer since.[56] Young Henry W. Norton got caught up in the drama also. "There was a traction engine threshing and grinding machine passed the school house this afternoon," he wrote in March 1885. "They had a team on the separator, then came the engine pushing and trailing the wagon with the feed grinder which was also the water wagon to which was fastened a barrel mounted on two wheels which the engine pumps water from at work. It was quite a procession and looked much like a R.R. train when coming towards a person."[57] Certainly machinery was vital to the picturesque aspect of farming: the machine in the garden was an irresistible image. The 1879 *Scribners* reporter, it will be recalled, felt that reaping machines had "a kind of Homeric character." His description of the working of the self-binder must have excited every farmer to own one, whether he could afford it or not.[58]

The editor of the *Osborne County Farmer* put well the feeling that people arriving on the plains—struggling with claim-jumpers, the land office, and their own feelings of being "strangers in a strange land"—had about life there as time passed. In the years when "the heaven over our heads was as brass, and the earth beneath our feet was as iron," he wrote, these families learned the true basis of civilization by creating it from its elements. Perhaps they could be excused for sentimentality. "The sod was broken, and the virgin soil upturned; the dugout and the log cabin sheltered purer and holier homes than brownstone fronts and marble halls; the sod schoolhouse and private dwelling were God's first temples here." Seldom had people—not men speculating on a mining frontier but families working together—met and survived such challenges, and it was the everyday details that loomed larger with the passing years rather than those hopes that had seemed so grand at the time. The tumble-down sod house where children played along a limitless horizon eventually evoked more emotion than the memory of a screw harrow, and the simple meal was recalled more often than the voting of railroad bond issues. "Still o'er these scenes," the Osborne editor wrote, "my memory wakes / And fondly broods with wiser care; / Time but the impression deeper makes, / As streams their channels deeper wear."[59]

Chapter Twelve

Home

Historians in recent decades have moved away from strictly political and intellectual history and placed increasing emphasis on understanding the small patterns that constitute the lives of ordinary people in their everyday existence. For western Kansas settlers, the psychological experience of arriving in an unfamiliar country and the stresses of dealing with the land-office bureaucracy were pieces of this personal pattern. But these things were likely to happen only once, whereas other, seemingly more trivial aspects of their lives assumed vast importance because of their constant challenge, their closeness, their inescapable nature. Included among these were adjustments in sex roles and relations among family members; creating and maintaining adequate shelter; balancing income and expenses; finding and creating food, clothing, and recreation on the High Plains; and the periodic contacts with prairie dangers from farm machinery, from fires, from disease.

While some may suspect the tendency of the "new social historians" to "treat individuals as illustrations of large groupings or trends," most can agree with such historians that "the great and famous cause less than we used to think, while ordinary people cause more."[1] A social-history focus disciplines scholars to ex-amine source materials they might once have ignored and to add complexity to the picture of the past by making it impossible to ignore any longer the significance of so many. The study of social history and popular culture, even on the level of a few families, is neither simple nor disconnected from broader trends. When a western Kansas family of the 1880s sat down to discuss its budget, when a mother gazed sadly out the door wondering when her husband might return, or when all gathered around a child with a fever, the stakes of civilizing the region, in all their complexity, were represented. At this level came the real test, for it was here that speculations and theories of settlement had to be made workable by experience.

Sod houses and the dugouts that often preceded them were not much to look at; their virtues were that they were cheap, fireproof, well insulated, and readily made from available materials. The settler cut strips of sod from the virgin prairie, whose dirt and grass were bound by a dense root system. With a grasshopper plow he cut bites three to four inches deep, yielding bricks of turf one foot wide by two feet long. These were laid grass side down, two wide, often with an occasional bonding layer placed sideways, to fashion a two-foot-thick wall and deep window wells where plants and

Home. Sod House in Decatur County.

children could sit. No roof style but shingles kept rain out well. Prices for these shelters ranged from the $10.05 Howard Ruede paid for materials for a ten-by-fourteen-foot dugout (some claimed $5 dugouts without providing precise budgets) to $80 or $100 for a more typical, family-sized, aboveground dwelling.[2]

Sod homes were not viewed with great affection by those who lived in them until much later, and then more for their nostalgic value than for admiration of their physical qualities. But there was grudging admission that these uncivilized hovels were well adapted to the environment. Luke Pembleton of Ness County noticed that "the settler who had a little money would haul lumber and build a cheap frame dwelling, in which he would freeze in the winter and cook in the summer and the house would be tossed around by every wind storm." He remembered one man putting up such a frame house, living in it for a year, then building sod structures to serve as house, barn, and chicken house. The sod house also had the advantage of being able to be built quickly, in one or two days with the help of neighbors, to provide the first cozy shelter for people who had lived for some time in wagons or tents. In fact, some settlers seemed at first to enjoy the cavelike but prairie-fire-proof, windproof, and sunproof sod interiors so universally lamented after a few years of living in one. "It was a long, crooked way they traveled—a tiresome drifting under the open sky and storms," wrote one settler. "But now the walls are complete, the stout ridgepole and rafters in place, the last piece of the roof on and together they go in. How wonderful the four walls enclose them, the sky shut out."[3] This calls to mind the image of Beret, whom Ole Rölvaag called "The Heart That Dared Not Let in the Sun" in his 1927 prairie novel *Giants in the Earth*. One long western Kansas poem, "Dugout Echoes," suggested that a reluctant, buried pride at the independence that inexpensive housing gave was the "True Inwardness" of the sod-house dwellers: "You'll be perfectly delighted / At the paradise you've found. / As you build your castles in the air / And dugouts in the ground."[4]

The sod house's most fundamental problem was leakage. This ranged from the streams of "yellow mud" pouring into the house, remembered by a Lane County resident, to the complete collapse of houses saturated with water, such as an 1880 incident in Rooks County that killed one and injured two at the Lloyd Shelby home.[5] At the least there was considerable inconvenience during the few days of heavy rain likely in the spring, and there was the additional galling fact that sod roofs were likely to drip for several days after the sun came out again. On the night of 22 December 1877, Howard Ruede slept only a few hours because it was raining and he had to move his bed and provisions under the ridgepole where the roof leaked least.[6] One Easter Sunday in the 1880s during a wind-driven rain, the Sprague family, living near Dighton in Lane County, had to put the youngest children to sleep in a dry-goods box to protect them from inside showers.[7] The Pembleton family in Ness County had a ceiling made of flour sacks, but this did not protect them when it rained. Their solution was to twist table forks into the ceiling to direct the streams of water to containers below.[8] The Vincent Kahle sod house in Wallace County, built in 1887, had a dirt roof topped with cane bundles at which the oxen nibbled, reducing even further its originally inadequate ability to deflect water. Dishpans were set on beds during rainstorms, but mud, not merely water, poured through the footing boards that held the roof in place. "When one of my children was ten days old," wrote Mary Kahle,

> we had a three-day rain. The house leaked so badly that we rolled the bedding up and tied it with a rope, and put the oil cloth from the table over it to keep it dry. I put the baby on top of the roll and put the parasol over it to keep her dry. Soon the rain ran off the ribs of the parasol and soaked around the baby so I fixed a place for her in the cupboard shelf—the only dry place in the house. I walked around with a slicker, a man's hat and overshoes to keep dry.

The Kahles, who may have thought rain would not be much of a problem along the desertlike western edge of Kansas, had to get a wagonload of tin cans from the town of Wallace and

High Plains Victorian. Exterior and interior of the Mead family dugout near Bloom, Kansas. Photographs of sod-house interiors are rare; this one suggests little adaptation to the unique geographical environment.

construct a metal roof. Mary remembered in 1960: "I used to think that if I EVER had a house that didn't leak, I would never complain of any house. I still enjoy hearing the rain on the roof as long as it doesn't come through."[9]

Some features of the interiors of sod houses were almost universal. Most often there was an attempt to somehow cover the dirt walls. Settlers usually plastered native lime onto walls and trimmed it smooth with a spade. Even this would wash off in streaks during a rain, but it was often not available and innovation was required.[10] One family hung building paper on wooden pegs driven into the sod walls; another hung gunny sacks and plastered newspapers on top of these.[11] Ideally, there was a wood floor and a ceiling: for homemakers, these and covered walls were essential to make rudimentary cleanliness possible. Ceilings could be most primitive—flour sacks or unbleached muslin

sheets sewn together and washed when dirty. This type of ceiling also could trap a mouse or a snake.[12]

In the absence of a wood floor, there were numerous recipes, most of them heavy on salt, for concoctions to spread on the bare dirt floor to harden it. Another stopgap, more difficult to maintain but surprisingly often employed, was wall-to-wall rag carpets stretched over straw laid directly on the dirt. These had to be untacked during hot weather and the considerable amount of dust beaten out of them. Then the whole family pitched in to try to stretch

them again, a job that could wear the skin off fingers and knees.[13] A last universal furnishing was a pile of dried buffalo or cow manure—chips—for fueling the stove in a timberless country. Women and children were assigned the duty of gathering these, and usually did it with gunnysack aprons, as a tub was too heavy to carry and a dragged sack would break these delicate items.[14] There had to be a box of them inside, with the mother of the family always trying to get the children to wash their hands after handling chips, but the main supply was piled outside, usually in a twelve-to-fifteen-foot-high cone that shed water.[15]

Within these parameters there was infinite room for individual variation, and the occasional pictures of sod house interiors show that pioneering and poverty did not always prevent an earnest try at Victorian decorative excess. Bonnie Bailey Vaughn of Scott County described in detail the inside of her family's 1880s soddy. A coal shovel with a snow scene painted on it hung on a red ribbon; wooden spoons with similar painted scenes were also hung up. Footstools kept feet off the cold floor. These were made of a size 2½ tin can encircled by others, padded, sewn together, and covered with carpet or velvet. Framed, cross-stitched mottos were popular. The Baileys' was "Nearer My God to Thee," but Bonnie said the most common was "God Bless Our Home." Large pictures and mirrors had scarves draped over them to add elegance.[16] There were flour-sack dishtowels, and covers were made from these sacks sewn together with unravelled gunnysack thread, stuffed with cotton, and tacked with red yarn.[17]

Harrie Jennison of Lane County remembered lots of utensils visible also: a barrel churn, steel knives and forks with wooden handles, wooden potato mashers, cast-iron teakettles, a coffee grinder, and a nutmeg grater. The beds, filled with straw or cornhusks because springs were unavailable, were high and comfortable at first but soon settled and got hard.[18] Christine Barnett Stormont gathered buffalo horns in Lane County, which her father scraped, polished, and used for hatracks.[19] Margaret Raser of Hodgeman County made a partial inventory of her family's sod home. There were a home-made cupboard, kitchen utensils on nails, a bench for the water bucket and wash basin, a roller for the towel, a swill bucket, a box for buffalo chips, beds high enough for a trundle bed to slide under, one rocker, coal-oil lamps, a bureau, a trunk or two, a cradle. The refrigerator was the well, where food was suspended on a small rope. The washtub, boiler, and dishpan hung on nails outside the house. Clothes were spread on the grass or bushes to dry.[20]

Of course, no number of household amenities could completely mask the regular reminders in everyday life that these families were living in an isolated semiwilderness containing elements that at times seemed demonic. The primary culprits were the rattlesnake, the bedbug, and the flea. Wrote the "Lane County Bachelor," Frank Baker, in the mid-1880s:

How happy I feel when I crawl into bed,
And a rattlesnake rattles a tune at my head.
And the gay little centipede void of all fear,
Crawls over my neck and down into my ear.
And the gay little bedbugs so cheerful and
    bright,
They keep me a-laughing two-thirds of the
    night.
And the gay little flea with sharp tacks on his
    toes,
Plays, 'Why don't you catch me' all over my
    nose.[21]

Many were not able to apply a sense of humor to what was sometimes a grim situation. Wrote a Rush County man: "Rattlesnakes, bedbugs, fleas, and the 'prairie itch' were what kept us awake nights and made life miserable."[22]

Snakes in general are frightening even to most people who pretend to be blasé about them, and the thick-bodied, ill-tempered prairie rattlesnake native to western Kansas is a far from gentle introduction to that variety of wildlife. In the case of the nineteenth-century settler, there was, on top of a fear naturalists believe comes from the totally alien appearance and behavior of snakes, a biblical connection of snakes with evil—a sinister meaning as thoroughly built into those people's subconscious as interpretations of plagues of locusts.[23]

Rattlers were present on that early prairie in an abundance hardly imaginable now, after one hundred years of exterminating them. "That sod had never . . . known the tread of human foot," wrote Dee Posey of Edwards County. "The rattlesnakes held supreme sway, and the children and I had to walk right across the prairie, there was not a sign of a road to [the] schoolhouse."[24] The Reverend R. J. Crumley had by 1878 killed 133 rattlesnakes on his farm seven miles southeast of Kingman, and a neighbor of his killed 127.[25] About the same time a nearly six-foot-long specimen was captured near Medicine Lodge.[26]

In contrast to the present day, when fear of snakes is usually not based on personal experience, most settlers had direct contact with snakes, often rattlesnakes. Mary Kahle's dog one day barked at a pair of shoes in the corner. She moved them. He kept barking. She moved them again and this time saw a rattlesnake stick its head out of one of the shoes. It had crawled in through a hole in the wall.[27] Mary Northway was combing her hair in her sod house near Portis in Osborne County when a blue racer dropped through the shrunken roof boards past her face and onto the floor: "Needless to say I could imagine I could see snake heads sticking through the roof in different places for a long

time." People put sheets up over their beds so that snakes would not fall on them as they slept, and it was not unusual for a snake to drop through the roof onto the dinner table during a meal.[28] All families kept snakebite remedies handy, the most usual being turpentine or coal oil sometimes mixed with wet soda in which to bathe the bite. One could also suck the poison out after washing one's mouth out with salt.[29] "It was nothing to be surprised," said Mrs. S. A. Morris, a neighbor of Mary Northway, "to look up at the ridge log in our little sod house and see a snake watching you or one sticking his head out from between the roof and the wall."[30]

The author of "Dugout Echoes," a Dr. Zoliger of Ness County, touched on the topic of rattlesnakes in a revealing way when advising about dugout construction. Dugouts, he said, were low to the ground and helped insure that "your wife will not be afraid of the high winds that we often have here."

Of course, it makes it handy for the rattler to climb onto when they are out on a lark of a summer night in July or August. And if one that has been doing a little trapeze performing on one of your rafters overhead happens to lose its grip and drop down by the side of your bed along about midnight, you don't want to get excited about it. Such things have happened to others here and may happen to you. All you have to do is slip off the foot or opposite side of the bed, locate the sound of the rattler and circle away around so as to give him plenty of air, until you have found the match box. No, there is no use to ask your wife where the matches are, for she has fainted. Just run your hand along the dry-goods box you use for a cupboard. When you have found the matches strike a light, then grab the hoe that your wife always has in the house to sweep with and make short work of the rattler. Of course, in your excitement you have upset the water bucket and your well of gypsum water is a quarter of a mile from the house and it is as dark as a stack of black cats out of doors. . . . Then quit swearing about the pleasures of life in the west and tie up the toe you have knocked the nail from against the corner of one of the empty cracker boxes that you use for seats.[31]

The smallest but mightiest inconvenience was insects. Although individually less fearsome than the rattler, they were far more numerous and were, among the famous western Kansas "varmits," the only class that no settler could entirely avoid.

The chief insect offenders were fleas and bedbugs—fleas by day and bedbugs by night. Fleas multiplied in the grass, and bedbugs found appealing the combination of wood and sod in the roofs of settlers' homes. "You don't have to keep a dog in order to have plenty of fleas," wrote Howard Ruede in June 1877, "for they are natives too and do their best to drive out the intruding settlers." As for bedbugs, "if you want to measure them in a spoon, you can gather them up in that way from between the sods in the wall."[32] Virginia Barr from Smith County noted that the so-called "buffalo fleas" become particularly bothersome on hot summer nights when families would sleep in the grass to catch the cool breeze. When the resulting "Kansas itch" got

too severe, they would all return to the house, light a kerosene lamp, and take turns picking fleas off one another.[33] A Hays poet put the problem in verse:

How we wake up in the night, bugs
And scratch with all our might,
While with vengeful appetite,
And with venomous delight,
Bit them bugs. . . .

Despite of human woes—
Through the night,
Ah, the bugs, bugs, bugs, bugs
Bugs, bugs, bugs,
Oh, the crawling and the mauling of the bugs![34]

Would that this had been all! There were orange centipedes to give variety to the visitors one might find in one's bed.[35] There were flies "by the millions" and no screen doors or sprays for protection.[36] Elam Bartholomew made a frame covered with mosquito netting for his sons George and Elbert's bed "as a protection against disturbance from the flies during their peaceful day slumbers."[37] There were potato bugs, and it was often the duty of children to pick them one by one from potato vines and dump them into a can with kerosene at the bottom.[38] June was noted for miller moths, always an annoyance when the men worked till dusk and the family had to eat supper by lamplight. "Papa always told Mama that they lived on miller gravy," remembered Mattie Beal of Wallace County. "This, of course, would arouse her and she would become quite indignant at such an expression."[39]

Bugs were truly a special pain for women. At

least with snakes, they were expected only to scream and call for help, but control of other vermin was included in the nineteenth-century expectation that women were to make a house a clean and healthy home.

Dee Posey was appalled that she slept, or tried to sleep, each night with "two children and I don't know how many bedbugs."[40] Broomsticks were the weapons of choice to dispatch "his centipedeship."[41] Fleas had to be dealt with by mashing them between the fingernails, a job regularly assigned to small girls. Bedbugs could be crushed too, but a more elegant method was to go to the bedsteads with a feather dipped in carbolic acid to finish off the nighttime offenders with a touch. Women cut newspapers into strips and pasted them on long sticks as sweeps to keep the flies off the table during meals.[42] Still, children wandering on the prairie could not be protected. Rosie Ise left her infant Billy in the care of his young sister Laura one day, and while the girl was intent on picking corn, the boy crawled into an ant heap. As the baby screamed and waved his hands in the air, the horrified mother first picked at the red swarm by hand and then tried to scrape them off with a knife, but she succeeded only in pulling the witless beasts in two, leaving their mandibles in the child's skin. She and her husband Henry packed the boy with a mud mixture, but his limbs swelled and he fussed for days in pain while his mother dreamed at night of "ants crawling on her arms."[43] A farmer's wife in Bazine in Ness County wrote in 1879 that something must be done about the "deplorable fact of filthy vermin" in homes. "Ladies of Ness, let us arise with the air of no sluggard, but with the grit that never says 'I can't,' and rid our homes of such that makes

them impure, unhealthy, and very unpleasant, that when we lay our tired bodies down cleanliness will soon lull us away into that land of sweet rest."[44]

The necessity for all in the family to share every kind of work sometimes masked the strict sex-role separation typical of Gilded-Age America. But scholars of frontier families have found that temporary changes in behavior did not necessarily guarantee permanent changes once things returned to normal.[45] There is abundant evidence in Elam Bartholomew's diary that his wife Rachel was a true companion to him, with whom he shared hardships, with whom he socialized, whom he much loved. Yet in July 1879, he quoted a contemporary writer's traditional view of sex roles. "Man is great in action," he copied, "woman in suffering; man shines abroad, woman at home; man talks to convince, woman to persuade; man has a rugged heart; woman a soft and tender one; man prevents misery; woman relieves; Man has science, woman taste; man has judgment; woman sensibility; man is a being of justice, woman an angel of mercy."[46] Another woman of whom we know much through a diary in which all family members wrote, Mary Norton from Pawnee County, felt the pressure of her role. In her forties when the family moved to western Kansas and with ten children ranging in age from twenty-two to one, she was understandably often tired and "blue." And when she was, she felt she had failed in her role as a woman. "Oh, I've been so cross all the afternoon, I'm ashamed to think of it," she wrote on 28 May 1880. "The rain kept the children indoors and it seemed as if poor little Georgie could do nothing but tease." Mary Norton's husband and older boys were away often, working in towns, once for over six months, and the burden of keeping the inside in order while they adventured outside was sometimes overwhelming.[47]

Part of the expectation was that women should nurture and support their families while hiding their own needs and disappointments. A few, such as Flora Heston in Clark County, adapted easily. Flora wrote jaunty letters home, loved the beauty of the place, and was cheerful right up to the time she died her lonely death in childbirth on the Plains.[48] But most did a good deal of secret pining, and their outward cheeriness was an obligation more than a true response. Wrote Hattie Humphrey in 1873 of her life in Edwards County: "Mr. Downing is plowing. It is pleasant to see someone at work—some life about this region. Everything is so monotonous, almost unbearable even to me, who am not supposed to have any nerves."[49] Mrs. John Smith did not take to Clark County as well as Flora Heston but hid the difference. The evening after her arrival, while her husband John was out doing chores, she went to the door of her one-room sod house. "I saw a vast expanse of prairie country in sunset, but it looked so very lonesome, and so I cried, in a moment of longing for my family so far away and the lure of our Illinois home." When John returned, however, she quickly dried her tears, and explained later that "the fact that we never gave up together kept us here thru the lean years."[50] Mrs. S. S. Button, who grew up in a Hodgeman County sod house, as a child watched her mother closely: "Oh, the long lonely days and nights especially for mother, who had left everyone she held dear excepting her own little flock. She was a brave woman and only when letters and the home

paper came did she give way to tears. But when she saw how it worried the children she would brighten up and read the funny pieces, and we would forget all about it." That mother had been a schoolteacher in Pennsylvania, "a refined gentle woman" who was frustrated by the unrefined, ungentle nature of a place where guests spit tobacco juice on her clean floor. Her escape was to play vigorously on the walnut organ they had brought along. "Mother never became quite satisfied with Kansas," Mrs. Button wrote, "but father loved it."[51]

The escape from these thoughts came in work, which was always available. One night when most of the family was at a spelling bee in Larned, Mrs. Norton and the girls felt lonely: "Mary missed the noise so much that she was uneasy and the wind rattling the doors frightened her. I made a little molasses candy to console her and Georgie and then sat in with them till M. was asleep. . . . Lottie washed."[52] The Norton women and others talked about wanting more leisure, at least to do creative work such as sewing. The constant round of "washed colored clothes" and "washed white clothes" that are such regular women's entries in the Norton diaries prevented creative leisure, but its monotony gave a sense of the familiar and kept them from brooding on the drawbacks of their situation.[53]

Whether or not it was really true that "it is the woman who bakes the bread and not the man who makes the laws that runs a country up hill and down," it is certain that food was fundamental to life.[54] Lack of income combined with high local prices and the unavailability of some items made it difficult to put together a healthful, not to mention tasty, diet. Pigs could be raised and butchered by families, so every possible use was made of pork. Sausage was fried up in large quantities on cold days (Mary Norton mentioned cooking a five-gallon crockful in January for spring use) and stored in stone jars with hot grease poured on top as a preservative. Months later the grease was used to fry doughnuts. Men, for reasons not usually understood by the rest of the household, would chew on preserved pigs' feet.[55] Wild game, usually rabbits, was welcome.[56]

For carbohydrates there was a great deal of plain corn bread sweetened with a "poor man's preserves" mixture (the exact ones were family secrets) involving sorghum molasses. Sometimes there was hominy made from the family's corn and placed in a washbasin to simmer on the stove for two or three days, mixed with lye to loosen the hulls.[57] Some had black-eyed peas, potatoes, or beans. Fruit was so scarce that its role as a Christmas stocking treat meant more than can now be imagined. Families regularly went out in season to look for wild currants, hackberries, chokecherries, and plums for plum butter.[58] However, one woman born on the prairie remembered that she did not see a banana until she was twelve years old; another did not see a grapefruit until high school.[59] "Of course a can of fruit don't last long," said a Ness County man, "but when we devour the contents we can place the empty can on the table and look at the pictures on it for dessert."[60] If that did not satisfy, there was sorghum cake or Indian pudding made of corn meal and cooked in a sack. But there were no expectations that that last dessert, as prepared in western Kansas, would contain the traditional raisins.[61]

It was not so much that groceries were unavailable in the railroad towns as that it was difficult to get to town, and prices were high enough to discourage people imbued with the Protestant work ethic from buying personal luxuries when they could make do with the necessities. Elam Bartholomew spent $8.20 on dried and canned fruit in 1883. This no doubt represented the minimum needed to ward off scurvy but cost a substantial sum considering that the fuel bill for the year was $7.00, boots and shoes for his large family cost $9.40, and he was selling eggs for 7 cents a dozen.[62] In Lane County in the 1880s, socks were 25 cents a pair and calico 10 cents a yard when $1.50 a week was not an uncommon wage for farm family members trying to supplement their income.[63] But a dollar did go a long way. At a sale at Bice Brothers at Schoharie in Ness County in 1884, a dollar would buy any of the following: twelve pounds of soda crackers, nine pounds of cream, twelve pounds of rice, sixteen pounds of beans, eleven pounds of prunes, sixteen bars of soap, eight three-pound cans of tomatoes or peaches, five pounds of oysters, or six pounds of pears.[64] And store prices declined through the 1880s. In Ness City in 1879 a dollar would buy only thirteen bars of soap; in 1890 it would buy fifty.[65] But prices for farm products went down even faster than store prices, and acquiring a dollar was still a challenge for settlers.[66] When they did have cash, they usually preferred to invest it in machinery or seed rather than in household items the family could make for itself.

No matter how much scrimping went on, there was still usually a shortfall in cash. Part of this was made up by packages from back home, generally clothes but sometimes food. One Lane County family received a barrel of navy beans and a barrel of buckwheat flour every winter from its Michigan relatives.[67] For early settlers, there was money to be made by picking up cattle and buffalo bones. In March 1879, the Nortons took 1,500 pounds of bones to Larned and traded them for a barrel of salt and 12 pounds of nails.[68] At about $6 to $8 a ton if traded for supplies, it was hard work, and soon there were few bones to be found.[69] Similarly competitive was sewing for sale and selling butter and eggs.[70] Both were so common that the market was flooded and prices declined accordingly. Yet the need for cash existed, and the only way to get it was to have the men and boys seek temporary jobs far from home.

The only moonlighting activity that both offered adventure and required only short absences from home was wild-horse hunting. Though this activity disappeared for lack of a supply when the boom populations appeared in the 1880s, it provided good income for a time to those clever and fit enough to chase horse herds for sometimes fifteen days at a time until the lead stallion wore out. It was a great event when an exhausted herd was brought back to a little town, put into a corral, and every boy tried to ride the wildest one. Horse hunting could be profitable, too, as horse outfits could round up as many as 250 animals on a single outing and sell them for a minimum of $5 to $40 or $50 each. The top figures applied if the horse was tame enough for a local farmer to use, the lowest if the outfit was selling to a wholesaler in return for his financing the expedition.[71]

Most often it was not a fast, fun trip followed by a large payday but a long absence for little return. The women who were left behind sometimes combined households and coped as best they could. When Ella Ferrell and Tillie Bell saw longhorns in their millet fields near Utica in 1879, they could not call on their husbands to drive the cattle off; they had to be resourceful and rush at them with sheets over their heads. They tried also to shoot some cranes, but firing Bell's big army gun knocked Tillie down and Ferrell's shotgun was found to have no caps.[72] If a baby came due while the husband was gone, an older daughter helped. "My mother told me what to do," remembered a woman who was twelve at the time of the birth of a younger brother, "and I took care of him myself."[73] Still, life was not complete. "It seems a long, long time," Mary Norton wrote when her husband and boys were away six months. "I am so tired of managing alone."[74]

With such a burden of loneliness to bear so often, it is no wonder that settlers took enthusiastically to company where they could find it. Frank Mallory and L. L. Scott, out on a cattle drive in 1879, stopped at a dugout and found that the woman there, though alone while her husband was getting supplies, was eager to give them a meal. Unfortunately she served onion soup, which neither of them liked, but they dared not complain and left her, over her protest, with two dollars for her trouble.[75] Church and school activities became social gatherings, and denominational differences were forgotten. "A Roman Catholic and a Hardshell Baptist or a Methodist," Howard Ruede observed, "are on just as friendly terms as though both had precisely the same creed."[76] Next to gathering new species of fungi, trips to such civilized places as WaKeeney for Presbyterian meetings were the highlight of Elam Bartholomew's life and merited an inordinate amount of space in his diary.[77] There were harvest home and Fourth of

Family Frontier. An 1890s household in Finney County.

July picnics with homemade amusement park rides and lots of food; there were lyceums and temperance lectures and political meetings.[78] And there was the simple joy of visiting with neighbors and with strangers passing through. Tracks soon led in all directions over the roadless prairie.[79] The Bartholomews did some quantification on this in 1880 when they recorded guests day by day: a grand total of 1,081 visitors and 783 meals served for the year.[80]

Family life in nineteenth-century western Kansas exhibited foremost a variety that is not well reflected in the scholarly literature. One reason is that the western family has not been extensively studied as an interacting unit. Men have been studied incidentally, women overspecifically, and children almost not at all.[81] Focus on the frontier family as an aspect of women's history has resulted in a tendency to concentrate on sex-role differentiation and on abstract questions such as whether frontier women took the Victorian "domestic fantasy" with them to places like Kansas.[82] The danger here is in creating a new stereotype of the family, dominated by the mother rather than the father and by a mother image more sophisticated but ultimately as incomplete and inaccurate as the "Madonna of the Prairies" or "Gentle Tamer" popular images that historians properly question.

Those who have concentrated on women's incidental writings (mostly letters) have discovered an unmetaphoric style, a matter-of-factness about sex and death, and a variety in outlook that make sweeping generalization suspect. Elizabeth Hampsten in her extensive study of the private writings of Midwestern women from 1880 to 1910 has noted that the style of these documents (which she calls "a literature of omission") is almost conversational. Yet, she observed that it does not take "reflective generalization" to reveal a "complex life" and a "strong presence."[83] This lack of generalization and metaphor in the sources creates complex problems of description and categorization for the historian. Sandra Myres, whose *Westering Women* is one of the most extensively researched studies of frontier women, concluded not only that "many women simply could not afford the luxury of the pedestal" but also that "if there is a truth about frontierswomen it is that they were not any one thing."[84]

Just as it was necessary and revealing to isolate aspects of the frontier—economics, exploration, warfare, women's role—from their context in the total mosaic of life to gain a broad perspective, it is equally important to portray women as part of families and family life. Perhaps the kind of family studies that Phillippe Aries and John Demos have done will be attempted soon for the frontier West.[85] Meanwhile, books such as this one can suggest how the family dynamic worked, as well as illuminate relationships between the personal sphere and the public sphere that are crucial to understanding either aspect of life.

Life in a sod house in western Kansas was a rich experience, especially for children, and one that, once survived, became ever more pleasant in retrospect. "I remember bright spots on that far away scene," went a typical memoir, "the ecstasy of gathering the first prairie flowers in spring, the beauty of the meadowlark's song. . . . And I can yet see Mother, Dad and Uncle Will sitting beside the little iron cook stove, their only light that of the flickering fire on the tiny hearth."[86] Life was hard, but it turned the children into "towers of strength" and good citizens.[87] Their parents, meanwhile, had the independence they had long craved. "Daddy wanted to be his own boss," wrote a woman whose family had come from the Pennsylvania coal-mining district. "Mother wanted freedom from the nightmare of knowing Daddy could be killed. . . . Then too she wanted with intense fervor to know her children were the equal of others and not suffer the stigma of a 'coal miner's brat!' In later years, I remember her saying that the price was not too great to pay."[88]

But there was a price, often a terrible price, that time could only soften, never erase. Mrs. John Cole shared with innumerable other pioneer mothers the painful experience of losing a child. In 1930 she visited the homestead in Ness County where she and her family had set up housekeeping in 1878. "Oh the memories that came rushing and crowding into our minds of the days and hours spent in that sacred place. Surely every one of those remaining stones were precious in my sight." They found only a mound where their house had been with a little of the magnesia limestone they had used to shore it up and some pieces of "that precious little cupboard" where Mrs. Cole had kept her store-bought cooking utensils. But seeing the remains of the house was not enough. Off they walked, round and round, looking for another mound—a small grave where they had buried one of their children in those difficult years. Time, however, had done its work and there was no sign of it—nothing to mark that amid the activities of that hopeful homestead, a life had flickered briefly and been swallowed without a trace.[89]

Chapter Thirteen

Abide With Me

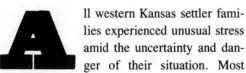ll western Kansas settler families experienced unusual stress amid the uncertainty and danger of their situation. Most were able to suppress the mental anguish so that its only outward effect was an occasional blue day. Some, however, were not. Their ravings and their crimes against themselves and others, along with untimely deaths of the weak and the young from disease, isolation, or the elements, were unwelcome reminders that paradise was not there for the taking. The sad events that symbolized failure and defeat therefore created a special intensity of community emotion and response. It was almost as though some corporate liturgy were required to exorcise the evil that seemed sometimes so near and to reassure those returning to work that the worst of it was unfortunate accident, not inevitable design. Gathered at funerals under the large, bright sky, they often offered the hymn "Abide With Me" to the howling wind, for there were things that could neither be comprehended nor borne by humankind alone.

In October 1879, the Barton County commissioners were called upon by settlers to investigate the situation at the dugout home of a family named Baumer (or Broomer). The wife had become ill some six weeks earlier and, because the husband would do nothing for her, the neighbors had tried to bring in food, only to be cursed by the man and told he did not want any "God damn Yankees" in his house. When the commissioners finally did enter the dugout, they were overwhelmed by a foul smell. The emaciated woman told them she had been bedfast for six weeks, could not help herself, and could not convince her husband to feed her. She begged the public officials not to leave her alone as she feared her husband would kill her. Despite new curses from the husband against "intermeddling Americans," the commissioners decided to take her to a neighbor. When they tried to lift the woman from the couch, however, they were horrified to find that she had lain for five weeks in her own excrement and that the flesh on her buttocks and hips was in an advanced stage of decay. Two days later she died. All the community could do was to arrest the man whose behavior was such a threat to its image of itself. "Great God!" wrote the *Register* reporter. "Do we live in a civilized country, and yet harbor wretches worse than barbarians?"[1]

Apparently so. Or maybe it was better to believe that they were barbarians when they arrived than to conclude that the difficulties of prairie living had either created or escalated their mental illness. In July 1874 near Bull City (now Alton) in Osborne County, a merchant named Charles Cook killed his sleeping baby, tried to kill his wife, and then committed suicide by striking himself in the head with a hatchet.[2] In June 1883, Louis Vulliet, a Swiss living in the eastern part of Hodgeman County, began attacking his neighbors, who bound him and dispatched him to the state insane asylum.[3] In 1885 a woman was found wandering in the sand hills near Larned in "pitiable condition." She said she had lost her dog and baby in the hills. No trace of either could be found, and she was judged insane and sent to the asylum.[4] In February 1886 a twenty-year-old woman was murdered by her husband, one Charles A. Fellows, near Cleveland (now Oakley). After he had shot her once, she got down on her knees and begged him not to shoot again. He then fired three more times until she fell at his feet. Fellows told townspeople he was drunk at the time and remembered nothing. His father, however, a devout Christian and a postmaster in Ohio, was broken up over the incident and wrote his apologies for his boy to western Kansas.[5] The same year Sam Purple, a stockman and farmer living seven miles east of Jetmore, the county seat of Hodgeman County, killed most of his family members one by one with a revolver and shotgun. Jetmore residents lynched him the next morning but not before Purple told them that his brother's spirit had come out of heaven and told him to do the deed. "I am Blendon the White Scout," he called to the assembled farmers as they threw the rope over the ridgepole of his sod house, "and I have killed my enemies. I am the man that jars the world." They stood him on a barrel and put the noose round his neck. "Oh, I wish that I could shake it."[6]

Pressures led to crimes against others more often than they resulted in self-destruction. However, the cause of suicide seems more often to have been romantic passion combined with Victorian moral sensibilities than weather or finances. A reading of newspaper accounts of western Kansas suicides leaves the strong impression that the vast majority of those who took this course were women and that the preferred method was strychnine.

Typical was an incident in Russell in March 1878. The night clerk of the Russell House Hotel heard noise in the room of a seventeen-year-old hired girl. He knocked and when there was no response went in to find the girl dead of strychnine poisoning. To her dress was pinned a note:

I do not want any one to open me to find out what is the matter of me, and for that reason I wrote to you. . . . I want a white shroud that looks decent, and that is enough. I want you to sing 'Sister, thou wast mild and lovely.' I want you to live so you can all go to heaven, and hope that I will reach that happy place, but I am afraid that I can't because I have committed suicide and shall have to be a murderer with the rest. Good bye forever. YOUR DEAR DAUGHTER.[7]

In July 1879 Anna Sayiz, a young Bohemian woman living south of Ellsworth, quaffed a deadly portion of strychnine because of a scandalous association with Frank Seckavic. Her sister, who had been Seckavic's wife, had taken her life the year before.[8] In November, Valiska Jacobs, a waitress at a Wilson hotel, was preparing to marry when her beau received a letter from a man claiming to be her former lover. Too proud to explain or defend herself from the groundless accusations by a disappointed suitor, she broke the engagement and "likewise her heart." Soon, after finishing her milking one afternoon, she put on her best clothes and drowned herself in the river.[9] In 1881, a woman in a wagon train, hearing that her husband was "flirting with the Amazons of Dodge City," shot and killed herself.[10] Hundreds of other such events are alluded to in the press with few details: Jacob Fowle hangs self; J. H. Hicks shoots self with .38-caliber Smith & Wesson; LaCrosse woman puts a shotgun in her mouth and blows the back of her head away.[11] Or they are almost casually mentioned in diaries. "Since we left New York state these things have happened here," wrote fourteen-year-old Bertie Canfield of Osborne County in 1880. "Samuel Sackett died in the spring; Mr. Twitchell moved to Nebraska and Mrs. Van Orter died; Helen Martin committed suicide by drowning."[12]

As surprisingly many as they were, however, the deaths by human agency in western Kansas were not numerous compared with those that resulted from the dangers of pioneering and carried away both weak and strong at random. Most primitive were those natural disasters so much more common in a virgin region than in one that had been modified by humankind. On the High Plains of Kansas these took the most symbolic of forms: water, fire, and ice.

Water should not be a threat in a desert, but it is often precisely in arid or semiarid regions, where unexpected and concentrated rains can create violent electrical effects and turn dry gullies and small creeks into torrents, that accidents with water occur. J. F. Nay of Phillips County was caught in a torrential storm that came up with little warning in the early 1870s. The next morning he found a Mr. Potts, his wife, and one child clinging to the upper branches of a large tree. Their wagon with all their belongings and three other children had washed down the Solomon River.[13] In June 1867 eight men were drowned at Fort Hays by a flood of Big Creek, and Libby Custer, among many others, found herself in a tree.[14] Those who were far from home faced dangers from cold and exposure. In April 1884, for example, Joe Foy, twelve years old, was sent out from his home near Garden City too look for some stray cattle and never returned. In the fall of 1885 his bones were found, and his parents identified the body by the patched boots on the feet. There were no marks of violence and the probability was that he got lost, drifted in the wind and cold rain, and died from exposure.[15]

Casualties from lightning were more common than from the rain itself, but the suddenness and violence of rainstorms were likewise at the root of these deaths. Lightning deaths had an additional diabolical element because of near complete inability to escape such a blow and the disfiguring consequences. A. H. Johnson, a manager for the Prairie Cattle Company, was riding near Cimarron Station west of Dodge in 1882 when he was struck by lightning. When his body was brought into Dodge on a caboose, a crowd gathered to see him: his hair was singed, his face and neck blackened, and his back and chest covered with blisters. His metal shirt buttons had melted, and his face was "much disfigured by discoloration and swelling."[16] More terrifying yet was the fate of a twelve-year-old adopted orphan boy in Ness County who was struck while carrying a metal bucket in each hand. The boy was charred beyond recognition by the voltage from the sky, and when neighbors tried to remove the bails of the buckets from his hands, the fingers all broke off at the joints and fell in pieces on the ground.[17]

Fire from the sky, however, was not as likely to threaten as fire from the land—the immense prairie fires that were a regional feature considerably more romantic to eastern readers than to those who might see one on the horizon bearing down on their home. A reporter with a penchant for color described in 1879 an experience that was common:

> The black mass grows blacker than ever, the rolls higher and higher, and you can scent the burning grass, and hear the distant roar of the fire—an awful roar resembling the sound of artillery in heavy timber. And it is so calm immediately about you that you do not so much as miss the ticking of your watch in your pocket; there is not breath of air stirring and the sun is shining, and the heavens above you are blue and placid. But the stillness will be broken soon. The oncoming cloud is only a few miles away now, and you easily trace the scarlet and terrific energy at its base; the smoke begins to hurt your eyes, too, and the heat becomes heavily oppressive. And then, all at once, the wind strikes and staggers you, that appalling roar deafens you, and the sun in blotted out, and you are in a darkness as of a midnight without moon or star.[18]

The fires could cover immense areas (one in 1884 damaged parts of seven western counties), use the time and energy of hundreds of settlers in trying to construct firebreaks, and result in numerous deaths.[19] Those who escaped were marked by the experience. Mrs. W. H. Gill cut up her precious Brussels carpet, brought from Iowa as her sod home's only symbol of civilization, and soaked the strips in water to try to slow a fire.[20] J. W. Chaffin fought the 1884 blaze by soaking rope in coal oil, setting it on fire, and dragging it behind his horse to try to burn a fireguard into the ground.[21] A. S. Kimball had no such sophisticated methods but knew when he looked up from the garden near his Pawnee County sod house in 1879 to see flames that he had to try something. "It came rushing down upon me, roaring, cracking, thundering!—on it flew with lightning speed like a devouring demon." Kimball got into a space in the shadow of his earth home to try to cool off and planned how to fight with two buckets of water and a long-handled dipper a conflagration he surmised only a "second adventist" would enjoy. He lost his crops and the trees that had provided for him a "sociability for one all alone," but he saved his house by fighting the fire for six hours with his hands and feet until they became bloody and sore. When it moved past him he ran to help his neighbor until "all charred and huffing like a horse" he was finally able to go to bed.[22] Sometimes, after a long night of fighting a fire, the blackened men of a community would gather and a minister would give thanks for what was spared.[23] After such a scrape with death from elemental force, Kimball could only comment, "God lives."[24]

As harrowing as was trial by fire, suffering by ice and snow was worse. As with everything else natural in western Kansas, hail and snowstorms there tended to extremes. A Clark

Out of Control. Settlers fighting a prairie fire; illustration from Harper's Weekly,
28 February 1874.

County man living in a dugout described an 1888 hail when the bark was stripped from trees, the fields mown low, cattle stampeded, rabbits killed, and windowpanes shattered on the north and east sides of all buildings. The man was not amused when his dog sat in the middle of the floor and howled "while those hailstones pounded on the roof and door as if someone with an ax [were] trying to beat an entrance."[25] More common and more devastating were blizzards, which in the 1880s became as identified nationally as a terror of western Kansas as grasshoppers had been in the 1870s. The most cruel was the unprecedented series of storms characterized by twenty-degree-below-zero temperatures and steady winds at near fifty miles per hour, collectively known as the "Blizzard of '86." But there were other snow emergencies nearly as dangerous; they came as a special shock because early promotion had emphasized the mild, clear winters that did indeed occur in some years. During the 1886 storm, a man was found in the southwest part of Kansas frozen to death. He had on linen pants, a nankeen coat, gaiters, a chip hat, and a linen duster for an overcoat. In his pocketbook was a flyer, "Ye people of the frozen north," it went, "why will you continue to shiver in the boreal blasts of a country where the icy chains of winter fetter the step of spring. . . . Come to Kansas, the Italy of America, whose skies are as calm as a painter's canvas and where hoary winter has yielded permanent possession to laughing spring.'' The Hays City paper commented: ''Had he struck this portion of the state he would have pulled through.''[26]

On 7 January 1875, after eight days in camp waiting out a snowstorm, S. S. Van Sickel and three other hunters started out along the plain of the Cimarron River some forty miles south of Dodge City under a cloudless sky. After a fifteen-mile day, they camped. All was quiet until midnight when Van Sickel was awakened by a companion crying, ''I am smothering. I am smothering. I shall freeze. I shall freeze.'' A gale was blowing and snow had covered the mess box and buffalo-hide shelters the men had made, trapping them. Unable to escape they yelled at each other all that night and the next day, the conversation turning in the day to the disposition of their property. On the second night the groans stopped and only Van Sickel, who managed to push out a small air passage, lived.[27]

One Christmas, a brother and sister holding down claims west of Ness City were preparing their sod house for a visit from their parents, coming from the East to spend the holidays.

Prairie Zephyr. The difficulties of strong winds; illustration from Harper's Weekly, *30 May 1874.*

The sister, however, got pneumonia in the middle of a snowstorm when help was unavailable. The next day a neighbor came to stay with the dead girl while the brother went to town to wait for the parents. For three days she preserved the body, carrying it outdoors at night to keep it frozen "and thus gave the father and mother an opportunity to gaze upon the form of that loved one ere it was laid away."[28]

What the fire of 1884 was to prairie blazes, the blizzard of 1886 was to snowstorms. The howling ice and snowstorm lasting forty hours on 6 and 7 January was probably the worst for most places, but conditions were bad enough to stop trains and strand passengers in western Kansas for the better part of two months.[29] Storms in 1871, 1875, 1878, and 1883 had been nearly as severe at times, and Elam Bartholomew recorded a low of minus thirty-one degrees and thirteen days of below-zero temperatures in 1885.[30] But no previous winter was as bad or as long as that in 1886 or had its deadly combination of heavy snow, extremely cold temperatures, and high winds. Snowdrifts of twenty feet were reported all over the region as new snowfalls piled on unmelted old and were blown about by winds which, when accompanied by icy snow, made walking in the horizontal fury a painful experience. The weather station at Dodge City hoisted the cold-wave signal flag on 1 January 1886 and left it flying for over a week of constant storm. The first siege lasted three days there, from noon of the first to 7 P.M. on the third, dropped 7½ inches of snow, and brought temperatures of twelve above zero with a steady wind of 37–39 miles per hour from the north. The storm beginning on midnight of the sixth was worse. Although only two inches of new snow fell, the average temperature at Dodge during the storm's forty-hour duration was eleven below, and it dropped to as low as sixteen below. Winds, meanwhile, raged at 44 miles per hour, moving a total of 888 cold miles from 11 P.M. of the sixth to 7 P.M. of the eighth and cutting residents with an incredible windchill.[31] Victor Murdock of the *Wichita Eagle* called the 1886 blizzard, or blizzards, "the most perilous experience prairie people ever encountered."[32]

Stories of effects on humans became nearly legendary. Western Kansas editors were quick to point out that there had been "only" sixteen documented human snow deaths in central western Kansas during January, rather than the one hundred reported by the Associated Press and that the figure for cattle loss was closer to twenty-five thousand than to the one hundred thousand widely reported. Still, the cattle were about 20 percent of the entire western Kansas stock, and the human cost, even in its least embellished version, is an incredible litany of pain.[33]

Some incidents could be laughed about later. Late in January a crew of 300 men had just gotten the Santa Fe passenger train dug out of a cut when another storm buried it again. It was there for a total of 121 hours, and local photographers made a good living selling views of the scene to stranded passengers.[34] Dr. William Workman of Ashland packed an unconscious man in snow in the hotel bathtub to thaw him out.[35] Harrie Jennison's mother, alone in Lane County with six children, went after the family cow tethered 100 yards from the house. She made it to the cow after several failed tries but could not find her way back. She then tied her shawl to the animal and released it. It went straight into the house, and the family and the cow waited out the storm there together.[36] Less welcome was a range steer drifting with the storm which, "eyes and nostrils covered with ice, burst through the window and fell into the kitchen" of the Walker residence in the same county. The man of the house skinned the animal on the spot, put the wet hide over the break in the sod wall, and cooked the family fresh steaks.[37] E. E. Frizell remembered crawling along the side of the house into the lashing storm to try to reach a pile of coal and his brothers trying to get to the barn along a clothesline, with instructions to fire a shot if they could not return to the house. On clear days the children sledded seventy-five yards down a drift with the top of a thirty-five foot high cottonwood tree sticking out of it.[38] A boy at Beeler, Frank Houghton, decided to see if his tongue would stick to a steel girder. It did. His mother had to heat water to free him.[39]

A number of the stories with more tragic endings turned upon the isolation of settlers and the lack of any means of communication between dwellings short of the personal appearance the blizzard made hazardous. Doubtless the brothers E. T. and W. T. Hayter and their companion Robert Wade, who were in Dodge City shopping for provisions when the 6 January storm struck, might have simply telephoned their families at the Eureka Irrigating Canal Company camp five miles west of town had a telephone been available. Instead, they set out on foot. Wade reached a house but was too frozen to ask for help, and the brothers died. "The men who perished in the snow," the local paper said, "were anxious about their families and hastened to join them; but death and separation under such distressing circumstances must be extremely painful and heartrending."[40]

Similarly, had there been a telephone Eliza and Mahaley Boucher and their mother might have called a brother a half-mile away rather than setting out for his house through the same blizzard as it affected Clark County. The mother was found and revived but died a month later from the shock of amputations. Both girls froze to death, Mahaley in the yard of her brother's house within an arm's length of the door. "Her hands were tangled in her hair," wrote a relative, "showing she had died a terrible death, no doubt thinking she was lost."[41] Lack of communication and a feeling of responsibility also led an Ellis County teacher, snowed in with her students on the night of 16 November 1886, to lead them in the Lord's Prayer, supervise a dinner from lunch boxes, and then start out to get help. Several days later, when the drifts had diminished, the teacher was found, her red shawl covered with ice, "her rigid face buried in two frozen hands."[42]

What, though, of the most famous Kansas weather threat of all, the tornado? It was present also, destroying towns with some regularity and leading homesteaders to hide underground when they saw funnels approaching.[43] But in some ways the tornado was less of a danger then than now, as these furious winds tend to skip down out of the clouds for brief periods and do the most appalling damage where property and population are concentrated. Also, ironically, western Kansas had so many greater threats to face that tornadoes were well down the list among things likely to kill or maim.

Actually, many seemingly insignificant aspects of living on the prairie were as dangerous as tornadoes, particularly to children, for whom none of the paraphernalia of civilizing the prairie was designed.

Guns, for instance. Very young boys hunted unsupervised and had frequent, sometimes fatal, accidents. A twelve-year-old shot himself in 1877 while hunting muskrats in Rush County. He had been tired and had grabbed the muzzle of the gun to aid him in scrambling up a bank. Two days later his wounds reopened, and he bled to death.[44] At Vernon in Ness County in October 1879, W. H. Dewey was cleaning a revolver when Willie Musselman, eight, and his sister Mollie, five, came to the door of his store. The gun discharged: Willie was injured and Millie killed.[45] In April 1887 twelve-year-old Adolphus McFessell, living near Larned, shot his three-year-old stepbrother, and then, in anguish at the result, shot himself.[46]

Or machinery. A man mowing grain in Phillips County in 1877 spotted a curly head before him. Unable to bring his sixteen-hundred-pound team to a stop, he raised the sickle and saw it pass over his daughter, cutting her toe badly. A doctor was called and, as her brother with horror remembered it, simply clipped off the damaged member "and threw it out in the yard and the writer saw a big red rooster gobble it up."[47] A boy helping his father move the Presbyterian Church building at WaKeeney in 1879 was severely injured when a rope broke and a bar hit him in the head.[48] A six-year-old died in 1878 while playing at the grain elevator in Russell. He had been told by another boy to go up and jar the wheat loose. Not knowing he was there, the owner opened the chute and the child smothered.[49] The greatest danger of all was trains, a great attraction to children, who ignored local ordinances against playing at the depot and chasing after engines. Accounts of

deaths and cripplings of children by trains abound, and the moral lesson the editors managed at each telling of a new tragedy helped but little.[50]

Danger could come, when far enough from neighbors or medical care, from even the most innocuous of farm elements. Runaway teams of horses killed children sitting in wagons.[51] Boys fell off horses they were trying to break.[52] Children were hooked by bad-tempered oxen.[53] Well-digging killed older boys, while falling into wells was the death of younger girls.[54] Chip stoves caused burns, and scrub water scalded. The two-year-old daughter of N. H. Stidger was sitting in a chair in December 1881 while her mother scrubbed the floor. She ran after her parent, upset a pan of boiling water and, confused when some splashed on her, fell backward into the bucket. The funeral was two days later. "She was a sweet little cherub," said the paper, "and the bereaved parents have the sincere sympathy of the entire community."[55]

It might be nothing more unusual at first than a child wandering away and becoming lost—usually a minor problem in a suburb but a major one on the prairie. On Christmas Eve 1890 Bessie Barker, three years old, clutched her rag doll and started from a neighbor's sod house toward home. One of the boys there had told her, falsely, that her mother was no longer inside but had left. When Bessie was missed she was out of sight, and a community search over the next two days in the vicinity of Laird in Ness County failed to find her. T. P. Levan could not sleep at night thinking of that child out in the cold and spent hours on his hands and knees in the dark looking for some trace. Finally he discovered tracks near a creek where she had fallen in and found her doll where she had slept one night. Approaching an abandoned house, he saw the print of her wet body on the door and then, as he was about to leave, a shoe extending from under the porch.

I looked under the steps and there laid little Bessie. My heart went to my throat. Friends, you can't imagine the shock that came over me. I tried to pick her up but found that her face was frozen to the ground. I sat down on the steps and wept like a child and the tears again come to my eyes as I write this article [1929]. After I recovered from the shock I took my pocket knife and dug the dirt away from her face until I could lift her. The sun was just rising as I picked her up and started to tenderly carry her to my house. . . . It was a mighty sad trip. Her little body was frozen like a chunk of ice and was all out of shape so it took us a long time to thaw out the body and make her look like Bessie.[56]

The most likely cause of all for suffering and death, however, was not crime or weather or accident but disease. The greatest terrors to the pioneers were lung fever (pneumonia), inflammation of the bowels (appendicitis), diphtheria, cholera, spinal meningitis, scarlet fever, and even the flu when the fever had to be borne so far from effective medicine or aid that they might as well not have existed. If parents were taken ill, they could regard it as part of the risk of an adventure freely chosen, but when children were stricken there was guilt that the innocent should suffer to support dreams that were not their own.

The death of a child on the Plains, with no reassurances from doctors, no muting of the experience by hospitals, no immediate comfort from friends or ministers, could be more devastating than any other single challenge of settler life. Rosie Ise had too much milk for her infant son Albert and her breasts hurt. Using a folk remedy involving live steam scalded her nipples and, no formula being available, her child got dysentery, then constipation, and finally cholera infantum. Rosie watched him convulse and cursed the wind that would not allow her even to concentrate on how to help. When he at last lay dead, she could only hug the body to herself, rock back and forth, and say "Oh, my poor little boy, oh my poor little boy."[57] Mrs. Mary Northway lost a two-year-old without even getting a diagnosis, though she thought it was pneumonia. "It was so pitiful to see the little one waste away day by day and suffer so with no medical assistance to be had."[58]

Probably the most wrenching account surviving of the death of a western Kansas child is Elam Bartholomew's characteristically detailed diary entry written within hours of the death of his infant son Hubert on 15 January 1887:

Our dear little boy having failed very rapidly during the past two days and having obtained no rest last night nor relief from the medicines administered, the time was passed as on previous days until the middle of the afternoon, when it became evident that the hour of dissolution was near at hand and as the death dews began to gather on his pallid little brow, I took him from the arms of Mrs. O. P. Coy who had been holding him, and sitting down in the rocking chair held him tenderly until about

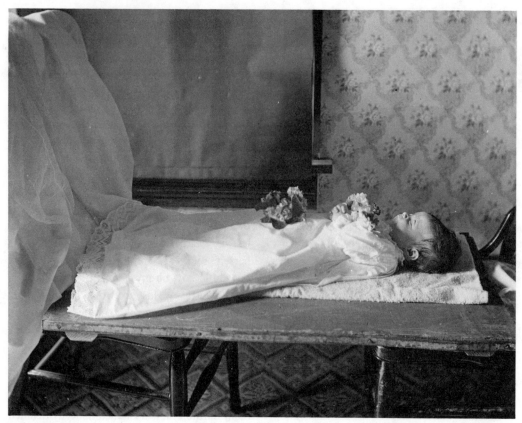

Baby's Gone.

---

half past three o'clock when the dreaded summons came from the dark angel and with a light struggle his spirit, embers from his birth, and made while in the blood of the Lamb, took its flight, and went to mingle with the angelic hosts beyond the river, in the boundless ocean of God's love.[59]

Bartholomew's religious interpretation was typical of the way families tried to deal with such losses. Alice Stormont on the night of her two-year-old sister's death in 1886 heard a rustling overhead and said it was the angel coming after Judy, whom she loved so well because as the next oldest sister she had most of the care of her. She wrote a poem about her dead sister and kept it in a box with other keepsakes for several years.[60] The Northway family curtained off a corner of the dugout and, unable to get a casket in Osborne, laid out their child in a pine box lined with "white goods."

"We read a chapter in the Bible . . . and then the little one was taken out and buried in a nook in the creek, there to rest until our Savior shall come to claim His own."[61] Mrs. Canfield of Osborne County visited her only son's prairie grave in August 1882 and recalled a dream she had had in which her son had beckoned to her from across a stream. She took it as a sign she would die soon but wrote that "if my little girls are left motherless, the Lord will be both father and mother to them."[62] "Dear mother-heart," went a poem called "Baby's Gone" printed in memory of a dead Ness County infant,

> "this sorrow deep
> Perhaps to you was given
> As one more link to bind you
> Closer to God and Heaven.
>
> For far above this dreamless sleep
> Safe in Christ's upper fold
> Your baby's feet securely rest
> From winter's chill or cold.
>
> And when the still small voice
> Calls from the other shore
> You'll clasp again your baby boy
> And meet to part no more."[63]

Still, neither religious comfort nor the "earnest sympathy" of friends could quite compensate James and Jennie Minnis of Barton County, who in 1878 lost their fourth child in as many years.[64] "Those who have never lost a child," wrote the editor of the *Larned Chronoscope* in 1879, "are unable to understand how great a void the death of one darling baby can make."[65] A woman talking to a *Scribners* reporter the same year said she had learned to live with the loss of her baby, though at first she noticed that "the grave was so little and pitiful and the prairie widened out from it so far; I hadn't mistrusted before how big the prairie was." Time helped her feel that the death had in a way made the site her home. Still, she was always glad "when the grass comes in spring to cover up the grave and make it look less like it did that winter day of the burying."[66]

All the talk about comfort found in death and the prospects of heaven backfired for the family of six-year-old Willie Sams, who after attending the funeral of a child near Wilson in July 1885, killed his infant brother with a stick and buried him with appropriate ceremony on a river bank. He told his mother about it with great pride. After all, if heaven were so wonderful, anyone should prefer being there to continuing to live in western Kansas.[67]

Chapter Fourteen

Dam the Draws

L ike the grasshopper plague of 1874 and the drought of 1880, the western economic boom-and-bust cycle of the 1880s has received little scholarly attention as a regional phenomenon with national importance. In the case of the former events, there may be justification for that neglect in their scattered impact, short duration, and limited economic result; no such conclusions are possible with the boom. It *was* without question regionally based in the western United States and was complex and variable in its timing, degree of effect, and causations. But the western boom-and-bust cycle of the 1880s was widely recognized at the time as a major outlet for investors' funds nationally in its up phase and, in its down phase, as a significant factor contributing to the national depression of 1893. In a June 1887 Bradstreet's survey of the volume of real-estate transactions in American cities, Kansas City ranked second (next to New York City), Wichita third, and Topeka tenth. Population increase for 1887 was 30 percent in New York City and 500 percent in Wichita, the fastest-growing city in the nation at the time.[1] Further research into this boom should, at the very least, lead to important qualifications to Joseph Schumpeter's classic analysis of business cycles, in which the mid-1880s appears as a trough.[2]

Some broad trends applicable to the West in the 1880s and contributing to the boom can be easily isolated. Most fundamental, the decade was the time of the true filling of that region with settlers, and it happened so quickly that by 1890 the census office could declare the American frontier closed. Western Kansas was not unusual in achieving a more rapid growth rate in this period than in any other in its history and doing a land-office business all the while. The 1880s were generally wet years in the West (though to say so is a great simplification), and it was the decade when the initial stimulus of the building of trunk railroad lines in the 1860s and 1870s was followed by infilling with constructed and projected lines to connect nearly every point in the West with every other. Each railroad charter created speculative possibilities for counties, town, industries, and land speculators along its route. Everywhere, also, was the excessive boomer rhetoric, which must be assessed as a contribution to boom psychology rather than dismissed as Victorian fluff.

The magnitude of possible gain combined with the uncertainties of the precise eventual level of achievement to create the high risk, great opportunity, and desperate need for credit characteristic of most "bubbles" in economic history. Investors saw in the West a tempting array of vehicles for appreciation, from cattle herds to town lots, and with attention focused on the region during the great emigration, it became as faddish to direct funds there as to the sun belt of a century later. "It seems," wrote Kansas Senator John Ingalls, "as if the great column of migration, in its western march across the continent, had paused upon these tranquil plains to accomplish the triumph and marvel of civilization."[3]

The difficulty in placing this boom and bust in its proper place historically, however, is the complexity of analyzing it as a single phenomenon. There is evidence that the boom did not have uniform causes over a wide area but rather created similar economic effects in different western subregions through various combinations of national, regional, and local factors. Its manifestations in the Pacific Northwest, southern California, and eastern Kansas were, for example, heavily urban, while in the Dakotas, Nebraska, and western Kansas the mix depended far more on rural factors.[4] In one place town-lot speculation loomed especially large, in another lumbering, in another mining, in another the possibilities for irrigation, a sorghum-sugar industry, or wealth in range cattle. Subregional variation also, as has been suggested in the discussion of the 1880 drought, led to different dates for boom and bust: wet years in the Dakotas in the early 1880s and drought in the mid-1880s insured, despite all other factors, that the boom and bust years there were the reverse of those in western Kansas. Naturally, also, different individuals with different styles, strengths, and weaknesses assumed leadership roles in each geographic area and were important to the way the boom unfolded and died there.

Thus does a general description become more and more difficult and building up regional accounts appear more and more important. Rendigs Fels, who in his *American Business Cycles 1865–1897* (1959) added more subtlety to Schumpeter's analysis, confessed that just as American cycles were found to be different from European, there might be regional variations within America as well. As he put it, "Business cycles are so complex and disorderly—i.e., the regularities are so undependable—that it is an exceedingly difficult field in which to make progress."[5] Charles Gates, who made an early and as yet unsurpassed attempt to analyze the specific western American boom of the 1880s as a whole, noted that there was no agreement about it: "Was a boom a local circumstance, to be observed and recorded as taking place uniquely in Washington or Michigan or Kansas? Or was it only a local manifestation of the upswing of a general business cycle? Was it a youthful distemper which occurred but once, conferring immunity thereafter, or was it a recurring surge of economic vitality, which periodically carried a regional economy to successively higher levels?" Gates believed that one could conclude only that there was a transition time for the West, the 1880s, when it was losing its frontier status and becoming integrated with the rest of the country. This time was one of rapid growth and unique opportunities. However, the boom, he thought, could not be reduced to a single formula but must be carefully studied in its regional manifestations before a sophisticated and complex synthesis might be possible.[6] To analyze it in western Kansas, therefore, is to add a piece to a fascinating historical puzzle.

The boom-and-bust cycle in western Kansas was, as it must have been elsewhere, caused by a combination of local, regional, and national factors. Probably none of these was unique to the area, but the combination and the strength of each, and therefore the flavor of the boom, was unique. Town-lot speculation, for example, was inescapable in any version of a boom but was much less prominent in western Kansas than in the Northwest or even in eastern Kansas. There were claims that Garden City, Liberal, Kinsley, and Dodge City might outdistance such cities in the antiquated eastern region as Chicago and Philadelphia, but the most enthusiastic publicists there freely admitted that the growth of their neighbor Wichita was unapproachable. But while the western Kansas boom might not result in the metropolitan areas that were blossoming in southern California, there were possibilities for the region that made it competitive with any other for the dollars of people whose eyes were focused on the trans-Mississippi West.

Two of the earliest of these, the development of a profitable range-stock industry and experimentation with irrigation based on river and stream diversion through canals, were examples of adaptation to a subhumid environment. In their first form early in the decade, these businesses did not represent unrealistic dreams for sale to eastern speculators but practical responses to the conclusion many drew from the 1880 drought that it had finally been proved, after over a decade of settlement, that western Kansas could never support extensive unaided agriculture. Ironically, the financial promise of these attempts to utilize what the natural environment provided to support a small population attracted a larger population for whom these mechanisms were neither adequate nor appropriate.

Given the flight of grangers in the wake of the drought and experience with cowboys and trail herds in the Texas drives, large-scale stock raising was a natural for western Kansas. Facilities for marketing cattle existed to serve the Texas longhorn trade, which thrived at Dodge City at a 300,000-head-a-year clip until a state-ordered quarantine on the driving of southern cattle into a land filling with farmers stopped it late in 1884. Chicago prices for cattle rose until 1882, when they were at their highest since 1870.[7] Ranchers could start inexpensively by purchasing longhorn calves at Dodge and then upbreed using Durhams, black Galloways, and Aberdeen Angus to create a herd for which the differential in cost and selling price was attractive.[8] Reports of cattlemen tripling their investment over two years from the sale of herds were common at the price maximum in 1882, and annual costs of maintaining cattle ranging freely over unclaimed public domain was only forty to seventy cents per head through the mid-1880s.[9] An 1878 broadside claimed that cattle and sheep in western Kansas could live on range grass 350 days a year and that there was "hardly a limit" either to the capacity of the range or the delight of the cultivated herdsmen's vagabond life. "The cattle business is SAFE AND PROFITABLE," wrote the publicist. "The cattle *grower* of western Kansas has the surest business under the sun. He rarely fails. Why should he, and how can he fail?"[10]

Indeed, such prospects resulted in the creation of some of the largest private businesses since the building of the trunk railway lines. George Grant has been mentioned. His success in Ellis County encouraged others. Thomas R. Clark, member of a mercantile firm in New York City, had twenty-four miles of fence containing 2,200 pounds of barbed wire in Ellis County. His herd of 800, including some Angus, was managed for him by agents.[11] The principals of Eldridge, Beach & Company, all from Norfolk, Connecticut, came to live on their 6,400-acre ranch in the southeast corner of Ellis County but admitted to knowing at the outset "about as much of western stock raising as the man in the lunar luminary."[12] It was simply an attractive investment. Likewise drawn by a good place for his money was Frank Rockefeller, brother of the Standard Oil president. Rockefeller bought a ranch in Comanche County in the late 1870s and through the 1880s worked with both cattle and Arabian horses from the commodious white ranch house headquarters of the firm of Wilson & Rockefeller.[13] Clarence D. Perry, developer of the Chicago suburb of Englewood, took his winnings from that speculation to Clark County, where in 1884 he purchased 10,000 acres and helped found Englewood, Kansas. Perry promoted irrigation and sugar manufacturing as well as cattle and sheep as panaceas for the western Kansas region and was even involved in advancing the unsuccessful Cattle King Railroad to serve the range country of southwest Kansas.[14] Henry Mudge was less interested in turning a profit than in spending his inheritance lavishly and living a good life in a free land. That too could be done on a Kansas ranch, as Mudge's almost legendary activities at his complex of stone ranch buildings in Hodgeman County attest.[15]

In the mid-1880s the contract books of the Santa Fe railroad began to show more large sales than previously. Most were to speculators for resale, but many were to cattle companies. In 1881, for example, a New York company, the New York & Western Cattle Company,

bought 10,000 acres of railroad and public lands southwest of Dodge City for a cattle operation. It had a capital stock of $250,000, and its plans merited a major article in the *New York Sun*.[16]

But the purchase of large tracts was expensive, even with large discounts given by railroads to corporate buyers, and fencing acreages of 2,000 to 5,000 could equal the cost of purchase.[17] Stock raisers therefore preferred, partly to upgrade herds and raise prices but mostly to pool cattle and make roundups over miles of unfenced public domain, to join together in organizations. An early stockmen's organization formed at Ellis in February 1878 included twenty-six ranchers owning 11,000 head. It divided the range into districts and arranged for community spring roundups.[18] At a similar meeting in April 1883, it was estimated that the capital represented, which had been $200,000 in 1878, was approximtely $50 million.[19] The Comanche Cattle Pool was formed in 1880 and controlled a range including most of Comanche County and parts of Barber County and the Cherokee Strip. It had its headquarters in Medicine Lodge and operated for five years with at times 26,000 head bearing twenty different brands.[20] The Smoky Hill Pool, formed in 1882 to organize grazing along a thirty-by-twelve-mile strip adjoining that stream, had 15,000 head by 1884 and required 150 men and 600 horses for its annual roundup.[21] The Pawnee Valley Stock Breeders' Association, headquartered at the buildings of old Fort Larned, had by 1882 a capital stock of $200,000 and specialized in registered shorthorn bulls, Clydesdale stallions, and sheep.[22] There were 80,000 sheep within twenty-five miles of Larned as early as 1880, and the local

Open Range. Cowboys of the Comanche Cattle Pool, 1884. This was probably taken at the annual round-up.

paper printed wool prices from the Boston market.[23] In 1883, sheep numbers for western Kansas were calculated at 2 million.[24] Stock interests even had their own newspaper, the *Kansas Cowboy,* printed first at Sidney in Ness County and then at Dodge City and supported by the Western Central Kansas Stock Association.[25]

Stock raising with the economies of the open-range grand scale and the Texas cattle trade were both, however, fundamentally incompatible with the population growth essential to the boom model. Farmers who disliked the effect splenic fever carried by longhorns had on their blooded stock, the effect rumbling herds had on their crops, or the effect transient cowboys had on the morals of their towns pushed for more and more comprehensive state-imposed "dead lines" banning the Texas trade from more settled regions. They lobbied locally for county herd-law ordinances requiring both trail drovers and area ranchers to control their stock or pay farmers damages. Both forms of legal restriction increased rapidly and became universal by the mid-1880s.

The Texas trade was the initial target. In 1877, Mennonite farmers captured Mike Dalton's trail herd between the dead line at the west boundary of Ellis County and the stockyards at Ellis five miles east of that boundary. The Mennonites got $800 for their trouble, and the trail boss had to pay a fine nearly equal to the value of the herd into a fund for the support of the Farmers' Protective Association.[26] "The Texas cattle trade and agriculture are in direct antagonism to each other," wrote the editor at Russell in 1875. Because there had to be a choice, it should be in favor of husbandry as that was "the one grand pursuit that develops the country . . . that lays the foundation for all other pursuits." More to the point, farmers were permanent and paid taxes.[27]

Restrictions on local open-range herding came simultaneously. There were debates between cattlemen and farmers about the necessity of herd laws, particularly in counties that seemed ill suited to agriculture. A rancher in Ness County complained in 1881 that "this county is too wet to be prosperous," having just enough rain to encourage farmers who ruined the cattle business.[28] A cattleman near Larned wrote in 1883 that "there has been enough money wasted in vacated buildings, and in savagely mutilating the virgin soil to no purpose, to fence every section of land in the country," put windmills on them, and stock them with cattle. Why try to raise wheat "in a climate where the Almighty has made the conditions impossible almost?"[29] The key

word was almost. Herd laws came everywhere. An attempt by cattlemen to gain title to large tracts cheaply by promoting a change to the homestead law allowing them to "cattlestead" up to 2,000 acres failed in 1884.[30]

The traditional explanation for the end of the investment boom in cattle has been three severe winters, with the difficult early months of 1886 at the center.[31] While it is true that Kansas ranchers lost as much as 40 percent of their stock during the storms of 1884 to 1887, the blizzards were only the *coup de grâce* to an industry already doomed by a changing settlement pattern and a renewed confidence that the environment could be manipulated. The great problem with the rancher was that his form of business was seen as holding back civilization. Wrote a Dodge City farmer in 1885: "The cowmen look upon us the same as the Indians do the white man, driving them off their hunting grounds."[32] A Ness City man who signed his letter "ONCE A COWBOY BUT NOW A FARMER" chimed in four years later, arguing that only an agricultural county could support churches, schools, and other essentials of civilization. If the herd law were repealed, these and the families that patronized them would disappear and in their place would be "nothing but cattle and a hankering after the almighty dollar."[33] The trend was clear even in Clark County, a region so suited to cattle that, after a ten-year experiment with wheat in the late 1880s and early 1890s, it would be returned almost entirely to open-range ranching for the next 100 years. "The granger is on the tear," wrote a Clark County resident in 1885 when the area was still mostly prairie. "If half the enthusiasm had prevailed amongst the Israelites Moses would have led them into the 'promised land' in forty days instead of forty years."[34]

More durable was irrigation. Like the cattle business, irrigation in its early form was a type of adaptation to an arid land, if not a desert, that Kansans of the late 1870s and early 1880s temporarily accepted as a given. Reporting on a small river-irrigation project begun at Garden City in 1880, a Dodge City man commented that gardens along the river were enough because "the drouth in two years has demonstrated the futility of making this an agricultural country." Modest goals were best. "We shall not talk any more about climatic changes, and so forth, but pursue the wisest and safest course under the circumstances; and when we shall adapt ourselves to these we shall become prosperous."[35]

Irrigation ideas took two forms. One model was a passive system of damming draws to create reservoirs that it was thought would provide for stock during dry seasons and perhaps increase rainfall and decrease the effect of hot winds on crops by raising the humidity. A second was an active design based on diverting rivers and streams into canals and laterals to water large gardens for the production of vegetables and fruits. These two approaches paralleled in a less sophisticated way the two moisture solutions that have dominated western Kansas agricultural development in the twentieth century: dry-land farming techniques and pump-driven irrigation from wells. The early methods had the advantage of not requiring widespread specialized knowledge or expensive, energy-using, sometimes unreliable technology. They did not employ nonrenewable resources, did not require massive federal aid, and had as sole disadvantages, critical as they turned out to be, inability to accommodate a large population and intensive cultivation of vast areas. Though it can be argued that the long-term fate of the twentieth-century successor solutions to the problem of transforming the desert to commercial use may yet be in doubt, it is no surprise that the early irrigation experiments, providing as they did a great initial improvement for a small investment, generated much enthusiasm.

Those advocating the damming of draws and creation of natural reservoirs tended to be more conservative about regional agricultural prospects than were the proponents of more expensive canal systems that would have to be built by corporations rather than individuals. H. R. Hilton in an 1880 speech before the Scientific Club at Topeka entitled "Effects of Civilization on the Climate and Rain Supply of Kansas" argued that western Kansas settlement would have to be more compact to have the effect on climate that had been so long advertised. Instead of scattering on homesteads, people should concentrate in towns, plant taller grass, protect the prairie from drying fires, intensively cultivate the soil, and create reservoirs to moisten the atmosphere.[36] The *Sterling Gazette* at the same time suggested that wind power could be utilized by individual farmers to fill these ponds with ground water.[37] More elaborate was a proposal that same year from William Manning of Hays to request federal aid to build 1,050 dams over the Plains states at a cost of nearly $3 million. "We have suffered from drouth, from potato bugs, from grasshoppers, every year since the county was settled, and are suffering, and will suffer from the above causes, until something is done to prevent it."[38]

Such schemes were bandied about for a long

time with the claim that even small ponds would "soften the hot winds" and "have a mellowing, fertilizing effect upon our atmosphere."[39] J. C. Hopper was still promoting this kind of thinking in Ness County in the 1920s.[40] However, this low-technology adaptive response was not attractive to nineteenth-century people once the rain started falling again, and it had too much of the dreamy rhetoric of the 1870s in it to appeal to the 1880s types who liked to feel they had been hardened by experience. W. J. Colvin of Dodge thought that "in these dry, hard times it is well to have something new to agitate the mind, and we might as well discuss the dam question as not; but I would prefer to discuss a subject of more practical importance."[41] A writer for the *Larned Chronoscope,* having waded through four columns of Manning's seemingly chimerical hopes for a federal reclamation system, put his reaction more simply. "It appears," he said, "that this part of the State has been damned enough already."[42]

Ditch irrigation began at least as early as 1873 when George Allman dammed the Smoky Hill River near Fort Wallace, constructed a mile-long irrigation ditch, and sold rich crops of vegetables to the soldiers.[43] Substantial activity of this type, however, waited for the next dry cycle at the end of the decade. In 1878, C. J. Jones and W. D. Fulton founded the town of Garden City along the Arkansas River in the southwest quarter of Kansas. The next year was so dry that the few who had gathered there decided to expand upon their millrace by digging crude ditches to garden plots in order to have something to show for their town's optimistic name. Jones, who over the next decade dominated Garden City's business leadership

and its canal companies, claimed that the formation of western Kansas' first irrigation company was his. However, the organization was perfected, financed, and initially promoted by Garden City general store owners G. W. Hollinger and Charles S. Landis. Their manager, Levi Wilkinson, and an associate, W. H. Armentrout, agreed to help, and Hollinger and Landis wrote letters to the Topeka papers to get backing. Their canal, four miles long, eight feet wide, and two feet deep, ran from a headgate four miles west of town to the edge of Garden City, cost $2,000, and was capable of watering only about one hundred acres.[44] It, however, began an irrigation experiment that was to be essential to western Kansas' greatest boom.

Over the decade of the 1880s more than four hundred miles of canals and ditches with a net worth of about $3 million were built in the Garden City area.[45] The name to reckon with was that of C. J. Jones. Jones became directly involved in promoting the Kansas Canal in 1880, the first to be financially backed by eastern capitalists. By 1882 its twenty miles of ditch, sold by Jones to raise capital for other projects, were operated by the Illionis Irrigating and Water Power Company. In 1880 also he promoted irrigation at Lakin, twenty-five miles west of Garden City, through the Minnehaha Ditch Company. This was sold to a group of Ohio men, renamed the Great Western Canal, and opened as a twenty-four mile stretch in 1884. Jones's most ambitious completed projects were the Great Eastern and the Amazon Canals. The Great Eastern was surveyed in July 1881 and benefited from an investment by Lawrence, Kansas, capitalists of $70,000 the first year. When it opened in 1884, it had forty

Charles Jesse Jones. The imaginative promoter of Garden City and a chief developer of the ditch irrigation system of western Kansas.

miles of ditches and in 1888 extended over 96 miles in Finney and Kearny Counties. The Amazon, constructed from 1887 to 1889 with the combined resources of Jones and A. T. Soule of Dodge City, was the largest canal ever constructed in Kansas and added 102 miles of main canal and 100 miles of laterals to an already impressive network centered at Garden City.[46]

These developments produced the earliest of the genuine boom rhetoric, genus 1880s, in western Kansas. In July 1882, a Garden City weekly, appropriately titled the *Irrigator,* surrounded news of the arrival of a colony of Presbyterians in their unorganized county (then known as Sequoyah) with some puffy prose:

What has transformed that once bleak
desert, Utah, from its former natural
barrenness and unproductiveness to the
garden spot of the entire country? Irrigation. What has placed the country between
Cairo and Alexandria, Egypt, in advance of
all European agricultural regions? Irrigation. And what, twenty years hence, will
place Garden City and Sequoyah County
upon the highest plane of agricultural
development of which it is possible to
conceive? Irrigation.[47]

At the state fair at Topeka in September, Clark E. Carr of Galesburg, Illinois, raised the rhetorical ante further. Carr was an investor in Garden City irrigation enterprises. He had been the first subscriber to the *Garden City Irrigator,* and a quotation from him about man's power to control rainfall was printed in every issue under its masthead.[48] Carr contended to his fair audience that with the western Kansas ditches,

"the valleys and basins of the Rocky mountains have been converted into a vast watering pot," and that "the Arkansas river is the spout, and the artificial ditches men have made the perforated nozzle." The Arkansas would give Garden City people all the advantages of the Nile without the disadvantage of flooding: "To form any conception of the wealth in store for the people who are to inhabit that region, one must study the history of ancient Egypt, of the Pharaohs, the Ptolemies, the Rameses, and the whole line of dynasties. The opulence and splendor which has continued for ages in the country watered by the Nile, is to be repeated in western Kansas."[49] The mistake made by settlers in the 1870s, wrote a Santa Fe land agent to the *Kansas Farmer* that same month, was to have ignored historical conversions of other deserts through irrigation. Correcting this error would lead "within less than a generation" to conversion of the western plains of Kansas "to abodes of the highest civilization, contributing by the hundreds of millions yearly to the national resources."[50]

These rhetorical flourishes drew crowds to Garden City to observe accomplishments that made the claims seem not entirey overblown. J. Simon showed his farm east of town to visitors in 1880. In that drought summer, Simon had good-looking crops of corn, potatoes, onions, cabbage, lettuce, and watermelons. He said that the value of his land had not been $500 before the ditch went through, though he would not take $2,000 for it now that it had water.[51] Tours in 1882 were told that H. W. Crow's forty acres produced 80-bushel-per-acre oats, selling at 60 cents a bushel. He raised 1,400 bushels of onions worth $1.50 a bushel on 3½ acres and 50,000 watermelons, which would sell for ten cents each, on 10 acres.[52] Visitors from Kinsley that year reported on Garden City area farms that produced 90-bushel-per-acre oats, 400-bushel-per-acre Irish potatoes, 600-bushel-per-acre sweet potatoes, and 4,000 cabbages per acre.[53] Similar reports filled the area press through the mid-1880s as reasonable rains kept supply and demand for irrigation water balanced. In 1884 C. P. Stafford, owner of 160 acres adjoining the Garden City townsite, harvested 40 acres of oats, 20 of wheat, 10 of barley, 7 of millet, 4 of potatoes, and a half-acre of sweet potatoes. He then published the financial results in detail, showing a total expense, including $100 (the largest single item) for water from the ditch company, of $564, leaving a single year's profit after sale of his crops of $1,190.45.[54] In 1886 a fifty-five-year-old man named Worrel farming west of Garden City had an income, including his cattle operation, of $8,000. Worrel said he had been all over the west half of the continent but had found "no place where a poor man can settle down and get rich on as little capital as right here in Western Kansas."[55]

Thanks to the efficient efforts of Garden City's Santa Fe land agent I. R. Holmes, canal building there was accompanied by brisk land sales and quick political evolution. The railroad first offered its lands around Garden City in March 1882, having concluded earlier that they were too close to worthless to merit the effort. In the first sixteen months of railroad land sales, over 100,000 acres were sold in the county at prices ranging from $2 to $12 an acre.[56] In November 1882 the Santa Fe's chief land officer A. S. Johnson reported the sale of a tract of twenty-one sections located south of

Lakin and in the region watered by the Great Western ditch to S. F. Covington, president of the Globe Insurance Company of Cincinnati. Covington paid $60,000.[57] Although Garden City was described by its own newspaper in 1882 as "shabby in appearance," it was incorporated early the next year.[58] In March 1883 came the creation of Finney County, the largest county in the state.[59] Garden City not only became the county seat but gained the more important distinction of being chosen the location of the latest new federal land office in western Kansas.[60] The ditches had brought about a rapid change from the first days of Garden City when Santa Fe trains would not stop there but, until the town founders deeded the company half the new townsite, required town residents to disembark six miles west of their homes.[61]

Next to Garden City, the place most influenced by canal building was Dodge City. There the role occupied by C. J. Jones in Garden City was taken by Asa T. Soule, who had made a fortune estimated at $5 million to $6 million in Rochester, New York, marketing a hop-bitters medicine and in 1883 was convinced by J. W. Gilbert of the Eureka Irrigating Canal Company of Dodge City to invest some of it in the West.[62] It was surely one of the great promotional coups of the decade, as it was estimated that by 1887 Soule had invested $2 million in Ford County.[63] He built a large house in Dodge; helped finance its streetcar system; owned several local business blocks, the bank, the electric light plant, and the water works; supported a local university; was involved in branch-railroad schemes to benefit the town; and even played a key role with his own town

Water to Spare. The weir used to divert water from the Arkansas River into the Eureka Canal, Ford County.

promotion in the county-seat war in adjoining Gray County.[64] For this one-man boom, irrigation was the initial attraction.

The Eureka Canal was surveyed in the fall of 1882, construction began in April 1884, and the main canal was complete from twelve miles above Dodge City at Ingalls to Kinsley in the spring of 1886.[65] The impact on the general economy of the area began long before water was available. Irrigation projects, according to one western Kansas visitor, produced in the communities where they centered "a feverish excitement, like to discovery of a gold mine or the striking of oil."[66] Things heated up further when construction began and the company created jobs and demand for tools and equip-

ment. A local editor reported in the spring of 1884 that the crew working on the Eureka Canal looked like a small army, as it had sixty horses and a number of New Era ditchers and needed to have twenty carloads of lumber on hand most of the time.[67] That fall 150 men were employed on the ditching and it was estimated the seventy-mile-long canal might cost close to a half-million dollars.[68] In May 1885 the construction gangs were four miles west of Dodge and pushing forward at two miles a week with the aid of five ditching machines pulled by twelve horses each. Along the way, company camps were established with deep wells (the latest was 96 feet) drilled by Chapman's hydraulic driller.[69] At the time of completion of the main canal, it was said Soule had invested about $750,000 in it and indirectly in the Dodge City and Ford County economy.[70] Perhaps at last there was a technique and financial backing sufficient to make a great change in the "wild, weary waste" Dodge Citians saw around them.[71]

Smaller projects abounded across the region. The Kinsley Irrigating and Water Power Company, though always "somewhat cramped financially" and hampered by the flooding of Coon Creek, added water power for manufacturing to irrigation.[72] The Pawnee Irrigation and Water Power Company undertook projects at Larned.[73] Hamilton County, at the far west end of the Arkansas River in Kansas, also had irrigation ditches, though development there was slowed by unfavorable geography. Completion of the system operated by the Alamo Irrigating and Manufacturing Company came in 1889, too late to allow its headquarters town of Syracuse full participation in the boom enhancement otherwise accompanying such events.[74]

Although irrigation in California, Utah, Colorado, and a few other western areas was more advanced than in Kansas during the 1880s, the western Kansas ditch experiments preceded the general western pursuit of the irrigation rage touched off by the first regional irrigation congress at Salt Lake City in 1891 and sustained by federal aid provided by the Newlands Reclamation Act of 1902.[75] Neighboring Nebraska, for example, had nothing like the extent of irrigation projects of Kansas before the 1890s, and Oklahoma was in the hands of the Indians.[76] Therefore, for people like Soule, who believed in the future of irrigation and saw opportunity for profit from the privately fi-

nanced development of it, western Kansas—arid enough to need irrigation but not so dry as to make relatively inexpensive ditch systems impossible, near sources of machinery, and served by railroads—was an especially attractive field for enterprise. While there were other reasons for the growth of Garden City from 378 to 8,000 people in less than ten years, irrigation was doubtless the most important.[77] And even where it did not benefit towns or counties directly, it created an atmosphere of promise. Irrigation, more than any other adaptive response to the 1880 drought, was a central element of the regional boom.

In hindsight more unrealistic than the cattle-raising and irrigation projects but equally an adaptive response to the drought of 1880 and equally important in beginning the boom was the idea of decentralized manufacturing. In the early 1880s it was not yet entirely obvious nationally that the trend toward industrial centralization in a few large cities would continue, and it was thought by some that occupation of the West would require that industries for processing that region's products be located nearer their sources. Western Kansans agreed and saw in this possibility an escape from exclusive dependence upon agriculture, freedom from the vagaries of distant markets, a savings in transportation cost, an invigorating introduction of machines and capital (which might expand to other objects) to their towns, and the creation of a more diverse and therefore more universally attractive society.

Many of the elements of decentralized industry that individual towns pushed could almost be guessed at: roller mills, creameries, cheese factories, broom factories, packing plants. Less predictable but most prominent among indus-

A New Egypt. Canal construction in Ford County in the mid-1880s. Race discrimination was laid aside when there was work to be done.

tries promoted beginning in 1880 as boom candidates was the sorghum sugar mill. Local factories to transform a new crop into a commodity that homesteaders found scarce and expensive had an attraction that created hopes far out of proportion to the modest accomplishments actual western Kansas companies showed.

The career of the initial western Kansas sugar operation, the Pioneer Sugar Mill begun by John Bennyworth at Larned in 1880, was typical. Bennyworth planted a section of land himself to early amber sorghum.[78] He saw to the incorporation of the Central Arkansas Valley Sorghum Sugar Association with a capital stock of $50,000 and a board of directors of Larned business and political leaders.[79] Farmers could get $10 worth of stock in the corpora-

tion for each acre of cane they planted and then be paid for the final crop in cash or in products of the plant.[80] Bennyworth ordered sugar-making machinery from Caldwell Brothers of New York and had a steam engine and accessories sent from Chicago and Kansas City.[81] The townspeople were fascinated to watch the heavy machinery for the $20,000 plant arrive at the depot and to see progress on the factory which, it was said, would be able to produce 10,000 pounds per day of sugar and molasses syrup and would employ seventy-five people.[82] Pawnee County's sorghum acreage in 1880 was 2,826, up from 141 acres two years earlier.[83] The Pioneer Sugar Factory, wrote Henry Inman, a director of the Association and editor of the *Larned Chronoscope,* "is attracting more attention than any one thing in Kansas."[84]

Things did not work out as advertised. The machinery did not arrive on time, and the plant, which should have been ready in August, did not start operating until early October. For a time, it was exciting, even operating on only one of two expected crushers. Twenty wagons hauled cane to the plant, three boilers steamed away, fifty men worked about the factory, and one hundred men worked cutting and hauling the crop. But just when the plant's Cuban overseer was ready to boast of success, an early frost killed about three-quarters of the sorghum crop and activity came to a halt.[85] Privately the operators admitted that there was a question whether the crusher method could make a high-quality sugar from sorghum (though molasses had been made from it in Nebraska since the 1860s) and whether the sorghum grown in western Kansas was the best sort. Even the molasses produced by the factory in 1880 was dark because there was not enough help to strip the leaves on the cane and it did not have a high sugar content. Also, the principals admitted that "the machinery is all new and so far away from any foundry that the least accident causes more or less delay."[86] The next year the Santa Fe Railroad loaned Bennyworth $4,000 to continue his mill, and Bennyworth himself, having been elected to the state legislature from Pawnee County, introduced a bill to give state sugar manufacturers (he was the only one) a premium of $100 for each 1,000 pounds manufactured and a subsidy of 10 percent of the cost of machinery up to $1,000.[87] The state subsidy bill failed, and the 1881 sorghum crop was so damaged by chinch bugs and drought that Bennyworth shut down his mill in September after only a few trial runs and sold the cane he had contracted for to stockmen.[88] A man

who visited Larned that first promising year was much saddened just a couple of years later when he saw only rusting machinery at Bennyworth's deserted sugar house "and some barrels of something that looked like petrified rosin."[89]

So exciting was the prospect of such an industry, however, that the region's sugar promoters pushed on. John H. Edwards offered to back a sugar mill in Ellis in 1880 and convinced some skeptical farmers. "If recognized capital is to be squarely interested . . . we can see our way clear," said an editor. "Capital is the big thing."[90] A Hays City man expressed the opinion in 1881, when J. B. Eldridge of Norfolk, Connecticut, visited there to invest in cattle, that people should "victimize him" to put some money in a sugar mill.[91] There was talk in 1881 of a mill in Ness County and one at Ellsworth, the latter to be financed by L. Squire & Brothers of Buffalo, New York.[92] Garden City received offers to build sugar mills in 1882 from both J. Harrison Clark of the Hutchinson Sugar Refinery and Bennyworth himself.[93] In 1882 J. B. Brinkman began extracting sugar on a small scale at Dundee near Great Bend.[94] Kinsley organized a company with $10,000 in capital stock in 1881 and in 1883 had a plant operated by Bennyworth and using some machinery moved from Larned.[95] The town of Sterling in Rice County began agitating for a mill in 1881. In 1883 the Kansas Sugar Works there, backed by capitalists from Illinois and Massachusetts, went into production. Its plant cost $45,000, used a new patented process, paid a $500-per-week payroll, and was powered by 350-horsepower steam boilers.[96] Still, it was able to make only thirty-five pounds of sugar per ton of sorghum. This was only

Dreaming Onward. Finney County Fair, heavy with windmill promotion, 1895.

marginally better than the twenty pounds per ton Bennyworth had made and far from commercially attractive.[97]

But there was hope—hope for improvements in the roller process of extraction, hope for better crops, hope for a state subsidy, hope to attract eastern capital. And upon hope, booms thrived. W. L. Parkinson established a sugar mill at Ottawa in eastern Kansas in 1884 and in a crisis went to Washington to seek federal aid. With the help of Kansas Senator Preston Plumb, Parkinson got a $50,000 appropriation in 1884 for solving the technical problems of the sorghum-sugar industry through the introduction of a diffusion process involving heating the sorghum in vats. The same amount came

from Washington in 1885. Still, Parkinson's results at Ottawa were a disaster. He moved his operation to Fort Scott, and Congress in 1886 appropriated $90,000 for study of sugar technology in Louisiana, New Jersey, and Kansas. The next year, against opposition from the secretary of agriculture, Senator Plumb managed to have $20,000 appropriated directly to Parkinson's experiments at Fort Scott.[98] The Kansas legislature that year passed ''An Act to Encourage the Manufacture of Sugar,'' which over the next several years paid a subsidy of two cents a pound on products that were at least 90 percent crystallized sugar made from sorghum cane grown in Kansas.[99]

If problems could be solved, demand was

surely there. It was estimated in the late 1880s that Kansas consumption of sugar was 84 million pounds a year, purchased at a cost of $5 million. Were all this to be provided by Kansas plants, it could keep fifty-six large mills going and fifty-six Kansas towns thriving.[100] Perhaps it would never equal the vision of the Larned newspaper editor who in 1881 imagined "two large lakes of sorghum molasses in this county, on each side of the Arkansas, with trees on the banks that grow fritters, so the hungry population can crowd around with sharp sticks, and gobble up the sweetness," but there continued to be reason to believe that sugar mills could have a major impact in the western half of Kansas.[101]

The three solutions born of desperation in the 1880 drought—range cattle, irrigation, and sugar manufacture—were important factors in spawning a boom that again encouraged western Kansans, as the rain increased, to forget the lessons of adaptation some thought were once and for all learned. A careful observer would have seen that all of these plans for renewed economic development were flawed as supports for the great population influx they were partly responsible for and that boomers' hopes for them took insufficient cognizance of the semi-arid and unpredictable climate of western Kansas. However, when local ripples from these new beginnings joined in the mid-1880s the national tide of western boom to create pandemonium about western Kansas land-office statistics, census figures, and railroad bonds, the wave was irresistible. It seemed that something limitless had at last arrived, and the only question was how best to dam the draws so that it would not once again escape.

Chapter Fifteen

Ties That Bind

The boom that activity in cattle, irrigation, and sugar mills set off, substantial renewed interest in expanding the western Kansas railroad system seemed to confirm. It was no accident that the period of the greatest expansion of railroad mileage for the nineteenth-century United States was in the 1880s when many western areas were filling and it appeared there would be traffic for numerous trunk and feeder lines. The statistics of railroad building in the decade indicate a heavy concentration in the western region, where the average miles per year built increased from 2,728 in the 1870s to 4,297 in the 1880s.[1] The contrast in Kansas, where railroad building in the 1880s equaled that of any other state, was greater than this average. Kansas led the nation in the mid-1880s in miles of railroad built per capita, and, considering that nearly all this mileage was in the relatively sparsely settled western part of the state, it can be seen that the booming impact of railroad building there, its speculative potential one might say, was far more intense than at any other place in the country.[2] For the study of the way in which railroad construction and promotion contributed to the western-based national boom of the 1880s, a western Kansas focus is therefore uniquely appropriate. The size of investment there and in the rest of the Great Plains by American rail corporations in the 1880s is one reason to suggest that in its spectacular rise and its fall just preceding the depression of 1893, the boom as a whole was a case in which the regional tail may have wagged the national dog.

Despite the lessons that might have been learned from the Kansas Pacific and the Santa Fe in the 1860s and 1870s, railroad building, or rumors of railroad building, had lost none of its invigorating magic. Major corporations were backed by serious money, and their intentions were serious. But even paper railroad corporations, which were designed, according to one editor, to go up rather than to go down, had impressive capitalizations and boards of directors studded with well-known names that local luminaries could associate with through the expedient of a county bond issue.[3] Given such seeming confidence in the region by the eastern experts, would it not be inappropriate for local residents to drag their feet just as the consummation they had devoutly wished for was approaching? Then, too, railroads made towns. Topography was less important in setting exact alignments than bond aid, and backing a winner among railroads could mean for a struggling village not only victory in the county-seat contest but eventual domination of a sizable agricultural market area. Because there were so many promised routes in the mid-1880s, perhaps, thought practical town leaders, it would be well to issue bonds on behalf of every possibility. Suddenly huge financial figures, the kind that bolster boom psychology, were being tossed about, many of them representing bonds that were never to be collected for railroads that were never to be built.

In their hope, their will to believe, and their pride, however, it was difficult for westerners to imagine that so much promotional rhetoric could come from so little substance or that towns with seven paper railroad prospects would be lucky to see rail from one. "It costs but little to secure a charter for a railroad that starts from some town that banks on a boom by securing one," wrote an editor at Kinsley in 1886, "and building a tissue paper road from their place diagonal across the state tapping every quarter section and frog pond along the route, which makes the people of the neighboring counties look upon the projective points as one inhabited only by Jay Goulds and Cyrus Fields." To a western Kansan who had sometimes for years fought drought and hot wind, ignored or laughed at by the rest of the state, it satisfied ambition fully "when he can see his name in print which reads, 'For director of this new route, which will be completed yet this year, Hon. Ephrem Augerhandle, one of the most prominent, wealthiest and influential men of our town.' "[4] Some of these prairie people might have been sobered and tempered by their environment: most remained all too human. "It is a bold spirit," wrote a western Kansan in 1886, "that dares to oppose a railway subsidy in Kansas, and there are not many of them here."[5]

The new regional railroad system in the mid-1880s was certainly more, however, than empty promises and false hope. New giants (i.e., major rail corporations) invested millions to tap previously isolated parts of the region, and the Kansas Pacific and Santa Fe, particularly the latter, did substantial defensive building in response to the intrusion. Particularly important were transregional lines constructed in 1886 and 1887 by subsidiaries of the Chicago, Rock Island & Pacific and the Missouri Pacific. These lines more than doubled the extent of western Kansas railroads that actually came from and went to somewhere other than the next county. The northwestern part of the state was influenced by some building from Nebraska backed by the Chicago, Burlington & Quincy, and the St. Louis–San Francisco built a few miles in west central Kansas. Perhaps just as important, the Santa Fe, seriously worried by intrusions into a territory it had considered its own, built new branches in the southwest, where the Rock Island's line toward El Paso ran, and in west central Kansas paralleling the new Missouri Pacific trunk line across the western half of the state. The Santa Fe also bought up a number of local promotions in order to absorb them before they grew.[6]

Beginning in 1886 there was, therefore, all at once, great rail activity in Kansas. For the fiscal year ending in June 1884, the total rail mileage in the state was 4,038; the increase in that year had been 225 miles. The next year 176 miles were built. In June 1886, however, the Board of Railroad Commissioners reported an increase in the previous year of 607 miles, and the next fiscal-year report communicated with wonder that 1,998.31 miles had been added to the Kansas system in a single twelve-month period.[7] By the end of 1888, total rail mileage in Kansas was 8,799.16, more than half of which had been constructed in the previous three boom years. The state Board of Railroad Commissioners estimated that rail mileage in Kansas was exceeded among the states only by that of Illinois and claimed that for rate of building in the period 1886 to 1888, Kansas had no peer. Compared to population, Kansas in 1888 was "the best equipped with railroads of any State in the Union, or any country in the world," with 5.5 miles per 1,000 population, compared, for example, with 2.3 per thousand for neighboring Missouri.[8] Perhaps the web image so often used to describe the western Kansas rail system at this time was exaggerated, but its share of this boom building surely outdated the thought of the region's railroads as a few lonely rivers through a wilderness. And it was natural that hopes should escalate accordingly.

The railroad commissioners noticed the obvious fact that "the immediate effect upon the prosperity of the State of the employment of an army of men in the work of new construction and the disbursement of the many millions of dollars which this has occasioned, has been marked."[9] A reporter for the *Dodge City Times* claimed in November 1886 that the Rock Island had 1,500 men in the field and that the Missouri Pacific held half a dozen Kansas charters and could move in virtually any direction. Wherever the giants went, they spawned local feeders that made "a good show on paper" and were supported by a willingness to give aid that "amounts to a mania in Kansas just now." The reporter said that politics was calm, as all the men that usually made a living at it were in the pay of railroad companies warming things up in towns, counties, and townships so that aid

might be voted to projected lines. There were Lehigh Valley cars, Mobile & Ohio cars, Union Pacific cars, and Milwaukee, St. Paul & Pacific cars emblazoned with signs suggesting they should be returned to Grand Rapids or Omaha but all heading for western Kansas loaded with bridge timbers.[10]

In Ness County it was said then that the town in western Kansas that was not reasonably certain of having six or seven railroads within the next year, preferably one of the trunk lines and several local feeders, was not much of a place. "And even if they get that many lines but do not secure 'end of divisions' and machine shops with each road, it does not appear as if much of a 'boom' is on." Few experiences compared with it: "For big prospects we commend our eastern readers to the way things are done at the average crossroads away upon the Great American Desert."[11]

Perhaps the most important impact upon the boom came from the Missouri Pacific. It built its share of mileage, expanding rapidly in eastern Kansas and completing a railroad all the way across western Kansas and into Pueblo, Colorado, between January 1886 and December 1887.[12] Also, the Missouri Pacific was headed by a famous, mysterious, and legendarily canny mogul named Jay Gould, whose mid-1880s interest in Kansas gave the boom a boost with his regular visits there, speeches about the promise of the place, and personal investment that freed Missouri Pacific subsidiaries from depending for construction speed entirely upon the outcome of bond-issue debates.

The Missouri Pacific, like other companies forced to conform to the corporation laws of Kansas, took over or formed many state-char-

Links to Everywhere. Repairing the new Rock Island Line near Arkalon, c. 1897.

tered companies with local directors to under-
take the construction phase. It happened that
the primary corporate shell used for western
Kansas construction, the Denver, Memphis &
Atlantic (DM&A), had a particularly appealing
independent history of high hope since being
formed in 1883 to build a narrow-gauge line
between Denver and Memphis, and it retained
some of this glamor as a Missouri Pacific front
organization.[13] The "Darling Mary Ann," as
the DM&A was popularly known, pursued the
Missouri Pacific's strategy of developing the
trade territory between the Kansas Pacific and
the Santa Fe by pushing quickly straight across

the central region of western Kansas to the
Colorado line via Hoisington, Brownell, Scott
City, Tribune, and a town called Halcyon.[14] It
threatened to and actually did construct part of
a second trunk line somewhat to the south and
along the original projected route of the independent DM&A. This line reached Kingman
and Larned with plans to go on into Hodgeman
County and organized to extend a branch from
the second trunk to a junction with the Rock
Island in Ford County when construction was
halted by a break in the boom.[15] This building
represented the largest investment and greatest
corporate activity ever in the developing region

between Dodge City and WaKeeney, and its like had not been seen anywhere on the Kansas High Plains in nearly twenty years. The bitter struggle on that long-neglected playing field between Gould and the equally powerful Santa Fe officers trying to stop him and the promise of branches to everywhere by both companies kept towns throughout the region keyed up to a high pitch.[16]

The Missouri Pacific efforts were also especially important to the general boom because of the reaction to them by the Santa Fe. In 1886 the Santa Fe announced that it would build 450 miles of new track in Kansas, to cost $5 million. The most active of the subsidiaries formed to carry out the western Kansas portion of this work (which was most of it), the Chicago, Kansas & Western (CK&W), built 903 miles of track in the region before the end of 1887.[17] An extension straight west from Great Bend through Ness City, Dighton, and Leoti paralleled the new Missouri Pacific line, often at a distance of only a few miles, all the way across western Kansas. A branch begun from Larned reached Jetmore in Hodgeman County and raised hopes at the then-booming town of Ravanna in old Garfield County just to the west.[18] Like the Missouri Pacific, the Santa Fe collected charters for the purpose of preempting desirable routes. In the case of the Chicago, Kansas & Western, plats were filed for fifty-two lines, which, if all constructed, would have added 7,274 miles to the Kansas railroad system. Of course, there was no intention of building them all, but Dodge City could still advertise that numbers 18, 20, 49, and 50 ran through Ford County.[19] When Ness County defeated bonds for a Santa Fe subsidiary called the Walnut Valley & Colorado in 1886, the

parent company could return with the name Chicago, Kansas & Western and eventually prevail.[20]

In addition to these Santa Fe lines north of the original route, there were two 1880s extensions to the south of it running through western Kansas. The longest of these struck west south of Wichita, passed through Rago and Coldwater and proceeded to Ashland and Englewood, where it stimulated farming in the Clark County stronghold of the cowboy and the open range. That line was a response to the second great intrusion of a "giant" into the region, the Chicago, Rock Island and Pacific. Through its whole length, the Santa Fe branch to Clark County paralleled at distances of ten to fifty miles the Rock Island's El Paso line which, on its way toward that Texas city, had in the *annus mirabilis* of 1886 opened far southwest Kansas and added the names of Meade Center and Liberal to the list of towns vying for regional dominance. Liberal did not mind being a terminus town for the moment; few imagined when the railroad arrived there in 1888 that it would remain the end of the line for thirteen years.[21]

The Rock Island construction subsidiary in western Kansas was the Chicago, Kansas & Nebraska (CK&N), and for speed, total mileage, adaptability in getting bond subsidies and variety of regions served, it had the top statistics of the western Kansas railroad revival. In addition to the line cutting across western Kansas in a southwesterly direction as bond issues from counties directly west failed, the CK&N constructed a major trunk line in the northern section of the region in the traffic gap left between the KP route and the northern border of the state. Passing through Smith,

Phillips, Norton, Decatur and Sheridan Counties, it entered almost empty territory in Thomas County, where Colby was established, and in Sherman County, where after a rousing county-seat fight, Goodland emerged as the prime town. From 1886 to 1889, the Rock Island, which had for some years waited on the eastern border of Kansas "like a Roman sentinel on the border of the Rhine," constructed 1,126.92 miles of track in the state.[22]

Equally influential in fueling the boom, though far behind these railroads in construction progress, was the Chicago, Burlington & Quincy. With the southwestern, west central, and northwestern potential traffic areas taken, there remained the opportunity of constructing a north-south trunk line, which the western section of Kansas entirely lacked. Under the *noms de guerre* Burlington & Missouri River; Chicago, Nebraska, Kansas & Southwestern; and Kansas, Texas & Southwestern, the "Q" promoters competed with representatives of all the others at the suddenly lively railroad meetings across western Kansas. While the Burlington lines never did more than compete with the Rock Island in the northwest region when the KP failed to respond to the challenge, the plan of the Kansas, Texas & Southwestern to build diagonally from north to south across western Kansas, connecting the prosperous Solomon River area with Hays, Dodge City, and the new southwest, was highly exciting to towns that had long found it easier to communicate with Colorado than with nearby regional population centers. The exact route was flexible; Garden City was courted by Burlington people along with Dodge. Surveys were made along several lines, and there were promises of branches if enough bond aid were forthcoming.[23] Ulti-

mately, it was not, and north-south communication in western Kansas remains crippled to this day. But through 1885, when the idea of connecting the Burlington & Missouri River in Nebraska with Texas through Kansas was broached, through 1886 and into 1887, the chance of such a line was a factor in the boom.

Far less promising in chance of completion than the longest shot among major corporations were dozens, perhaps hundreds, of local and regional lines chartered in the mid-1880s to take advantage of connections with the major routes in order to serve some specific area or interest. Yet these, with their local directorates, local offices, and sometimes grand aspirations, appealed perhaps most of any railroads to regional pride and the psychology of the boom. They allowed regional centers to boast that they were certain soon to have the services of not just one or two, but six or seven, railroads, some of which would headquarter in that western Kansas town and push out trade feelers through surrounding states. Dodge City in 1887, for example, was as proud of its own Dodge City, Montezuma & Trinidad—slated to tap the Colorado coal fields but destined only to complicate the battle over the Gray County seat—as it was of its existing connection (through a short, locally financed "bobtail" line) with the Rock Island, its service from the Santa Fe, or its immediate prospects of being reached by the Chicago, Nebraska, Kansas & Southwestern; the Wichita & Western (Frisco); or the Denver, Memphis & Atlantic.[24] For some places, everything was a prospect and all the prospects were paper thin.

The names of the local lines born in the wake of aggressive expansion by major companies are a model railroader's dream of color and

We Have Arrived. The Rock Island Depot and Hotel at Liberal, probably in the 1890s.

obscurity. It would be difficult, however, for such a hobbyist to find designs for locomotives and cars because no such equipment ever existed for most of the road names despite their prodigality in producing bonds. There was the Arkansas Valley, Iuka & Northwestern; the Anthony, Attica & Northwestern; the St. Louis, Kansas & Arizona; the Russell, Great Bend & Texas; the Kiowa, Ashland & Trinidad; the Southern Kansas & Panhandle; the Larned & Northwestern; the Omaha & Mexican Air Line; the Larned, Ness City & Wallace; the Ellsworth, LaCrosse & Western; the Chicago, Oswego & Western; the Walnut, Ninnescah & Fort Dodge; the Garfield, Pawnee Valley & Colorado; the Hutchinson, Greensburg & Western; the Kansas, Scott City & Colorado; the Kansas, Colorado & California; the Larned, Garden City & Denver; the Harper & Western; the Beatrice & Great Bend; the Topeka Western & Pacific; the Newton, Walnut Valley & Denver; the Cattle King Railroad; the Nickerson & Panhandle; the Geuda Springs, Caldwell & Western; the Omaha, Dodge City & Southern; the Mulvane, Ulysses & Trinidad; and the Montana, Syracuse & Texas.[25] As has been mentioned, the filing fee for corporate charters was low. And, like Nathan Bedford Forrest's small group of Confederate cavalrymen circling the enemy and calling out the names of nonexistent units, the effect was more impressive than its cause.

There were conservative farmers who, at least initially, took to the railroad boom with skepticism. Commenting on the promises of the Anthony, Attica & Northwestern, a Kinsley resident said most of the town had no faith in its ever being built, though it would fill a void by providing hotels with fresh ice from its projected far northern terminus "while as many trains would run north loaded with sorghum and sunflower seed for the Alaska canary birds." There would be no problem with financing: "British America has already bonded all her possession for its construction to be paid ten years after the admission of Queen Victoria into the Greenback party." And its route and facilities were first class: "The road is a bee line past the door of Will Bolton's wigwam to a polar bear's burrow at the head of Yum-Yum river, striking nothing but county seats from one end to the other. Foul air brakes, political platforms, and skating rink bumpers on every car."[26] A Ness County editor described one railroad proposition advanced on behalf of the Kansas & Colorado by a townsite speculator named O. P. Hamilton and defeated by the county voters as " 'Grandma Hamilton's' Patent, Elliptical, Automatic, Self-Adjusting, Double-Curve Line, Stem-Winding Railroad Project." There were too many of these, the editor thought. "Give us a real railroad."[27]

Ultimately, however, the railroad lobby was too strong for doubters. Ness County, for example, was a problem that became famous among promoters after it defeated three railroad bond issues between March and May 1886—for the Chicago, Nebraska, Kansas &

Southwestern, the Walnut Creek & Colorado (later the Chicago, Kansas & Western), and the Kansas & Colorado. Even here, however, it was found that resistance was not philosophical and could be overcome with better tactics. With several propositions before them, each township tended to vote for the road that would benefit it most and against the others, and in Ness City the west side and the east side split about promises of a depot location. Through the summer there were several major railroad meetings with representatives from the defeated roads and new contenders present to align the interests, and in September the county voted by a good margin to aid the Chicago, Kansas & Western and the Burlington north-south project, now dubbed the Kansas, Texas & Southwestern. Perhaps it would have been easier for an impractical project to have gained support. "Is it not about time," wrote a local wag, "that our citizens take some measures to secure a proposition from the Pensacola, Ness City, Puget Sound Railroad. This is the only line that will suit everybody as it proposes to run its track through every man's dooryard."[28]

The arguments advanced by pro-bond forces in Ness County were typical of the winning arguments over the region. The bonds would not have to be issued unless the railroads were actually built, so it was no risk to vote them. Interest would not be due until the roads were complete, but taxes could be assessed on them before that time. Railroads could lower taxes for individuals, lower prices for the goods they bought, and lower the taxes they paid while increasing government services.[29] The savings in the cost of coal alone could pay for the tax the county would have to levy to issue the bonds: "It is all well enough for a family to burn chips and weeds when they cannot afford anything better, but it is shameful for any man to deliberately plan to keep his family shivering about cow-chip fires for all time to come. . . . Let no man worthy of the name plan to keep his wife and children picking cow chips and breaking weeds for fuel one day longer than necessary.''[30] Not to have a railroad was to reject the modern age (the defeat of the bonds in Ness was characterized by an editor as taking ''us back to the days when the value of steam was unknown and the lightning had never been chained'') and to give an advantage to others who would surely take what you had despised.[31] Ness City was chided with the success of Trego County, which had had the KP since the 1860s.[32] When bringing C. J. Jones to New York and introducing him through banker Nathaniel Niles to Jay Gould, Russell Sage, August Belmont, and other business leaders did not automatically bring forth bond issues in Finney County, railroad people there tried threats.[33] Kansas, Texas & Southwestern lobbyists told Garden Citians in 1886 that if they would not vote bonds, other towns would. ''If the people of Wichita had pursued a similar course to that pursued by many of your people in this matter,'' wrote railroad representatives to C. J. Jones, ''do you suppose it would have been the prosperous and prominent city that it has become?''[34] At a rail meeting at Garden City, A. C. McKeever ''made a few telling remarks taking Wichita as his text, giving the history of their magnificent university, and also referred to Platt City, Mo., which was literally killed by their failure to vote bonds.''[35] The Finney County bond propositions passed.

The greatest attraction of the new railroads to western Kansas communities, however, was the importance of ''premature'' transportation in creating the regional population and industry, the market, it would need to prosper. Meanwhile the money brought to the region by rail construction would sustain its economy until the direct efforts by land grant railroads to sell and settle their lands, and the large indirect effect of railroads building into previously market-isolated areas on activity at the public land offices bore fruit. Railroad promotion, bringing eastern money into the region, seemed a kind of magic. Agricultural prices were low in the mid-1880s, the weather was not particularly favorable, and the state railway commissioners were sure that without the ''extraordinary stimulus'' to Kansas business from the railroad building there would have been declines in real-estate values and widespread bankruptcy. Instead, there was a boom. True, these special conditions could not last forever. But in its 1887 report the board repeated the argument that rain followed the plow, and that climatic changes, combined with the ''general spirit of enterprise and activity'' the railroad building had generated, would eliminate the marginality and the cyclic nature of the High Plains economy. Western Kansas, the commissioners said, was yet only ''meagerly supplied'' with railroads, and would likely see more building in the next few years in response to market needs than it had previously as a matter of speculation.[36]

There is no question that in 1886 and 1887, the Kansas Pacific and the Santa Fe, forced by competition to lower their rates and increase their business, became the most effective immigration agents western Kansas ever had. Employing agents both in western Kansas and in cities in the upper Midwest, the land-grant roads advertised extensively and brought excursion train loads of prospects to specific townships where they would have the chance of meeting the hazards of the West in the company of familiar faces from back home. These agents sometimes organized into land companies like the Santa Fe's Arkansas Valley Land & Town Company or the Rock Island's Kansas Town and Land Company to speculate in former railroad property, but often they worked on their own by purchasing large amounts of land from the railroad and then selling it to actual settlers or holding it for speculation.[37] The result was a sudden large increase in railroad-land sales in western Kansas, the quick filling of the plat books if not entirely the landscape of previously empty counties, and a clamor at the federal land offices for title to the alternate public sections this checkerboard railroad bonanza surrounded.

The surviving land-sales records for the Kansas Pacific are incomplete, but boom-period records that do exist for sales in Wallace and border townships of Sherman and Logan Counties demonstrate well what the boom meant quantitatively to the KP land department's western Kansas operation.[38] Between 1 January and the end of June 1887, the KP made 487 sales, mostly in Wallace County, totaling 123,414 acres. By 1 October, the sales total stood at 837 and the acreage transferred in nine months was a remarkable 197,938 acres.[39] Because Wallace County, where most of the sales were, contained twenty-five townships or 576,000 acres total, one must assume that this run of sales represented a substantial percentage of the land the company had available in the area.

Several interesting patterns appear. First, one can notice the targeting the railroad did of specific areas in seeking settlers. People who bought KP lands in Wallace County did not come from around the country at random but from a few states and from relatively few cities and towns within those states. For the period studied, 244 of the buyers (29 percent) were from Illinois, 235 (28 percent) from Kansas, 184 (22 percent) from Nebraska, 86 (10 percent) from Iowa, and 40 (4.8 percent) from Colorado. Nearly 80 percent came from three states; five states accounted for 95 percent. The existence of buying excursions organized for particular towns can be inferred both by the clustering of sales to people from these towns at certain dates and by the unusual percentages of sales that derive from certain small towns. It is obvious, for example, that the KP was especially active at Wymore, Holdrege, and Loomis, Nebraska; at Monmouth, Moline, and Roseville, Illinois; and at Keokuk, Iowa.[40]

Nor were the lands these people bought in Kansas chosen at random. Either through their choice or the railroad's design, sales to persons from the same state or town clustered in certain townships. Plotting the sales on a sectional map using different colors for buyers from different states reveals not a kaleidoscopic pattern but blocks of solid color. Townships 9 and 10 south, range 37 west (Sherman County), for example, were Nebraska townships. By contrast, township 14 south, range 38 west (Wallace County), just southeast of Sharon Springs, was dominated by people from Iowa, while nearby township 15 south, range 39 west, had most of the Coloradans that bought land. Township 13 south, range 39 west, just northeast of Sharon Springs, was heavy on people from Illinois.[41] Boom settlers did not come in organized colonies, as had been so common in the 1870s, but the association and familiarity the colonies provided was reproduced in purchase decisions that were not entirely individualistic.

Given that this was railroad land, which would attract buyers wanting larger tracts than the homestead and timber-culture acts provided, and given that the far western counties probably required larger farms, it is not surprising that, though the average purchase was just 236.5 acres, 28 percent of the transactions involved tracts larger than 160 acres and 11.2 percent were for more than a half-section at once. Of the total acreage sold, over half was in farms or ranches larger than the traditional 160-acre family farm, and multiple purchases by the same buyer, or by buyers from the same family who consolidated their adjoining smaller tracts (both common practices), meant that these figures underestimate the actual size and number of large unified land holdings in Wallace County. Neither the railroad nor the county, however, cared in what form the money was coming, nor, to the later chagrin of both, what the real chances were that the buyers would move to Wallace County and hold their property until the generous ten-year time payments the KP allowed were all made. They could only see that the contracts negotiated in these frantic boom months could, given the average KP land price there of $4.72 an acre, bring in $934,413.25 plus interest, and who knew how much in eventual taxes, from what had recently been considered wasteland.

Although the surviving Santa Fe land sales records for the boom period in western Kansas are complete and though it is obvious that there was a spectacular increase in volume of transactions and acreage sold in the mid- to late 1880s, it is actually more difficult than with the KP to determine who the final buyers were. This is because the Santa Fe in the 1880s sold land in large blocks to speculators or agents (it amounted to the same thing) and left it to these men to handle the paperwork and gain the profits, if there were to be any, from reselling farm-sized pieces.[42]

The role of these agents is what modifies superficial resemblances to the KP. Individual transactions of over 160 acres during the boom years on the Santa Fe are just under one-third of the total, almost exactly the ratio on the KP. However, the Santa Fe price to large buyers varied more widely than with the KP, was always at least $1.00 an acre lower, and regularly reached a "wholesale" level for real-estate agents close to the public domain price of $1.25 an acre. Also, the sales over 160 acres along the KP were likely to be a half-section or a section, while those on the Santa Fe were often immense, consisting regularly of twenty or thirty sections in various counties sold to a real-estate agent or several thousand acres to a cattle or irrigation corporation. While there were multiple transactions involving the same individual in the KP records, what was an exception there was the rule with the Santa Fe, where page after page of the contract books contains the same familiar names.

This pattern was in stark contrast to the Santa Fe approach in the 1870s, when the average land price was $5.72 an acre, there were very few multiple sales to the same individual, and the average sale was right at 160 acres. Perhaps the company believed its remaining lands were of lesser quality and had to be sold at a discount. Perhaps it needed the quick cash that sale to agents would bring. Whatever this policy did for the Santa Fe, it is certain what it did for western Kansas. It tied the financial interest of dozens of aggressive real-estate men, both from Kansas and the settler-recruiting states of the upper Midwest, directly to "selling" western Kansas as a home for the thousands of customers they needed. Their individual vigor and their range of promotional imagination made the best previous efforts of the corporation look sluggish.

The most active of the agents from Kansas who dealt in Santa Fe lands west of Wichita during the boom were David Heizer and J. V. Brinkman of Great Bend; Alexander and Fred Forsha of Hutchinson; Simon Ott, George Tewksbury, and the Reverend John Knox of Topeka; George Wadsworth of Larned; and A. J. Hoisington and I. R. Holmes of Garden City. These men were highly influential in their communities and were enterprising and sometimes flamboyant in the extreme. David Heizer, forty years old in 1886, had been one of the first residents of Barton County and was a well-educated man who had taught school in Iowa and been a school principal in Manhattan, Kansas, before coming to homestead near Great Bend. He had represented his county in the state legislature, was the founder of a major bank in Great Bend, and was a large investor in business blocks there.[43] I. R. Holmes, only thirty-three in 1886, reached Garden City in 1882, invested in the local irrigation ditches, and in 1887 built the Wildwood, a brick building that was one of the showplaces of the town.[44] He was president of the Bank of Western Kansas, was mayor of Garden City in 1885, and used the earnings from his and partner A. C. McKeever's real-estate firm to build a $12,000 home.[45] Holmes could and did buy

two pages of the Sunday *Topeka Capital* to advertise Garden City and Finney County.[46] A. J. Hoisington, formerly the editor of the *Great Bend Register,* was one of the most silver-tongued, ambitious, and controversial men in the state and, at thirty-five, receiver of the new Garden City land office and president of the Finney County Bank.[47] The Reverend John Knox had a perfect theory, for a combination Methodist minister and land agent, of the relationship of the spiritual to the material. In his 1883 book *Paths to Wealth,* he included a long chapter on "Investments in Land." While Knox generally advised against going in debt, he thought it was a good idea to borrow in order to buy land. Ownership of land, he wrote, "stimulates industry, promotes economy, arouses hope, and brings out the best energies of the man. He trusts the air and clouds and sun and soil and God."[48]

Agents from out of state with heavy Santa Fe investments in western Kansas included Edward G. Hudson, an attorney from Lincoln, Illinois; John C. Fahnestock, a former bookseller from Galesburg, Illinois; Fredericksen & Co. of Chicago; W. H. Garrett of Mansfield, Ohio; S. D. Davis and J. M. Strahan of Malvern, Iowa; and J. Wilkes Ford and M. M. Towle of Chicago.[49] Apparently being remote from the scene was no disadvantage. Fredericksen & Co. had local representatives across western Kansas as well as district agents in towns such as Galva, Toulon, and Andover, Illinois, from which, not surprisingly, many of the ultimate buyers of their land came. "This land firm works as systematic as a clock," wrote a reporter in Dodge City announcing the arrival of a Fredericksen excursion train in June 1887. Sales in township 27, range 27W in Gray

County, where all the railroad land had been purchased by this firm for resale, were given in full for the previous week. Investors from Toulon, Galva, and Elmira, Illinois, and one from Koszta, Iowa, had paid $25,560 that week for land in odd-numbered sections in the township, paying between $8.50 and $9.50 an acre.[50] The motivation for getting into the railroad land resale business along the Santa Fe was obvious.

A sample of the activity of George Wadsworth of Larned and John Fahnestock of Galesburg, Illinois, illustrates the scope involved. Wadsworth tended to limit his purchases to the counties near Larned: the bulk of his land was in Pawnee County. On 15 May 1884, he signed up at the Santa Fe land office for forty-two quarters and an eighty in Pawnee County and four quarters in Edwards County, a total of 7,360 acres. This was typical of the kind of purchase Wadsworth made regularly over the next year and a half. Wadsworth's May purchase and another of just over 10,000 acres late in July apparently lasted him through 1884. However, early in 1885 he stepped up his buying considerably as the boom began. He made large purchases (5,000 to 12,000 acres) on 25 January, 18 April, 4 June, 20 June, 6 July, 6 August, and 22 October of that year. In the year 1885 alone, Wadsworth bought 56,887 acres of Santa Fe land, over 50,000 acres of it located in Pawnee and Edwards Counties. Fahnestock, having no particular local loyalties, chose land all over western Kansas and, when he had good financial backing, bought very large acreages. On 20 March 1886, he purchased 20,779.08 acres in Ford, Edwards, Barton, Pawnee, Finney, Hodgeman, and Rush Counties for $73,451.21 ($3.50 per acre). An-

other big day for him was 4 December 1885 when he bought 13,627.31 acres, all in Ford County, for $23,348.47 ($1.71 an acre), and still another was 14 January 1886 when he purchased 11,554.54 acres with seventeen sales contracts at prices ranging from $3 to $4 an acre. Fahnestock began his constant large purchasing in 1884 when he bought 6,450.99 acres in Stafford County one August day and kept it up until mid-1886 when so much of the Santa Fe land was in the hands of agents like himself that direct sales from the company slowed dramatically.

People like Wadsworth and Fahnestock, with 50,000 to 75,000 acres of Santa Fe lands to be paid for on four-year contracts and who had not the financial resources the railroad might have had to hold them indefinitely, were a major factor in the boom. And there is evidence in the Santa Fe contract books that not only did these buyers sell to settlers, but they transferred contracts to other speculators who took over their payments and joined the force of western Kansas land promoters.

The stimulus of the new phase of railroad building and prospects of railroad building accelerated the momentum of the economic recovery of western Kansas from the recession of 1879–1882, against which the cattle, irrigation, and local agricultural-processing industries had been the initial salvos. Competition enlivened the original regional trunk lines to the benefit of the areas they served, while new lines created for the first time the possibility of large-scale commercial agriculture, big towns, and local industry for the central corridor, the southwest, and the far northwest.

Approximately the westernmost one-third of western Kansas had lain empty, though part of it had early railroad service, while experiments with agriculture proceeded in the wetter areas. Wallace County, for instance, had a small population during the early years of the KP, but lost it in the 1870s so entirely that it reported nothing to the agricultural census. That county revived so rapidly in 1887 that within a year it achieved a population as great as it was to have nearly a century later.[51] Other far-west areas had not even been organized into counties before the railroad flurry of the mid-1880s, and the new counties that emerged all at once spawned activity to establish towns quickly that could vie for county-seat status in regions that now seemed worth struggling for.

Railroad projectors, railroad land agents, and registers and receivers at new public land offices, working in and through new towns and revitalized older towns, contributed mightily to creating in western Kansas of 1886–1887, for the first and last time in its history, the gaudy atmosphere of high boom.

Chapter Sixteen

Ravanna Rhymes with

Hosanna

igh boom" in western Kansas was statistical, rhetorical, and psychological, each element fanning the others. Next to miles of railroad built and projected, the most impressive statistics representing what would have seemed to an observer at the time accomplished fact were those concerning land taking and population. Railroad land sales and the extension of railroads into previously isolated regions stimulated people to take western Kansas public land, mostly under the homestead and timber-culture acts, more rapidly than ever before. Consequently, population surged at an unprecedented rate. Kingman County had 3,125 people in 1880, dropped to 2,757 in 1881, and only slowly recovered until 1885 when population jumped to over 10,000. It reached a claimed 20,000 in 1887, more than double what the population has been since the 1930s despite the county's commuting proximity to Wichita. But whatever its impact on the countryside, the climax of the boom was particularly felt in and almost wholly communicated through towns. Old towns blossomed in western Kansas, new towns were born, and all of

them felt their potential was limited only by the imagination of their political and economic leaders and the ability of their editors to create the "high-falutin" prose every place on the make required. Description beggared logic and so was often metaphoric or even poetic. A Kingman County man wrote that the boom there "made a landscape strange, / Which was the living chronicle / Of deeds that wrought the change."[1]

As boom editors were fond of saying before launching into a flight of windy hyperbole, the raw statistics of the land rush hardly needed embellishment. Among western land offices, Larned alone remained fairly steady in volume of business through the period, at about 2,000 entries a year encompassing about 200,000 acres. Garden City had 2,467 homestead entries (390,690.1 acres) and 2,838 timber-culture entries (452,025.76) in the fiscal year ending in June 1885 out of total entries of 8,036 (864,739.58 acres). In fiscal 1886 there were 7,454 original homestead entries at Garden City (1,181,736.33 acres) and 4,501 timber-culture entries (724,510.50 acres). Preemption entries were up from 140 (21,683.36 acres) the year before to 811 (127,785.86 acres), and the total for June 1885 to June 1886 was 18,958 entries covering 2,036,598.18 acres, not including more than 4,000 filings made at Garden City on former Osage Indian lands. Through June 1887 the activity at Garden City remained high: 16,604 entries that fiscal year for 1,536,945.21 acres. There was some decrease in timber-culture entries and increase in pre-emption sales, but this suggested confidence by cash investors. It was not until the final report of June 1888, when entries over the past year dropped to 11,997 at Garden City and acres entered to 970,296.89, that statistics buttressed the common-sense conclusion that there would not forever be unsettled land to transfer nor unsettled people to grasp frantically at getting it quickly.

Similar increases took place at Kirwin, Oberlin, and WaKeeney, though Kirwin, serving a more settled area, reached only a 4,000-entry-per-year level compared with 10,000 to 15,000 for the others and had a higher percentage of preemption sales. In addition, Kirwin, Oberlin, and WaKeeney all experienced a decline in activity in fiscal 1887, about a year earlier than Garden City's first hints. At the peak in 1885 and 1886, Oberlin had 11,357 entries on 1,347,172.99 acres, indicating that the new northwest was developing as rapidly as the new southwest. WaKeeney, reflecting movement into the central area between the KP and the Santa Fe opened by the Missouri Pacific, peaked with 15,831 entries on 1,655,315.90 acres.[2]

Heady western Kansas population increases during the boom resulted in many new county organizations. In fact, the twenty-five counties (all of them in western Kansas) organized between 1885 and 1888 were equaled in only one other similar period (1870–1874) in Kansas history, and at that time not only were there still unsettled central Kansas areas to dilute the impact on western Kansas, but the counties were smaller.[3] The pattern in boom-population increases indicates the importance of these new county organizations in giving a perhaps exaggerated sense of the regional growth rate. Some well-established counties did experience amazing increases. Ford County went from 2,450 people in 1886 to 9,218 in 1887 and Finney from 1,487 in 1885 to 13,662 in 1886. But Ford and Finney were the two counties most affected by irrigation, a major boom factor, and both experienced especially large drops in the later bust—Ford to 7,429 in 1888 and Finney to 5,294 the same year.

More typical were Edwards (3,519 in 1885; 4,388 in 1886; 4,717 in 1887; 4,447 in 1888), Ellis (5,046; 5,582; 7,034; 7,461), Ellsworth (10,009; 10,624; 10,774; 11,321), and Russell (6,665; 7,791; 9,072; 7,791)—impressive but not unprecedented growth. In the new counties, however, an influx of similar numbers of new people meant a rapid move from nothing to something, complete with instant towns, and that created more excitement. Gove County (organized in 1886), went from almost nothing in 1885 to 3,032 in 1886 to 4,113 in 1887; Hodgeman (1887) from 1,799 to 4,023 to 4,259; Lane (1886) from 278 to 2,726 to 3,630; Sherman (1886) from only scattered residents to 2,820 to 3,879 to 5,115 in 1888; Thomas (1885) from 981 to 3,411 to 5,629 to 6,174; and Comanche (1885) from 907 in 1886 to 5,284 in 1887.[4] The new railroads were making a substantial percentage difference in these areas, and the hopeful liked to project their growth rates and the accompanying geometrical

"Everybody Was Making Money." The Garden City U.S. Land Office entrance, 1885. During the boom years, just getting into the land office to file on a claim was a major logistics problem. Strict rules for queuing up had to be established to prevent violence.

effect on the western Kansas region as a whole into the future.[5]

The land business was a boon for all towns in the districts where lands were being taken, but it was a special stimulus for some. Because all the federal land office functions for the region were concentrated in a few towns (WaKeeney, Oberlin, Kirwin, Larned, and Garden City in 1887), these hosted people entering lands in vast areas. The Garden City Land Office, established in 1883, covered business for Finney, Ford, Clark, Meade, Gray, Seward, Stevens, Haskell, Grant, Morton, Stanton, Kearney, Hamilton, Garfield, and Hodgeman Counties. This was an area of 11,350 square miles, or 7,264,000 acres.[6] The land-office towns experienced a crush of activity and a large flow of money, causing an artificially high demand there for everything from boots to newspapers. Therefore, land office locations were fought over as the greatest asset a western town could have.

As early as August 1885 a man moving to WaKeeney found two- to three-room houses there renting for $15 a month and sixty men in that town engaged in the real-estate or government land office business.[7] Even so, land paperwork was a week or more behind, as every day that month 10,000 acres were entered at WaKeeney. Business was even more brisk that fall, when in one day there were 158 entries covering 25,280 acres.[8] Although this was just the beginning of the upsurge, the sidewalk in front of the land office building at WaKeeney was always crowded in the summer and fall of 1885, and some people slept on its steps at night. There was a system of giving out information to homesteaders and land attorneys at a set time of one half-hour each morning and evening only; otherwise, repeating the information to everyone would leave no time for the other work of the office. "Everybody," the new resident wrote, "was making money."[9]

Naturally the land-office towns, both because of the wealth the office brought and in order to keep this asset from rival towns by providing superior services, underwent flurries of improvement. WaKeeney had gotten the land office away from Hays City in 1879 by a campaign around urban amenities.[10] Dodge City made similar arguments in 1887 and sent representatives to Washington to try to encourage consolidation of the land offices of Garden City and Larned at Dodge City. Garden City, the editor of the *Dodge City Times* wrote, "never had anything but wind and the land office business to keep her up."[11] Just at the time of the Dodge City campaign, the Garden City land office experienced what people there said was the largest number of land entries ever made in a single day at one land office in the United States—375 entries on 25 April 1887. True, C. J. Jones' Buffalo Block, where the land office was, was for the moment unroofed to add a third story, and a rain storm had gotten things wet, but, said Garden Citians, "comparing the Buffalo block with Dodge City's build-

ings makes their proposition extremely ludicrous."[12] The office was centrally located at Garden City, its defenders said. There were no saloons or gambling dens as there were at Dodge but instead an opera house, lectures, and first-class plays. One could ride around town on streetcars at a five-cent fare, have water from the new waterworks by turning on a faucet, and walk on lighted streets at night. Most important, Garden City deserved the land-office business because it was in Garden City that people had first invested in the idea that southwest Kansas could be agricultural. If Dodge City had prevailed, "these plains would today have been in the hands of cattle barons, and what towns would have existed in this country would have been simply cow camps and whisky would have been as free as water and crime would have run riot."[13] A Dodge City editor's response to that was bitter. "Larned and Garden City have both grown rich and haughty from the crumbs that have dropped from the land office tables, and while the removal of the office from Larned would not injure the town's business and prospects, there is a faint surmise that Garden City would suffer irreparable damage in stone blocks, wind, and highfalutin enthusiasm."[14]

This struggle for the land office between towns was a typical western Kansas boom phenomenon. So tenuous was growth, so relatively small was the base, and so important was a confident psychology to urban development on the High Plains that any differentiating asset—an irrigation ditch, a sugar mill, a newspaper, streetcars, waterworks, a college, or a county seat—was sought and protected by rival towns with an intensity surprising to outsiders.

During the boom, any improvement, no matter how impractical or in advance of need, seemed to have an immediate beneficial effect on town-lot prices and thus seemed justified. Garden City business lots in 1885, two years after the location of the land office there, were held at prices from $500 to $1,500, while residence blocks in the suburbs cost $1,200. "The prices are exorbitant," wrote the local editor, "but buyers are plenty and sellers on the alert."[15] Two years later, business lots were $2,500 in Garden City, and Governor St. John predicted the town would have a population of 75,000 within the decade.[16] According to the *Kansas Real Estate Journal,* business-lot prices ranged up to $30,000 in Wichita in 1887; to $12,000 in Hutchinson; $5,000 to $10,000 in Great Bend, Larned, Kinsley, and Dodge City; and as much as $500 in western Kansas towns of under 1,000 population.[17] Kinsley, with three weeky newspapers and one daily in 1887, advertised that it had $140,000 in real-estate transfers in a single day and that its population had gone from 623 in 1884 to 1,102 the next year.[18] A Dodge City newspaper in 1885 had a simple headline that to 1880s Kansas residents said it all: "LIKE WICHITA."[19]

As in all booms, however, anticipations were outsized. Towns acted like cities and villages acted like towns. Rival towns thought it was ludicrous when Larned chartered a street railway in 1885, intending to have most of the equipment home built by the talented Allen Ditson of the Larned windmill factory and iron foundry.[20] Wrote a jaundiced observer:

Of all the ganzy schemes for advertising a town, that of the charter is the most industriously worked. This, that and the other fool thing is chartered into existence, the stockholders are chartered out of their spare cash, and not infrequently a large portion of the public is chartered into a swindle. All manner of enterprises are thus galvanized into a feeble existence to create an impression abroad that the community is immensely prosperous and approaching that condition of financial plethora where money goes a-begging. On the frontier of Kansas this harmless amusement greatly flourishes.

The latest announcement in this line is the chartering of the Larned Street Railway Company! Holy Moses, what next? Imaging the throngs that will wait at the crossings for the cars! Imagine the wild rush for seats! The treading of toes, the gouging of ribs, the wild whir of nickels into the money box! We can see it all.[21]

The laughter changed to jealousy, however, when Ditson began operating his two mule cars on a mile of street railway in Larned the next year and got in addition a twenty-one-year contract for an electric-light plant there.[22] Garden City ordered two cars from Ditson for its own proposed street railway, planned during the blizzard of 1886, and within a year granted franchises and voted municipal bonds for an electric-light plant, a waterworks, a sewer system, and a natural-gas plant.[23] People there professed concern that there were not enough low-rent "tenements" in town to accommodate its workmen.[24] Dodge City started a waterworks and an electric-light plant, formed a company to bore for gas, graded the streets, built sidewalks, chartered a street railway, and ordered streetcars from the East.[25] Smaller towns were not immune. Ness City, which did not make the summer 1887 list of towns over

1,000 population, planned a $25,000 water-works and a street railway.[26] Even Jetmore in Hodgeman County thought its claimed 1,500 people, three banks, and two hotels deserved to be served by a street railway, and one was chartered there.[27] A Garden Citian's explanation was typical: "We have grown out of our village clothes and as a city must have what belongs to us."[28]

Kinsley, which advertised 3,000 people but which an 1887 count set at 1,266 (ninety-eighth in the state), represented a middle ground in western Kansas towns.[29] A publicist there wrote in 1877 that if "Satan had stood upon the elevation north of Kinsley, instead of the mountains of Palestine; and offered all of the valleys and plains visible, in return for homage and loyalty, had our Lord and Savior been less divine than human, the results would have been different," but there were initial local doubts about the boom.[30] The first attempt to fund a waterworks failed in July 1886 when a $32,000 bond issue was defeated by thirty-five votes.[31] However, the town's five lumberyards were kept busy supplying material, the Edwards County Bank built a $20,000 structure, and the town got two new hotels at $10,000 and $35,000, a library, and a new Santa Fe depot of pressed brick with a sixty-foot tower.[32] Convinced by these physical signs that the boom was real, Kinsley residents proceeded to go "wild" in the improvement business. Waterworks bonds, this time $41,000, passed in June 1887 by a margin of 148 to 33 (for a town of just over 1,000 in a time of male-only suffrage, that was not a bad turnout), and there was immediate talk of a sewer system and subsidies for industry.[33] The *Mercury,* the evening representative of Kinsley's two daily papers, printed 25,000 copies of one special edition for distribution in the East and included columns on the proposed Cooperative Cracker Factory, mattress factory, packing plant, bottling works, paper-box factory, and sorghum mill. The newspapers predicted that Kinsley would have a population of 15,000 to 20,000 within five years and within a decade would be replete with steel mills, rolling mills, a plow works, and a college. Much would come immediately. "What Wichita is to Kansas City today," the *Mercury* man attested, "Kinsley will be to Wichita one year from this time."[34]

Towns born in the boom had no uneven past to restrain them and so produced a verbal picture of themselves further out of line with actual accomplishment than did older towns. A Dodge City man noticed in 1885 that it was very cheap to found a western Kansas town. All you had to do was give it a name, organize a city government, grant yourself and your friends charters for a street railway, a gas company, and a couple of banks, donate lots for a courthouse, and pass a resolution to call the attention of eastern capitalists to the town "as a place offering superior advantages for manufacturing." The whole thing took only twenty minutes, and the only expense was for whisky to keep up the confidence of the promoters.[35] Hodgeman Center, founded in October 1885, already had high hopes by November. "They want the county seat, a newspaper, brass band, and skating rink," said the Dodge press of the dozen-house town, "and will then be in shape to move on to glory."[36] Dodge City writers looked equally askance at Meade Center, which it said had a bad location and "has nothing but strife and speculation to keep it up."[37] Wendell's sole advantage was its location at the

Taming the Wilderness. Hays City, 1885.

center of Edwards County; Ravanna (formerly Cowland) had a euphonious name and county-seat hopes in a county (Garfield) too small to continue; Kalvesta and Nonchalanta boasted only scenic locations, and many other new towns had nothing but the accumulated wind of their residents. But how that breeze did blow!

Fine lithographs of tiny, dusty places met the eyes of readers of the late 1880s series of *Handbooks* on western Kansas counties produced by the C. S. Burch Company of Chicago, looking for all the world as though the town pump and the hardware store might be gathering places for serious urban planners. There were "bird's eye" views of towns that would fit in a bird's eye and whose multiple newspapers were made up with plates purchased from national subscription firms.[38] They did, however, compose their own ads and raised the two-column boom spread to a kind of art form: "All Roads Lead to Ravanna—Gaze on the

Map and See For Yourselves—YOUR WIFE KNOWS! Your minister knows! Your physician knows! Your children know! Your neighbors know! In fact IT IS WELL KNOWN THAT the best opportunity for EXCELLENT BUSINESS LOCATIONS and remunerative investments is Afforded by the New Town of Ravanna.—Lakin is THE ONLY TOWN west of Garden City destined to be the county seat that has not yet had any boom.—If happiness you seek, and wealth you crave; / If town you want and form you need; / Be sure you go to the town of the brave, / And constantly sing as now you read: 'Her name is KALVESTA / In her I'll invest.—Leoti City. In the exact CENTER OF WICHITA COUNTY. . . . Buy lots there now before the BIG BOOM gets on.—There is a city in sunny Kansas / Ness City is its Name / That now enjoys a building boom / And getting there all the same.—Don't Fail to go to TERRY, the thriving town of North Finney.—Nonchalanta

Spins—Play well your part my boys, / Distribute the Havanna, / You surely are the people's choice, / We'll shout the loud Hosanna.—HECTOR, Greeley County, Kansas, The Infant Wonder of the Plains.—HAROLD. The New Town in Southern Ness County . . . in the beautiful Pawnee Valley, equi-distant between Ness City and Jetmore . . . on the line of the P.V.&D. Railroad, and the C.V.K.S.W.R.R., and is without doubt the PRETTIEST TOWN SITE IN KANSAS."[39] In an alliterative nightmare drawn probably from Wichita's success with slogans like "Peerless Princess" and "Athletic Ajax of the Aboundful Arkansas," the *Ness City Times* reported county doings under the heads "Beeler Buglings," "Harold Happenings," "Franklinville Facts," "Cyrus Chips," "Dots from Drake," "Utica Utterances," "Brownell Buds," and "Notes from Nonchalanta," little imagining that before the twentieth century was well opened, few county residents would have more than a vague recollection that several of these wide-awake boom towns had even existed.[40]

If confidence could make things happen or mind influence matter, the future of western Kansas would have been unlimited. The *Western Empire* of Bull City in Osborne County claimed to be "the only reliable paper on earth! It is red-hot every week." Its ads for itself advised that "mortals wishing to soak in the beautiful gems of fricasseed thought that scintillate throughout the six horse power columns of this eighteen-carat journal can do so by calling at the office."[41] Hays people were advised by an editor in 1886 that they needed to "wake up" and "pull together" with "vim and push" or they would be outdistanced by people

in other towns that had fewer advantages but flashier advertising.[42] The Kinsley rule was to be upbeat and not to mope, so as to encourage the visitor.[43] "While we may not believe the sun, moon and stars were created only for us," went an editorial there in the discouraging year of 1881, "we can herald the advantages of our town and the surrounding country and by the combined effort of the community build up a good live town."[44] A few years later the same thought was more simply put: "He that bloweth not his own horn," wrote a Kinsley resident in 1886, "the same shall not be blown."[45]

For a time it seemed that it had worked. Western Kansas cities, where a few years earlier the best entertainment was the amateur literary society, sported roller rinks, secret music clubs (the Sequoyah United Mastodon Minstrels, for example), polo clubs, elaborate expositions, and enough opera houses to justify the Southern and Western Theatrical Association, formed in 1886 to coordinate their productions.[46] This boom of 1886 and 1887 was bigger than any of the region's previous cyclic upswings, and it was not based, as most had been, purely on accidental good weather or a single outside factor such as a railroad or a colonization scheme. Perhaps some of the industrial prospects would fail to materialize, perhaps the climate had not permanently changed for the better, perhaps some of the land buying was speculative, maybe not every village would become a city. But surely too much was at stake this time to again abandon the quest for polished civilization in western Kansas. Surely the time was past when it would ever again make sense to speak of it as one of those "natural" areas where climate dominated all. "The Struggle for life in Western Kansas,"

A Mixture of Things. Another view of Hays City, 1885. Needless to say, there was no zoning.

said a Hays City editor, ''is fast passing away, and our fruitful seasons are bringing comforts and luxuries.''[47]

At the Norton farm near Larned, family diarists recorded in 1879 a comment by George Norton that was teasing nonsense but reflected well enough the attitude that, as soon as the material was there, spawned the western Kansas boom. Norton updated a popular 1850 poem by Urania Bailey that ran: ''I want to be an angel / And with the angels stand / A crown upon my forehead / A harp within my hand.'' The new version went: ''I want to be an angel

with a town on my head and a *Harpers Weekly* in my hand.''[48]

Western Kansans of the 1880s, like all pioneers, wished not to become something new but to reproduce something old—civilization and culture as it was defined elsewhere. And now, after so many years of frustration in the region, it appeared that all at once, as it happened in ''an Arabian Knight's tale,'' the region west of Wichita would at last share the blessings of that vigorous city and the nineteenth-century glories of the world beyond.[49]

Chapter Seventeen

Red-Haired Men

in Silk Ties

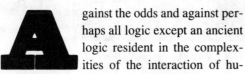gainst the odds and against perhaps all logic except an ancient logic resident in the complexities of the interaction of human beings and nature in western Kansas, even the mid-1880s boom turned out to be a bubble, a mirage, an illusion, part of yet another wrenching cycle. There were signs of instability in 1887, but when the bottom dropped out suddenly in 1888, it was a great and unpleasant surprise to most. All that had gone up, it seemed, as dramatically went down. The rain stopped, the wind and snow started, population dropped, crops failed, credit tightened, railroad companies withdrew, the land-office business shriveled, cattlemen gave up, irrigation ditches dried up, sugar mills burned up, towns had safes full of worthless bonds to give away, and farm families found that suddenly it was 1880 again. The "red-haired men in silk ties" who had been so courted on their arrival from the East disappeared from their cluttered offices in the towns; in their place came New Mexico and Texas sand blown in from the southwest by hot scirocco winds.[1] The very names Garden City and Goodland were an ironic taunt to the mortgage-laden, dust-covered remnants of the great bust of 1888.

The number that went back east "to see their wife's folks" after 1887 was large. A common population loss for a western Kansas county in the initial bust was 2,000 people, with a slower but steady decline thereafter until the early twentieth century. This was a greater shock to counties that had only 4,000 to begin with than those with 10,000, but to all that had made plans based on a continuance of a rapid growth rate, it required mighty adjustments. The pattern can be glimpsed by a few county population samples from 1887 to 1891: Ford (9,218; 7,429; 6,647; 5,491; 4,992); Finney (10,000?; 5,294; 4,300; 3,170; 2,951); Russell (9,072; 8,324; 6,882; 6,783; 6,626); Lane (3,630; 3,684; 2,519; 2,061; 1,679). Only the new counties in the far west and southwest remained temporarily stable before they too began declining in population as the 1890s drought deepened.[2] Between 1887 and 1898, Comanche County went from 5,004 to 1,369; Greeley from 4,646 to 502; Stanton from 2,864 to 326; Morton from 2,560 to 255; and Stevens from 2,663 to 519.[3] The total population in Kansas west of the 100th meridian was 81,279 in 1889 and only 49,850 in 1895.[4]

The population drop had many effects. Postmasters' salaries in western Kansas towns were reduced in 1889, and several towns dropped a class in their incorporation status due to population losses.[5] The need for aid for suffering western Kansas farmers was again the dominant news from the region—when there was any news from there at all.[6] At Larned in 1888, things were changing so little that a *Chronoscope* reporter was reduced to writing stories on a farmer's four-legged chicken and a bean-counting contest at the drugstore. "If more horses would run away," he mused, "houses burn down or something else sensational would happen it would be a boon to the reporter."[7] In Kinsley, twenty columns of the paper were taken up by delinquent tax notices for a quiet town. It had returned, in the words of historian James Malin, to the status of country town "where farmers brought their eggs and butter on Saturdays and traded for a few groceries. Its only distinction was the doubtful one of a county court house with an empty treasury."[8]

The ultimate and simple explanation for any business downtown anywhere, particularly in a boom-and-bust cycle, is loss of confidence. Signs of this were always present in western Kansas among those who suspected too much of a good thing. Will Mace of Garden City returned to the East in the spring of 1887 and, in a newspaper interview there, suggested the boom was doomed. There was no substantial farming community for the services of Garden City to fall back on, he said, once the temporary stimuli of the land office and irrigation were gone: "Every form of business . . . is terribly overdone. There are about four hundred real-estate agents in the city; nine or ten lumber yards, and I am afraid to say how many groceries. All the professions are crowded. And when you consider that almost every man is living off his neighbor, in some shape, things aren't so rosy at Garden City as the real estate men would have the stranger believe. . . . It is all outlay. We produce nothing."[9]

The early response to this sort of criticism by boomers whose short-term interest would be damaged by planning and restraint was that it was the carping of the weak. "Men who shudder at the sight of a surge," wrote a Garden City editor, "have no business in a land where such things run loose."[10] Once the money flow into the region slowed, however, there was a chorus of "I told you so's" from people who could suddenly afford the time and discipline it took to be wise. The *Kinsley Mercury* in March 1888 replaced its usual boom editorial with a copy of the Ten Commandments. Its rival found that a refreshing change from a former pursuit of "ignotum per ignotius."[11] The boom, the *Kinsley Graphic* man thought, was "like that which inflates a balloon, it loses its buoyancy, and, in fact, its existence, utterly, after a little time and the balloon descends to earth or water in an exceedingly crushed and wrinkled condition."[12] At Larned, the editor suspected it was the men in the silk ties who had led honest farmers astray—"it is the fellow who came here and wanted to get rich without work; it is the fellow who saw twenty dollar gold pieces under every clod of dirt; it is the fellow who tried to buy a controlling interest in the earth without any capital; it is the fellow who thought the world was full of 'suckers' and he was the best

"Another Wichita." Garden City's Main Street during the boom, 1887. The special wealth that hopes for irrigation brought to Garden City is evident in this view.

fisherman in existence."[13] The old negative stories and jokes about the hard, sometimes wild life in western Kansas began again to circulate as confidence waned. There was the one about the man who, reaching the gates of heaven, was told his life had been sinful and he should apply to hell. Upon reaching there, he was told the devil did not want him either. "Oh, Lord," he exclaimed with a sorrowful heart, "will I have to go back to Dodge?"[14]

These comments suggest some of the specific causes of loss of confidence in its western Kansas 1880s manifestation. First, there was the weather. Despite all efforts to convince people otherwise, western Kansas remained almost entirely dependent on farming and ranching; thus, there were limits to how long it could continue to boom when rainfall was short and winters were long. Second, the rairoads, in an unregulated competitive fury (the Interstate Commerce Commission was not organized until 1887), overbuilt substantially in western Kansas, as they did all over the country. The trunk lines experienced financial difficulty too great to invest much in booming towns or even to pay their taxes, and the paper lines lost all hope of any construction. Third, credit, which had fueled investment for investment's sake, retracted nationwide, people reneged on promises, and assets, real or otherwise, which had once been levers for borrowing, became at best useless, at worst millstones which kept costing, but ceased paying. The red-haired men in silk ties proved unequal to the emergency. Fourth, in direct response to this and consequent disillusion with the silk-tie types, western Kansas farmers became active in opposition to the boom establishment and, through the Kansas Farmers Alliance and later the People's party, began to pursue very different economic and political goals than had been typical in the boom.

Fifth, towns were seriously overexpanded and overcommitted to projects designed for a rapidly growing population, and they were therefore not flexible in meeting a reverse gracefully. Towns were fooled by the old economists' joke about a society that lived by people taking in each other's washing. Much of the activity there (land-office business, for example) had a special temporary cause, and it was naive for towns to assume it could go on forever. Sixth, and a related factor, western Kansas towns became nationally known in the late 1880s for vicious county-seat wars, often involving killings and requiring a calling out of the state militia to maintain order. Like the earlier gunfighter news from Dodge City, this made good copy for eastern newspapers but was no compliment to "civilization" west of Wichita. Seventh, the three solutions that had held promise independent of the outside excitement—cattle, irrigation, and sugar—all failed because they were not properly structured to

succeed in the western Kansas of the 1890s. Eighth, regional newspapers, the majority of whose readers were newcomers with no experience of the region, pandered to their advertisers, who were mostly land speculators, rather than communicating the experience of older residents consonant with the reality of the place. One could in fact summarize all the causes of the bust with the statement that in western Kansas in the latter 1880s, there was an escalation of a long-standing but ultimately ill-fated attempt to manipulate a natural environment through the application of values fundamentally alien to it. Boys who talked about towns on their heads were clever: men who accepted similar visions were dangerously gullible.

Nothing was more important in influencing regional history than the weather. And the weather did not cooperate with the real-estate speculators. Rainfall diminished. For central western Kansas, which advertised over-30-inch years in the best times, average rainfall in 1887 was 25.25 inches; in 1888, 18.95 inches; in 1889, 32.52; and in 1890, 21.40 inches. In the far western section, the equivalent figures were 20.45, 18.62, 19.79, and 13.44.[15] While this was a consistent shortfall, depleting ground moisture, and while, as always, averages did not mean much to areas that got no rain at all, this was not an unprecedented drought and did not compare to the under-10-inch average rainfall figures that would be recorded in the 1890s. More significant to the post-boom discouragement were hot winds that cooked crops and raging blizzards that punished those who stayed on for the cool season. The year-round violence of the climate in these years dashed the spirits

A Plethora of Real Estate Offices. This block in Garden City seems to have been devoted in 1887 entirely to dealing in real estate. It soon became evident that towns had to do something else.

of homesteaders, investors, and culture seekers on the Kansas High Plains.

The hot winds became as nationally famous a western Kansas liability as the grasshoppers had once been. Charles Francis Adams, whose investments in railroads led him to be concerned about the health of the region, visited western Kansas in September 1888 and was shocked by the heat at a time a New Englander like himself expected autumn. The wind was strong from the southwest, and farmers told him that it was so damaging because the region to the south and west of them was wilderness. Adams, while admitting that he was "not an expert on meteorology," wrote a letter to the *Kansas City Times* suggesting it would be in the interest of western Kansas to press for the rapid settlement of Indian Territory and New Mexico if it would diminish the force of these terrible winds.[16] Elam Bartholomew recorded in his diary for 31 July 1888 that it was 113 degrees in Rooks County that day and had been 111 in the shade the day before. On 1 August, it was 107 and on the second, 106.[17] Another settler, Frank Wilkeson, sent a vivid description to the *New York Times*. Wilkeson had, like Bartholomew and many others in the region, lain awake nights with the temperature at 106 degrees, listening to the howling wind and worrying about his future:

The mental anguish which the agriculturalists of the semiarid belt suffer when the scirocco blows is beyond description. Mortgages, the children of the high protective tariff, hang heavily over the land. The hot southwest wind decreases the interest-paying capacity of the farmers. They labor in heated air all day. They lie awake nights, their minds ever busy in vainly attempting to solve the problem of how to obtain money with which to pay the interest on their mortgages. And the weird voices of the night threaten them with bankruptcy. Then that strange quality of mind which make it exaggerate all difficulties in the night, springs into life and enrolls picture after picture for the financially-embarrassed farmer to look at. He sees his wife, his children and himself thrown into the hopper.[18]

There was relief from the heat in the winter, but it went too far. If people surmised that they had paid their winter dues in 1886–1887, they were mistaken. The winter of 1887–1888 was nearly as severe and led to such widespread suffering in the western counties that major aid campaigns were necessary for the first time since the drought of 1880. The Santa Fe and the Missouri Pacific offered to haul relief goods to starving settlers free, and meetings and charity performances were held over the eastern part of the state in response to the difficulty.[19] A. H. Gibble of Clark County addressed a mass meeting at Wichita in December at which he claimed that half the people of his county were

"utterly destitute" and that there had been several deaths because of inadequate fuel supplies. Gibble said he did not care about the speculators who criticized him for painting a bleak picture of the country but only for the women and children isolated in a forbidding crisis.[20] "None can fully understand the situation of these poor people," a Wichita editor commented, "unless they have been through that part of the state and investigated their life personally. There are but few of them who live in anything but dugouts or sod-houses and although these are often tastefully arranged inside they are poor protection from the blizzards." J. T. Hanning of the Kansas Steam Laundry at Wichita donated all his unclaimed clothing. Grocers and hardware merchants pitched in with tools and food.[21]

The weather affected corporations as seriously as individuals, notably the railroads that had built so much line in western Kansas during the boom in anticipation of increased traffic from bumper crops and new industries. A sober analysis of the railroad phenomenon by the State Board of Agriculture in 1888 included the confession that a "very large proportion" of the new western railroad mileage "has been built in anticipation of future growth and material development, rather than to meet present demands" and that this had increased the fixed expenses of the railroads to a degree that now left them in poor financial condition. Nearly 7,000 miles of the state's railroads failed that year to return expenses. "The freight traffic has not kept pace with reasonable expectations."[22] The Board of Railroad Commissioners surveyed the scene with similar diminished enthusiasm. Kansas since 1885 had experienced, wrote the commissioners, "a succession of unfavorable seasons which have no precedent in her history'' (they could have used more study of history), and in the time since the railroad construction boom, ''the conditions for the rapid development of business have not been favorable.''[23] In 1890 the commissioners found that only 85 miles of railroad had been constructed in the entire state over the previous twelve months. They could summarize the situation more succinctly now: ''After the 'boom' the 'boomerang.' ''[24]

Not only did railroad construction cease, but benefits it was thought the companies had already brought to the region turned out to be illusory. This was especially true of land sales, which, because of credit arrangements with buyers, could just as easily result in abandonment of the contract as in the arrival of a farmer. The Kansas Pacific lands, purchased during the boom on ten-year credit terms at 6 to 7 percent interest, were extremely vulnerable to abandonment by buyers. The company tried to discourage this by offering a 20 percent discount on the purchase price for any land cultivated within two years of the sale by a purchaser actually residing on it, but this did not prevent mass abandonment of contracts during the bust.[25] Of the 837 sales contracts negotiated by the KP for land in Wallace, Sherman, and Logan Counties between 1 January and 1 October 1887, 468 were canceled due to abandonment of payments by buyers before 1890. Only 205 parcels, or less than one-fourth, showed completed payments on the initial ten-year contracts, and many of these had been transferred to others, possibly speculators, by the original buyers.[26] Records of the General Land Office indicate there was a simi-

larly high rate of abandonment of homestead and timber-culture entries all over western Kansas. There were two to five times as many canceled homestead and timber-culture certificates at all the western Kansas land offices than there were final certificates issued.[27] What had seemed hard, quantitative evidence of a permanent boon to Wallace County simply evaporated when confidence in the blooming of the desert waned.

Historian Vernon Parrington once said that the long boom that was the American Gilded Age had been manufactured by ''steam and credit.'' But credit was a two-edged weapon, and it showed its dangerous side to western Kansas in more ways than abandonment of railroad land contracts. Kansas real estate, which for a time looked like something solid and tangible to investors with extra cash when millions of dollars of government bonds were called in in 1886 and 1887, now was just another fad as money moved elsewhere.[28] State legislators, who for seven consecutive sessions had worked to revise the credit laws of Kansas to make the state more attractive to investors, were now convinced too late by ''the recklessness of some brokers'' that steps must be taken to protect debtors rather than to encourage creditors.[29] However, farmers fighting the weather and their mortgage payments in an attempt to stay on the land appeared to be the only ones who could not or would not transform their western Kansas boom obligations into something equally artificial elsewhere. James Malin has noticed the strange similarity between the boom and bust in their unrealistic extremism: ''An unfailing earmark of a boom is an abiding faith in the impossible; for in-

A Little Weather. Cattle in the blizzard of 1886, illustration from Harper's Weekly, *7 February 1886. The depth of the drifts along the fence line indicates an early stage of the storm. Later most fences and some trees disappeared under the snow.*

stance, that cash is unnecessary and credit a cardinal virtue. And equally, the same implicit faith in the impossible marks a depression; a cash basis is a necessity and credit a sin. Both conditions are alike in that there is little or no cash in either, and they are different only in the matter of credit and the factors upon which it rests."[30] The Garden City land office, which had entered 1,536,945.21 acres in 1886–1887, handled 142,764.25 in 1889–1890.[31] Credit had abandoned the Kansas frontier.

Frank Spearman, who visited western Kansas in 1888 to report to readers of *Harpers Monthly* on the reappearance of the "Great

American Desert," wrote that credit problems were the fault of the improvidence of the pioneer as well as the greed of the silk-tie people. It was tempting to create more loan agencies than a community could justify and to charge extraordinary interest when customers were so carried away by hope and so enamored of the idea of "big-time" farming of large acreages with the latest expensive machinery. Most of the loans were forwarded to banks in Omaha, Kansas City, Minneapolis, St. Paul, Lincoln, and Sioux City, and the local agent was really a kind of fee-supported conduit, whose financial backing could disappear as fast as it had appeared if his eastern sources had other ideas.[32] J. C. Lohnes, who himself negotiated loans at Riverside at 2-percent-a-month interest for the Merrill Loan & Trust Company of Ness City, noted that during the boom, W. D. Miner represented Lew Darrow of Iowa and that other Ness County agents were getting money from John D. Knox & Co. of Topeka, the Loan & Guaranty Company of Connecticut, and J. B. Watkins & Co. of Lawrence, Kansas. "Money is a good thing to have in a new country," Lohnes mused later, "but when a few dozen loan agents fall over each other, bound to make you a loan, whether you really want it or need it, I fear it is foolish and dire in effect."[33]

Scholarly analysis of boom credit in Kansas, incomplete as it is, tends to confirm this contemporary minority impression. Allan Bogue, whose knowledge of farm credit in the nineteenth century is unsurpassed, made a careful study in 1951 of the extensive records of the J. B. Watkins Land Mortgage Company, which between its incorporation in 1883 and the year 1893 sold obligations in the West totaling $18

million, two-thirds of these in Kansas and Texas. Watkins Company interest rates varied in different areas and times but for western Kansas in the 1880s averaged only about 12 percent annually, an amount not inappropriate to the perceived risk, and loans were usually not more than $500 in lands west of the 100th meridian. The Watkins Company contributed to the bust, not, as the farm radical movements had it at the time, by continuing to loan money at outrageous rates but rather by withdrawing from the loan business in western Kansas on the grounds that the future of the area was uncertain. Watkins in a letter to a friend in 1891 said the Farmers' Alliance groups in attacking the mortgage business were "really beneficial" in one way: "Instead of making improvements, extending their operations, and living extravagantly, they are being urged to cancel their mortgages." Bogue emphasized that there must be more differentiation among types of credit suppliers historically, as well as better balance of the blame for errors.[34] For there to be irresponsible use of credit, there must be ready demand as well as ready supply.

Typical of opportunistic purveyors of credit and watchers for the first chance was Silas D. Aulls, who arrived at Pratt, Kansas, in the spring of 1888 from Avoka, New York, with the intent of putting money from his New York bank to more lucrative use. "This is no Avoka banking business," he wrote to his brother from a Pratt hotel. "A man is a fool to loan any money in the East when he can come here and get any such rates and security." He reported that annual interest rates in western Kansas were 36 percent at a minimum and that he had just made a four-month loan to a farmer with two cosigners of his note at 6 percent a month, or 72 percent a year interest.[35] Aulls also invested in town lots, though he said, "It is like speculating in Wall Street . . . to buy village lots," and started a clothing store in Bucklin, near Dodge City, on the promise of large markups.[36] "They double their money on cheap suits," he wrote his brother, "and make a big profit on the more expensive suits." A suit that cost $12.50 could be sold in Bucklin for $22.50 to people "who are not so particular about buying as they are in the East."[37] Aulls thought he could do fine, even as the bust began, as long as he did not trust anyone. "There is no need of trusting people. This country is more prosperous to-day than N.Y. and yet people here pay high rates of interest and security is required."[38]

As the depression deepened, however, the spirit left the speculators. "Business is rather dull here just now," Aulls wrote in June 1889.[39] At the same time M. S. Stokes, a Philadelphia investor looking for chances to buy cheaply in what might be a temporary downturn, bought several western Kansas town lots from W. C. L. Beard, who had advertised in a flyer that he had 5,180 town lots in western Kansas for sale at $8.00 each. "Don't think from the price named," Beard claimed, "and the manner in which this property is offered for sale that this is a lottery scheme or a steal to rob the public by working off worthless trash." Yet in fact that is just what it was. Though Beard claimed to have 686 lots in Leoti, 753 in WaKeeney, and 1,505 in Scott City, he also had 1,500 lots in Jerome, a town in Gove County not served by any railroad. Buyers were to send the $8.00, and the lots they were to get would be determined at a drawing at WaKeeney. Not surprisingly, Stokes was informed that his lots

were to be at Jerome, that there was not enough response to have a drawing on all the towns, and that the buyer, not the seller, had to pay the $1.10 per lot for registering the deeds.[40] H. L. Lark, who was Stokes's loan agent in Kansas, complained in 1890 that he could no longer provide his Philadelphia backers with the returns they wanted. Lark said he was "an honest, upright, Christian man" and was offended that Stokes's trust officer suspected fraud: "It looks as if he was determined to find a 'mountebank' somewhere." Perhaps it was time to abandon the region altogether: "I am getting tired of walking the floor & spending sleepless nights for other people's debts."[41]

Where creditors were annoyed, debtors were enraged. Prices of farm products declined precipitously. Corn was 83 cents a bushel in 1881 and 23 cents in 1890. Wheat fell from $1.19 in 1881 to 49 cents in 1890.[42] Expenses for machinery increased as the farm machinery business consolidated in a few companies; mortgage payments were high due to the effect of the boom on land prices and interest rates; elevators and railroads, themselves hard pressed, raised rates to try to pay fixed charges on plants they had optimistically expanded; and the local tax burden, as population fell, descended more heavily on farmers who remained. The census of 1890 revealed that 60 percent of the taxed acres in Kansas were mortgaged, a higher figure than in any other state, and that the per capita debt in Kansas was four times the national average.[43] It also showed that the vast majority of farmland in western Kansas was still cultivated by its owners rather than rented for cash or a share of the crop; thus, the full burden of debt fell upon men who had only sale of crops at distressed prices to pay for it.[44] Given such circumstances, it is not surprising that Kansas, so recently famous for untrammeled economic boosterism, became known for the enthusiastic participation of its farmers in the radical regulatory activities of first the Farmers' Alliance (the Kansas manifestation was organized in December 1888) and then the People's party.[45] The defeat of Republican candidates statewide in the elections of 1890 and the success of third-party candidates showed the depth of disappointment in Kansas with the leadership that had brought the boom and bust.

The Farmers' Alliance and its more politically oriented successor, the People's party, were national movements but with heavy concentration in western farm and silver-mining states and significant subregional variation in the reasons for their support. The most obvious examples are the widely differing motivations of Colorado silver miners, Kansas farmers, and eastern factory workers in supporting Populist inflationist planks. But within the farm community, experiences and appeals varied enough that historians have been able to find contemporary quotations supporting general conclusions as widely divergent as that the farm movement was protosocialist, that it was protofascist, or that it was not radical at all but sour grapes on the part of farmers who had failed to learn commercial techniques. Pressures varied and responses varied: the alliance and the Populists were surely patchworks of interests. But there is no question that Kansas was a center for early agitation, and it is clear that in Kansas a major element in the accompanying rhetoric was a desperate search for a new outlook in the wake of the failed dream of the 1886–1887 boom.

Western Kansas debtors were most pressured of all, and the radical rhetoric there became shrill indeed. "Farmers cannot always live on prospects," wrote an Edwards County granger in 1889. "The prices we receive for our grain and the prices we pay for bread stuffs shows too large a margin in favor of the latter."[46] A headline in Kinsley in October read "DOWN WITH THE RING" and attacked the silk-tie crowd "who came here with satchel in hand and hats drawn over their eyes . . . men who pay no taxes, but are continually slipping their hands in the treasury. . . . We are not slaves that we need to cower before the party lash."[47] In Pawnee County, the alliance organized a cooperative store and coal exchange and boycotted local merchants.[48] In Ness County, the alliance called for the repeal of all debt-collection laws and passed formal resolutions endorsing state laws that would reduce interest, stay execution of foreclosures, provide for redemption of foreclosures, exempt homesteads from some taxation, bring about secret ballots, elect the state railroad commissioners by a vote of the people, and assess taxes on mortgaged land to the owner only to the extent of his equity.[49] "Great Caesars!" wrote the editor at Larned when he heard of the Ness County resolutions, "can it be that in this enlightened country, where the highest type of civilization prevails . . . that such anarchists are found in our midst?"[50]

Alliance members, listening to shouting candidates on the backs of wagons at picnics or going to the now little-used opera house in town to hear a Medicine Lodge speaker whose claim to their attention was that he did not wear socks, may have seemed like anarchists to some.[51] Their own interpretation, however, was that they had only returned to reason and mutual dependence after a period of individualism, illusion, and artificial hope. They had learned, they thought. "Farmer voters were wild to elect bankers to represent them in our national legislative bodies," wrote one man, "but find by sad experience that they made a mistake. . . . We the people should do the electing and not boodle and whisky."[52] They were no longer interested in new railroads, which would be a convenience too costly at taxpaying time, nor could towns be created by acts of will. "The people of this portion of Kansas have awakened to the realization of the fact that it is detrimental to boom a town or advance it ahead of the country in which it is located. Why agitate when it does not stand to reason?"[53] It was with barbed irony that the *Ness City Times* reported in October 1890 that Jay Gould had passed through town on another of his grand tours. "We haven't received quotations on town lots but it is safe to say they are still going up if not gone up."[54] There could be no boom without a corps of true believers, and those believers had been forced to open their eyes.

There was a sadness about western Kansas towns at the close of the decade, like the sadness of an aging former superstar or of a reformed alcoholic in the midst of withdrawal. What had in better times been interpreted as drive, even vision, among townspeople now looked like selfishness and peevishness as they fought, often violently, among themselves and against representatives of rival towns over prizes that were no longer worth the trouble. While the killings and town sieges of the western Kansas county-seat wars drew front-page headlines in the eastern press until many must have thought Winchesters were again the law in Kansas, projected streetcar lines and water works failed in execution, and the large number who had returned to the old-time religion at the first hint of an economic reverse attacked the tawdry big-city morality that had attached itself to several villages during their bloated time.[55] The greatest pain was having to see so clearly that the great boom had been only a grosser caricature of the illusory hopes for easy success that had come to the region before. "One trouble with . . . a number of our esteemed contemporaries," went an editorial in the *Larned Chronoscope* at the end of 1887, "is that they have over-estimated the efficacy of downright, bare-faced, absurd and ridiculous lying." People would consume some of this, but newspaper readers as a class were not fools: "They know, when a comparison is made between Kinsley and Chicago, and the latter city is made [to] appear as a tallow dip alongside an electric light, that it is either intended as an extravagant joke or is written on the presumption that its readers are idiots."[56]

There had been county-seat feuds in western Kansas since there had been counties. The struggle between LaCrosse and Walnut City (now Rush Center) for county seat of Rush County lasted from 1878 to 1888, used immense amounts of time in courts all the way to the Kansas Supreme Court, and required numerous moves of the county building as one town or the other gained an advantage.[57] Stafford County's struggle among St. John, Kennelworth, Stafford, Milwaukee, and several other towns peaked in 1879.[58] Ness County experienced high rhetoric in competition in

1880 among Clarinda, Ness City, Sidney, and Waterport—all within a mile of one another at the county center, all with newspapers, and none with a reliable water supply. Ness City won by "outgeneralizing" Sidney.[59]

However, with the rapid organization of new counties spurred by the railroad building of 1885 and 1886, the number of county-seat contests increased, and when the broken boom made it clear there would not be enough business to sustain any more than one town in many counties, the physical as contrasted with the rhetorical violence of the contests escalated dramatically. Late 1880s contests in Hamilton, Morton, Gray, Garfield, Kearny, Seward, Wallace, Rawlins, Grant, Wichita, Sherman, and Stevens Counties were all characterized by double sets of county officers, charges of fraud and intimidation, multiple law suits, and in several cases killings, national headlines, and the calling out of the state militia. It was, as one participant later remembered, "a most demoralizing industry" where otherwise honorable men seemed to deteriorate.[60] Wrote a Ness City editor: "Any county that can't sustain a bitter and disgraceful county-seat warfare for years is 'mighty small potatoes.' Next to a regular rough-and-tumble fight, give us a red-hot county-seat tussle, where everybody hates everything not after a certain kind."[61]

The details are depressingly similar. In March 1887 the *New York Times* gave front-page attention to the "Cowboy War" in Kansas between the towns of Leoti and Coronado in Wichita County. Three men were killed and three badly wounded. Squads of armed citizens patrolled the streets in both towns, one man from Leoti telling a reporter that "they don't want to hurt any one but the men who killed

their friends, and they are going to have them if they have to kill everyone in Coronado." No one paid attention to the findings of the governor's commission sent to resolve the matter.[62] Later in the year the county-seat election in Gray County, with Cimarron, Montezuma, and Ingalls the major competitors, was complicated by the free use of money on behalf of Ingalls by Asa T. Soule. Recriminations about the honesty of that election led to violence, beginning when the ballot box was put under a guard of armed ruffians and peaking when an estimated 1,000 shots were fired in a January 1889 raid on Cimarron by Ingalls residents in an effort to capture county records. The state militia put both towns under martial law and all business was suspended.[63] Violence erupted at Kendall in 1887 when officers from rival Syracuse tried to arrest a man there.[64] Ravanna and Eminence both claimed victory in the Garfield county-seat election in November 1887, and the county building at Ravanna was turned into a fortress against any ballot counting by Eminence people.[65] Armed raids on Eustis, the temporary seat of Sherman County, by partisans of Sherman Center (Goodland), who had organized into a secret terrorist group known as the Homesteaders' Union Association (HUA), brought troops there early in 1888.[66]

In Stevens County, Sam Wood, a man who many thought richly deserved killing, complicated the county-seat contest in the interest of his town of Woodsdale against the ambitions of Hugoton, thus precipitating probably the greatest bloodshed of any contest. The Stevens County violence started with a pistol whipping at a railroad bond meeting and climaxed with the killing of seven men at the so-called "Haymeadow Massacre" when posses from the rival

Cowboy Wars. Troops with Gatling gun during the Stevens county-seat war. This scene was repeated distressingly often in western Kansas in the late 1880s.

towns chased each other in Indian Territory in July 1888. Troops journeyed to Stevens County to restore order on two different occasions, and it was estimated that the lawsuits instituted by attorney Wood to boom his town lots cost the state $5,000.[67] Tension between Springfield and Fargo Springs in Seward County (both of which ironically disappeared when the railroad favored Liberal) led to the murder of the county sheriff at the "Battle at Big Canyon" in January 1892, and the state militia was again on a train west.[68]

At places where county-seat battles raged, some people were aware of how absurd it was that these pitiful contests should be the means through which their region was mostly known. They might have been more annoyed still at the

prominence they would take also in written history. "No tragedy was ever more farcical, nor any farce more tragical," wrote a New York reporter, "than the succession of events that brought about a state of civil war in Wichita County, Kansas."[69] The Larned editor agreed:

The county seat business in Kansas has arrived at that stage where there is little more fairness in an election than a straight out and out warfare. Resort in almost every case is had to the gun and revolver, which might as well be used to decide the matter before as after the vote is taken. Such a state of affairs is a disgrace to any county, and especially to the fair name of Kansas.[70]

In Sherman County the peaceable majority became tired of being caught in the center:

> The air is full of rumors. The county records are to be taken from Eustis by force! The commissioners are to be strangled, or sent to the pen for life! Blood knee deep is to run down the streets of Eustis! Fire, famine and pestilence are to be let loose. All for what? Because two Town Companies have got into a little squabble over whose lots are to command the most money in the market. Personally we don't propose getting in the way of anybodies Winchester if we can help it. Some other fellow who carries a larger life insurance, and has no babies to cry after their pa, may play target if they have any fancy for having their skin perforated with cold lead.[71]

Even the HUA received appeals to stop it all. One man suggested that the seat be located at a new town independent of all warring factions. "The question of locating the county seat," he wrote, "has become a great trouble & is eating the very life blood out of our people."[72] At the very least these wars, leftovers of unrealistic puffery, discouraged any potential settlers not already discouraged by the drought and the depression from joining in the attempt to civilize western Kansas.

It was clear that agriculture was in trouble, and it should have been clear enough, especially after the severe winter of 1887, that a combination of low prices, bad weather, loss of range, and the greed of cattlemen in overstocking the range they did have doomed the cattle business as a single solution for the Kansas

High Plains.[73] But, even as the men and money from the East once again fled and the hot winds blew, there remained optimism about those two local trump cards, irrigation and sorghum sugar mills, that had helped start the boom. That these also proved useless was the unkindest cut.

As with so many other aspects of the boom, the difficulty with irrigation was that its imagined benefits were blown out of proportion to reality. In fact, the reality became less and less as drought and diversion upstream in Colorado diminished the flow of the Arkansas, which had been impressive at times in the mid-1880s, to a trickle or nothing. The famous subterranean flow that was often mentioned when the river was dry was not adequate to fill existing ditches, much less the dreamed-of Suez Canal system, which, according to C. J. Jones, was to serve seven counties. In the summer of 1890, the Arkansas River was, partly due to drought and partly to diversion farther upstream, completely dry in western Kansas.[74]

Studies by experts were not encouraging. E. M. Shelton of the State Agricultural College at Manhattan analyzed western Kansas irrigation in 1889 and concluded that large-scale irrigation by ditches was impossible there. Perhaps something could be done with underground water, but for the moment the technology of electric pumps was too expensive for farmers there and such a system would be unreliable if used only occasionally.[75] The men at the State Board of Agriculture were slightly more optimistic about ground water, which could be pumped into reservoirs by windmills and combined with dry-land farming techniques to yield crops. But they too rejected the idea that cheap ditches could provide easy yield increases through diversion of river water.[76] Ditch irrigation using private resources was in fact failing all over the West, and promoters and users were joining in a series of regional irrigation congresses which would lead eventually to the Newlands Reclamation Act of 1902 and federal sponsorship of an activity that was too legally problematical and too expensive for local advancement.[77] An 1890 census report noted that the Arkansas flow was insufficient, that western Kansas farmers were not skilled in irrigating, and that consequently there was "more or less dissatisfaction, intensified by the too sanguine hopes of great benefits to be received from this method of agriculture."[78] It was the old story. "We can't run railroads by the gas generated through the human body," one man had prophetically noted in 1882, "nor quench the thirst of a Texas steer at a Dodge City electric lamp post."[79]

Sorghum sugar was an even hollower shell. Senator Preston Plumb kept getting increased appropriations in agricultural bills for study of the diffusion process of manufacturing crystal sugar from sorghum, and the Kansas legislature offered bounties on such sugar. However, the yield in Kansas continued to be too low for profit.[80] The problem, as the 1900 census report finally explained it, was that while sorghum contained a large percentage of sucrose and a small percentage of glucose, it contained also much "starch," dextrin, and other substances that worked against its being as successfully refined as, for example, sugar beets.[81]

Although there were nine sugar plants in Kansas in 1889, and six were in western Kansas (Attica, Medicine Lodge, Meade Center, Arkalon, Liberal, and Ness City), a great deal of evidence began to show that these were more effective as speculations than as sugar producers.[82] "Several Farmers" wrote to the *Dodge City Times* in January 1888 that they would not vote for a $100,000 bond issue for a sugar mill at Dodge because the mill would pay for sorghum only half what it was worth as feed and because they were personally tired of being "deceived, cajoled, swindled, and robbed" by boom schemers.[83] Investigations in 1889 revealed massive fraud in the building of sugar mills. A great amount of bad publicity came to the American Sugar Company, which had built a mill at Meade Center and started one at Minneola. That company had "salted" its syrup with imported sugar in order to make a good showing to the local citizenry voting bonds.[84] There was no longer a chance of a profit. The "sugar cranks," the *New York Times* commented, had proceeded in "utter disregard of the experience of men who have experimented for years with sorghum in Kansas."[85] Because of this kind of fraud and the impracticality, the U.S. Department of Agriculture issued a formal warning in 1890 to communities of western Kansas not to be taken in by proposals to build sorghum sugar plants. The report was critical of building plants in such dry regions as around Meade Center and Ness City and concluded that "it would be criminal rashness to multiply factories in such localities and a most reprehensible advocacy of the industry to persuade communities or capitalists to invest in them."[86]

The largest of these latter-day sugar mills and a symbol in many ways of the passing boom was the $150,000, five-story behemoth that opened at Ness City in September 1889. It was a true wonder, with seven boilers sixteen feet high and six feet in diameter, three steam

Hope in Stone. The Ness City Sugar Mill, c. 1890, said to be the largest sorghum sugar mill in the world at the time.

engines, two cutting machines, three shredding machines, an eighteen-coil evaporator, an eighteen-foot strike pan, and ten steam pumps.[87] The company was to employ 150 people and use the products of 5,000 acres of sorghum.[88] It was said to be the largest sorghum sugar factory in the world, and its 242-foot length of Ness County post rock, illuminated at night by 125 electric lights, was a marvelous vision. Wrote a Topeka visitor: "The structure looks like a monster indeed, situated as it is on an unbounded track of level prairie."[89]

It was, however, the incarnation of a kind of hope that after a nearly thirty-year trial in the region was clearly inappropriate. There was no magic in the mill that could transform the dusty community of under 1,000 people into a center of national or even regional trade. The first year's cane crop turned out poorly, the mill produced nothing, and local banker N. C.

Merrill, who held most of the stock in return for financial services, searched for devices to keep the enterprise afloat.[90]

Theories abounded about the fire that was discovered at the mill at 1:30 on the Saturday morning of 23 August 1890, one week before the mill was to begin its second and critical year of operation. But from the fire's rapid spread in an area inaccessible to the internal water-tank fire protection system, most concluded it must have been arson. "It was an awful sight," wrote an eyewitness. "The country was illumined for miles and the flames seemed to lick the very heavens. Every now and then a piece of machinery would fall with a crash that sounded like a terrific peal of thunder." The mill burned to its stone shell, all its expensive machinery reduced to twisted wreckage. And then on Sunday evening came one of those violent storms typical of western Kansas. Ness City residents stood quietly as the sky came alive with lightning and the fury of the wind caved the walls into the remains of the engines and casings, "filling the air with a succession of reports like the continuous firing of canons."[91] They watched and they wondered.

They talked a little about how this mill might finally have brought on the "New West" of regional legend. But that evening they knew, knew at last for certain, that it was the end of an era on the High Plains west of Wichita.

Chapter Eighteen

Nature and Civilization

in Western Kansas

The late nineteenth century, the so-called Gilded Age in America, was a period of unprecedented economic growth, rapid technological advance, and remarkable innovation in the application of large-scale organization, centralization, and standardization to the mobilization of capital and the efficient utilization of resources. The general population, including western Kansas pioneers, were conditioned by media interpretations not only to take a reasonable pride in these accomplishments but to imagine that the challenge of nature to the progress of mankind was about to become of purely historical interest.

"Such was the awesome power of American energies," wrote David Emmons in summarizing the imagery of the western approach, "that, should the need ever arise, deserts could be brushed aside quite as easily as any other environmental obstacle." The Republican party promised "Free Land, Free Labor and Free Men" in the West, assuming that the country could be quickly cleansed of Indians and deserts and settled by families and towns set in place at railroad speed.[1] "Faustian

Man," as environmental historian John Opie went so far as to label the late-nineteenth-century settler, defined "the civilizing process and desirable human progress as the ability to win man's separation from and independence of the natural world."[2] Nature was seen, according to Mary Young's trenchant analysis, "as logically and historically prior to civilization, a condition to be overcome and transformed for the sake of higher culture."[3]

While it is important to apply to historical overgeneralization the lesson of restraint the settlers should have learned, legitimate general conclusions may be drawn from the early history of western Kansas, seen as an example of what Donald Pickens has called a dialectic between the rise of mass expectations encouraged by nineteenth-century politics and science and a given environment's promise in the West.[4] That early history provides material for analysis of the slow modification of the post–Civil War American outlook in the face of new realities—a modification, it may be argued, that is still in process.

At the most fundamental level, one must conclude that this history is strong evidence for

A Matter of Scale. Man and nature in Finney County, 1880s.

the power of mental assumptions as communicated through popular imagery to modify not only behavior but the perception of reality that is taken by individuals to be experience. More important, it provides examples of the relationship between stimulus and response in a specific environment.

The theory that stereotypes influence behavior was popularized in Walter Lippmann's *Public Opinion* (1923). Both social scientists and historians since have made numerous calls for the study of this process in the West. Yet most histories are too specialized to reveal much of the dynamics of total human experience. The myth/symbol school concentrates on imagery, the quantitative school eschews subjectivism, and innumerable studies focus on slices of life titled "Economic History," "Social History," "Urban History," or "Political History."

West of Wichita has not made the dream of

"total history" much less a dream, nor does it fully answer Bruce Kuklick's request for a model of the relationship between myth and experience.[5] But its attempt to integrate several aspects of life, mental and physical, as lived at a definite place and time at least provides examples of that interaction. It is no accident that claims to total history "have been most clearly approximated in a variety of exciting local studies, rather than in a larger regional or national frame."[6] For, as suggested in the introduction, the limitations of scholars' capabilities mean that deeper, more integrated examinations of historical life must be chronologically and geographically narrower.

The complexity of the relationship between myth and reality and the contribution of illusion to experience in western Kansas can be suggested by noting, first, that the reality to be experienced there over the long term would not have been easy to grasp even by the most neutral observer; second, that the stereotypes of settlers not only precluded such an unbiased learning process but were internally conflicting; and third, that both these complications can affect written history through selective source survival and oversimplified methodology. Perhaps the significance of this is best understood by reexamining a few examples.

However much accurate perception of reality may have been inhibited by culture, it was also complicated by the famous variability of the Great Plains. Rainfall varied not only year to year but over distances of a few miles. Droughts, floods, insect invasions, Indian attacks, blizzards, and fires existed in different combinations for different people arriving at different locations at different times. And of course each individual had a unique manner of communicating. Therefore, even assuming initial homogeneity, one could not expect a single response.

In all locations, however, there was throughout the period an appearance of short-term activity and prosperity that was understandably deceiving to all but the most analytical and/or cynical. This surface appearance was due to temporary factors connected with the initial occupation by modern civilization of any large body of land: increased employment and urban sales during railroad construction activity; an unusually large physical and economic presence by the military while defense was required; federal and state subsidies for the purposes of disaster relief and to encourage experimental and developmental enterprise; the substantial ancillary business created by the operation of land offices in a region where occupation was more sudden than on earlier frontiers; and the stimulation of economic solutions of unknown future from paper railroads to irrigation to the sorghum sugar craze. These features created "hard statistics" showing sometimes spectacular population growth, increases in bank clearings, urban building activity, and other "indicators," and it is understandable that residents, who were desperate not to miss the apparent opportunities for lack of facilities, were led to overexpand.

The speed of such development made it difficult to evaluate what aspects would be lasting and led to serious planning errors. Given the number of economic irons the region had in the fire and the number of examples of some types (feeder railroads and ditch irrigation canals, for example) that were projected, few imagined that so many projects would fail to live up to their initial promise.

The overexpansion of city services—western Kansas towns competing to install waterworks, streetcar lines, and colleges to match a growth rate that reversed by the time construction was under way—is one example. Not only were towns the "spearheads of the frontier," to employ urban historian Richard Wade's phraseology, but they overran considerably the development of the hinterland upon which they would ultimately depend and confused the settlement boom with permanent markets.

This is not only to stand the Turnerian picture of frontier growth stages on its head but to argue that for a time effects were likely to be confused with causes. Such feverish if insubstantial activity was made to order for the men in the silk ties—the outside speculators who would come and go with the rest of the boom entourage—but it damaged the process of agricultural adaptation that needed to occur before western Kansas could establish a sustainable population and business base. For western Kansas, one can agree with Howard Lamar's laconic statement about the Dakotas: "The early citizens seemed to be engaged in almost every occupation but that of farming."[7]

Another important confusing factor about seeming unimpeachable "reality" in early western Kansas was the power of technological masking to create special effects. Robert Berkhofer, in a seminal 1964 article entitled "Space, Time, Culture and the New Frontier," argued that the impact of environment on culture (not to be confused with temporary behavior modifications) was proportional to the technological level of the society experiencing that environment. Societies with more technology have to bend their institutions and modify their cultures less in response to varying natural environments.[8] While there is surely truth in this, Berkhofer's idea that technology can create a "secondary environment" that masks people's direct perception of the natural world fits the history of western Kansas better than his implication, which seems to match the nineteenth-century illusion, that high enough technology levels may make adaptation permanently unnecessary.

Evidence of technological masking was everywhere in early western Kansas. The railroad's "metropolitan corridor" brought both instant accessibility to a highly sophisticated civilization, hiding earlier frontierspeople's sense of awe and isolation, and instant towns with imported features, from sewers to opera companies. Modern communications made possible the nationalization of the settlement process, an important factor in its rapidity and variety. It allowed immediate distribution of good and bad news about the region and immediate and substantial responses. The breaking of the virgin prairie was not possible before the development of the steel plow, and it was understandably thought that the combination of machinery and nineteenth-century soil and crop science would allow agricultural prosperity in the country even if civilization did not change its climate. This kind of technological masking—encouraged further after 1890 by the development of electric motors and superior pumps, dry-land farming techniques, hybrid grains, oil well technology, feed lot technology, and fertilizing chemicals—has remained an important intermediary influencing western Kansans' perception of the place.

Also important in creating a range of experiences was the high rate of population turnover during the cycles of early western Kansas history. Historians have speculated that adaptation to the West may have been slowed by differences between the perceptions of newcomers and the more realistic outlook of long-time residents. The cycles of renewed optimism in western Kansas history document that. They also demonstrate that disaster leads to population replacement, which itself insures dominance of future policy by newcomers who are back at the beginning on the learning curve.

No great psychological probing is required to understand that climatic variability, temporary but positive statistics, technological masking, and constant population turnover contributed to the cycles characteristic of early western Kansas. The strength of the Farmers' Alliance movement in the 1880s in Kansas and of the later Populist party was due not only to immediate hard times but to errors tied to these cycles. Residents' flexibility in dealing with a down cycle was, after the 1880s boom, severely diminished by their eagerness during that decade to exploit fully an up cycle through breaking large, sometimes agriculturally marginal acreages; purchasing larger farms with high-interest mortgages; investing in irrigation; floating bonds beyond the current capabilities of the tax base for local industry, new railroads, or buildings to attract the county seat; and buying agricultural machinery on credit. It was a capitalization of a hope based partly on observation, at least on short-term observation. When the things observed changed and it was discovered that "nature" was in a way as much a myth as "civilization," the obligations remained. The only course was political action.

Of course, an analysis of appearances is not enough: there is also the matter of the settlers' goals, their conditioning—in short, the culture

they brought with them. It is not surprising to a modern historian that the settlers of western Kansas should think that they would conquer the High Plains environment. What is surprising in analyzing the content of this book, and less adequately explained by the literature, is that, even after such humiliating experiences as that with western Kansas before 1900, Kansans felt in retrospect that they had done so. An explanation of that requires examining how these mental constructs operate in the dynamic context of history, as it has been the goal of this volume to do, as well as understanding something about the way local heritage is created through source selection.

The goals and assumptions of those interested in western Kansas from the Civil War to 1890 were powerfully influenced by effective propaganda, which itself was tied to the economic self-interest of several of the nation's wealthiest rail corporations as well as numerous investors interested in changing hope into reality through a combination of force and illusion. The stereotypes, the mythological combinations of idea and emotion tested in the environmental cauldron of nineteenth-century western Kansas, were many: that the Indians would be easily swept away to open the field for a superior civilization; that railroads and the creation of railroad towns were capable of creating a kind of "instant civilization" imported from the East; that the climate could be changed by settlement; that technology could cushion individuals from the effects of the natural world; that western Kansas was a divine testing ground where virtue and hard work would triumph; that government aid was required only temporarily; that rain was regularly adequate for agriculture and winters regularly mild enough to sustain cattle without feed; that decentralized manufacturing would create economic diversity and enliven western Kansas towns; that insects were insignificant creatures; that the frontier was best understood and developed by white Americans; that women were to be protected and provided for by their husbands; that families were strongest when they were together; that individualism, not cooperative ventures, led to better economic results; that the people one met were usually honest. Then there was the ruling mind set, strong particularly in the boom years of the 1880s, that western Kansas could sustain a dense population and that the degree to which it could be exploited depended only on the skill and imagination of those involved.

As should be obvious from the text of this volume covering the fate of each of these constructs and others, when settlers did not believe in something, they were remarkably slow to see it, and when they did strongly believe, they could conjure it up despite evidence that they were banking on a mirage. For example, the strong Gilded-Age emphasis on individualism, combined with the myth of the virtue of the yeoman and the family farm, made it possible for western Kansans to ignore all sorts of evidence about what worked and what did not work economically in the region. A dispassionate account could not overemphasize the importance of corporations, cooperative colonies, and government in every area important to regional viability. Analysts since, particularly Walter Webb and Carl Kraenzel in the 1950s, have argued that not only history but simple observation indicates that residents of the Great Plains will have either to fundamentally change their way of living, accept heavy

subsidy from other regions of the country and colonization by them, or both. "It has not yet been demonstrated," Kraenzel wrote in 1955, "that civilization can thrive, or even survive, in the American Plains without subsidy."[9] Yet western Kansans did not and do not yet accept this, as it conflicts fundamentally with some treasured concepts of what life ought to be about.

Such mental stubbornness contributes greatly to the irony so central to western Kansas history: that in a limited environment shaped or reshaped only by eons, then approached by persons of unlimited ambition and short-term vision, "success," as the invaders define it, can be a kind of ultimate failure. It reminds one of the impossibility of using old techniques in new situations to which these techniques are inapplicable: struggling in quicksand, for instance, or steering in a frictionless, directionless setting such as space. The future is likely to bring more situations involving limited resources, and the interest of humanity is not likely to be best served by repeating such responses to true novelty as are documented in the history of western Kansas settlement.

Another factor having to do with the way vision becomes perception, then experience, and finally history became obvious in researching and writing this book. It would seem remarkable that so many historical accounts share the optimism of Ole Rölvaag's Per Hansa and ignore the terrified madness of the Berets at daily punishments. While this may be due partly to a bias shared by much of the general public, it is also explained by the nature of the source materials that remain.

For one thing, not everyone wrote about pioneer experiences, and there is a marked tendency for those who were successful to be more interested than those who failed in documenting their experiences for public consumption. Wrote Earl Pomeroy in *The Pacific Slope:* "In later years, when most of the coast had prospered more than anyone expected in pioneer days, and when the men and women who had decided to live there had more to say about why they had gone than others had to say about why they had remained in the older states, it was easy to build up a picture of a pioneer who was stronger, wiser and more virtuous than other Americans."[10]

Those with a literary bent were more likely to view their experience through a heavy cultural screen of sometimes romantic preconceptions than those who wrote nothing and whose views we therefore do not know. Most who wrote for public perusal, whether it was a book, a memoir, a letter to the editor, or just a letter home, were to some degree defensive about their decision to commit their lives to the Plains region. Bayard Taylor once wrote a letter to his fiancée advising her not to take seriously the western descriptions he provided the *New York Tribune:* "Don't be frightened at what I may say of Indians, grizzly bears, and the like; the greatest thing to be feared in this country is *fleas.*"[11] That the real enemies might be insects and boredom did not fit the heroic mold; thus, description of life as it was could be embarrassing.

Ironically, just such a tendency to make a literary genre, ordinary or profound, out of the pioneer experience meant also that the life style the environment forced on residents trying their best to live otherwise became in retrospect sacred. Howard Lamar saw it in his study of the Dakotas: "What had been merely a technique

of survival during a temporary pioneer phase often had lasting effects: the means sometimes became the end, and the pioneer spoke in glowing terms of his enforced self-sufficiency, his lack of neighbors, and his political and economic independence. Pioneering had become a way of life with highly desirable moral, social and political qualities."[12]

It is important too to recognize that those who wrote about Plains pioneering often did not do so at the time but much later when some of the negative aspects had either been conveniently forgotten or placed in the nostalgic perspective of "character builders." Such memoirs, which filled small-town Kansas papers in the 1920s, 1930s, and 1940s, are of great importance in discovering the everyday detail of pioneer life, but for an assessment of spontaneous reactions, diaries and letters are superior.

Most regions do not have the luxury of the variety of this latter type of source such as is preserved at the Kansas State Historical Society, one of the earliest western state historical societies to become active in collecting such diaries before they were destroyed. Particularly revealing for this history because they were kept every day over long years and contain on-the-spot reactions are the voluminous Elam Bartholomew diaries from Rooks County and the Norton family diaries from Pawnee County. Bartholomew was an educated man but could not impose a barrier between himself and reality every day for twenty years. The Nortons were not as highly educated, and their account has the added advantage of having been written by children as well as adults.

A last reason for the positive bias in sources is that the twentieth-century memoirs were most commonly written by women and very often by people who were children at the time of their experience on the Plains. Needless to say, a little girl experienced the Plains quite differently from her mother and father. The relative lack of responsibility for the family's survival and the superior awareness of children of the aesthetic glories of the High Plains, as well as the closeness the experience brought to the family and the environment's great potential for just plain fun, tended to make their recollections of it positive. It was certainly *the* great formative experience of their lives, and to criticize it is in a way to criticize themselves and by indirection their parents for bringing them there. All these factors affect the way experience becomes perception, not only among settlers but also among historians.

As suggested in the introduction, penetrating such a subtle screen of bias and illusion to provide a picture closer to truth is aided by a regional focus and chronological limits. Specifically, choosing a limited region and time allowed the use of several techniques and the drawing of a number of conclusions that would doubtless not have appeared in a broader study.

The technique of quantification, for example, cannot be employed as it is here for a very broad area or long chronological era, nor is it likely to be much employed by the amateur historians who write much local history. Its usefulness in finding patterns that may run counter to newspaper rhetoric and in isolating points at which the statistics of western Kansas make events there nationally significant is, however, enormous. While the audience and narrative design of *West of Wichita* made it imperative that the techniques themselves be largely transparent to the reader, the knowledge gained from computer databases created during the research contributed in many ways to the content of the story that was told.

Anyone who has made a quantitative study of land records, either generated by land offices or railroad companies, recognizes both the significance of such studies in balancing subjective impressions and the impossibility of grasping detailed settlement patterns for a unit larger than a township. Those few studies that have reached a subtle level of analysis for even a state across thirty or forty years (Paul Gates's *Fifty Million Acres* and Leslie Decker's *Railroad's Lands and Taxation*, to mention outstanding studies of Kansas land policy) have required many years of research to discover the real outlines of only a single factor influencing the region. By comparison, *West of Wichita* has generalized irresponsibly, but the focus has at least allowed it to apply Gates's and Decker's technique to new quantitative data and to learn such things as the ubiquity of colonization as a settlement technique of 1870s western Kansas; the precise timings of booms and recessions there; the impact of railroad excursions in creating clusters of settlers from the same home region in adjoining townships; variation in the size of purchases from railroads at various dates and therefore a gauge on speculative buying at times in and out of booms; a sampling of prices, types, and locations of land sold at given times; a comparison of acreages taken and prices paid in railroad and nonrailroad grant areas; and a comparison of significant intraregional variation in land use, even in an area so small by traditional standards of scholarly focus on the West—between, for example Rooks County on the eastern border of the region and Wallace County on its west.

Quantification combined with a regional focus contributed also in many other areas not so predictable as land sales patterns. It allowed use of price data—for consumer goods, for agricultural equipment, for transportation, and for crops farmers had to sell—in building a picture of the actual situation of specific groups of pioneer families. It allowed study of the relative contributions of individuals, corporations, and government to relief during disasters as well as an assessment of the size and importance of that relief effort. It encouraged more detailed analysis of census data to reveal patterns of population and depopulation in given eras, to note concentrations variously defined, and to suggest questions about differences in nearby counties that led to other sources in search of answers. One could "see" the irrigation belt and its times of fortune and misfortune as an anomaly on a computer graph loaded with census data compared with less localized trends. Regional concentration made possible study of genealogical relationships among area families, inventories of their household goods, and analysis of what specific Indians were met under what specific circumstances by what particular settlers during raids that otherwise become almost clichés. The limited scope made it feasible to study the microclimate of western Kansas through the use of monthly weather records and to correlate not only cycles several years in duration but variations in rainfall and snow within given years with the level of prosperity and mood of settlers as derived from other types of sources. It allowed the study of hundreds rather than dozens of memoirs, written by a cross-section of ordinary and extraordinary people, turning upon the same series of large events as well as upon the many smaller ones that form the body of social history.

For all the importance of ambiguous appearance and faulty perception in explaining the interaction of nature and civilization in pre-1890 western Kansas, the analysis would be incomplete without touching on an internal contradiction in the goals and outlook of its settlers that led to inconsistent expectations and therefore the near impossibility that any result would be fully satisfying. Simply put, the contradiction was between seeing pioneering in western Kansas as a commercial enterprise and at the same time as a way of life—to seek in it simultaneously wealth and freedom.

Several western historians have suggested that such an interpretation may be an appropriate one to apply to specific histories. Mary Young approached the problem when she concluded in an analysis of the cultural identity of the West that technology and transportation applied to the Edenic garden was bound ultimately to change it. The pastoral ideal, however, remains, and then "the agrarian myth functions as a rationalization for interested groups, but inhibits understanding of the problems of industrial civilization."[13] The agrarian myth inhibits understanding, one might add, of the very industrial civilization the settler thought he desired as much as the independence of a family farm and the aesthetic glories of the landscape. A more direct statement comes from Jackson Putnam's recent reappraisal of the Turner thesis. "Far from being a self-confident extrovert supremely self-assured that he was executing 'God's will,'" Putnam has written, "the frontiersman seems frequently to have been a creature of ambivalence." To develop the wilderness was to destroy it, to gain wealth was to recreate the eastern society from which he had often fled, to be rich was to be less free. In short, the values of wealth and power in a civilized setting versus freedom and innocence in a primitive one were conflicting and forced the settlers to make agonizing and frustrating choices. Putnam thinks this was the primary contributor to the "strange melancholy" observers noticed in settlers as well as modern-day disillusionment. They and we, he concludes, are haunted by the possibility that their choices may have been foolish ones.[14]

Perhaps the most powerful statement of this theme of internal division and flawed choice has come not from a professional historian but from poet, novelist, and farmer Wendell Berry in his prophetic book *The Unsettling of America: Culture and Agriculture.* Berry has argued that historically Americans have always had choices that were aspects of the same fundamental choice: between moving on and staying put, between "succeeding" and living well, between exploiting and nurturing, between masculine and feminine values, between immediate surroundings and the big picture. Civilization always won over domesticity for the majority, exploitation over nurture, quantity over quality, and in the process, Berry has written, both humanity and nature suffered. The farmer was pulled along with the rest of the country, but, because of the nature of his work and his relationship to the land, he could not be entirely comfortable ever with inattention to the "mother" he partly was. Still, to choose was difficult, for the land was both mother and father, and the farmer, Berry wrote, "crosses back and forth from one zone of spousehood to another, first as a planter and then as a gatherer."[15] Agricultural pioneers in a place like western Kansas had to try to live lives in which conflicting values coexisted. They knew the secret in a way, but were powerfully drawn to ignore it. The tensions and behavioral inconsistencies that psychological situation created help explain the region's history, and its history is the key to its future.

What are the lessons, then, of the history of western Kansas before 1890, stated in the most general terms? They are that humankind cannot limitlessly manipulate physical environments and that when traditional ideas of the civilizing process are applied to an environment with obvious and immediate limits, success itself, as defined by the civilizing culture, breeds an ultimate failure. Western Kansas marked the exact beginning of the zone John Wesley Powell warned in the 1870s would require a change in attitude, laws, and technology to utilize efficiently. Yet the history of the American "attack" demonstrates the dominance of the old "more is better" attitude—more population, more capital, more technology, more exploitation, and, later, more tractors, more pumps and more chemicals—with results ambiguous at best.

There will be those who disagree with the conclusion that the results were ambiguous. The first and loudest objection might well come from present residents of the region, who can surely present evidence that the vaunted victory, while slow in arriving and certainly not evident by 1890, when this book ends, did eventually arrive. But the Great Plains and western Kansas as a commercial enterprise depend heavily on technology and on such temporary factors as oil and gas exploration and the pumping of a limited underground aquifer. As Jerome Steffen noted recently, the phenomenon of Great Plains commercial agriculture is only about one hundred years old and "man's so-called victory may represent only a dysfunctional stage of adaptation."[16] Webb did not think victory over the desert was complete by the 1950s, and western chambers of commerce said he was a typical academic pessimist. It is no more complete in the 1980s.

That such was the case was, to use an exactly appropriate phrase, disillusioning. As Theodore Salutos has written: "Perhaps no development of the nineteenth century brought greater disappointment to the American farmers than did their failure to realize the prosperity that they had expected from industrialism."[17] But absorbing such a lesson does not imply abandoning western Kansas or avoiding all commercial exploitation of it. It does mean an approach more balanced by the lessons of its history. And those lessons are clear.

The alternative may be glimpsed in the accepting, adaptive attitude of the settlers' children—in their love and respect for the natural region they saw through uninitiated eyes and in the adaptability of youth. John Madson, the well-known environmentalist, suggests such a change of perspective in discussing his "use" of a piece of "loafing prairie" in his *Where the Sky Began: Land of the Tallgrass Prairie.*[18] John Opie took a more academic tack in a fascinating essay entitled "Frontier History in Environmental Perspective." Opie's thesis, confirmed here, I believe, is that nineteenth-century Americans made the High Plains into a "dream landscape" of their own imagining, tried to substitute technology for organic process, and attempted not only to mask the natural world but to obtain their final separation from and independence of it. When there were

choices to be made, they were influenced by their greed and by the men in the silk ties more than by their other dream of a peaceful though modest home. There was consequently an attempt to reduce a complex ecosystem, fraught with regional variability, into a more manageable "uniform environment," with consequent disastrous losses both to the physical setting and to its exploiters, economically and spiritually. "Our proper interest," wrote Opie, "should not be the role of nature in the larger history of man, but to position the activity of man properly within the larger framework of the monumental history of nature."[19] The relative strengths of man and nature in a fair fight cannot be better demonstrated than in the history of western Kansas. The conclusion is that in the future we had better not see our relationship with nature as a battle.

Given their early experience with climate and pests, it is little wonder that the first settlers of western Kansas did not fully appreciate the necessity for a "kindly" use of nature. Just as the word "civilization" is related to the word "city," so "wilderness" and "bewilderment" have a common root. John Stilgoe notes in his *Common Landscape in America* that through much of American history, the medieval fear of wilderness as an abode of wild beasts and wild men—gypsies, "crazed magicians," and Indians—remained an important and understandable influence on the attitudes of those who found themselves in it.[20]

It is therefore not so much they who should be taken to task as ourselves for learning so little from the passage of so much time. We have the advantage of seeing the long-range results of choices made in the nineteenth century, including the negative effects on human

Survivors. A Western Kansas family, 1907.

spiritual health of too much masking of distinctive regions like Kansas' High Plains. Berry complained that the "Vagrant Sovereign" created by nineteenth-century attitudes toward the land is now king of nowhere. By assuming that "there is nothing that he *can* do that he should not do, nothing that he *can* use that he should not use," humankind has standardized things and hopelessly generalized the sense of worldly whereabouts. "Geography is defined for him by his house, his office, his commuting route, and the interiors of shopping centers, restaurants and places of amusement—which is to say that his geography is artificial; he could be anywhere, and he usually is."[21] The antidote is, in the view of landscape historian John Jackson, the appreciation of regional variation. Particular physical and cultural landscapes remind us that we "belong—or used to belong—to a specific place," and their special look, weather, and history provide people a setting for their life experiences—"spaces that never change and are always as memory depicted them." Western Kansas unquestionably had strong defining characteristics, and it is these, writes Jackson, "that give a landscape its uniqueness, that give it style. These are what make us recall it with emotion."[22]

Ideas change. Western Kansas remains, and for all the manipulation by puny man over the last few thousand years modestly and the last one hundred twenty intensely, it is still an awesome natural setting, the "glorious upland" that a geologist in 1888 called "*the* feature of Kansas." Farmers looking at the sky and feeling the wind have not been replaced there by "automatic men and machinery," as a Wichita editor predicted they would be in 1885, nor has the landscape's capability to generate loyalty and emotion been subsumed by franchise restaurants and cable television. The blue hills on the horizon have been subjected to every human hat trick, superficial modifications coming with lightning speed. In the period of this study, railroads were flung across a wilderness in months, forts brought instant population and security, towns imported the essense of St. Louis, farm machinery broke miles of virgin prairie and created orderly patchworks of plowed fields. Yet the mystery and the mirage that generated such great hopes and such chilling fears remained and remains. The area west of Wichita was always a highly defined physical region: Josiah Copley's 1867 conclusion that it was "as unique as it is stupendous" still applies. What is less appreciated is that it has become equally identifiable historically and culturally. Learning the process by which this happened may contribute to the eventual solution of the puzzle that was and is western Kansas.

Notes

Introduction: On Regional History

1. Jerome Steffen, *The American West: New Perspectives, New Dimensions* (Norman: University of Oklahoma Press, 1979), 4.

2. John Williams, "A New Look at an Old Field," *Western Historical Quarterly* 9 (1978): 281–96.

3. Fernand Braudel, *The Structures of Everyday Life: The Limits of the Possible* (New York: Harper & Row, 1981), 23.

4. Henry Nash Smith, "The West as an Image of the American Past," *University of Kansas City Review* 18 (1951): 29–35.

5. Gilbert Fite, "Daydreams and Nightmares: The Late Nineteenth-century Agricultural Frontiers," *Agricultural History* 40 (1966): 285.

6. One historian who has applied such analysis to the historical Great Plains is Roger Barker. See his "The Influence of Frontier Environment on Behavior," in Steffen, *The American West,* 71–91.

7. Andrew Clark, "The Great Plains: Perception by Any Name," in Brian Blouet and Merlin Lawson, eds., *Images of the Plains: The Role of Human Nature in Settlement* (Lincoln: University of Nebraska Press, 1975), xi.

8. Howard Lamar, *Dakota Territory 1861–1889: A Study of Frontier Politics* (New Haven, Conn.: Yale University Press, 1956), viii.

9. Donald Meinig, *Imperial Texas: An Interpretive Essay in Cultural Geography* (Austin: University of Texas Press, 1969).

10. Clark, "Perception by Any Name," xi, xii.

11. Laurence Veysey, "Myth and Reality in Approaching American Regionalism," *American Quarterly* 12 (1960): 31, 37, 43.

1. The Blue Hills

1. Huber Self, *Environment and Man in Kansas: A Geographical Analysis* (Lawrence: Regents Press of Kansas, 1978), 40.

2. A typical dust-bowl map is in the frontispiece of Vance Johnson, *Heaven's Tableland: The Dust Bowl Story* (New York: Farrar, Straus and Company, 1947).

3. Technically, the climate zones in Kansas moving east to west are humid subtropical, temperate continental, and middle latitude steppe, the last two encompassing western Kansas. Self, *Environment,* 63–64.

4. John Romey et al., eds., *This Remarkable Continent: An Atlas of United States and Canadian Society and Cultures* (College Station: Texas A&M University Press, 1982), 16. Useful throughout this book for reference will be Homer Socolofsky and Huber Self, *Historical Atlas of Kansas* (Norman: University of Oklahoma Press, 1972); Rex Buchanan, ed., *Kansas Geology: An Introduction to Landscapes, Rocks, Minerals, and Fossils* (Lawrence: University Press of Kansas, 1984); Robert Richmond, *Kansas: A Land of Contrasts* (St. Charles, Mo.: Forum Press, 1974); and for a county-by-county overview collected from the pioneers, A. T. Andreas, *History of the State of Kansas* (Chicago: A T. Andreas, 1883).

5. Self, *Environment,* 42.

6. W. D. Pratt in *Larned Chronoscope,* 6 January 1888.

7. A delightful account of this aspect of the western Kansas environment is Grace Muilenberg and Ada Swineford, *Land of the Post Rock: Its Origins, History, and People* (Lawrence: University Press of Kansas, 1975).

8. A more recent interpretation of the same sort is Elwyn Robinson, "An Interpretation of the History of the Great Plains," *North Dakota History* 41 (1974): 5–19.

9. David Emmons, *Garden in the Grasslands: Boomer Literature of the Central Great Plains* (Lincoln: University of Nebraska Press, 1971), 154.

10. *Climate and Man: Yearbook of Agriculture* (Washington, D.C.: Government Printing Office, 1941), 12.

11. C. Warren Thornwaite, "Climate and Settlement in the Great Plains," *Climate and Man,* 179.

12. Ibid., 177.

13. Atchison, Topeka & Santa Fe Railroad, *How and Where to Get a Living* (Boston: By the Company, 1876), 3, 7.

14. Josiah Copley, *Kansas and the Country Beyond* (Philadelphia: J. B. Lippincott & Co., 1867), 5.

15. *Russell County Record,* 22 November 1877.

16. L. D. Burch, *Kansas as It Is* (Chicago: C. S. Burch and Co., 1878), 11.

17. *Dodge City Times,* 25 August 1877.

18. Frank Waugh, "Pioneering in Kansas," typescript in Manuscripts Division, Kansas State Historical Society, Topeka, 27, 50.

19. *Osborne County Farmer,* 7 July 1876.

20. William H. Dixon, *New America* (8th ed., London: Hurst and Blackett, 1867), 28–29.

21. *Osborne County Farmer,* 5 November 1931.

22. *Protection Post,* 2 May 1947, 31 May 1957. A pair of contemporary rather than remembered accounts are in *Valley Republican* (Kinsley, Kans.), 15 December 1877 and 19 January 1878.

23. *Wichita Beacon,* 16 April 1886.

24. *Dodge City Times,* 10 September 1885.

2. Savages

1. M. Windsor and James Scarborough, *History of Jewell County, Kansas, with a Full Account of Its Early Settlements and the Indian Atrocities Committed within Its Borders* (Jewell City, Kans.: "Diamond" Printing Office, 1878), 4, 5. This pamphlet was reprinted in the 1920s in *Kansas State Historical Society Collections* 17 (1926–28): 389–409.

2. Ibid., 5–7. The *Osborne County Farmer,* 22 July 1880, says that nine people were killed in this 9 April raid. Of the details of the deaths of the others, nothing is known. The settlement was abandoned for less than one year.

3. *Osborne County Farmer,* 22 July 1880.

4. A. W. Burton to Isaac, 11 July 1863, misc. Burton, and Cardella Brown to Aunt, 8 February 1866, misc. Brown, MSS Division, Kansas State Historical Society, Topeka. Both letters were sent from Fort Larned.

5. For a general discussion of these concepts, see Robert Berkhofer, *The White Man's Indian: Images of the American Indian from Columbus to the Present* (New York: Vintage Books, 1979), 38–54.

6. A great deal of policy is summarized here. Of the vast literature, a reader might consult Loring Priest, *Uncle Sam's Stepchildren: The Reformation of United States Indian Policy, 1865–1887* (New Brunswick, N.J.: Rutgers University Press, 1942); Francis Prucha, *American Indian Policy in Crisis: Christian Reformers and the Indian, 1865–1900* (Norman: University of Oklahoma Press, 1976); Robert Mardock, *The Reformers and the American Indian* (Columbia: University of Missouri Press, 1971); H. Craig Miner and William E. Unrau, *The End of Indian Kansas: A Study of Cultural Revolution, 1854–1871* (Lawrence: Regents Press of Kansas, 1978); and Douglas Jones, *The Treaty of Medicine Lodge* (Norman: University of Oklahoma Press, 1966).

7. A summary of fort building can be found in Robert Fraser, *Forts of the West: Military Forts and Presidios and Posts Commonly Called Forts West of the Mississippi River to 1898* (Norman: University of Oklahoma Press, 1965). For reliable, brief accounts, see Leo Oliva, *Fort Hays* (Topeka: Kansas State Historical Society, 1980) and *Fort Larned* (Topeka: Kansas State Historical Society, 1982).

8. Hancock's campaign is described in Robert M. Utley, *Frontier Regulars: The United States Army and the Indian, 1866-1891* (New York: Macmillan, 1973), 111-119.

9. Samuel Crawford, *Kansas in the Sixties* (Chicago: A. C. McClurg & Co., 1911), 321. Crawford's views on the Indian situation in Kansas in the late 1860s are found throughout the last fifth of the book.

10. Samuel Crawford to E. G. Ross, 29 June and 5 July 1867, Governors' Papers, Crawford, box 1, folder 8, Archives Division, Kansas State Historical Society, Topeka.

11. A good account of the battles of the Saline River and Prairie Dog Creek, fought that year, is in Lonnie White, *Hostiles and Horse Soldiers: Indian Battles and Campaigns in the West* (Boulder, Colo.: Pruett Publishing Company, 1972), 49-67.

12. The definitive account of the 1867 cholera outbreak is Ramon Powers and Gene Younger, "Cholera on the Plains: The Epidemic of 1867 in Kansas," *Kansas Historical Quarterly* 37 (1971): 351-93.

13. Robert Utley, "Campaigning with Custer," *American West* 14 (1977): 5, 58.

14. White, *Hostiles,* 50.

15. Joseph Snell and Robert Richmond, "When the Union and Kansas Pacific Built through Kansas," *Kansas Historical Quarterly* 32 (1966): 346.

16. *Osborne County Farmer,* 22 July 1880; White, *Hostiles,* 50-51.

17. *Rooks County Record,* 29 March 1912.

18. *Hays Sentinel,* 18 January 1878.

19. E. S. Lane, "Account of Killing of Thomas Parks by Indians, WaKeeney, Sept. 19, 1867," misc. Lane, MSS Division, Kansas State Historical Society, Topeka.

20. Ibid.

21. Ibid. The site of this incident was the "badlands," about which vague rumors of some connection with Indian atrocities survived in my father's childhood. Lane almost exactly a year later was part of the rescue party that brought back the volunteers who had been trapped by Indians at Beecher's Island on the Arickaree fork of the Republican River.

22. W. T. Sherman to Secretary of War, 1 November 1868, in *Annual Report of the Secretary of War For the Year 1868-69* (Washington, D.C.: Government Printing Office, 1869), 3-4.

23. P. H. Sheridan to W. T. Sherman, 26 September 1868, ibid., 11.

24. Hill P. Wilson, "Black Kettle's Last Raid— 1868," *Kansas State Historical Society Collections* 8 (1903-4): 11.

25. John Whiteford to S. J. Crawford, 27 August 1868, Governors' Papers, Crawford, box 1, folder 8, Archives Division, Kansas State Historical Society, Topeka.

26. *Annual Report of the Secretary of War for the Year 1868-69,* 5. In the *Annual Report* for 1869-70, 52-55, there is a table of lives lost, people captured, and property destroyed in the entire military Department of the Missouri, including Kansas, in 1868 and 1869. The total for the region for the two years was 158 killed and 14 women raped. The number killed did not include those who died during official military engagements.

27. Glenda Riley, "The Specter of a Savage: Rumors and Alarmism on the Overland Trail," *Western Historical Quarterly* 15 (1984): 427.

28. *Annual Report of the Secretary of War for the Year 1869-70* (Washington, D.C.: Government Printing Office, 1870), 55.

29. The best one-stop source for captivity stories is Lonnie White, "White Women Captives of Southern Plains Indians, 1866-1875," *Journal of the West* 8 (1969): 327-54.

30. The Weichell experience is described in detail in reminiscences by another German settler. See Ferdinand Eberhardt, "Reminiscences," MSS Division, Kansas State Historical Society, Topeka.

31. V. B. Osborn to S. J. Crawford, 13 August 1868, Governors' Papers, Crawford, box 1, folder 8, Archives Division, Kansas State Historical Society, Topeka.

32. The reader can follow military actions in Utley, *Frontier Regulars,* 142-62; Lonnie White, "The Cheyenne Barrier on the Kansas Frontier

1868–69," *Arizona and the West* 4 (1962): 51–64; Oliver Knight, *Following the Indian Wars: The Story of Newspaper Correspondents among the Indian Campaigners* (Norman: University of Oklahoma Press, 1960); and Lonnie White, "Indian Raids on the Kansas Frontier, 1869," *Kansas Historical Quarterly* 38 (1972): 369–88.

33. White, "White Women," 345–46. An account of the Morgan and White experience is also in Joanna Stratton, *Pioneer Women: Voices from the Kansas Frontier* (New York: Simon and Schuster, 1981), 122–25.

34. James Hadley, "The Nineteenth Kansas Cavalry and the Conquest of the Plains Indians," *Kansas State Historical Society Collections* 10 (1907–8): 453.

35. Mrs. Olive Clark, "Early Days along the Solomon Valley," *Kansas State Historical Society Collections* 17 (1926–28): 728. Stratton, in *Pioneer Women*, 125, quotes Mrs. Morgan as saying her Indian husband was kind to her and expressing regret that whites had found her. The possibility that her deep shame changed to acceptance is an interesting one, but the sources are not adequate to explore it.

36. D. S. Bacon to J. M. Harvey, 13 May 1872, Governors' Papers, Harvey, box 2, folder 12, Archives Divison, Kansas State Historical Society, Topeka.

37. Julia Chase, "Mother Bickerdyke," *Kansas State Historical Society Collections* 7 (1902–3): 189–92.

38. Chase, "Mother Bickerdyke," 193; Hiram Bickerdyke to his brother, 11 February 1902, B-5-2; S. C. Pomeroy to O. O. Howard, 1 January 1869; and John Logan to ?, 28 December 1868, relief 1868–69, MSS Division, Kansas State Historical Society, Topeka.

39. Alfred Sully to James Harvey, 12 February 1869, Governors' Papers, Harvey, box 2, folder 12, Archives Division, Kansas State Historical Society, Topeka.

40. N. H. Davis to James Harvey, 25 February 1869, ibid.

41. O. P. Hamilton to James Harvey, 17 June 1869, ibid.

42. Nelson Miles to James Harvey, 28 June 1869, ibid.

43. R. G. Kshenka to James Harvey, 15 May 1870, box 2, folder 12, ibid.

44. N. O. Wilke to James Harvey, February 1870, ibid.

45. *Register* (Great Bend), 15 May 1897.

46. C. Delano to J. M. Harvey, 4 May 1871, Governors' Papers, Harvey, box 2, folder 12, Archives Division, Kansas State Historical Society, Topeka.

47. Mrs. Frank Montgomery, "Fort Wallace and Its Relation to the Frontier," *Kansas State Historical Society Collections* 17 (1926–28): 254; Bernice Webb, "First Homesteader and the Battle of Sappa Creek," *Kansas Quarterly* 10 (1978): 52–58.

48. *Russell County Record,* 4 May 1876.

49. *Hays Sentinel,* 24 January 1877.

50. An excellent source on the Jordan affair, employing all the extant primary material, is Minnie Millbrook, "The Jordan Massacre," *Kansas History* 2 (1979): 219–30.

51. Mrs. F. C. Montgomery, "United States Surveyors Massacred by Indians," *Kansas Historical Quarterly* 1 (1932): 266–72.

52. White, "White Women," 347–49. The date of the killing was 11 September.

53. *Russell County Record,* 8 April 1875.

54. Mrs. O. F. Short to Thomas Osborn, 25 May 1876, Governors' Papers, Osborne, box 3, folder 5, Archives Division, Kansas State Historical Society, Topeka.

55. S. S. Van Sickel, *A Story of Real Life on the Plains: A True Narrative of the Author's Experience* (N.p., n.d.), Indian pamphlets, vol. 1, Kansas State Historical Society, Topeka, 30–31.

56. *New York Times,* 20 August 1868, p. 4, col. 5.

57. Thomas Osborn to the President, 6 July 1875, quoted in *Russell County Record,* 22 July 1875.

58. *New York Times,* 11 July 1869, p. 4, col. 3.

59. *Osborne County Farmer,* 1870, Osborne County clippings, vol. 1, 51, Kansas State Historical Society, Topeka.

60. *Dodge City Times,* quoted in *Edwards County Leader* (Kinsley), 31 May 1877.

61. *Hays Sentinel,* 7 June 1876.

62. Sandra Myres, *Westering Women and the Frontier Experience 1800–1915* (Albuquerque: University of New Mexico Press, 1982), 38, 53, 57.

63. *Kansas City Times,* 2 July 1957; *Oakley Graphic,* 27 June 1957; *Hays Daily News,* 5 July 1957.

64. Pictures of her are in *Hays Daily News,* ibid.

3. The Steel Nile

1. John Stilgoe, *Metropolitan Corridor: Railroads and the American Scene* (New Haven, Conn.: Yale University Press, 1983), ix–xii, 52.

2. William Goetzmann, *Exploration and Empire: The Explorer and Scientist in the Winning of the West* (New York: Alfred A. Knopf, 1966); Robert Berkhofer, "Space, Time, Culture and the New Frontier," *Agricultural History* 38 (1964): 21–30; Earl Pomeroy, "Toward a Reorientation of Western History: Continuity and Environment," *Mississippi Valley Historical Review* 41 (1955): 579–600.

3. *Senatorial Excursion Party over the Union Pacific, E.D.* (St. Louis: S. Levison, 1867), 46. For evidence that the manipulating influence of railroad technology may have appeared still earlier, see H. Craig Miner, "Stereotyping and the Pacific Railway Issue, 1845–65," *Canadian Review of American Studies* 6 (1975): 59–73.

4. A good example of the quantitative approach is Lloyd Mercer, *Railroads and Land Grant Policy: A Study in Government Intervention* (New York: Academic Press, 1982). For an American studies–style interpretation, see Miner, "Stereotyping."

5. William Petrowski, "The Kansas Pacific: A Study in Railroad Promotion" (Ph.D. diss., University of Wisconsin, 1965), 89–127; R. M. Shoemaker et al., *Reports of Preliminary Surveys for the Union Pacific Railway, Eastern Division*

from Fort Riley to Denver City (Cincinnati: Robert Clarke & Co., 1866); George Anderson, *Kansas West* (San Marino, Calif.: Golden West Books, 1963), 11–15.

6. Petrowski, "The Kansas Pacific," 147, 149; Paul Gates, *Fifty Million Acres: Conflicts over Kansas Land Policy, 1854–1890* (New York: Atherton Press, 1966), 251. (Gates's book was originally published in 1954.)

7. Petrowski, "The Kansas Pacific," 147.

8. *The Ellsworth & Pacific Railroad. Some Facts and Information as to the Routes of the Ellsworth & Pacific Railroad and the Country through which It Would Pass* (Leavenworth, Kans.: Bulletin Office, [1868]), 5, 16, 27.

9. Snell and Richmond, "Union and Kansas Pacific," 185.

10. Ibid., 337–38.

11. *Senatorial Excursion,* 8.

12. Snell and Richmond, "Union and Kansas Pacific," 338–41, 345.

13. A detailed account of this incident is found in two letters from Adolph Roenigk to J. C. Ruppenthal in Hist. Russell County, MSS Division, Kansas State Historical Society, Topeka. Less complete but more available is A. Roenigk, "Railroad Grading among Indians," *Kansas State Historical Society Collections* 8 (1904): 384–89.

14. Ibid.

15. Ibid.

16. *Russell County Record,* 27 November 1877.

17. Snell and Richmond, "Union and Kansas Pacific," 339.

18. *Russell County Record,* 27 November 1877.

19. "A Trip to the End of the Union Pacific in 1868," *Kansas Historical Quarterly,* 13 (1944): 199.

20. Petrowski, "The Kansas Pacific," 181–82.

21. The most careful analysis of the way this kind of financing was done is Robert Fogel, *The Union Pacific Railroad: A Case in Premature Enterprise* (Baltimore: Johns Hopkins University Press, 1960). See also Lloyd Mercer, *Railroads and Land Grant Policy* (New York: Academic Press, 1982). For the UPED, see William Petrowski, "Kansas City to Denver to Cheyenne:

Pacific Railroad Construction Costs and Profits," *Business History Review* 48 (1974): 206–24. Petrowski quotes (208) a government official who said UPED construction devices were just like the Crédit Mobilier, "only the financial maneuvering was more cleverly done."

22. *Ness City Times,* 6 March 1880.

23. Anderson, *Kansas West,* 21.

24. Snell and Richmond, "Union and Kansas Pacific," 342.

25. Keith Bryant, *History of the Atchison, Topeka and Santa Fe Railway* (New York: Macmillan, 1974), 26–30, 34–35; Joseph Snell and Don Wilson, "The Birth of the Atchison, Topeka and Santa Fe," *Kansas Historical Quarterly* 34 (1968): 345–54.

26. *Pioneer Plows and Steel Rails; Outriders of Civilization in the Valley of the Solomon* (Downs, Kans.: Downs News & Times, 1961), 12–14. This line was built to Cawker City, Downs, and Alton in 1879 but never went much farther. *Downs News,* 22 January 1959.

27. S. C. Pomeroy, "Report of Senator S. C. Pomeroy of a Ten Days Trip West from Waterville, Kansas," 5 September 1870, misc. Pomeroy, MSS Division, Kansas State Historical Society, Topeka.

28. *Statement of the Condition and Resources of the Kansas Central Railway (Narrow Gauge) from Leavenworth, Kansas, to Denver, Colorado* (Leavenworth: Office of the Kansas Farmer, 1871), 4, 14–15.

29. Leslie Decker, *Railroads, Lands, and Politics: The Taxation of Railroad Land Grants, 1864–1897* (Providence, R.I.: Brown University Press, 1964), 253–325, contains a township-by-township mapping of taxable railroad lands in Saline, Russell, and Trego Counties from 1872 to 1887. Another source for visual confirmation of this pattern is *Centennial Edition of the Fourth Annual Report of the State Board of Agriculture* (Topeka, Kans.: Geo. W. Martin, 1876). In contains a complete set of county maps showing railroad and public lands still available and therefore, by omission, the settlement pattern at

mid-decade. A detailed map showing lands taken in Russell County is in *Russell County Record,* 23 August 1877.

30. James Forsythe, "Environmental Considerations in the Settlement of Ellis County, Kansas," *Agricultural History* 51 (1977): 39.

31. Webb's book *Buffalo Land: An Authentic Account of the Discoveries, Adventures and Mishaps of a Scientific and Sporting Party in the Wild West* (Philadelphia: Hubbard Brothers, 1872) is addressed primarily to the sportsman and thrill-seeker but does contain an appendix on settlement possibilities.

32. *Hand Book for the Kansas Pacific Railway Containing a Description of the Country, Cities, Towns & C., Lying along the Line of the Road and Its Branches* (St. Louis: Aug. Wiebusch & Son, 1870), 62–63.

33. Gates, *Fifty Million Acres,* 267, 271; Decker, *Railroad Lands,* 107, 113.

34. Forsythe, "Environmental Considerations," 39–42. The idea that, in contrast to Frederick Jackson Turner's thinking, cities were actually "spearheads" of the frontier was most forcefully advanced by Richard Wade, *The Urban Frontier* (Chicago: University of Chicago Press, 1964).

35. Gates, *Fifty Million Acres,* 271.

36. D. L. Lakin to T. Nickerson, 7 March 1872, AT&SF land dept. correspondence, RR 308, MSS Division, Kansas State Historical Society, Topeka.

37. Gates, *Fifty Million Acres,* 271.

38. List of sold and unsold lands, 1 January 1878, AT&SF, land dept. correspondence, RR 308, MSS Division, Kansas State Historical Society, Topeka.

39. Records of the AT&SF Railroad, contract books, vols. 7 and 9, MSS Division, Kansas State Historical Society, Topeka. Original KP sales books for this period are not now known to exist, but, as shall be seen, 1880s manuscript records for the KP indicate similar targeting of buyers. The great number of actual settlers hailing from Illinois and a few other Midwestern states can be seen in *Centennial Edition of the Fourth Annual Report of*

the *State Board of Agriculture* (1876), which offers a table for each Kansas county in 1875 showing from where its settlers came.

40. 1870 Census, Population Schedules, Kansas, Microcopy 593, Roll 442, National Archives, Washington, D.C.

41. Nyle Miller and Robert Richmond, "Sheridan, A Fabled End-of-Track Town of the Union Pacific Railroad, E.D., 1868–69," *Kansas Historical Quarterly* 34 (1968): 435–38.

42. 1870 Census, Microcopy 593, Roll 442, National Archives.

43. Miller and Richmond, "Sheridan," 429.

44. This theme is especially prominent in the work of western historian Robert Athearn.

45. Francis Walker, *A Compendium of the Ninth Census* (Washington, D.C.: Government Printing Office, 1872), 191, 193, 466, 627.

46. Raymond Welty, "Supplying the Frontier Military Posts," *Kansas Historical Quarterly* 7 (1938): 159.

47. The definitive work here is Robert Dykstra, *The Cattle Towns* (New York: Alfred A. Knopf, 1968). For a more detailed look at Wichita, see H. Craig Miner, *Wichita: The Early Years, 1865–80* (Lincoln: University of Nebraska Press, 1982).

48. Especially perceptive on the settler-cattlemen conflict is Minnie Millbrook, "North from Dodge: Troubles along the Trail," *Kansas Quarterly* 6 (1974): 5–14.

49. Recent interpretive studies of the vice question and the end of the trade are David Galenson, "The Profitability of the Long Drive," *Agricultural History* 51 (1977): 737–58; Gary Cunningham, "Gambling in the Kansas Cattle Towns: A Prominent and Somewhat Honorable Profession," *Kansas History* 5 (1982): 2–22; Carol Leonard and Isidor Walliman, "Prostitution and Changing Morality in the Frontier Cattle Towns of Kansas," *Kansas History* 2 (1979): 34–53.

50. Walker, *Compendium of the Ninth Census*, 736–37.

51. *Report of the State Board of Agriculture to the Legislature of Kansas for the Year 1873* (Topeka, Kans.: State Printing Works, 1874), 93.

52. *Centennial Edition of the Fourth Annual Report of the State Board of Agriculture*, 120, 126, 132, 232.

53. An encapsulated history of the establishment of Kansas land offices is part of the inventory of Record Group 49 land records at the National Archives and Records Administration, Kansas City, Missouri. The basic changes can be followed through the *Annual Report of the Commissioner of the General Land Office to the Secretary of the Interior.*

54. *House Executive Document* 1, 44th Cong., 2d Session (Serial 1749), 138–39.

55. *Larned Press*, 8 December 1876.

56. Quoted in Bryant, *History of the Atchison, Topeka and Santa Fe*, 35.

57. J. H. Tice, *Over the Plains, on the Mountains; or Kansas, Colorado and the Rocky Mountains; Agriculturally, Mineralogically and Aesthetically Described* (St. Louis: Industrial Age Printing Co., 1872), 54.

4. "This Ocean of Bloom"

1. G. M. Lewis, "Changing Emphases in the Description of the Natural Environment of the American Great Plains Area," *Transactions and Papers, Institute of British Geographers* 30 (1962): 76–80.

2. Will Mitchell to his sister, 1 August 1864, misc. Mitchell, MSS Division, Kansas State Historical Society, Topeka.

3. *Liberal News*, 21 February 1934.

4. *Larned Progress*, 24 June 1888.

5. John Morrill to family, 23, 26 September, 9 October 1865, Morrill collection, MSS Division, Kansas State Historical Society, Topeka.

6. Edwards in *Kansas Daily Commonwealth* (Topeka), 18 February 1872.

7. *Senatorial Excursion*, 25.

8. *Hand Book*, 57–60.

9. "A Trip to the End of the Union Pacific in 1868," 201–2. The observer was John Putnam.

10. William Bell, *New Tracks in North America* (London: Chapman and Hall, 1870). Bell wrote the book partly to encourage British emigration to Kansas Pacific lands and so was not generally given to negative exaggeration.

11. Francis Richardson to his wife, 21 July 1872, misc. Richardson, MSS Division, Kansas State Historical Society, Topeka.

12. Tice, *Over the Plains,* 52–53.

13. James Malin, *Winter Wheat in the Golden Belt of Kansas: A Study of Adaption to Subhumid Geographical Environment* (Lawrence: University of Kansas Press, 1944), 1, 8.

14. *Compendious History of Ellsworth County, Kansas* (Ellsworth, Kans.: Reporter Office, 1879), 25–26, 34.

15. *Hays Sentinel,* 18 January 1878.

16. Ibid., 8 March 1876, 8 August 1879, 16 July 1880, 11 February 1881.

17. Bernard Smyth, *The Heart of the New Kansas* (Great Bend, Kans.: B. B. Smyth, 1880), 89.

18. Malin, *Winter Wheat,* 32–33, 66.

19. David Emmons, *Garden in the Grasslands: Boomer Literature of the Central Great Plains* (Lincoln: University of Nebraska Press, 1971), 132, 143. See also Emmons, "Richard Smith Elliott, Kansas Promoter," *Kansas Historical Quarterly* 36 (1970): 390–401.

20. Richard Elliott, *Notes Taken in Sixty Years* (St. Louis: R. R. Studley & Co., 1883), 305–6.

21. Ibid., 306–7.

22. Emmons, *Garden,* 144–46.

23. Elliott, *Notes,* 307–11.

24. *Hays Sentinel,* 16 February 1878.

25. Tice, *Over the Plains,* 44–49.

26. The exact location of Watson's sections is known, but all references to the Elliott farm simply say "at Ellis." The only reason for believing operations were separate is Martin Allen's comment when mentioning Watson's farm that "the KP Railroad also commenced experiments there" (*Hays Sentinel,* 18 January 1878).

27. *The Western Kansas Agricultural Association, Chartered June 6, 1870* (Quincy, Ill.: Whig Company, 1871), 1. I am indebted to book dealer Michael Heaston of Austin, Texas, for sending me a photocopy of this rare pamphlet.

28. Louis Watson to his mother, 1 August, 4 December 1870, Jennings coll., MSS Division, Kansas State Historical Society, Topeka.

29. *Western Kansas Agricultural Association,* 4–5.

30. Watson to directors, [1872], Jennings coll., MSS Division, Kansas State Historical Society, Topeka.

31. Watson to his mother, 17 July 1871, ibid.

32. Watson to stockholders, 11 January 1872, ibid.

33. Watson to his mother, 22 January 1872, ibid.

34. Watson report, 30 December 1872; J. B. Cahill to Louis Watson, marked "Personal," 19 December 1871, ibid.

35. Watson to his mother, 24 June 1873, ibid.

36. Watson to his mother, 2 August 1874, ibid.

37. Watson to his mother, 29 October 1875, ibid.

38. Watson to his mother, 24 June 1873, ibid.

39. John Bonnell to A. E. Touzalin, 9 January 1872, RR 308, MSS Division, Kansas State Historical Society, Topeka.

40. W. H. Droze, "Changing the Plains Environment: The Afforestation of the Trans-Mississippi West," in Thomas Wessel, ed., *Agriculture in the Great Plains, 1876–1936* (Washington, D.C.: Agriculture History Society, 1977), 8, 12, 15.

41. C. H. Longstreth to A. S. Johnson, 25 January 1879, ibid.

42. Copley, *Kansas and the Country Beyond,* 26.

43. *Hand Book,* 66–67.

44. F. H. Snow, "Is Kansas Rainfall Increasing" (1884), in William Seiler, "Magazine Articles about Kansas Published from 1864 to 1904," 3 vols., typescript, 458–60, Kansas State Historical Society, Topeka. For an overview of the literature on this question, see Paul Travsi, "Changing Climate in Kansas: A Late 19th-Century Myth," *Kansas History,* 1 (1978): 48–58.

45. For comment on this idea through the entire

Great Plains region, see Emmons, *Garden in the Grasslands.*

46. *Hays Sentinel,* 23 November 1877.

47. B. B. Smyth's detailed reports, including notes on wind velocity, plant life, and temperature as well as rainfall appeared nearly every month in the *Great Bend Register* during the 1870s. For examples, see *Great Bend Register,* 8 February 1877, 14 March 1878, 11 March 1880.

48. *Clark County Clipper,* 31 March 1886.

49. A convenient source for detailed breakdown of weather from several western Kansas reporting stations are this board's reports. For the wet year of 1877, see *First Biennial Report of the State Board of Agriculture to the Legislature of the State of Kansas, for the Years 1877–78* (Topeka: Kansas State Board of Agriculture, 1878), 427–28. That year, even while Hays, Dodge, Larned, Kinsley, and Osborne stations were soaked with 25 to 30 inches of rain, Smith Center had only 19 and Wallace 13.31. This was 2 inches less for Wallace than during the previous year.

50. 7 July 1876.

51. *Dodge City Times,* 9 January 1878.

52. *Hand Book,* 67.

53. C. C. Hutchinson, *Resources of Kansas* (Topeka: Published by the author, 1871), 97. Hutchinson's book contains an extended section, "Western Kansas and the Buffalo Grass" (94–114).

54. *Dodge City Times,* 29 September 1879.

55. *Hays Sentinel,* 16 January 1876.

56. *Larned Press,* 8 August 1878.

57. Edgar Guild, "Western Kansas—Its Geology, Climate, Natural History, Etc." (1879), in Seiler, "Magazine Articles," 461–67.

58. Howard Lamar, *Dakota Territory 1861–1889: A Study of Frontier Politics* (New Haven, Conn.: Yale University Press, 1956).

59. The classic treatment of the "myth of the garden" is in Henry Nash Smith, *Virgin Land: The American West as Symbol and Myth* (Cambridge, Mass.: Harvard University Press, 1950).

60. *Wichita Eagle,* 29 May 1932.

61. Of buffalo draft animals, the *Osborne County Farmer,* 7 October 1880, said: "They

pulled admirably, but there was no obstacle in the way of their sweet wills. In summer they took the shortest road to water, regardless of intervening obstructions, and they thought nothing of flinging themselves over a perpendicular bank, wagon and all." For prairie chickens, see *Larned Chronoscope,* 10 June 1881.

62. John Madson, *Where the Sky Began: Land of the Tallgrass Prairie* (Boston: Houghton Mifflin, 1982), 104–5.

63. *Great Bend Register,* 8 May 1879.

64. Ibid., 3 July 1879.

65. *Dighton Herald,* 27 March 1957.

66. The game is described in *Osborne County Farmer,* 5 November 1931.

67. Burch, *Kansas as It Is,* 96.

5. The Ravaging Hopper

1. Percy Ebbutt, *Emigrant Life in Kansas* (London: Swan, Sonnenschein and Co., 1886), 127.

2. *The Rocky Mountain Locust or Grasshopper, Being the Report of Proceedings of the Governors of Several Western States* (St. Louis: R. P. Studley Company, 1876), 38–39.

3. Louis Watson to his mother, 2 August 1874, Jennings coll., MSS Division, Kansas State Historical Society, Topeka.

4. Clipping (N.p., n.d.), vol. 1, 85, Edwards County Clippings, Kansas State Historical Society, Topeka.

5. *Portis Independent,* 23 September 1937.

6. *Wichita Eagle,* 13 August, 1874.

7. *Kinsley Republican,* 4 January 1879.

8. Ebbutt, *Emigrant Life,* 127–28.

9. Mrs. W. A. Gill in *Larned Tiller and Toiler* (N.d.), vol. 1, 148, Pawnee County Clippings, Kansas State Historical Society, Topeka. Other descriptions of women's experiences are in Stratton, *Pioneer Women,* 102–6.

10. Mrs. M. V. Washington, "The Grasshopper Raid" (1891), in Seiler, "Magazine Articles," 531–32.

11. Ebbutt, *Emigrant Life,* 132. Description of the devouring of curtains and household plants is in John Ise, *Sod and Stubble* (Lincoln: University of Nebraska Press, 1967), 51. Ise's book was first published in 1936.

12. *Wichita Eagle,* 3 June 1875.

13. Ebbutt, *Emigrant Life,* 132.

14. For an immigrant reaction, see the fine description of the invasion in Ole Rölvaag, *Giants in the Earth: A Saga of the Prairie* (New York: Harper & Brothers, 1927), 350–52. Rölvaag's chapter is called "The Power of Evil in High Places."

15. *Kansas City Journal of Commerce,* quoted in *Wichita Eagle,* 3 December 1874.

16. C. P. Austin, "Early Days at Bulls City," Hist. Osborne County, 73–74, MSS Division, Kansas State Historical Society, Topeka.

17. A. A. Green to O. G. Guttery, 24 May 1930, ibid.

18. *Osborne County Farmer,* 25 November 1880.

19. The verse is Eccles. 12:5. Actually the Authorized (King James) Version's "the grasshopper shall be a burden" is a misleading translation. The Revised Standard Version, which came out a number of years after the Kansas invasion, puts it, "The grasshopper drags itself along," and the New English Bible translates the phrase as "the locust's paunch is swollen." The comparison is to old age. However, "shall be a burden" seemed just right to the settlers in 1874.

20. C. K. Holliday to his son Charlie, 12 September 1874, Holliday letters, MS. 70, Kansas State Historical Society, Topeka.

21. *Wichita Eagle,* 22 July 1875.

22. John Schlebecker, "Grasshoppers in American Agricultural History," *Agricultural History* 27 (1953): 86; Davis Britton and Linda Wilcox, "Pestiferous Ironclads: The Grasshopper Problem in Pioneer Utah," *Utah Historical Quarterly* 46 (1978): 354–55.

23. *Rocky Mountain Locust,* 24; *Kansas City Star,* 22 July 1891.

24. Joseph Gambone, "Economic Relief in Territorial Kansas," *Kansas Historical Quarterly* 36 (1970): 151, 154, 173.

25. Britton and Wilcox, "Ironclads," 341.

26. Britton and Wilcox, "Ironclads," 342.

27. Gilbert Fite, *The Farmers' Frontier 1865–1900* (New York: Holt, Rinehart and Winston, 1966), 68.

28. Cox's research proposal is entitled "The Grasshopper Plague in the Trans-Mississippi West, 1874–1878: A Laboratory for Reform and Community Organization."

29. List [1874], Records of Kansas Central Relief Committee, hist. relief 1874–75, MSS Division, Kansas State Historical Society, Topeka; W. H. Odell to Thomas Osborn, 25 August 1874, Governors' Papers, Osborn, box 4, folder 7, Archives Division, Kansas State Historical Society, Topeka.

30. J. A. Walker to E. S. Stover, 12 December 1874, Records of Kansas Central Relief Committee, hist. relief 1874–75, MSS Division, Kansas State Historical Society, Topeka.

31. Circular from Smith County, 2 October 1874, ibid.

32. George Butler to Central Committee, 23 February 1875, ibid.

33. *Chicago Tribune,* quoted in *Wichita Eagle,* 21 January 1875.

34. Printed circular signed by Alfred Gray in destitution report for Edwards County, 7 January 1875, Records of the Kansas Central Relief Committee, hist. relief 1874–75, MSS Division, Kansas State Historical Society, Topeka.

35. Smith County circular, 2 October 1874, ibid.

36. J. B. Schlichter to Central Committee, [1875], ibid.

37. *Sedalia Democrat,* 24 December 1874.

38. Thomas Byrne to B. F. Hartshorn, 19 December 1874, Records of the Kansas Central Relief Committee, hist. relief 1874–75, MSS Division, Kansas State Historical Society, Topeka.

39. E. B. Foster to E. C. Redington, 31 December 1874, misc. Redington, MSS Division, Kansas State Historical Society, Topeka.

40. R. S. Osborn to E. C. Redington, 29 December 1874, ibid.

41. Louisa Seaver to E. C. Redington, 27 December 1874.

42. Isaac Irey to E. C. Redington, 1 January 1875, ibid.

43. E. D. Redington to R. R. Hayes, 15 January 1925, ibid.

44. R. K. Smith to Central Committee, 12 November 1874, Records of the Kansas Central Relief Committee, hist. relief 1874–75, MSS Division, Kansas State Historical Society, Topeka.

45. R. S. Stevens to E. S. Stover, 28 November, 28 December 1874, ibid.

46. R. K. Smith to Central Committee, 12 November 1874, ibid.

47. Everett Dick, *Conquering the Great American Desert: Nebraska* (Lincoln: Nebraska State Historical Society, 1975), 191–215, treats the Nebraska situation, as does Robert Manley, "In the Wake of the Grasshoppers: Public Relief in Nebraska 1874–75," *Nebraska History* 44 (1963): 255–76.

48. Harold Briggs, "Grasshopper Plagues and Early Dakota Agriculture, 1864–1876," *Agricultural History* 7 (1934): 58.

49. Fite, *Farmers' Frontier,* 56–68.

50. For debate on Sedgwick County relief bonds, see H. Craig Miner, *Wichita: The Early Years, 1865–80* (Lincoln: University of Nebraska Press, 1982), 91, 95.

51. Donnell, Lawson and Company to Thomas Osborn, 7 September 1874, Governors' Papers, Osborn, box 4, folder 7, Archives Division, Kansas State Historical Society, Topeka.

52. R. K. Smith to Central Committee, 12 November 1874, Records of the Kansas Central Relief Committee, hist. relief 1874–75, MSS Division, Kansas State Historical Society, Topeka.

53. Smith County circular, 2 October 1874, ibid.

54. "Address of Kansas Central Relief Committee," 20 November 1874, ibid.

55. *Russell County Record,* 25 February 1875.

56. Ibid., 1 April 1875.

57. John Edwards to Thomas Osborn, 7 February 1875, Governors' Papers, Osborn, box 4, folder 8, Archives Division, Kansas State Historical Society, Topeka.

58. *Western Times* (Wallace), 1 May 1958.

59. "Address of Kansas Central Relief Committee," Records of the Kansas Central Relief Committee, hist. relief 1874–75, MSS Division, Kansas State Historical Society, Topeka.

60. A completed form from Jewell County, 5 January 1875, is in Records of the Kansas Central Relief Committee, ibid.

61. R. K. Smith to Central Committee, 12 November 1874, ibid.

62. M. M. Murdock to E. S. Stover, 5 December 1874, Records of the Kansas Central Relief Committee, ibid.

63. Chase, "Mother Bickerdyke," 194–96.

64. G. L. Brinkman to E. S. Stover, 28 December 1874, Records of the Kansas Central Relief Committee, hist. relief 1874–75, MSS Division, Kansas State Historical Society, Topeka; clipping, June 1909, Ford County clippings, vol. 1, 128, Kansas State Historical Society, Topeka.

65. Alex McLean to Mrs. M. A. Bickerdyke, 25 December 1874, Records of the Kansas Central Relief Committee, hist. relief 1874–75, MSS Division, Kansas State Historical Society, Topeka.

66. William Whitney to E. S. Stover, 23 December 1874, ibid.

67. H. C. St. Clair to E. S. Stover, 25 December 1874, ibid.

68. Mrs. E. L. Williams to E. S. Stover, 5 January 1875, ibid.

69. C. C. Hutchinson to E. S. Stover, 1 December 1874, ibid.

70. William Frielly to E. S. Stover, 16 December 1874, ibid.

71. William Blackburn to Thomas Osborn, 17 December 1874, ibid.

72. Judson Learned to Central Committee, 27 January 1875, ibid.

73. J. B. Schlichter to E. S. Stover, 27 November 1874, ibid.

74. J. B. Mitchell to E. S. Stover, 25 December 1874, ibid.

75. *Wichita Eagle,* 18 February 1875.

76. A good summary of federal relief is Gilbert Fite, "The United States Army and Relief to Pioneer Settlers," *Journal of the West* 6 (1967): 99–107.

77. Speech of Stephen Cobb, 1 February 1875, *Congressional Record,* 43d Cong., 2d Sess., III, 887. For discussion of the extension of the homestead time, see ibid., 66–67.

78. Fite, "The United States Army," 103–4.

79. Charles Aldrich to T. Osborn, 5 December 1874, box 4, folder 7; and A. Kimball to T. Osborn, 8 February 1875, box 4, folder 8, Governors' Papers, Osborn, Archives Division, Kansas State Historical Society, Topeka.

80. Fite, "The United States Army," 103–4.

81. Alfred Gray to County Commission in *Wichita Eagle,* 4 March 1875; *Wichita Eagle,* 22 April 1875; M. Sargent to E. S. Stover, 13 March 1875, Records of the Kansas Central Relief Committee, hist. relief 1874–75, MSS Division, Kansas State Historical Society, Topeka.

82. J. G. Brisbin to E. S. Stover, 20 April 1875, ibid. For the role of an officer in Nebraska, see Gary Olson, ed., "Relief for Nebraska Grasshopper Victims: The Official Journal of Lieutenant Theodore E. True," *Nebraska History* 48 (1967): 119–40.

83. H. C. Waterman to E. S. Stover, 16 December 1874, ibid.

84. H. Edwards to E. S. Stover, 23 January 1875, ibid.

85. W. H. Bancroft to M.S. Sargent, 27 January 1875, ibid.

86. Mrs. J. M. Smith to E. S. Stover, 26 January 1875, ibid.

87. Laf. Smith to E. S. Stover, 8 January 1875, ibid.

88. Geo. Bishop to E. S. Stover, 24 February 1875, ibid.

89. *Russell County Record,* 29 April 1875.

90. Ibid., 6 August 1875.

91. H. Edwards to E. S. Stover, 23 January

1875, Records of the Kansas Central Relief Committee, hist. relief 1874–75, MSS Division, Kansas State Historical Society, Topeka.

92. *Osborne County Farmer* (N.d.), Osborne County Clippings, vol. 1, 106, Kansas State Historical Society, Topeka.

93. *Dodge City Times,* 27 November 1880.

94. *Russell County Record,* 14, 28 January 1875.

95. Ibid., 21 January 1875; Van Sickel, *Real Life,* 34–49.

96. Van Sickel, *Real Life,* 49.

97. W. L. Bear to H. King, 21 January 1875, Records of the Kansas Central Relief Committee, hist. relief 1874–75, MSS Division, Kansas State Historical Society, Topeka.

98. H. C. Cone to E. S. Stover, 24 December 1874, ibid.

99. G. A. Atwood to T. Osborn, 26 December 1874, Governors' Papers, Osborn, box 4, folder 7, Archives Division, Kansas State Historical Society, Topeka.

100. W. H Odell to T. Osborn, 10 December 1874, ibid.

101. R. B. Foster to F. W. Giles, 29 December 1874, Records of the Kansas Central Relief Committee, hist. relief 1874–75, MSS Division, Kansas State Historical Society, Topeka.

102. *New York Times,* 26 December 1874, p. 6, col. 4.

103. D. W. Wilder, *The Annals of Kansas. New Edition 1541–1885* (Topeka: T. Dwight Thacher, Kansas Publishing House, 1886), 652.

104. Kansas Central Relief Committee, *Report of the Executive Board. Their Transactions From Date of Organization to Disbandment* (Topeka, Kans.: State Printing Works, Geo. W. Martin, 1875), 3–8.

105. Ibid., 17.

106. A fascinating account of the mechanical response is Douglas Hurt, "Grasshopper Harvesters on the Great Plains," *Great Plains Journal* 16 (1977): 123–34.

107. *Wichita Eagle,* 20 April 1876.

108. *Great Bend Register,* 19 April 1877.

109. Petition from Clay County for day of prayer (N.d.), Governors' Papers, Anthony, Archives Division, Kansas State Historical Society, Topeka.

110. Fite, *Farmers' Frontier,* 72–73.

111. *The Rocky Mountain Locust,* 2, 8.

112. *Dodge City Times,* 2 March 1878; Geo. Gaumer to Geo. Anthony, 21 August 1878, Governors' Papers, Anthony, box 4, folder 5, Archives Division, Kansas State Historical Society, Topeka. The Rocky Mountain locust became extinct altogether about 1902, though this did not stop invasions of grasshoppers of other kinds. Doren Buscemi, "The Grasshopper Years," *American History Illustrated* 12 (1978): 25.

113. Schlebecker, "Grasshoppers," 92.

114. Manley, "Wake," 275.

115. *Congressional Record,* 43d Cong., 2d Session, III, 887.

116. Manley, "Wake," 275.

117. *Wichita Eagle,* 20 August 1874.

118. Undated clipping in Osborne County Clippings, vol. 1, 54, Kansas State Historical Society, Topeka.

119. A. Essick, Speech at Harvest Festival, 15 October 1875, misc. Essick, MSS Divison, Kansas State Historical Society, Topeka.

120. Ibid.

121. *Centennial Edition of the Fourth Annual Report of the State Board of Agriculture,* 129.

6. Colonists

1. Henry Nash Smith, "The West as an Image of the American Past," *University of Kansas City Review* 18 (1951).

2. *Great Bend Register,* 9 June 1882.

3. Harry Pollack, "Colonies in Ellis County," typescript, library, Kansas State Historical Society, Topeka; Kenneth Miller, "Danish Socialism on the Kansas Prairie," *Kansas Historical Quarterly* 38 (1972): 156–68.

4. *Hays Sentinel,* 31 August 1878.

5. For an overview of colonies in other counties, see George Root, "Notes on Kansas Colonies," misc. Root, MSS Division, Kansas State Historical Society, Topeka; Nell B. Waldron, "Colonization in Kansas from 1861 to 1890" (Ph.D. dissertation, Northwestern University, 1923); Socolofsky and Self, *Historical Atlas of Kansas,* 42, graphically shows colony locations for foreign groups. It is no insult to the enterprise of these researchers to note that none of the lists is complete.

6. *Centennial Edition of the Fourth Annual Report of the State Board of Agriculture,* 118, 230, 257.

7. Francis Walker, *Compendium of the Tenth Census* (Washington, D.C.: Government Printing Office, 1883), 349, 505–6.

8. Burch, *Kansas as It Is,* 98.

9. *Osborne County Farmer,* 7 July 1876. For a thoughtful plea to western historians, not wholly heeded, to better recognize this conservatism among settlers in the entire West, see Pomeroy, "Toward a Reorientation of Western History."

10. Francis Swehla, "Bohemians in Central Kansas," *Kansas State Historical Society Collections* 13 (1913–14): 474.

11. Burch, *Kansas as It Is,* 98–99.

12. *Kinsley Graphic,* 4 May 1878.

13. Examples of early colony inquiries are John McClimont to James Harvey, 12 November 1869, and Cawker and Kshinka to James Harvey, 17 January 1870, Governors' Papers, Harvey, box 2, folder 11, Archives Division, Kansas State Historical Society, Topeka. McClimont was on the locating committee for the Excelsior Cooperative Colony of New York City, and Cawker, a Milwaukee attorney and real-estate dealer, brought 200 families to settle at Cawker City in Mitchell County.

14. Mrs. Alice G. Young, Reminiscences, hist. Osborne, MSS Division, Kansas State Historical Society, Topeka.

15. Paper read by F. R. Gruger before Old Settlers Reunion Osborne, 27 May 1896, Osborne County Clippings, vol. 2, 172, Kansas State Historical Society, Topeka.

16. Young, Reminiscences.

17. Paper read by F. R. Gruger, Osborne County Clippings, vol. 2, 172.

18. Jacob Sackman, letters on Pennsylvania colonies of the 1870s, hist. emigration, MSS Division, Kansas State Historical Society, Topeka. Sackman was with the so-called "First Pennsylvania Colony" from Cumberland County, which located near Wilson, Kansas, in 1872.

19. Paper read by F. R. Gruger, Osborne County Clippings, vol. 2, 172.

20. Ibid.

21. Ibid., 173.

22. Minutes of Pennsylvania Colony, 15, 25 April 1871, in *Osborne County Farmer,* N.d., ibid., 167.

23. Paper read by F. R. Gruger, ibid., 174–75.

24. Ibid., 175.

25. Minutes, 27, 30 April, 2, 4 May 1871, ibid., 167–68.

26. Paper read by F. R. Gruger, ibid., 176.

27. Ibid. It was not uncommon for colonies to become town companies. The Northwestern Colony from Ripon, Wisconsin, for example, was about the same size as the Osborne County group and converted itself at just the same time to the Russell Town Company. *Russell County Record,* 22 April 1875.

28. Paper read by F. R. Gruger, Osborne County Clippings, vol. 2, 176; Minutes, 24 February 1872, ibid., 178.

29. Gruger was one who expressed that opinion.

30. James Malin, "The Evolution of a Rural Community," in *Lewis Press,* 1 June 1933; James Malin, "J. A. Walker's Early History of Edwards County," *Kansas Historical Quarterly* 9 (1940): 259–63. The orange grove story is from *Kinsley Graphic,* 14 February 1880.

31. Malin, "The Evolution of a Rural Community," in *Lewis Press,* 1 June 1933.

32. *Topeka Capital,* 12 July 1885; *Report of the Commissioners Appointed to Investigate the Condition of Barbour, Comanche, and Harper Counties,* [15 September 1874], Kansas State Legislative Documents, vol. 1, Kansas State Historical Society, Topeka. The Barber County case is described

briefly in T. A. McNeal, *When Kansas Was Young* (Topeka, Kans.: Capper Publications, 1934), 20–24.

33. Minnie Millbrook, "Dr. Samuel Grant Rodgers, Gentleman from Ness," *Kansas Historical Quarterly* 20 (1953): 322, 325, 329–30.

34. Ibid., 322, 325.

35. Memoirs of J. M. Litton, 30 December 1922, in Ness County Clippings, vol. 1, 47, Kansas State Historical Society, Topeka.

36. Millbrook, "Dr. Samuel Grant Rodgers," 318, 324.

37. Ibid., 324, 327–28, 330–31, 334–36, 346–47. There is a list of distribution points in Records of the Kansas Central Relief Committee, MSS Division, Kansas State Historical Society, Topeka.

38. J. C. Lohnes, "History of Ness County," 1, 5, typescript in Ness County Histories, copied by Minnie Millbrook, 1955, Kansas State Historical Society, Topeka.

39. *Kinsley Republican,* 4 January 1879.

40. Lohnes, "History of Ness County," 1–4.

41. Ibid., 6–8, 14, 16.

42. *Hays Sentinel,* 30 March, 27 April, 4, 18 May, 8, 22 June 1878.

43. *Kinsley Graphic,* 8 March 1879.

44. C. Robert Haywood, "Pearlette: A Mutual Aid Colony," *Kansas Historical Quarterly* 42 (1976): 270–73.

45. Kenneth Miller, "Danish Socialism on the Kansas Prairie," *Kansas Historical Quarterly* 38 (1972): 156–68.

46. *Hays Sentinel,* 9 March 1878, 21 March 1879.

47. *Clark County Clipper,* 29 June, 28 December 1939, 23 May 1940; Peter Beckman, *Kansas Monks: A History of St. Benedict's Abbey* (Atchison, Kans.: Abbey Student, 1957), 100–2.

48. *WaKeeney World,* 30 April 1892.

49. Ibid., 22 December 1879; *Hays Sentinel,* 30 November 1877. Warren and Keeney at times advertised "400,000 acres for sale," and if they in fact purchased all the railroad land in the 600,000-acre county, plus some public lands, the 340,000-acre figure usually given is possible. However,

some comments in the press suggest that the partnership initially paid cash for only two townships, or about 46,000 acres, and held the rest of the county through options contingent upon being able to attract settlers. This idea is consistent with earlier company ads advertising 150,000 acres, perhaps an interim step.

50. *Hays Sentinel*, 23, 30 November, 1 December 1877.

51. *Trego County, Kansas: Its Soil and Climate and the Advantages It Affords to the Farmer and Stock Grower* (Chicago: Warren, Keeney & Co., [1877]), pp. 1–3, 14.

52. *Hays Sentinel*, 21 December 1878; *WaKeeney World*, 19 April 1879.

53. *Hays Sentinel*, 21 December 1878.

54. *WaKeeney World*, 3 May 1879.

55. Ibid., 15 March 1879; *Ness County Pioneer*, 23 August 1879.

56. *Ness County Pioneer*, 1 September 1879; *WaKeeney World*, 21 June 1879.

57. *Trego County, Kansas*, 13.

58. Decker, *Railroads, Lands and Politics*, 182; Andreas, *History of Kansas*, 1296.

59. Ibid.

7. Sheepskin and Teakettles

1. This account is drawn from C. B. Schmidt, "Reminiscences of Foreign Immigration Work for Kansas," *Kansas State Historical Society Collections* 9 (1905–6): 485, 490–93; C. B. Schmidt to A. S. Johnson, 23 March 1875, RR 308, MSS Division, Kansas State Historical Society, Topeka.

2. Ibid.

3. Schmidt, "Reminiscences," 494–95.

4. Norman Saul, "The Migration of the Russian-Germans to Kansas," *Kansas Historical Quarterly* 40 (1974): 58, 60.

5. Schmidt, "Reminiscences," 495. Waldron in "Colonization in Kansas," 113, records that one Mennonite said at the time, "Grasshoppers will go to none but a good country."

6. Saul, "Migration," 41–44, 48.

7. Schmidt, "Reminiscences," 493.

8. C. B. Schmidt to A. S. Johnson, 23 March 1875, RR 308, MSS Division, Kansas State Historical Society, Topeka.

9. Schmidt, "Reminiscences," 493.

10. C. B. Schmidt to A. S. Johnson, 9 June 1877, RR 308, MSS Division, Kansas State Historical Society, Topeka; *Hays Sentinel*, 22 March 1876.

11. Schmidt, "Reminiscences," 495.

12. *Hays Sentinel*, 1 March 1876.

13. Ibid., 22 March 1876.

14. Noble Prentis, "The Mennonites at Home," in *Kansas Miscellanies* (Topeka: Kansas Publishing House, 1889), 162–67. The piece originally appeared in *Topeka Commonwealth*, 20 August 1875.

15. John P. Swenson to Samuel Crawford, 6 February 1865, Governors' Papers, Crawford, box 1, folder 7, Archives Division, Kansas State Historical Society, Topeka.

16. Jacob Ruppenthal, "The German Element in Central Kansas," *Kansas State Historical Society Collections* 13 (1913–14): 524–25; Francis Laing, "German-Russian Settlement in Ellis County, Kansas," ibid., 11 (1909–10): 521.

17. Glen Schwendemann, "Nicodemus: Negro Haven on the Solomon," *Kansas Historical Quarterly* 34 (1968): 10–31.

18. Robert Athearn, *In Search of Canaan: Black Migration to Kansas 1879–80* (Lawrence: Regents Press of Kansas, 1978), 75–78. A summary of some of the pre-exodus colonies is also contained in Nell Painter, *Exodusters: Black Migration to Kansas after Reconstruction* (New York: Alfred A. Knopf, 1977), 146–59.

19. *Great Bend Register*, 22 May 1879.

20. *Weekly Champion* (Atchison), 31 July 1881, in Rooks County Clippings, vol. 1, 17, Kansas State Historical Society, Topeka.

21. *Topeka Commonwealth*, 7 May 1879.

22. *Edwards County Leader*, 15 May 1879.

23. *Hays Sentinel*, 16 March 1878.

24. Ibid., 21 September, 30 March 1877.

25. Athearn, *In Search of Canaan*, 179–81.

26. *Hays Sentinel*, 25 April, 7 May 1879.

27. Ibid., 12 October 1877.

28. *Advertiser* (Wakefield), 21 January 1878, in Ellis County Clippings, vol. 1, 71, Kansas State Historical Society, Topeka.

29. *Wilson County Citizen* (Fredonia), 6 August 1875, ibid., 25.

30. AT&SF Railroad, *How and Where to Get a Living*, 37–39.

31. James Forsythe, typescript of talk on George Grant, 22 May 1973, misc. Grant, MSS Division, Kansas State Historical Society, Topeka.

32. Ibid.

33. James Forsythe, "Environmental Considerations," 40–42. For the experience of other English colonies, see Waldron, "Colonization in Kansas," 53–67; William Chapman, "The Wakefield Colony," *Kansas State Historical Society Collections* 10 (1907–08): 485–533; and Nyle Miller, ed., "An English Runnymede in Kansas," *Kansas Historical Quarterly* 41 (1975): 22–62, 183–224.

34. Swehla, "Bohemians in Central Kansas," 470–85; Waldron, "Colonization in Kansas," 35–42.

35. Lillian Shimmick, *Early Pioneer Families in Decatur County, Kansas* (Hays, Kans.: Fort Hays State University, 1979), 6, 26, 34.

36. Waldron, "Colonization in Kansas," 43.

37. Emory Lindquist, *Smoky Valley People: A History of Lindsborg, Kansas* (Lindsborg, Kans.: Bethany College, 1953), 34–50; Alfred Bergin, "The Swedish Settlements in Central Kansas," *Kansas State Historical Society Collections* 11 (1909–10): 19–46.

38. *Hays Sentinel*, 9 May 1879.

39. Sister Mary Johannes, *A Study of the Russian-German Settlements in Ellis County, Kansas* (Washington, D.C.: Catholic University of America Press, 1946), 8–10.

40. Laing, "German-Russian Settlements," 491–92.

41. Ibid., 493–94.

42. Ibid., 522; Johannes, *Study*, 41–42.

43. *Topeka Commonwealth* in *New York Times*, 9 December 1875; Noble Prentis in *Kansas City Star*, 29 July 1891, in Biographical Clippings, vol. 10, 182, Kansas State Historical Society, Topeka.

44. Laing, "German-Russian Settlements," 494–95.

45. Noble Prentis in *Kansas City Star*, 29 July 1891, Biographical Clippings, vol. 10, 183, Kansas State Historical Society, Topeka.

46. Laing, "German-Russian Settlements," 495–96; Johannes, *Study*, 12–23.

47. Noble Prentis in *Kansas City Star*, 2 July 1891, Biographical Clippings, vol. 10, 183, Kansas State Historical Society, Topeka.

48. The phrase comes from Andreas, *History of Kansas*, 1289.

49. "The New Comers," *Hays Sentinel*, 16 August 1876.

50. Ibid., and *Great Bend Rustler*, 25 December 1905, in Barton County Clippings, vol. 1, 175, Kansas State Historical Society, Topeka.

51. *Hays Sentinel*, 16 August 1876.

52. Johannes, *Study*, 12–23, 29–33; Laing, "German-Russian Settlements," 513–14.

53. Laing, "German-Russian Settlements," 518–20.

54. *Hays Sentinel*, 11 October 1876.

55. Ibid., 1 November 1876.

56. Ibid., 13 July 1877.

57. Ibid., 17 August 1877.

58. Ibid., 21 February 1879.

59. Ibid., 27 April 1878.

60. Ibid., 19 October 1878.

61. Ibid., 30 November 1877.

62. *Russell County Record*, 7 December 1876.

63. *Hays Sentinel*, 27 April 1878.

64. For a good account of how immigrants were attracted on an earlier frontier, see Paul Gates, *The Illinois Central and Its Colonization Work* (Cambridge, Mass.: Harvard University Press, 1934), 188–224.

65. For Beersheba, see James Rudin, "Beersheba, Kan.: 'God's Pure Air on Government Land,'" *Kansas Historical Quarterly*, 34 (1968): 282–98; Elbert Sapinsley, "Jewish Agricultural Colonies in the West: The Kansas Example," *Western States Jewish Historical Quarterly* 3 (1971): 157–69; Lipman Goldman Feld, "New Light on the Lost Jewish Colony of

Beersheeba, Kansas 1882–1886,'' *American Jewish Historical Quarterly* 60 (1970): 159–68; Charles Davis, "A Colony in Kansas," *American Jewish Archives* 17 (1965): 114–39.

66. Frederick Luebke, *Ethnicity on the Great Plains* (Lincoln: University of Nebraska Press, 1980), xiv, xviii.

8. At the Front

1. Page Smith, *As a City upon a Hill: The Town in American History* (New York: Alfred A. Knopf, 1966), 18–33.

2. Lewis Atherton, *Main Street on the Middle Border* (Bloomington: Indiana University Press, 1954), 13–14.

3. Gunther Barth, *Instant Cities: Urbanization and the Rise of San Francisco and Denver* (New York: Oxford University Press, 1975), 130 and *passim;* Roger Lochtin, *San Francisco 1846–1856: From Hamlet to City* (New York: Oxford University Press, 1974).

4. Atherton, *Main Street*, 14.

5. *Russell County Record*, 18 March 1875.

6. *Hays Sentinel*, 9 April 1880.

7. Walter Prescott Webb, "The American West, Perpetual Mirage," *Harpers* 214 (1957): 25–31.

8. *Valley Republican* (Kinsley), 30 March 1878.

9. *Hays Sentinel*, 18 October 1876.

10. *Great Bend Register*, 11 May 1876.

11. *Valley Republican* (Kinsley), 15 December 1877.

12. *Kinsley Graphic*, 10 July 1880.

13. *Hays Sentinel*, 18 October 1876.

14. *Dodge City Times*, 6 July 1878, 8 December 1877.

15. Ibid., 3 August 1878.

16. *Hays Sentinel*, 23 March 1877.

17. *Dodge City Times*, 6, 20 September, 8 February 1883.

18. Ibid., 1 June 1882.

19. Ibid., 7 September 1878.

20. *Kingman Courier*, 18 October 1935.

21. *Hays Sentinel*, 31 May 1876.

22. Ibid., 23 March 1878.

23. Ibid., 16 April 1880.

24. Ibid., 20 July, 13 May 1878.

25. *Kinsley Graphic,* 26 April 1879.

26. Ibid., 19 June 1880.

27. Ibid., 6 December 1879, 7 February 1880.

28. *Larned Chronoscope,* 13 August 1880; *Hays Sentinel,* 6 February 1880.

29. *Garden City Irrigator,* 12 July 1883.

30. *Valley Republican* (Kinsley), 3 November 1877.

31. *Kinsley Graphic,* 3 August 1878. One problem with the bone pile was that E. I. Meeker, Kinsley's first mayor, was also the local bone dealer. Ibid., 7 June 1878.

32. Ibid., 31 August 1878.

33. Ibid., 5 October 1878.

34. Ibid., 31 May 1879.

35. *Great Bend Register,* 18 January 1877.

36. Ibid., 20 February 1879.

37. *Kinsley Graphic,* 7 June 1879.

38. *Hays Sentinel,* 31 December 1880.

39. Ibid., 7 January 1881.

40. Ibid., 25 June 1885.

41. Ibid., 27 July 1878.

42. Ibid., 25 January 1878.

43. *Great Bend Register,* 7 June 1877; *Hays Sentinel,* 9 July, 27 August 1880.

44. *Great Bend Register,* 1 March 1877.

45. Ibid., 27 December 1877.

46. *Kinsley Graphic,* 10 May 1879.

47. Accounts of local elections may be found in *Hays Sentinel,* 13 April 1877, and *Kinsley Graphic,* 30 November 1878.

48. *Hays Sentinel,* 19 July 1883.

49. *Larned Chronoscope,* 28 March 1884.

50. *Great Bend Register,* 9 November 1876.

51. *Larned Chronoscope,* 10 December 1880.

52. *Great Bend Register,* 29 August 1878.

53. *Kinsley Graphic,* 16 July 1881.

54. Ibid., 26 February 1881.

55. *Russell County Record,* 25 May 1876.

56. Ibid., 30 September 1875.

57. *Larned Chronoscope,* 6 August 1880.

58. *Russell County Record,* 24 December 1874.

59. *Edwards County Leader,* 10 May 1877.

60. *Great Bend Register,* 3 August 1876.

61. *Valley Republican* (Kinsley), 17 November 1877.

62. Ibid., 19 January 1878.

63. Ibid., 30 March 1878.

64. *Larned Chronoscope,* 10 December 1880.

65. *Valley Republican* (Kinsley), 16 March 1878.

66. *Kinsley Graphic,* 24 May 1879.

67. *Valley Republican* (Kinsley), 9 January 1878.

68. *Hays Sentinel,* 18 July 1879.

69. *Kinsley Graphic,* 6 December 1879.

70. Ibid., 12 February 1880, 7 December 1878.

71. Ibid., 5 July 1879, 16 August 1883; *Edwards County Leader,* 12 June 1879.

72. *Kinsley Graphic,* 25 December 1880.

73. *Great Bend Register,* 14 August 1879.

74. Ibid., 4 July 1878.

75. *Larned Chronoscope,* 3 February, 22 October 1882.

76. *Hays Sentinel,* 27 June 1883.

77. *Larned Chronoscope,* 28 March 1884.

78. *Kinsley Graphic,* 26 July 1879.

79. *Hays Sentinel,* 17 May 1883.

80. *Larned Chronoscope,* 24 December 1886.

81. *Kinsley Graphic,* 6 April 1882.

82. *Ellsworth Reporter,* N.d., Ellsworth County Clippings, vol. 1, 17, Kansas State Historical Society, Topeka.

83. *Larned Chronoscope,* 11 December 1878.

84. Entries of 24 November 1877, 26 December 1879, 2 January 1881, Elam Bartholomew diaries, MS. 1069, MSS Division, Kansas State Historical Society, Topeka.

85. *Hays Sentinel,* 28 February 1879.

86. *Dodge City Times,* 16 November 1882.

87. Ibid., 15 February 1883.

88. *Hays Sentinel,* 19 October 1878.

89. *Larned Press,* 9 March 1877.

90. *Valley Republican* (Kinsley), 2 March 1878. When this hall, built by DePuy and Frater, burned that fall in one of Kinsley's general conflagrations, its replacement by Calkins Hall was one of the first orders of business for the town.

91. *Kinsley Graphic,* 4 January 1879, 21 February 1880; *Valley Republican* (Kinsley), 1 December 1877.

92. *Great Bend Register,* 31 July 1879.

93. *Hays Sentinel,* 19 April 1876.

94. Ibid., 14 March 1879.

95. Ibid., 13 April 1882, 19 August 1881, 10 December 1880.

96. Ibid., 21 December 1878, 22 March 1883; *Edwards County Leader* (Kinsley), 20 November, 11, 25 December 1879; *Great Bend Register,* 24 July 1879.

97. *Kinsley Graphic,* 13 December 1879; *Bazine Advocate,* 6 August 1937.

98. Fern E. Cook reminiscences, N.d., Ness County Clippings, vol. 1, 31–34, Kansas State Historical Society, Topeka.

99. *Kinsley Graphic,* 5 April 1879.

100. *Hays Sentinel,* 28 March 1879.

101. *Second Biennial Report of the State Board of Agriculture* (Topeka, Kans.: Geo. W. Martin, 1881), 513–33.

102. One recent example of a call for process analysis in looking at western towns is Oliver Knight, "Toward an Understanding of the Western Town." *Western Historical Quarterly* 4 (1973): 27–42.

103. Populations for 1883 may be found in *Fourth Biennial Report of the State Board of Agriculture* (Topeka, Kans.: Kansas Publishing House, 1885). Town statistics are recorded by county.

9. Dull Knife

1. Ramon Powers, "Why the Northern Cheyenne Left Indian Territory in 1878: A Cultural Analysis," *Kansas Quarterly* 3 (1971): 79–80. Powers has made by far the most extensive study of the Dull Knife raid and has aided me personally as well as through his writings in forming this chapter.

2. Ibid., 77–78.

3. *Dodge City Times,* 14 September 1878.

4. *Indian Raid of 1878. The Report of the*

Commission Appointed in Pursuance of Senate Joint Resolution No. 1, Pertaining to Losses Sustained by Citizens of Kansas by the Invasion of Indians during the Year 1878 (Topeka: Geo. W. Martin Kansas Publishing House, 1879), 3; *Dodge City Times*, 2 November 1878.

5. *Dodge City Times*, 21 September 1878.

6. Ibid., 28 September 1878.

7. Ibid., 5 October 1878.

8. Ibid., 2 November 1878.

9. Ibid., 23 November 1878.

10. Ibid., 2 November 1878.

11. Ramon Powers, "The Northern Cheyenne Trek through Western Kansas in 1878: Frontiersmen, Indians and Cultural Conflict," *Trail Guide* 17 (1971): 13.

12. *Kinsley Graphic*, 5 October 1878.

13. Powers, "The Northern Cheyenne Trek," 14.

14. *Kinsley Graphic*, 5 October 1878.

15. Powers, "The Northern Cheyenne Trek," 14–15.

16. *Dodge City Times*, 28 September 1878.

17. Powers, "The Northern Cheyenne Trek," 14; *Hays Sentinel*, 28 September 1878.

18. Mari Sandoz, *Cheyenne Autumn* (New York: McGraw-Hill Book Company, 1953).

19. Powers, "The Northern Cheyenne Trek," 15, 18.

20. *Hays Sentinel*, 28 September 1878.

21. *Kinsley Graphic*, 21 September 1878.

22. *Dodge City Times*, 21 September 1878; Powers, "The Northern Cheyenne Trek," 16.

23. *Kinsley Graphic*, 28 September 1878.

24. Powers, "The Northern Cheyenne Trek," 11, 14; *Hays Sentinel*, 28 September 1878.

25. Powers, "The Northern Cheyenne Trek," 16. Powers points out that General John Pope, commanding the Department of the Missouri, did not at first believe in the possibility of an Indian outbreak in 1878.

26. After bypassing Dodge City, the Indians had moved as much west as north, and after the battle in present Scott County, they turned back northeast. For the general route, see Socolofsky and Self, *Historical Atlas of Kansas*, 29. Famished

Woman's Creek was sometimes called Punished Woman's Creek and today is known as Ladder Creek. John Rydjord, *Kansas Place Names* (Norman: University of Oklahoma Press, 1972), 70, 477.

27. Powers, "The Northern Cheyenne Trek," 16–17; *Hays Sentinel*, 5 October 1878.

28. Governor John P. St. John in his January 1879 report to the state said the Indians had committed "outrages upon defenseless women and children, so brutal, heinous, and revolting in their nature as to never be forgiven or forgotten." *Dodge City Times*, 25 January 1879.

29. *Hays Sentinel*, 23 November 1878. Some of the names come from Powers, "The Northern Cheyenne Trek," 19.

30. *Hays Sentinel*, 23 November 1878.

31. Powers, "The Northern Cheyenne Trek," 20.

32. J. B. Fuller, "Incidents in My Life," written by Mrs. A. H. King, Fuller MSS, MSS Division, Kansas State Historical Society, Topeka.

33. Ibid.

34. Ibid.

35. Ruth Hayden, *The Time That Was: The Courageous Acts and Accounts of Rawlins County Kansas 1875–1915* (Colby, Kans.: Colby Community College, 1973), 23–27.

36. Powers, "The Northern Cheyenne Trek," 12; Barry Johnson, "Cheyennes in Court: An Aftermath of the Dull Knife Outbreak of 1878," *English Westerners Brand Book* 4 (1962): 8.

37. *Dodge City Times*, 25 January 1879.

38. *Hays Sentinel*, 21 February 1879.

39. J. H. Hammond, U.S. Indian Inspector, Pine Ridge, D.T., to Geo. R. Peck, U.S. attorney for Kansas, 6 December 1878, Governors' Papers, Anthony, box 4, file 8, Archives Division, Kansas State Historical Society, Topeka.

40. Johnson, "Cheyennes in Court," 6–8.

41. *Dodge City Times*, 8 January 1879.

42. Ibid., 22 February 1879.

43. Ibid., 15 February 1879. One of the witnesses was A. J. French, the man who had spoken to the Indian group at Meade City shortly after they crossed into Kansas.

44. There is some disagreement on the names. This list is from the *Dodge City Times,* 22 February 1879, and is used by some historians. The *Leavenworth Times,* 28 February 1879, gave the names as Wild Hog, Old Crow, Big Head, Left Hand, Blacksmith, Porcupine, and No Eye Water. Still a third list appears in the *Dodge City Times,* 28 June 1879, listing six captives: Wild Hog, Left Hand, Big Thorn, Noisy Walker, Blacksmith, Tangled Hair, and Old Crow. In the proceedings, the only Indian to emerge individually as a spokesman is Wild Hog, who is on all lists.

45. Dexter Clapp to John St. John, 16 February 1879, Governors' Papers, St. John, box 15, folder 9, Archives Division, Kansas State Historical Society, Topeka.

46. *Dodge City Times,* 22 February 1879.

47. *Hays Sentinel,* 28 February 1879.

48. Ibid.

49. For accounts of the case, see Johnson, "Cheyennes in Court," 8–10, and a second part to the same study in the *English Westerners Brand Book* 4 (1962): 2–5; Todd Epp, "The State of Kansas v. Wild Hog, et al.," *Kansas History* 5 (1982): 139–46.

50. *Dodge City Times,* 28 June 1879.

51. *Hays Sentinel,* 11 July 1879; *Edwards County Leader,* 3 April 1879.

52. Powers, "The Northern Cheyenne Trek," 26–28. The claims were eventually paid through congressional appropriations from Indian Office funds, finally to be charged to tribal accounts there. Ramon Powers, "The Indian Claims Commission of 1879," typescript loaned to author.

53. *Indian Raid of 1878. The Report of the Commission,* 7–34.

54. Ibid.

55. *Kansas Monthly* in *Edwards County Leader,* 13 November 1879.

56. Margaret Smith to John St. John, 10 February 1881, Governors' Papers, St. John, box 6, folder 19, Archives Division, Kansas State Historical Society, Topeka.

10. The Weak Shall Flee

1. Quoted in *Hays Sentinel,* 14 September 1877.

2. Ibid.

3. *First Biennial Report of the State Board of Agriculture,* 427.

4. Ibid.

5. "Ness" in *Hays Sentinel,* 3 August 1877.

6. *Dodge City Times,* 10 September 1885; *Hays Sentinel,* 9 May 1879.

7. *Hays Sentinel,* 7 September 1877.

8. *First Biennial Report of the State Board of Agriculture,* 429.

9. Ibid.; *Hays Sentinel,* 9 May 1879.

10. *Great Bend Register,* 16 January 1879.

11. *Hays Sentinel,* 3 August 1877.

12. Ibid., 13 July 1877.

13. *First Biennial Report of the State Board of Agriculture,* 112, 121, 125, 129, 274, 316–17. The estimate is based on figures from Edwards, Ellis Ellsworth, Ford, Pawnee, and Russell Counties. Both this report and the next show the trend toward winter-wheat culture in all but the northeastern part of the region, where corn remained dominant. For an overview, see Robert Marple, "The Corn-Wheat Ratio in Kansas 1879–1959," *Great Plains Journal* 8 (1969): 79–86.

14. *Hays Sentinel,* 6 July 1877.

15. *Annual Report of the Commissioner of the General Land Office for the Fiscal Year Ending June 30, 1878* (Washington, D.C.: Government Printing Office, 1878), 153–54; *Annual Report of the Secretary of the Interior on the Operations of the Department for the Year Ended June 30, 1879* (Washington, D.C.: Government Printing Office, 1879), 605–6.

16. *Annual Report of the Commissioner of the General Land Office for the Fiscal Year Ending June 30, 1880* (Washington, D.C.: Government Printing Office, 1881), 212.

17. *Report of the Secretary of the Interior for the Fiscal Year Ending June 30, 1881,* vol. 1 (Washington, D.C.: Government Printing Office, 1881), 280–81.

18. For the pattern, see *Third Biennial Report of*

the State Board of Agriculture to the Legislature of the State of Kansas for the Years 1881–82 (Topeka: Kansas Publishing House, 1883).

19. *Second Biennial Report of the State Board of Agriculture,* 133–210, summarizes acreage in various crops 1879 and 1880 for all counties. *Fourth Biennial Report of the State Board of Agriculture,* 522–31, does the same for wheat and corn for 1883 and 1884.

20. *Hays Sentinel,* 25 May 1877.

21. Ibid., 7, 21 September, 2 November 1877, 16 February 1878.

22. *Valley Republican* (Kinsley), 10 November 1877, 20 April 1878.

23. *Kinsley Graphic,* 11 May 1878.

24. *Valley Republican* (Kinsley), 9 March 1878.

25. *Hays Sentinel,* 27 April 1878.

26. *WaKeeney World,* 9 August 1879.

27. *Hays Sentinel,* 13 April 1878.

28. Burch, *Kansas as It Is,* 11, 15, 21, 39, 141.

29. *Larned Chronoscope,* 2 October 1879.

30. Ibid.

31. Ibid., 1 October 1880.

32. *Great Bend Register,* 15 May 1879.

33. Ibid., 10 April 1879.

34. *Dodge City Times,* 13 August 1885; *Second Biennial Report of the State Board of Agriculture,* 158.

35. *Kinsley Graphic,* 2 August 1879.

36. *Hays Sentinel,* 20 June 1879.

37. *Garden City Irrigator,* 12 June 1884.

38. *Dodge City Times,* 13 August 1885.

39. *Second Biennial Report of the State Board of Agriculture,* 422–27. Not all monthly reports are available for all stations in this publication for 1880. The agriculture reports were a form of advertising widely read by persons interested in coming to Kansas, and it was not unusual for correspondents to hold off on submitting unfavorable crop, weather, or population statistics for a time, hoping for better news.

40. Rainfall statistics for Ness County from 1892 to 1950 are in Minnie Millbrook, *Ness: Western County Kansas* (Detroit, Mich.: Millbrook Publishing Company, 1955), 14.

41. *Kinsley Graphic,* 7 December 1878.

42. *WaKeeney World,* 23 August 1879.

43. Burch, *Kansas as It Is,* 101–3.

44. *Great Bend Register,* 8 May 1879.

45. *Dodge City Times,* 11 October 1879.

46. Ibid., 10 May 1879.

47. *First Biennial Report of the State Board of Agriculture,* 273; *Second Biennial Report of the State Board of Agriculture,* 518–19; *Third Biennial Report of the State Board of Agriculture,* 228, 388, 237, 221.

48. *Hays Sentinel,* 25 July 1879.

49. *Larned Chronoscope,* 29 January 1879.

50. *Ness County Pioneer,* 19 July 1879.

51. Ibid., 26 July 1879.

52. Ibid., 17 November 1879.

53. Ibid.

54. *Kinsley Graphic,* 9 August 1879.

55. *Hays Sentinel,* 26 September 1879.

56. Ibid., 12 December 1879.

57. *WaKeeney Leader,* 21 January 1880, quoted in *Ness County Pioneer,* 31 January 1880.

58. Ibid., 20 December 1879.

59. Ibid., 31 January 1880.

60. Ibid., 14 February 1880.

61. *New York Times,* 22 January 1880, p. 5, col. 2.

62. *Hays Sentinel,* 30 April 1880; *Larned Chronoscope,* 7 May, 4 June 1880; *WaKeeney World,* 1 May 1880. Brief debate on the bill is in *Congressional Record,* 46th Cong., 2d sess., XI, 3802.

63. *Hays Sentinel,* 23 July 1880; *WaKeeney World,* 22 May 1880.

64. *Ness City Times,* 12 August 1880; *Hays Sentinel,* 17 September 1880.

65. *Dodge City Times,* 23 October 1880.

66. *Kinsley Graphic,* 12 June 1880; *Eldorado Press,* 17 June 1880.

67. *Hays Sentinel,* 2 July 1880. Detailed breakdowns of aid to individuals in Ness County may be found in *Ness County Pioneer,* 5 July 1880, and *Ness City Times,* 15 July 1880. A complete listing of aid shipments to the West and their towns of origin for November is in *Hays*

Sentinel, 26 November 1880. A less complete accounting for July is in *Topeka Commonwealth,* 30 July 1880.

68. *Daily Press,* 14 August 1880, in Relief Clippings, vol. 3, 93, Kansas State Historical Society, Topeka, contains the number of destitute in each county compared with total population.

69. *Topeka Commonwealth,* 2 February 1881.

70. *Larned Chronoscope,* 18 February 1881; *Hays Sentinel,* 1 April 1881.

71. *Topeka Daily Capital,* 30 June 1881; *Third Biennial Report of the State Board of Agriculture,* 619. Rainfall figures for 1881 and 1882 are incomplete, but it was clear that totals were up and the rain better distributed.

72. *Topeka Daily Capital,* 11 January 1881.

73. *WaKeeney World,* 15 May 1880.

74. *Great Bend Register,* 15 July 1880.

75. *Larned Chronoscope,* 10 December 1880; *Ness County Pioneer,* 24 January 1880; *Kinsley Graphic,* 18 December 1880; *Topeka Commonwealth,* 23 July 1880; *Russell County Record,* 16 September, 23 December 1880.

76. *Inland Tribune* quoted in *Dodge City Times,* 25 September 1880; *Daily Champion* (Atchison) in Relief Clippings, vol. 3, 48–51, Kansas State Historical Society, Topeka.

77. *Iuka News* quoted in *Topeka Commonwealth,* 25 May 1880.

78. James Malin, "The Turnover of Farm Population in Kansas," *Kansas Historical Quarterly* 4 (1935): 339–72.

79. Fite, *Farmers' Frontier,* 116.

80. W. Eugene Hollen, *The Southwest: Old and New* (New York: Alfred A. Knopf, 1961), 316.

81. Herbert Schell, "Drought and Agriculture in Eastern South Dakota during the Eighteen Nineties," *Agricultural History* 5 (1931): 162; James Hamburg, "Railroads and the Settlement of South Dakota during the Great Dakota Boom, 1878–1887," *South Dakota History* 5 (2): 168.

82. Hollen, *Southwest,* 316; Schell, "Drought," 162.

83. *Ness County Pioneer,* 5 July 1879; *WaKeeney World,* 22 May 1880; *Hays Sentinel,* 27 August 1880; *Kinsley Graphic,* 6 June 1880.

84. "Memories," Jennie Snyder, Ness County Clippings, vol. 1, 26–29, Kansas State Historical Society, Topeka.

85. *Dodge City Times,* 21 September 1882.

86. Henry Tilley to his mother, 7 August 1881, Belle and Henry Tilley papers, MSS Division, Kansas State Historical Society, Topeka.

87. *Ness County Pioneer,* 24 January 1880.

88. *Topeka Commonwealth,* 1 July 1880, Relief Clippings, vol. 4, 94–95, Kansas State Historical Society, Topeka.

89. Ibid.

90. Ibid.

91. Thomas F. Saarinen, *Perception of the Drought Hazard on the Great Plains* (Chicago: University of Chicago Press, 1966).

92. *Ness County Pioneer,* 2 August 1880.

11. Heaven of Brass, Earth of Iron

1. Roy Robbins, "The Public Domain in the Era of Exploitation, 1862–1901," *Agricultural History* 13 (1939): 98.

2. Gilbert Fite, "Great Plains Farming: A Century of Change and Adjustment," *Agricultural History* 51 (1977): 244.

3. Quoted in Hollen, *The Southwest,* 7.

4. "Picturesque Features of Kansas Farming," *Scribners Monthly* 19 (1879): 132.

5. Ibid., 134–35.

6. The psychological impact of the three-phase process of departure from the familiar, journey, and arrival at the unfamiliar is analyzed in Stanley Elkins, *Slavery: A Problem in American Institutional and Intellectual Life* (Chicago: University of Chicago Press, 1959).

7. Mrs. S. S. Button in *Jetmore Republican,* 25 April 1930.

8. *Clark County Clipper,* 14 December 1939.

9. Entries of 31 July, 28 August, 2 September 1876, Elam Bartholomew diaries.

10. Cleo Langley, "Story of Ama Sharp Langley's Life," Typescript, Hist. Osborne County, MSS Division, Kansas State Historical Society, Topeka.

11. Nellie Fitzgerald LaRosh in *Osborne County Farmer,* 5 November 1931.

12. "Memories," Jennie Snyder [1915], Ness County Clippings, vol. 1, 26–29, Kansas State Historical Society, Topeka.

13. *Osborne County Farmer,* 5 November 1931.

14. *Utica Star,* 14 July 1932.

15. *Dighton Herald,* 6 August 1936.

16. Undated clipping in Ness County Clippings, vol. 1, 26, Kansas State Historical Society, Topeka.

17. "Memories," Jennie Snyder, ibid., 26–29.

18. *Kinsley Graphic,* 13 December 1928.

19. Entries of 10 September, 9, 14, 16–18 October 1876, Elam Bartholomew diaries.

20. Ise, *Sod and Stubble,* 3–4.

21. *Kinsley Graphic,* 13 December 1928.

22. In addition to the evidence of the obvious popularity of homestead and timber-culture entries compared to cash sales recorded in the General Land Office annual reports for these years, one sees this pattern by consulting the Bureau of Land Management, Kansas Tract Books, available on microfilm at the Kansas State Historical Society; the Santa Fe contract books previously cited, also available there; and a manuscript plat book from the Dodge City land office 1876–88, MS. 1053, MSS Division, Kansas State Historical Society, Topeka.

23. Gates, *Fifty Million Acres,* 238.

24. The tenth census showed that the average farm size in western Kansas was barely over 160 acres in 1880 and that tenancy was nearly exclusively cultivation by the owner. U.S. Bureau of the Census, *Report on the Productions of Agriculture* (Washington, D.C.: Government Printing Office, 1883), 52–54.

25. U.S. Bureau of the Census, *Report on the Statistics of Agriculture* (Washington, D.C.: Government Printing Office, 1895), 142. Gates, *Fifty Million Acres,* 240, indicates that by showing that by 1890, farm tenancy statewide was up one-half compared to 1880 while number of farms increased one-fifth.

26. Railroad comparisons come from AT&SF, contract books, Kansas State Historical Society and

Kansas Pacific Railway, land grant mortgage sales November 1870 to June 1888, subgroup 54, vol. 28, Records of the Union Pacific Railroad, Nebraska State Historical Society, Lincoln.

27. Detailed studies of individual township landholding patterns are James Malin in *Lewis Press,* 1 June 1933; Allan Bogue, "Farmer Debtors in Pioneer Kinsley," *Kansas Historical Quarterly* 20 (1952): 82–107; Leo Oliva, *Ash Rock and the Stone Church: The History of a Kansas Rural Community* (Ellsworth, Kans.: Ellsworth Printing Company, 1983), 282–372; James Malin, *The Grassland of North America: Prolegomena to Its History with Addenda* (Lawrence, Kans.: James Malin, 1956), 278–322.

28. Paul Gates, "The Homestead Law in an Incongruous Land System," *American Historical Review* 41 (1936): 652–81.

29. *Great Bend Register,* 8, 15 August 1878, 1 May 1879, follows the KP question. The quote is from the 8 August issue.

30. George Anderson, "The Administration of Federal Land Laws in Western Kansas, 1880–1890: A Factor in Adjustment to a New Environment," *Kansas Historical Quarterly* 4 (1952): 233–39.

31. Ibid., 246–47.

32. *Clark County Clipper,* 29 January 1885.

33. Issue of 26 November 1886, quoted in Anderson, "The Administration of Federal Land Laws," 244.

34. Ibid., 247.

35. *Hays Sentinel,* 19 August 1881.

36. *Russell County Record,* 3 December 1874.

37. Anderson, "The Administration of Federal Land Laws in Western Kansas," 240.

38. *Ness City Times,* 16 April 1885.

39. *Edwards County Leader,* 25 October 1877.

40. *Osborne County Farmer,* 13 December 1934, contains an extensive account of the case, and Ise, *Sod and Stubble,* 90–91, a brief one. Anderson's footnotes refer to similar incidents documented in the General Land Office records.

41. *Larned Press,* 2 March 1877, has one such calculation.

42. Malin, in *Lewis Press,* 1 June 1933, and

Malin, *Winter Wheat,* discuss experiments. The latter work gives some account of success of crops year by year.

43. *Ness City Times,* 28 April 1881; *Hays Sentinel,* 12 December 1879.

44. *Second Biennial Report of the State Board of Agriculture,* 133–212.

45. *Russell County Record,* 10 June, 26 August 1875, 10 June 1877; *Edwards County Leader,* 31 May 1877.

46. E. Sperry in *Russell County Record,* 24 June 1875.

47. Burch, *Kansas as It Is,* 96–98.

48. Howard Ruede, *Sod-House Days: Letters From a Kansas Homesteader 1877–78,* John Ise, ed. (New York: Columbia University Press, 1937), 88, 110, 127, 154, 164, 171, 201, 240. A paperback reprint of Ruede's book was issued by the University Press of Kansas in 1983.

49. Muir, "Elam Bartholomew," 189.

50. Bartholomew recorded his complete accounts in his diaries, usually at the back of the yearly volumes under no particular date. The ones used here are MS. 1069–1070, Kansas State Historical Society, Topeka.

51. Ibid.

52. Entries of 17, 18 July 1885, Henry W. Norton diary, Norton family diaries, unprocessed, MSS Division, Kansas State Historical Society, Topeka.

53. *Edwards County Leader,* 19 July 1877.

54. *Kinsley Graphic,* 8 March 1879; *Russell County Record,* 16 July 1881.

55. George Strauth, "Reminiscences of a Ford County Pioneer," Hist. Ford County, MSS Division, Kansas State Historical Society, Topeka; *Larned Chronoscope,* 18 September 1947; *Hays Sentinel,* 15 August 1879.

56. *Great Bend Register,* 27 July 1882.

57. Entry of 30 March 1885, Henry Wylie Norton diary, Norton family diaries.

58. "Picturesque Features of Kansas Farming," 134.

59. *Osborne County Farmer,* 31 December 1874.

12. Home

1. Peter Stearns, "The New Social History: An Overview," in James Gardner and George Adams, eds., *Ordinary People and Everyday Life: Perspectives on the New Social History* (Nashville, Tenn.: American Association for State and Local History, 1983), 6–7.

2. Everett Dick, *The Sod House Frontier, 1854–1890* (New York: Appleton-Century, 1937), has brief descriptions of the building and furnishing of sod houses. More detailed and specific to Kansas is Barbara Oringderff, *True Sod: Sod Houses of Kansas* (Newton, Kans.: Mennonite Press, 1976). The building of Ruede's dugout is described in Ruede, *Sod House Days,* 28. A description of a house in the hundred-dollar range is in *Dighton Herald,* 13 November 1957.

3. Luke Pembleton memories [c. 1930], Ness County Clippings, vol. 1, 71, Kansas State Historical Society, Topeka.

4. *Ness City Times,* 12 January 1888.

5. *Dighton Herald,* 23 January 1957; *Hays Sentinel,* 10 September 1880. Another account of a collapse is in *Utica Star,* 14 July 1932.

6. Ruede, *Sod House Days,* 197.

7. Nellie Sprague Cook in *Dighton Herald,* 16 October 1957.

8. Luke Pembleton, Memories [c. 1930], Ness County Clippings, vol. 1, 70.

9. *The Western Times* (Sharon Springs), 14 April 1960.

10. Unidentified clipping [*Western Times* (Sharon Springs)], 5 May 1960, Wallace County Clippings, vol. 1, 224, Kansas State Historical Society, Topeka. Innumerable accounts mention lime plaster using material dug from a riverbank.

11. Memories, Jennie Snyder [c. 1915], Ness County Clippings, vol. 1, 26–29, Kansas State Historical Society, Topeka; Bonnie Bailey Vaughn in *Scott News Chronicle,* 15 September 1960.

12. *Scott News Chronicle,* 15 September 1960.

13. Ibid. Another account of a carpet is Christine Barnett Stormont, unidentifed clipping, 19 June 1957, Lane County Clippings, vol. 1, 113,

Kansas State Historical Society, Topeka.

14. Margaret Raser in *Jetmore Republican,* 16 May 1957.

15. Unidentified clipping [*Western Times* (Sharon Springs)], 5 May 1960, Wallace County Clippings, vol. 1, 224, Kansas State Historical Society, Topeka.

16. Bonnie Bailey Vaughn in *Scott County News Chronicle,* 24 November 1960.

17. Ibid., 2 June 1960.

18. Harrie L. Jennison in *Dighton Herald,* 27 March 1957.

19. Christine Barnett Stormont, unidentified clipping, 19 June 1957, Lane County Clippings, vol. 1, 112, Kansas State Historical Society, Topeka. A number of Lane County memoirs have been collected in *Pioneer Days in Lane County* (Dighton, Kans.: Lane County Historical Society, 1959 and 1976).

20. Margaret Raser in *Jetmore Republican,* 16 May 1957.

21. *The Lane County Historical Society Museum Presents the Lane County Bachelor* (Dighton, Kans.: Lane County Historical Society, N.d.). The ballad was sung to the tune of "The Irish Washerwoman."

22. W. H. Russell in unidentified clipping, Ellis County Clippings, vol. 1, 216, Kansas State Historical Society, Topeka.

23. A sensitive essay on the psychology of snake fear is Peter Steinhart, "Fear of Snakes," *Audubon* 86, no. 2 (1984): 6–9. The photograph at the head of the article is of a prairie rattlesnake.

24. Dee Posey in *Kinsley Graphic,* 13 December 1928.

25. *Kingman Mercury* in *Hays Sentinel,* 16 November 1878.

26. *Great Bend Register,* 3 May 1877.

27. Mary Kahle in *Western Times* (Sharon Springs), 14 April 1960.

28. Mary Northway in *Portis Independent,* 2 September 1937.

29. Examples are J. F. Nay, Reminiscences, Hist. Phillips County, MSS Division, Kansas State Historical Society, Topeka; *Great Bend Register,*

29 November 1877; Mrs. Henry Mull in *Notes on Early Clark County, Kansas,* vol. 3 (Ashland, Kans.: Clark County Historical Society, 1942), 39.

30. Mrs. S. A. Norris in *Osborne Journal,* 1 July 1937.

31. *Ness City Times,* 12 January 1888.

32. Ruede, *Sod House Days,* 91–92.

33. Virginia Barr, "Reminiscences of Early Days in Kansas," Hist. Smith County, MSS Division, Kansas State Historical Society, Topeka.

34. *Hays Sentinel,* 13 April 1877.

35. Alice Stormont, "Memories," MSS at Lane County Historical Society, Dighton.

36. Harrie Jennison in *Dighton Herald,* 27 March 1957.

37. Entry of 3 June 1879, Elam Bartholomew diaries.

38. Harrie Jennison in *Dighton Herald,* 27 March 1957.

39. Mattie Beal Price in unidentified clipping, 19 May 1960, Wallace County Clippings, vol. 1, 227, Kansas State Historical Society, Topeka.

40. Dee Posey in *Kinsley Graphic,* 13 December 1928.

41. *Garden City Irrigator,* 31 August 1882.

42. Harrie Jennison in *Dighton Herald,* 27 March 1957.

43. Ise, *Sod and Stubble,* 84–87.

44. *Hays Sentinel,* 16 May 1879.

45. There is a vast literature on Victorian sex-role expectations. For the West, a start is John Faragher, *Women and Men on the Overland Trail* (New Haven, Conn.: Yale University Press, 1979); Sandra Myres, *Westering Women and the Frontier Experience 1800–1915* (Albuquerque: University of New Mexico Press, 1982); and Scott McNall and Sally McNall, *Plains Families: Exploring Sociology through Social History* (New York: St. Martin's Press, 1983).

46. Entry of 21 July 1879, Elam Bartholomew diaries.

47. Mary Norton, entries of 28 May, 11 November 1880, family journal, Norton family diaries, Kansas State Historical Society, Topeka.

48. " 'I think I will Like Kansas': The Letters

of Flora Moorman Heston, 1885–1886,'' *Kansas History* 6 (1983): 70–95. This delightful collection, carefully edited by Maxine Benson, is a model of the way primary materials should be prepared for publication.

49. Entry of 2 March 1873, diary of Hattie Humphrey, printed in unidentified clipping, 15 September 1899, Edwards County Clippings, vol. 1, 85, Kansas State Historical Society, Topeka.

50. Mrs. John B. Smith in *Clark County Clipper* (Ashland), 23 November 1899.

51. Mrs. S. S. Button in *Jetmore Republican*, 25 April 1930.

52. Mary Norton, entry of 27 January 1880, family journal, Norton family diaries.

53. Ibid., entry of 19 February 1879, talks about leisure. The washing entries are everywhere.

54. *Hays Sentinel*, 14 November 1879.

55. Bonnie Bailey Vaughn in *Scott County News Chronicle*, 29 September 1960; Mary Norton, entry of 3 January 1880, family journal, Norton family diaries.

56. Mrs. N. E. Dunham in *Osborne County Farmer*, 2 July 1925.

57. Guy Miller in *Dighton Herald*, 27 February 1957; Harrie Jennison, ibid., 27 March 1957.

58. The Bartholomew diary is filled with fruit-hunting expeditions; for example, the entry of 2 July 1883.

59. Harrie Jennison in *Dighton Herald*, 27 March 1957; Blanche Patten Trostle, ibid., 22 May 1957.

60. *Ness City Times*, 5 January 1888.

61. Harrie Jennison in *Dighton Herald*, 27 March 1957; Mrs. N. E. Dunham in *Osborne County Farmer*, 2 July 1925.

62. Accounts for 1883 and 1881, Elam Bartholomew diaries.

63. Nellie Sprague Cook in *Dighton Herald*, 16 October 1957.

64. *Ness City Times*, 9 October 1884.

65. Ibid., 8 May 1890; *Ness County Pioneer*, 24 May 1879.

66. Detailed comment on prices may be found also in *Osborne County Farmer*, 7 July 1876;

Dodge City Times, 28 May 1885; *Larned Chronoscope*, 16 November 1883. The *Wallace County Herald* commented on 17 May 1888: ''When the Kansas farmer pays two dollars for a few boards worth a dollar and a half, takes off his coat worth five dollars for which he paid ten dollars, rolls up the sleeves of a shirt which cost him a dollar and a half when it is worth a dollar, and proceeds to repair his dwelling using 15 cents worth of nails for which he paid 25 cents and using a hatchet worth 40 cents for which he paid a dollar, how he ought to bless the good old Republican party for the prosperity he enjoys.''

67. Kitty Kepner in *Dighton Herald*, 2 October 1957.

68. Mary Norton, entry of 28 March 1879, family journal, Norton family diaries.

69. *Hays Sentinel*, 13 June 1879.

70. Sewing operations are described in Raser, *Jetmore Republican*, and ''The Letters of Flora Moorman Heston,'' 87. Heston took three days to knit a pair of socks which she sold for fifty cents, a profit over materials of twenty-five cents. Raser's mother had a sewing machine and sold thirty shirts in the summer of 1878.

71. Accounts of horse hunting are L. L. Scott in *Bazine Advocate*, 2 July 1937; Mrs. John Cole, unidentified clippings, Ness County Clippings, vol. 1, 156, 255, Kansas State Historical Society, Topeka; *Larned Chronoscope*, 26 June, 1879, 22 July 1881; Guild, ''Western Kansas,'' 464–66; Charles Youngblood, *A Mighty Hunter: The Adventures of Charles L. Youngblood on the Plains and Mountains* (Chicago: Rand, McNally & Company, 1890), 163–73.

72. Ella Ferrell in *Utica Star*, 14 July 1932.

73. Clara Kahle Barton in *Western Times* (Sharon Springs), 5 May 1960.

74. Mary Norton, entry of 11 November 1880, family journal, Norton family diaries, ibid.

75. L. L. Scott in *Bazine Advocate*, 30 July 1937.

76. Ruede, *Sod House Days*, 32.

77. Entries of 26, 27 March 1884, Bartholomew diary.

78. L. L. Scott in *Bazine Advocate,* 18 June 1937; Alice Stormont, "Memories," Lane County Historical Society, Dighton.

79. Luke Pembleton in unidentified clipping, Ness County Clippings, vol. 1, 73, Kansas State Historical Society, Topeka.

80. Calculations at end of 1879 entries, Bartholomew diary, MS. 1069.

81. Elliott West has been at work on a book on frontier children that will help redress the balance.

82. For example, Julie Jeffrey, *Frontier Women: The Trans-Mississippi West 1840–1880* (New York: Hill and Wang, 1979), and Annette Kolodny, *The Land before Her: Fantasy and Experience of the American Frontiers, 1630–1860* (Chapel Hill: University of North Carolina Press, 1984).

83. Elizabeth Hampsten, *Read This Only to Yourself: The Private Writings of Midwestern Women, 1880–1910* (Bloomington: Indiana University Press, 1982), 20–21, 88, 89, 96–97.

84. Myres, *Westering,* 1, 8.

85. One beginning is Lillian Schlissel, "Families: Crisis in Ideology," in Sam Girgus, ed., *The American Self: Myth, Ideology and Popular Culture* (Albuquerque: University of New Mexico Press, 1981).

86. Grace Russell Shouse in *Dighton Herald,* 23 January 1957.

87. "The Way We Live," in *Ness County Pioneer,* 13 December 1879.

88. Grace Russell Shouse in *Dighton Herald,* 23 January 1957.

89. Mrs. John Cole, memories [1930], Ness County Clippings, vol. 1, 58, Kansas State Historical Society, Topeka.

13. Abide with Me

1. *Great Bend Register,* 9 October 1879.

2. *Osborne County Farmer,* 25 November 1880.

3. *Kinsley Graphic,* 25 January 1883.

4. *Larned Chronoscope,* 21 August 1885.

5. *Hays Sentinel,* 18 February 1886.

6. *Jetmore Reville* in *Kinsley Graphic,* 12 November 1886.

7. *Russell County Record,* 14 March 1878.

8. *Hays Sentinel,* 25 July 1879.

9. *Ellsworth Reporter* quoted in ibid., 7 November 1879.

10. *Dodge City Times,* 10 November 1881.

11. *Hays Sentinel,* 12 September, 1 November 1879, 30 January, 12 February 1880; *Dodge City Times,* 10 November 1881.

12. Entry of 3 July 1880 in *Osborne County Farmer,* 6 January 1972.

13. J. F. Nay, Reminiscences, Hist. Phillips County, MSS Division, Kansas State Historical Society, Topeka.

14. Leo Oliva, *Fort Hays,* 62.

15. *Dodge City Times,* 24 September 1885.

16. Ibid., 6 July 1882.

17. *Ness County News,* 25 May 1950.

18. "Picturesque Features of Kansas Farming," 139.

19. Accounts of the 1884 fire are J. W. Chaffin in *Scott County Record,* 16 March 1933 and *Kinsley Graphic,* 11 March 1884.

20. *Larned Tiller and Toiler,* N.d., Pawnee County Clippings, vol. 1, 149, Kansas State Historical Society, Topeka.

21. J. W. Chaffin in *Scott County Record,* 16 March 1933.

22. A. S. Kimball in *Larned Chronoscope,* 22 January 1879.

23. The story of one such morning meeting in western Kansas after a 1930s prairie fire was told to me by Beulah Paul, a minister's wife.

24. A. S. Kimball in *Larned Chronoscope,* 22 January 1879.

25. *Notes on Early Clark County,* vol. 4, 71.

26. *Hays Sentinel,* 4 February 1886.

27. Van Sickel, *A Story of Real Life on the Plains,* 39–48.

28. *Topeka Capital,* N.d., Ness County Clippings, vol. 1, 18–19.

29. Diarists were especially interested in the storms, and even those who were not usually regular with entries kept careful track of it. Of

course, the Bartholomew and Norton diaries provide complete detail day by day on the weather in Rooks and Pawnee Counties. Others with daily storm entries are William A. Gill diary in *Larned Tiller & Toiler*, 20 January 1944, and J. W. Dappert diary (Comanche County) in *Protection Post*, 28 March 1947. Henry Wylie Norton recorded a drifting snow on 28 March and feared his potatoes would freeze in the ground.

30. *Ness City Times*, 7 January 1886, 15 December 1887; undated entry, vol. 7, 140, Elam Bartholomew diary, MS. 1070.

31. *Dodge City Times*, 7, 14 January 1886.

32. *Notes on Early Clark County, Kansas*, vol. 4, 15.

33. *Topeka Capital* in *Dodge City Times*, 18 February 1886.

34. *Dodge City Times*, 21 January 1886.

35. *Notes on Early Clark County, Kansas*, vol. 3, 77.

36. Harrie Jennison in *Dighton Herald*, 27 March 1957.

37. Thorn Walker in ibid., 1 May 1957.

38. E. E. Frizell in *Larned Chronoscope*, 9 January 1936.

39. Frank Houghton, "Bits About Beelers," typescript, MSS Division, Kansas State Historical Society, Topeka.

40. *Dodge City Times*, 7 January 1886.

41. Ibid., 14 January 1886; Lillie Boucher Owings in *Notes on Clark County, Kansas*, vol. 2, 74–76.

42. *Topeka Capital*, 2 January 1916.

43. Some accounts of tornadoes are *Larned Chronoscope*, 2 May 1884; account of 18 June 1886 tornado by D. M. Adams in hist. meteorology, MSS Division, Kansas State Historical Society, Topeka; *Notes on Clark County, Kansas*, vol. 3, 45.

44. *Great Bend Register*, 22 November 1877.

45. *Ness County Pioneer*, 6 October 1879.

46. *Larned Chronoscope*, 8 April 1887.

47. J. F. Nay, reminiscences, Hist. Phillips County, MSS Division, Kansas State Historical Society, Topeka.

48. *WaKeeney World* in *Hays Sentinel*, 14 November 1879.

49. *Russell County Record*, 29 August 1878.

50. Typical accounts are *Hays Sentinel*, 10 December 1880, *Larned Chronoscope*, 29 October 1886.

51. *Russell County Record*, 29 August 1878.

52. *Dodge City Times*, 8 July 1886; *Larned Chronoscope*, 26 August 1887.

53. *Great Bend Register*, 8 August 1878.

54. A poignant example is in Mrs. John Cole, memories [1930], Ness County Clippings, vol. 1, 153, Kansas State Historical Society, Topeka.

55. *Ness City Times*, 8 December 1881.

56. Reprinted in *Hays Daily News*, 28 November 1954.

57. Ise, *Sod and Stubble*, 41–45.

58. Mary Northway in *Portis Independent*, 9 September 1937.

59. Entry of 15 January 1887, Elam Bartholomew diary.

60. Alice Stormont, memories, Lane County Historical Society.

61. Mrs. Mary Northway, *Portis Independent*, 9 September 1937.

62. *Osborne County Farmer* 6 January 1872.

63. *Ness City Times*, 10 May 1888.

64. *Great Bend Register*, 17 October 1878.

65. *Larned Chronoscope*, 1 January 1879.

66. "Picturesque Features of Kansas Farming," 137.

67. *Hays Sentinel*, 9 July 1885.

14. Dam the Draws

1. *Wichita Eagle*, 25 June 1887.

2. Joseph Schumpeter, *Business Cycles: A Theoretical, Historical and Statistical Analysis of the Capitalist Process* (New York: McGraw-Hill, 1939), 1: 169, 338–40.

3. *Garden City Sentinel*, 1 January 1888.

4. Analysis of the boom for regions are Emmons, *Garden in the Grasslands;* Glenn Dumke, *The Boom of the Eighties in Southern*

California (San Marino, Calif.: Huntington Library, 1963); Earl Pomeroy, *The Pacific Slope: A History* (New York: Alfred A. Knopf, 1965); Gunther Barth, *Instant Cities: Urbanization and the Rise of San Francisco and Denver* (New York: Oxford University Press, 1975); and James Hamburg, "Railroads and the Settlement of South Dakota during the Great Dakota Boom, 1878–1887," *South Dakota History* 5 (1975): 165–78. For a good contemporary description of Tacoma's boom, see Rudyard Kipling, *From Sea to Sea: Letters of Travel,* vol. 2 (New York: Doubleday & McClure, 1899).

5. Rendigs Fels, *American Business Cycles 1865–1897* (Chapel Hill: University of North Carolina Press, 1959), 21.

6. Charles Gates, "Boom Stages in American Expansion," *Business History Review* 33 (1959): 34–36.

7. Dykstra, *The Cattle Towns,* 329–35.

8. Charles Wood, "Upbreeding Western Range Cattle: Notes on Kansas, 1880–1920," *Journal of the West* 16 (1977): 18; *Dodge City Times,* 19 April 1883.

9. *Larned Chronoscope,* 28 April 1882; Mary Einsel, "Some Notes on the Comanche Cattle Pool," *Kansas Historical Quarterly* 26 (1960): 59.

10. Burch, *Kansas as It Is,* 55–56.

11. *Hays Sentinel,* 4 June 1880.

12. Ibid., 20 February 1880.

13. *Larned Chronoscope,* 4 January 1884; *Kinsley Graphic,* 8 December 1927.

14. Charles Wood, "C. D. Perry: Clark County Farmer and Rancher, 1884–1908," *Kansas Historical Quarterly* 39 (1973): 449–77; *Liberal Democrat,* 9 June 1921.

15. Margaret Caldwell, "The Mudge Ranch," *Kansas Historical Quarterly* 24 (1958): 285–304.

16. *Dodge City Times,* 7 April 1881. Additional detail on financing and life on ranches of the period may be found in Alice Rollins, *The Story of a Ranch* (New York: Cassell & Co., 1885), for a ranch near Ellsworth and the M. C. Campbell letters, 1880–1910, misc. Campbell, Kansas State

Historical Society, Topeka, for a Clark County ranch.

17. Costs of fencing various acreages are given in *Dodge City Times,* 25 January 1883. For a history of the introduction of barbed wire, see Earl Hayter, "Barbed Wire Fencing—A Prairie Invention: Its Rise and Influence in the Western States," *Agricultural History* 13 (1939): 189–207.

18. *Hays Sentinel,* 16 February 1878.

19. *Wichita Beacon,* 18 April 1883.

20. Einsel, "Notes," 59; *Coldwater Western Star,* 28 September 1951; Hal Herd, "The Comanche Cattle Pool," Hist. Washburn County, MSS Division, Kansas State Historical Society, Topeka; *Larned Chronoscope,* 17 December 1880.

21. W. P. Harrington, "History of Gove County (1917)," Hist. Gove County, MSS Division, Kansas State Historical Society, Topeka, 37–39; *Dighton Herald,* 14 April 1954; *Larned Chronoscope,* 27 June 1884.

22. *Larned Chronoscope,* 27 June 1884, 7 April 1882.

23. Ibid., 24 December 1880, 23 June 1882.

24. *Dodge City Times,* 1 March 1883.

25. *Ness City Times,* 1 May 1884. An excellent study of herd law legislation over the West is Rodney Davis, "Before Barbed Wire: Herd Law Agitation in Early Kansas and Nebraska," *Journal of the West* 6 (1967): 41–52.

26. *Dodge City Times,* 2 June 1877.

27. *Russell County Record,* 28 January 1875.

28. *Ness City Times,* 22 December 1881.

29. *Larned Chronoscope,* 21 September 1883.

30. The history of herd laws near cattle towns that would have the greatest interest in avoiding them is treated in Dykstra, *The Cattle Towns.* The homestead change lobby is found in *Garden City Irrigator,* 22 November 1883, 17 January 1884, *Dodge City Times,* 7 February 1884.

31. A sophisticated analysis that goes beyond this is Gene Gressley, *Bankers and Cattlemen* (New York: Alfred A. Knopf, 1966). However, the book contains little on Kansas. For a colorful description of the 1885–86 blizzard's effect on

cattle, see "The Great Winter Kill" in McNeal, *When Kansas Was Young,* 159–62.

32. *Dodge City Times,* 25 June 1885.

33. *Ness City Times,* 21 February 1889.

34. *Clark County Clipper,* 3 September 1885.

35. *Dodge City Times,* 17 July 1880.

36. Ibid., 1 May 1880.

37. Ibid., 15 May 1880.

38. *Topeka Commonwealth,* 23 July 1880.

39. *Ness City Times,* 30 April 1885, 21 February 1889. The *Clark County Clipper,* 8 March 1888, reported on a plan for a central reservoir and encouraged farmers to build their own dams.

40. My father remembers this.

41. *Dodge City Times,* 14 August 1880.

42. *Larned Chronoscope,* 30 July 1880.

43. Robert Hay, "Irrigation in Western Kansas: Its Water-Supply and Possibilities," in *Seventh Biennial Report of the State Board of Agriculture For the Years 1889–1890* (Topeka: Kansas Publishing House, 1891), 129.

44. Conner Sorenson, "A History of Irrigation in the Arkansas River Valley in Western Kansas, 1880–1910," (Master's thesis, University of Kansas, 1968), 12–14; James Tomayko, "The Ditch Irrigation Boom in Southwest Kansas: Changing an Environment," *Journal of the West* 22 (1983): 20.

45. Tomayko, "The Ditch Irrigation Boom," 20.

46. Sorenson, "A History of Irrigation," 15–24.

47. *Garden City Irrigator,* 13 July 1882.

48. Ibid., 24 October, 12 December 1885.

49. Ibid., 21 September 1882.

50. Ibid., 25 September, 5 October 1882.

51. *Kinsley Graphic,* 14 August 1880.

52. *Garden City Irrigator,* 3 August 1882.

53. *Kinsley Graphic,* 11 September 1882.

54. *Garden City Irrigator,* 14 August 1884.

55. Ibid., 30 September 1886.

56. *Kinsley Graphic,* 12 July 1883.

57. *Garden City Irrigator,* 9 November 1882.

58. Ibid., 30 November 1882, 29 January, 1 February 1883.

59. Ibid., 1 March 1883.

60. Ibid., 8 March 1883.

61. Ibid., 18 January 1883.

62. *Kansas City Star* [7 September 1902], Ford County Clippings, vol. 1, 85, Kansas State Historical Society, Topeka; *Dodge City Times,* 11 January, 5 April, 7 June 1883, records Gilbert's initial contacts with Rochester capitalists.

63. *Dodge City Times,* 26 May 1887.

64. Ibid., 19 May, 29 December 1887, 17 January 1889.

65. Sorenson, "A History of Irrigation," 27–29; Tomayko, "The Ditch Irrigation Boom," 22.

66. *Dodge City Times,* 5 October 1882.

67. Sorenson, "A History of Irrigation," 40.

68. *Dodge City Times,* 18 September 1884.

69. Ibid., 28 May 1885.

70. Ibid., 20 May 1886.

71. Ibid., 23 March 1882.

72. *Kinsley Graphic,* 12 July, 23 August 1883.

73. *Great Bend Register,* 19 October 1882; *Larned Chronoscope,* 20 October 1882.

74. Sorenson, "A History of Irrigation," 33–36.

75. Paul Taylor, "Reclamation: The Rise and Fall of an American Idea," *American West* 7 (1970): 27–33, 63.

76. Everett Dick, *Conquering the Great American Desert: Nebraska* (Lincoln: Nebraska State Historical Society, 1975), 383–86.

77. Tomayko, "The Ditch Irrigation Boom," 23.

78. *Larned Chronoscope,* 14 January 1881.

79. *Ness County Pioneer,* 6 March 1880.

80. *Dodge City Times,* 7 February 1880.

81. *Larned Chronoscope,* 14 January 1881.

82. Ibid., 6 August 1880.

83. Ibid., 10 December 1880.

84. Ibid., 1 October 1880.

85. Ibid., 14 January 1881; *Dodge City Times,* 9 October 1880.

86. Ibid., 8 October 1880; Dick, *Conquering,* 141–47.

87. Ibid., 4 February 1881.

88. Ibid., 23 September 1881.

89. *Dodge City Times,* 29 September 1887.

90. *Hays Sentinel,* 30 April 1880.

91. Ibid., 2 September 1881.

92. *Ness City Times,* 3 February, 5 May 1881.

93. *Garden City Irrigator,* 7 September, 2 November 1882.

94. *Seventh Biennial Report of the State Board of Agriculture,* 140.

95. *Kinsley Graphic,* 15 January 1881, 25 January, 16 August 1883.

96. *Hays Sentinel,* 13 September 1883; *Kinsley Graphic,* 13 September 1883.

97. *Seventh Biennial Report of the State Board of Agriculture,* 140–41.

98. *Ness City Times,* 5 January 1888.

99. *Sixth Biennial Report of the State Board of Agriculture For the Years 1887–88* (Topeka: Kansas Publishing House, 1889), 164.

100. *Ness City Times,* 5 January 1888.

101. *Larned Chronoscope,* 4 February 1881.

15. Ties That Bind

1. Michael Mulhall, *The Dictionary of Statistics,* 4th ed. (London: George Routledge and Sons, 1899), 508.

2. *Sixth Annual Report of the Board of Railroad Commissioners for the Year Ending December 1, 1888* (Topeka: Kansas Publishing House, 1888), 4.

3. *Dodge City Times,* 6 September 1888.

4. *Kinsley Graphic,* 14 May 1886.

5. Ibid., 25 June 1886.

6. Good county maps showing railways in Kansas in 1887, including many of the projected lines, are in *The Official State Atlas of Kansas* (Philadelphia: L. H. Everts and Co., 1887). A color-coded map of the state rail system as of the end of 1888 is folded in the back of *Sixth Annual Report of the Board of Railroad Commissioners for the Year Ending December 1, 1888* (Topeka: Kansas Publishing House, 1888). Comparing this to the map showing Kansas railroads in 1918 in Socolofsky and Self, *Atlas of Kansas,* 36, shows how little western Kansas building was done in the next twenty years.

7. *Fifth Annual Report of the Board of Railroad Commissioners for the Year Ending December 1, 1887* (Topeka: Kansas Publishing House, 1887), 5.

8. Ibid., 6; *Sixth Annual Report of the Board of Railroad Commissioners,* 4.

9. *Fifth Annual Report of the Board of Railroad Commissioners,* 6.

10. *Dodge City Times,* 11 November 1886.

11. *Ness County News* in *Garden City Irrigator,* 11 December 1886.

12. A. Bower Sagaser, "Building the Main Line of the Missouri Pacific through Kansas," *Kansas Historical Quarterly* 21 (1955): 328. Sagaser's article contains a detailed map from the company's 1888 annual report showing its lines in Kansas.

13. *Ness City Times,* 18 October 1883. Prominent men in Larned and Garden City were among the original DM&A directors.

14. *Dodge City Times,* 21 July 1887.

15. *Larned Chronoscope,* 2 October 1885; *Dodge City Times,* 7 July 1887.

16. *Larned Chronoscope,* 14 May, 22 October 1886.

17. Bryant, *History of the Atchison, Topeka & Santa Fe Railway,* 124–25.

18. The development can be followed on the maps mentioned above.

19. *Dodge City Times,* 14 October 1886.

20. The argument there can be found in *Ness City Times,* 1 April, 6 May, 1 July 1886.

21. O. P. Byers, "Early History of the El Paso Line of the Chicago, Rock Island & Pacific Railway," *Collections of the Kansas State Historical Society* 15 (1919–22): 574.

22. A. Bower Sagaser, "The Rails Go Westward," in John Bright, ed., *Kansas: The First Century,* vol. 1 (New York: Lewis Historical Publishing Company, 1956), 249.

23. A sample of the voluminous newspaper comment on this plan is *Hays Sentinel,* 2, 16 July 1885, 21 January, 29 April 1886; *Garden City Irrigator,* 8 May, 19 June, 11 September 1886; *Dodge City Times,* 24 September, 8 October 1885, 29 April, 30 December 1886; *Kinsley Graphic,* 7 October 1887.

24. *Dodge City Times,* 17 February, 12 May 1887.

25. In order, these roads are discussed in *Kinsley Graphic,* 18 March 1887, 28 August 1885, 25 March, 1 April 1887; *Dodge City Times,* 19 July 1879; *Great Bend Register,* 20 December 1877; *Clark County Clipper,* 1 September 1887, 19 August 1886; *Hays Sentinel,* 14 September 1878; *Larned Chronoscope,* 16 December 1887; *Ness City Times,* 15 September 1885; *Kinsley Graphic,* 17 July 1880; *Garden City Daily Herald,* 19 February, 22 June 1887; *Garden City Irrigator,* 3 October 1886, 1 January 1887, 12 December 1885; *Great Bend Register,* 6 June 1881; *Dodge City Times,* 29 December 1881, 28 May, 27 August, 3 September 1885, 26 April 1888, 11 November 1886; *Sherman County Dark Horse,* 23 December 1886.

26. *Kinsley Graphic,* 28 August 1885.

27. *Ness City Times,* 6 May 1886.

28. An excellent account of the dynamics of the railroad lobby in Ness County is in Millbrook, *Ness: Western County Kansas,* 113–21.

29. *Ness City Times,* 11 March 1886.

30. Ibid., 18 March 1886.

31. Ibid., 1 April 1886.

32. Ibid., 8 July 1887.

33. *Garden City Irrigator,* 10 October 1885.

34. Miller, Leman, and Chase to C. J. Jones, 3 September 1886 in *Garden City Irrigator,* 7 September 1886.

35. *Garden City Irrigator,* 29 September 1886.

36. *Fifth Annual Report of the Board of Railroad Commissioners,* 6–7.

37. The Kansas State Historical Society has a huge collection of records of the Rock Island's Kansas Town and Land Company (MSS Division, collection 130), which would seem to be a bonanza for this study. Unlike the complete sales records for the Santa Fe available there, however, the Rock Island material is mostly from the twentieth century. Nineteenth-century material concerns mainly town lots (the Rock Island had no land grant in Kansas) and is too fragmentary to be useful.

38. These records of Kansas Pacific Railway, Land Grant Mortgage Sales, nos. 1–7902 (November 1870–June 1888), are in Subgroup 54, volume 28, Union Pacific Railway records, Nebraska State Historical Society, Omaha, and have been microfilmed. The early sales records in this volume are all from Colorado; the Kansas sales pick up late in 1886 and run through 1888. It is possible that more Kansas Pacific records of this sort will be available as the Union Pacific Railroad transfers material to the Nebraska State Historical Society.

39. Conclusions based upon the KP land records were drawn from a study of sales for the first nine months of 1887 done using a database program on a microcomputer.

40. Thirty-one buyers from Wymore (1890 population of 2,420) and twenty-seven from Holdrege (population 2,601), both located just north of the Kansas line, purchased 14,078 acres in Wallace and Sherman counties between January and October 1887.

41. A good aid to precisely locating things in western Kansas is the detailed set of county maps available in two scales at nominal cost from the State Highway Commission of Kansas.

42. The quantitative analysis of Santa Fe land sales comes from the AT&SF, contract books, MSS Division, Kansas State Historical Society as cited previously. Every land sale the railroad made in Kansas in the nineteenth century is recorded in this collection of 150 large, heavy books.

43. Hill P. Wilson, *A Biographical History of Eminent Men of the State of Kansas* (Topeka, Kans.: Hal Lithographing Company, 1901), 569–71.

44. Finney County Historical Society, *History of Finney County, Kansas* (Garden City, Kans.: Finney County Historical Society, 1954), II: 221.

45. *Garden City Irrigator,* 25 June 1885, 1 January 1886.

46. Ibid., 2 January 1886.

47. L. E. Hoffman, "Ajax the Great," typescript biography of Hoisington in misc. Hoffman, MSS Division, Kansas State Historical Society, Topeka.

48. John Knox, *Paths to Wealth* (for the author, 1883), 500. Knox sold the book at his real-estate office through the boom.

49. Biographical information on Fahnestock, one

of the largest buyers of Santa Fe land, can be found in *History of Knox Co. Illinois* (Chicago: S. J. Clarke Publishing Co., 1912), II: 324.

50. *Dodge City Times,* 16 September 1886, 23 June 1887.

51. The Wallace County population was 2,644 in 1888 and 2,400 in the 1970 census.

16. Ravanna Rhymes with Hosanna

1. *Kingman Journal,* 31 March 1939.

2. A detailed breakdown of all classes of transfer from each western Kansas land office can be found in *Annual Report of the General Land Office* for the fiscal years 1885 to 1888 (Washington, D.C.: Government Printing Office, 1885–88).

3. *Garden City Sentinel,* 1 January 1888; Helen Gill, "The Establishment of Counties in Kansas," *Collections of the Kansas State Historical Society* 8 (1904): 449–72.

4. Population statistics are from the Fifth, Sixth, and Seventh Biennial Reports of the Kansas State Board of Agriculture. The Sixth (1886–87), 3–4, lists county organization dates, size of counties, and populations for the years 1887 and 1888.

5. It was claimed at various points during the boom that 1,500 people a day were coming into western Kansas, and in both 1885 and 1886, newspapers calculated that if the land being sold were actually occupied, one person per quarter section, there would be 200,000 new people in western Kansas each year. *Dodge City Times,* 3 December 1885; *Garden City Irrigator,* 10 July 1886; *Clark County Clipper,* 10 June 1886.

6. *Garden City Sentinel,* 1 January 1888.

7. Special edition of *Western Kansas World,* March 1979, reprinting an 1889 WaKeeney newspaper.

8. *Larned Chronoscope* in *Clark County Clipper,* 19 November 1885.

9. Special edition of *Western Kansas World,* March 1979.

10. *Hays Sentinel,* 8, 21 February 1879.

11. *Dodge City Times,* 5 May 1887.

12. *Garden City Daily Herald,* 26 April 1887.

13. Ibid., 4 May 1887.

14. *Dodge City Times,* 5 May 1887.

15. *Dodge City Times,* 27 August 1885.

16. *Garden City Daily Herald,* 21 January, 5 February 1887.

17. Quoted in *Kinsley Graphic,* 27 May 1887.

18. James Malin, "The Kinsley Boom in the Late Eighties," *Kansas Historical Quarterly* 4 (1935): 29–30.

19. *Dodge City Times,* 15 October 1885.

20. *Larned Chronoscope,* 7 May, 4 June 1886; *Topeka Capital,* 24 June 1888; *Larned Tiller and Toiler,* 26 February 1943, 23 October 1947, describe Ditson's operation.

21. *Minneapolis Messenger* in *Dodge City Times,* 3 September 1885.

22. *Larned Chronoscope,* 4 June, 6 August 1886.

23. *Garden City Daily Herald,* 30 March, 1 April 1887; *Garden City Irrigator,* 1 November 1885, 9 January, 27 November, 18 December 1886.

24. *Garden City Irrigator,* 28 August 1886.

25. *Dodge City Times,* 4 February, 13, 20 May, 24 June, 14 October 1886.

26. *Ness City Times,* 12 August 1886, 21 July, 22 September 1887.

27. *Jetmore Republican,* 25 April 1930, 16 May 1957.

28. *Garden City Irrigator,* 21 August 1886.

29. *Dodge City Times,* 25 September 1887.

30. *Valley Republican* (Kinsley), 15 December 1877.

31. *Kinsley Graphic,* 14, 21 May, 16 July 1886.

32. Ibid., 24 July 1885, 3 June 1887.

33. Ibid., 24 June, 1 July 1887.

34. Malin, "The Kinsley Boom," 28–34. Kinsley is the best studied of the 1880s western Kansas boom towns, thanks to the interest of economic historians James Malin and Allan Bogue.

35. *Dodge City Times,* 16 July 1885.

36. Ibid., 19 November 1885.

37. Ibid., 3 December 1885, 27 May 1886. The editor at Meade Center became angry with the *Dodge City Times* reporter for saying that Meade Center was located on a hill and inaccessible. So

the paper changed: "Instead of being 'situated on a hill,' Meade Center is located on the 'bluff overlooking Crooked Creek,' with a magnificent view of the site where Meade Center ought to be situated."

38. *Ness City Times,* 24 November, 29 December 1887, reports on the preparation of the Burch handbook for Ness County, which had seventy-two views and was produced in an edition of 8,000 from company offices in Chicago. The state historical society has Burch handbooks produced at the same time for several other western counties that Burch himself had visited.

39. *Garden City Irrigator,* 25 June 1885; *Garden City Daily Irrigator,* 25, 27, 28 October 1886; *Ness City Times,* 10 June 1886, 14 April, 6 October 1887; Daisy Hatch, "Early Day History of Old Garfield County," typescript, Hist. Garfield, MSS Division, Kansas State Historical Society, Topeka; *Kinsley Graphic,* 14 May 1886, contain these ads.

40. *Ness City Times,* 5 January 1888.

41. F. L. Hulaniski to Walrond and Mitchell, 22 November 1884, Hist. Osborne County, MSS Division, Kansas State Historical Society, Topeka.

42. *Hays Sentinel,* 29 April, 6 May 1886.

43. *Kinsley Graphic,* 11 June 1886.

44. Ibid., 19 February 1881.

45. Ibid., 3 September 1886.

46. *Dodge City Times,* 15 January, 2 April 1885; *Garden City Irrigator,* 5 February, 19 March, 2 April 1885, 12 October, 11 December 1886, 25 January 1887; *Hays Sentinel,* 20 August 1885; *Larned Chronoscope,* 11 September 1885, 23 April, 10 December 1886.

47. *Hays Sentinel,* 20 August 1885.

48. Entry of 30 January 1879, Norton family diaries, MSS Division, Kansas State Historical Society, Topeka.

49. *Clark County Clipper,* 3 March 1887.

17. Red-Haired Men in Silk Ties

1. The phrase "red-haired men" comes from *Garden City Daily Herald,* 13 April 1887.

2. These population figures are from the sixth and seventh *Biennial Reports* of the Kansas State Board of Agriculture.

3. Emmons, *Garden in the Grasslands,* 170.

4. Sorenson, "A History of Irrigation," 53.

5. *Ellis Headlight* in *Ness City Times,* 18 July 1889.

6. *Hays Sentinel,* 16 December 1890.

7. *Larned Chronoscope,* 13 July 1888.

8. Malin, "The Kinsley Boom," 179, 183.

9. *Garden City Daily Herald,* 13 May 1887.

10. Ibid., 2 June 1887.

11. *Kinsley Graphic,* 30 March 1888.

12. Ibid., 13 January 1888.

13. *Larned Chronoscope,* 2 May 1890.

14. *Dodge City Times,* 13 May 1886.

15. Rainfall statistics are from the *Seventh Biennial Report of the Kansas State Board of Agriculture.*

16. *Kansas City Times* quoted in *New York Times,* 16 September 1888, p. 7, col. 2.

17. Entries of 31 July, 1, 2 August 1888, Elam Bartholomew diaries.

18. *New York Times,* 13 August 1888, p. 2, col. 3.

19. *Wichita Beacon,* 21 December 1887.

20. Ibid., 23 December 1887.

21. Ibid., 22 December 1887.

22. *Sixth Biennial Report of the Kansas State Board of Agriculture,* 152.

23. *Sixth Annual Report of the Board of Railroad Commissioners* (Topeka: Kansas Publishing House, 1888), 5.

24. *Eighth Annual Report of the Board of Railroad Commissioners* (Topeka: Kansas Publishing House, 1890), iv, ix.

25. *Sherman County Dark Horse,* 24 March 1887.

26. The KP mortgage sales records, cited earlier, contain complete listings of payments made and cancellations.

27. This information comes from an inventory of 1,508 feet of certificates for Kansas housed at the National Archives and broken down by land office. The inventory is at the Manuscript Division, Kansas State Historical Society, Topeka.

28. *Kinsley Graphic,* 9 September 1887.

29. Allan Bogue, "To Shape a Western State: Some Dimensions of the Kansas Search for Capital, 1865–1893," in John Clark, ed., *The Frontier Challenge: Responses to the Trans-Mississippi West* (Lawrence: University Press of Kansas, 1971), 224.

30. Malin, "The Kinsley Boom," 44.

31. *Annual Report of the Commissioner of the General Land Office for the Fiscal Year Ended June 30, 1890, Dated September 13, 1890* (Washington, D.C.: Government Printing Office, 1890), 281.

32. Frank Spearman, "The Great American Desert," *Harpers Monthly* 87 (July 1888): 238–40.

33. J. C. Lohnes, "History of Ness County," 24–25.

34. Allan Bogue, "The Land Mortgage Company in the Plains States," *Agricultural History* 25 (1951): 20, 25, 30, 32.

35. S. D. Aulls to his brother, 15 May 1888, misc. Aulls, MSS Division, Kansas State Historical Society, Topeka.

36. S. D. Aulls to A. W. Hewlett, 24 April 1888, ibid.

37. S. D. Aulls to his brother, 17 April, 3 May 1888, ibid.

38. S. D. Aulls to A. W. Hewlett, 13 April 1888, ibid.

39. Ibid., 14 June 1889.

40. W. C. L. Beard flyers, 22 August, 11 September 1889; Beard to M. S. Stokes, 28 October 1889, misc. Stokes, MSS Division, Kansas State Historical Society, Topeka.

41. H. L. Lark to M. S. Stokes, 8 November, 9 December 1890, ibid.

42. Peter Argersinger, "Road to a Republican Waterloo: The Farmers' Alliance and the Election of 1890 in Kansas," *Kansas Historical Quarterly* 33 (1967): 444.

43. Ibid., 445.

44. U.S. Census Office, *Report on the Statistics of Agriculture in the United States at the Eleventh Census: 1890* (Washington, D.C.: Government Printing Office, 1895), 142–44.

45. Robert McMath, "Preface to Populism: The Origin and Economic Development of the 'Southern Farmers' Alliance in Kansas," *Kansas Historical Quarterly* 42 (1976): 59. An account of the founding by a participant is W. F. Rightmore, "The Alliance Movement in Kansas—Origin of the Peoples' Party," *Collections of the Kansas State Historical Society* 9 (1905–6): 1–7.

46. A. N. Ironclad in *Kinsley Graphic,* 15 February 1889.

47. *Kinsley Graphic,* 25 October, 1889.

48. *Larned Chronoscope,* 10 January, 18 July, 19 December 1890.

49. *Ness City Times,* 17 April 1890.

50. *Larned Chronoscope,* 19 September 1890. How many of these suggestions found their way into law can be followed in Bogue, "To Shape a Western State," 226–27.

51. An account of an alliance picnic is in *Larned Chronoscope,* 18 July 1890. The speaker meant is of course "Sockless" Jerry Simpson, the Populist firebrand.

52. *Kinsley Graphic,* 21 February 1890.

53. Ibid., 22 December 1889.

54. *Ness City Times,* 30 October 1890.

55. Examples of failures of town improvements are *Dodge City Times,* 29 December 1887; *Larned Chronoscope,* 14 January 1887; *Garden City Daily Herald,* 4, 8 April 1887.

56. *Larned Chronoscope,* 23 December 1887.

57. Calvin Schwartzkopf, "The Rush County-Seat War," *Kansas Historical Quarterly* 36 (1970): 40–61.

58. *Great Bend Register,* 22 May, 21 August 1879.

59. The Ness County fight can be followed in *Hays Sentinel,* 28 February 1879; *Ness County Pioneer,* 10 May 1879, 6 March, 10 April, 3 May 1880; *Ness City Times,* 23 December 1880, 14, 28 April 1881.

60. *Topeka Capital,* 26 March 1941.

61. *Ness City Times,* 30 June 1881.

62. *New York Times,* 2 March (p. 5, col. 3), 3 March (p. 1, col. 7), 4 March (p. 1, col. 2), 5 March (p. 1, col. 5), 11 March (p. 8, col. 5) 1887; *Wichita Beacon,* 12 December 1887; McNeal, *When Kansas Was Young,* 163–70.

63. J. D. Neufeld, "The Gray County-Seat Fight," Hist. Washburn County, MSS Division, Kansas State Historical Society, Topeka; George Stauth, "Reminiscences of a Ford County Pioneer," Hist. Ford County, ibid.; *Dodge City Times,* 17 January 1889; *New York Times,* 13 January 1889 (p. 3, col. 6), 28 February 1890 (p. 2, col. 6).

64. *Garden City Irrigator,* 27 November 1886; *Clark County Clipper,* 30 June 1887; *Larned Chronoscope,* January 1888; "Some Lost Towns of Kansas," *Collections of the Kansas State Historical Society* 12 (1911–12): 456–63.

65. Hatch, "Early Day History of Old Garfield County"; *Larned Chronoscope,* 18 November 1887; *Ness City Times,* 19 September 1889.

66. Walter King, "The County Seat Dispute of Sherman County, Kansas 1885–1888" (Master's thesis, Wichita State University, 1970); *Wichita Beacon,* 18 January 1888; E. E. Blackman, "Sherman County and the H.U.A.," *Collections of the Kansas State Historical Society* 8 (1904–5): 50–62; *Sherman County Dark Horse* (Eustis), 3 February, 3, 17 March, 28 April, 26 May 1887, 12, 19, 26 January, 2 February, 22 March, 10 May 1888. Eustis residents eventually gave up and moved themselves and their newspaper to Goodland. Something can be learned also from the records of the Sherman County Homesteaders' Union Association, Hist. Sherman County, MSS Division, Kansas State Historical Society, Topeka.

67. A complete treatment is Joseph Snell, "The Stevens County Seat Controversy" (Master's thesis, University of Kansas, 1962). For the eastern view, see *New York Times,* 28 July (p. 2, col. 3), 29 July (p. 1, col. 4), 6 August (p. 5, col. 1) 1888.

68. *Hutchinson News Herald,* 1 December 1940. An overview concentrating especially on Seward and Stevens Counties is Henry Mason, "County Seat Controversies in Southwestern Kansas," *Kansas Historical Quarterly* 2 (1933): 45–65.

69. *New York Times,* 6 March 1887 (p. 8, col. 5).

70. *Larned Chronoscope,* 11 November 1887.

71. *Sherman County Dark Horse* (Eustis), 1 December 1887.

72. B. Taylor to HUA Grand Lodge, 13 August 1887, Records of the HUA, MSS Division, Kansas State Historical Society, Topeka.

73. A fine analysis of the decline of the cattle business in another region is Ernest Osgood, "The Cattleman in the Agricultural History of the Northwest," *Agricultural History* 3 (1929): 117–30. Osgood argues that it was not the blizzards or the farmers but the fascination of the cattlemen with the same sort of boom speculation that misled others that was the major cause of the industry's troubles.

74. Sorenson, "A History of Irrigation," 22, 52.

75. *New York Times,* 15 December (p. 1, col. 4) 1889.

76. Robert Hay, "Irrigation in Western Kansas: Its Water-Supply and Possibilities," in *Seventh Biennial Report of the State Board of Agriculture,* 129–33.

77. Taylor, "Reclamation," 27–33; Tomayko, "The Ditch Irrigation Boom," 24. An excellent account of federally sponsored pump irrigation around Garden City in the twentieth century and reasons for its failure is Conner Sorenson, "Federal Reclamation on the High Plains: The Garden City Project," *Great Plains Journal* 15 (1976): 114–33.

78. U.S. Department of the Interior, Census Office, *Report on Agriculture by Irrigation in the Western Part of the United States at the Eleventh Census: 1890* (Washington, D.C.: Government Printing Office, 1894), 275–76.

79. *Dodge City Times,* 2 December 1882.

80. A typical debate is *Congressional Record,* 48th Cong., 2d Sess., XVI, 1940–42. Congress was more concerned with the international balance of payments than the prosperity of Kansas. For the bounty, see *Topeka Commonwealth* in *Ness City Times,* 23 February 1888.

81. Dick, *Conquering the Great American Desert,* 147.

82. *Ness City Times,* 6 June 1889.

83. *Dodge City Times,* 12 January 1888.

84. *New York Times,* 12 December (p. 1, col. 2), 13 December (p. 2, col. 7) 1889, 9 January (p. 2, col. 4) 1890, follows the American Sugar Company fraud.

85. Ibid., 2 November (p. 1, col. 6), 10 December (p. 1, col. 7) 1889.

86. *Dodge City Times,* 24 April 1890.

87. *Ness City Times,* 9 May 1889.

88. Ibid., 14 March 1889.

89. *Topeka Daily Capital,* 13 September 1889.

90. *Ness City Times,* 3 October 1889, 25 September 1890.

91. *Ness City Times,* 28 August 1890.

18. Nature and Civilization in Western Kansas

1. David Emmons, "The Influence of Ideology on Changing Environmental Images: The Case of Six Gazetteers," in Blouet and Lawson, *Images,* 126–28.

2. John Opie, "Frontier History in Environmental Perspective," in Steffen, *The American West,* 10–13.

3. Mary Young, "The West and American Cultural Identity," *Western Historical Quarterly* 1 (1970): 140.

4. Donald Pickens, "Westward Expansion and the End of American Exceptionalism: Sumner, Turner and Webb," *Western Historical Quarterly* 12 (1981): 414.

5. Bruce Kuklick, "Myth and Symbol in American Studies," *American Quarterly* 24 (1972): 435–50.

6. Peter Stearns, "The New Social History: An Overview," in James Gardner and George Adams, eds. *Ordinary People and Everyday Life: Perspectives on the New Social History* (Nashville, Tenn.: American Association for State and Local History, 1983), 7.

7. Lamar, *Dakota,* 73.

8. Robert Berkhofer, "Space, Time, Culture and the New Frontier," *Agricultural History* 38 (1964): 21–30.

9. Carl Kraenzel, *The Great Plains in Transition* (Norman: University of Oklahoma Press, 1955), 4.

10. Pomeroy, *Pacific Slope,* 33.

11. Earl Pomeroy, "Rediscovering the West," *American Quarterly* 12 (1960): 24.

12. Lamar, *Dakota,* vii.

13. Young, "Cultural Identity," 141.

14. Jackson Putnam, "The Turner Thesis and the Westward Movement: A Reappraisal," *Western Historical Quarterly* 7 (1976): 402–4.

15. Wendell Berry, *The Unsettling of America: Culture and Agriculture* (New York: Avon Books, 1978), 3–8.

16. Jerome Steffen, "Insular vs. Cosmopolitan Frontiers: A Proposal for the Comparative Study of American Frontiers," in Steffen, *American West,* 95.

17. Theodore Salutos, "The Agricultural Problem and Nineteenth Century Industrialism," *Agricultural History* 22 (1948): 156.

18. John Madson, *Where the Sky Began: Land of the Tallgrass Prairie* (Boston: Houghton Mifflin, 1982).

19. Opie, "Frontier History," 10–25.

20. John Stilgoe, *Common Landscape of America* (New Haven, Conn.: Yale University Press, 1982), 20.

21. Berry, *Unsettling,* 53.

22. John Jackson, *The Necessity for Ruins and Other Topics* (Amherst: University of Massachusetts Press, 1980), 16–17.

Bibliography

Manuscripts

Kansas State Historical Society, Topeka

Adams, D. M. Account of the tornado of 1886, Hist. Meteorology.

Atchison, Topeka & Santa Fe Railway Co. Land Department Correspondence marked "Old Correspondence and Papers." RR. 308.

———. Land Sale Records, Contract Volumes. 15 vols. Santa Fe Railroad Collection.

Aulls, Silas D. Papers 1888–89. Misc. Aulls.

Baker, Fred. "A Local History of Jerome Township, Gove County, Kansas." Hist. Gove Co.

Barr, Virginia. "Reminiscences of Early Days in Kansas." Hist. Smith County.

Bartholomew, Elam. Diaries, 1 January 1871–21 December 1896. MS 1069–70.

Bickerdyke, Hiram. Account of 1868 Indian raids. B-5-2.

Brown, Cardella. Letter, 8 February 1866. Misc. Brown.

Burton, A. W. Letter, 11 July 1863. Misc. Burton.

Butcher Family. Letters from Sun City, 1871–90. Misc. Butcher Family.

Campbell, M. C. Letters, 1880–1910. Misc. Campbell.

Chicago, Rock Island & Pacific Railroad. Records of the Kansas Land and Town Company 1885–1930. Collection 130.

Clarke, D. Papers, 1868–69. Clarke Collection.

Constant, Rezin. Diary, 1877–78. Misc. Constant.

Davidson, Donna. "The Morrises as Pioneers." MS 70.

Edwards, J. B. Papers. Misc. Edwards.

Endsley, Niles. "From New York to Kansas in 1872." Misc. MSS.

Erhardt, Ferdinand. Reminiscences. Misc. MSS.

Essick, A. Speech at Harvest Festival, Fort Harker, 15 October 1875, Misc. Essick.

Fancher, N. C. Reminiscences of Early Sumner County. Misc. Box 2.

Farmers Loan and Trust Company. Tax Register, 1886–89. Collection 144.

Forsythe, James. Typescript address on George Grant. Misc. Grant.

Fort Wallace. Telegrams Sent, 1871–80. Hist. Forts.

Fuller, J. B. "Incidents in My Life." Misc. Fuller.

Harrington. W. P. "History of Gove County." Hist. Gove County.

Hatch, Daisy. "Early Day History of Old Garfield County." Hist. Garfield County.

Herd, Hal. "Commanche Cattle Pool." Hist. Washburn University.

Hoffman, Earl. "Ajax the Great." Misc. Hoffman.

Holliday, Cyrus. Scrapbook and Letters. MS 70.

Homesteaders Union Association. Sherman County, Record Book, 1887–88. MS 70.

Houghton, Frank. "Bits About Beeler." Misc. Houghton.

Hunnius, Adolph. Diaries and Papers, 1876. A. Hunnius Collection.

Jay, Ira. Letters, 1884–85. Misc. Jay.

Kansas Central Relief Committee. Records, 1874–75. Hist. Relief 1874–75.

Kansas, State of. Correspondence Files of the Governor's Office. Correspondence received, for Governors Crawford, Harvey, and Osborne.

Lane, E. S. Account of Killing of Thomas Parks by Indians, 19 September 1867. Misc. E. S. Lane.

Leavenworth Times, MS. Article 1867. Hist. Ind.

Lohnes, J. C. "History of Ness County." Library.
Lone Tree Alliance Gove County. Minutes,
    1890–91. Hist. Farmers Alliance.
McConnell, J. W. "McConnell and the Indians."
    Clipping in library.
Mitchell, William. Letter, 1 August 1864, Misc.
    Mitchell.
Moon, Franklin. Account Books, 1867. Misc.
    Moon.
Morrill, John. Letters, 1865. Morrill Collection.
Nay, J. F. "Reminiscences of the Nay Family and
    Their Friends of Pioneer Days." Hist. Phillips
    County.
Neufeld, J. D. "The Gray County Seat Fight."
    Hist. Washburn.
Norton Family. Diaries, 1876–95. Unprocessed.
Osborne County. Misc. Items. Hist. Osborne
    County.
Plat Book. Ranges 21–31W, 1876–88. MS. 1053.
Pollack, Harry. "Colonies in Ellis Co." Type-
    script in library.
Pomeroy, S. C. Report of Senator S. C. Pomeroy
    of a Ten Days Trip West from Waterville,
    Kansas, 5 September 1870. Misc. S. C.
    Pomeroy.
Popular Grove Grange. Minutes, 1874–76. Hist.
    Republic County.
Raymond, Henry. Diary and Letters. H. Raymond
    Collection.
Redington, E. D. Letters, 1874–75. Misc. MSS.
Richards, James. Diary, 1867. MS. 70.
Roenigk, Adolph. Letters on Fossil Creek Raid.
    Hist. Russell County.
Root, George A. Notes on Kansas Colonies. Misc.
    Root.
Sackman, Jacob. Reminiscences of Pennsylvania
    Colony. Hist. Emigration.
Seiler, William. "Magazine Articles about Kansas
    Published From 1864 to 1904." 3 vols.
    Typescript in library.
Stokes, M. S. Letters, 1889–90. Misc. Stokes.
Strauth, George. "Reminiscences of a Ford
    County Pioneer." Hist. Ford County.
Thoburn, Joseph. Account of Short Massacre.
    Misc. MSS.

Tilley, Belle and Henry. Letters, 1880–93. Misc.
    MSS.
Union Pacific Railroad, Central Branch. Reports to
    Secretary of the Interior, 1867–79. Microbox
    317.
U.S. Bureau of Land Management. Kansas Tract
    Books. Microfilm.
Watson, Louis. Letters and diaries, 1868–91.
    Misc. Jennings.

Lane County Historical Society, Dighton

Stormont, Alice. "Some Memories of Childhood
    Life on a Western Homestead."

Nebraska State Historical Society, Lincoln

Kansas Pacific Railway. Land Grant Mortgage
    Sales, November 1870–June 1888. Subgroup 54,
    vol. 28. Union Pacific Archives.

Newspapers

The Kansas State Historical Society has been
clipping Kansas newspapers by county and subject
since 1870. The county clippings books contain
articles thought to be of historical interest and are
a rich source of memoirs of western Kansas
people, written primarily between 1880 and 1930.

Barton County Clippings. Vol. 1, 1879–1915.
Clark County Clippings. Vol. 1, 1886–1940.
Comanche County Clippings. Vol. 1, 1885–1959.
Dodge City Times. 1876–90.
Edwards County Clippings. Vol. 1, 1878–1955.
Edwards County Leader (Kinsley). 1877–80.
Ellis County Clippings. Vol. 1, 1873–1930.
Ellsworth County Clippings. Vol. 1, 1865–1943.
Finney County Clippings. Vols. 1–2, 1879–1955.
Ford County Clippings. Vol. 1, 1873–1925.
Garden City Daily Herald. 1887.
Garden City Irrigator. 1884–87.
Great Bend Register. 1876–83.
Hays City Sentinel. 1876–90.

Hodgeman County Clippings. Vol. 1, 1916–62.
Kansas Biographical Scrapbooks. Vols. 4 and 10.
Kansas Relief 1880–81. Clippings. Vol. 3.
Kingman County Clippings. Vols. 1–2,
   1881–1974.
Kinsley Graphic. 1878–87.
Lane County Clippings. Vol. 1, 1880–1963.
Larned Chronoscope. 1878–91.
Larned Press. 1876–78.
Ness City Times. 1882–90.
Ness County Clippings. Vol. 1, 1881–1955.
Ness County Pioneer. 1879–80.
New York Times. 1865–90.
Osborne County Clippings. Vols. 1–3, 1872–1965.
Pawnee County Clippings. Vols. 1–2, 1873–1962.
Rooks County Clippings. Vol. 1, 1880–1930.
Russell County Record. 1874–77.
Scott County Clippings. Vol. 1, 1886–1967.
Seward County Clippings. Vol. 1, 1886–1943.
Sherman County Dark Horse. 1886–88.
Thomas County Clippings. Vol. 1, 1881–1956.
Trego County Clippings. Vol. 1, 1878–1954.
Valley Republican (Kinsley). 1877–78.
WaKeeney Weekly World. 1879–82.
Wallace County Clippings. Vol. 1, 1870–1961.
Wichita Beacon. 1880–90.
Wichita Eagle. 1870–90, 1932.

Printed Primary Sources

Adams, F. G. *The Homestead Guide, Describing
   the Great Homestead Region in Kansas and
   Nebraska.* Waterville, Kans.: F. G. Adams,
   1873.
"Along the Line of the Kansas Pacific Railway in
   Western Kansas in 1870." *Kansas Historical
   Quarterly* 19 (1951): 207–11.
Atchison, Topeka & Santa Fe Railway. *How and
   Where to Get a Living: A Sketch of the "Garden
   of the West." Presenting Facts Worth Knowing
   Concerning the Lands of the Atchison, Topeka &
   Santa Fe Railroad Company in Southwestern
   Kansas.* Boston: By the Company, 1876.
Bell, William. *New Tracks in North America.*

London: Chapman and Hall, 1870.
Boughton, J. S. *The Kansas Hand Book.* Law-
   rence, Kans.: Daily Journal Steam Printing
   Press, 1878.
Braudel, Fernand. *The Structures of Everyday Life:
   The Limits of the Possible.* New York: Harper
   and Row, 1981.
Burch, L. D. *Kansas as It Is: A Complete Review
   of the Resources, Advantages and Drawbacks of
   the Great Central State.* Chicago: C. S. Burch
   and Co., 1878.
Byers, O. P. "Personal Recollections of the
   Terrible Blizzard of 1886." *Kansas State
   Historical Society Collections* 12 (1911–12):
   99–120.
Compendious History of Ellsworth County, Kansas.
   Ellsworth: Reporter Office, 1879.
Congressional Record. 1865–90.
Copley, Josiah. *Kansas and the Country Beyond on
   the Line of the Union Pacific Railway, Eastern
   Division.* Philadelphia: J. B. Lippincott and Co.,
   1867.
Dixon, William H. *New America.* 8th ed. London:
   Hurst and Blackett, 1867.
Ebbutt, Percy G. *Emigrant Life in Kansas.*
   London: Swan Sonnenschein and Co., 1886.
Elliott, Richard Smith. *Notes Taken in Sixty Years.*
   St. Louis: R. P. Studley & Co., 1883.
*The Ellsworth & Pacific Railroad. Some Facts and
   Information as to the Routes of the Ellsworth &
   Pacific Railroad and the Country through Which
   it Would Pass.* Leavenworth: Bulletin Office
   [1868].
Gray, W. W. *The Emigrants Guide: A History and
   Description of Northwestern Kansas.* Kirwin,
   Kans.: W. W. & L. Gray, 1880.
Griswold, Wayne. *Kansas. Her Resources and
   Developments or the Kansas Pilot. Giving a
   Direct Road to Homes for Everybody. Also the
   Effect of Latitudes on Life Locations, with
   Important Facts for All European Emigrants.*
   Cincinnati: Robert Clarke & Co., 1871.
Guild, Edgar W. "Western Kansas—Its Geology,
   Climate, Natural History, Etc." *Kansas City*

Review of Science and Industry 3 (1879): 461–67.

Hamblin, George. *The Kansas Guide: Facts and Practical Suggestions to Those Who Intend Seeking New Homes in the "Far West."* Ottawa, Kans.: Ottawa Journal, 1871.

Hand Book for the Kansas Pacific Railway Containing a Description of the Country, Cities, Towns &c., Lying along the Line of the Road and Its Branches. St. Louis: Aug. Wiebusch & Son, 1870.

Hay, Robert. "The Central State. Its Physical Features and Resources." *Harpers New Monthly Magazine* 87 (June 1888): 39–51.

Indian Raid of 1878. The Report of the Commission Appointed in Pursuance of the Provisions of Senate Joint Resolution No. 1, Relating to Losses Sustained by Citizens of Kansas by the Invasion of Indians during the Year 1878. Topeka: Geo. W. Martin Kansas Publishing House, 1879.

Kansas as She Is. Lawrence: Kansas Publishing House, n.d.

Kansas Central Relief Committee. *Report of the Executive Board. Their Transactions from Date of Organization to Disbandment.* Topeka, Kans.: State Printing Works, 1875.

Kansas State Board of Agriculture. *Biennial Reports* 1872–1890. Topeka, Kans.: State Printer, 1872–90.

Kansas State Board of Railroad Commissioners. *Annual Reports.* Topeka, Kans.: Kansas Publishing House, 1884–90.

Knox, John. *Paths to Wealth.* Topeka, Kans.: John D. Knox & Co., 1883.

Lethem, John. *Historical and Descriptive Review of Kansas.* Vol. 1. *The Northern Section.* Topeka, Kans.: Jno. Lethem, 1890.

———. *Historical and Descriptive Review of Kansas.* Vol. 3. *The Central and Southwest Sections.* Topeka, Kans.: Jno. Lethem, 1891.

Phillips, William. "Lights and Shadows of Kansas History." *Magazine of Western History* 12 (1890): 6–15.

"Picturesque Features of Kansas Farming," *Scribners Monthly* 19 (1879): 132–40.

Report of the Commissioners Appointed to Investigate the Condition of Barbour, Comanche, and Harper Counties. [Sept. 15, 1874].

Reynolds, R. E. *Illustrated Southern Kansas, an Industrial Publication Devoted to the History of Kingman.* Kingman, Kans.: Daily and Weekly News, 1887.

The Rocky Mountain Locust or Grasshopper, Being the Report of Proceedings of a Conference of the Governors of Several Western States. St. Louis: R. P. Studley Company, 1876.

Roenigk, A. "Railroad Grading Among Indians." *Kansas State Historical Society Collections* 8 (1904): 384–89.

Rollins, Alice. *The Story of a Ranch.* New York: Cassell & Co., 1885.

Ruede, Howard. *Sod-House Days: Letters from a Kansas Homesteader, 1877–78.* Edited by John Ise. New York: Cooper Square Publishers, 1966.

Schmidt, C. B. "Reminiscences of Foreign Immigration Work for Kansas." *Kansas State Historical Society Collections* 9 (1905–6): 485–97.

Senatorial Excursion Party over the Union Pacific, E.D. St. Louis: S. Levison, 1867.

Shoemaker, R. M., George Wickes, and P. Golay. *Reports of Preliminary Surveys for the Union Pacific Railway, Eastern Division from Fort Riley to Denver City.* Cincinnati: Robert Clarke & Co., 1866.

Smyth, Bernard B. *The Heart of the New Kansas.* Great Bend, Kans.: B. B. Smyth, 1880.

Snow, F. H. "Is the Rainfall of Kansas Increasing?" *Kansas City Review of Science and Industry* (1884): 457–60.

Spearman, Frank. "The Great American Desert." *Harpers Monthly* 87 (1888): 232–45.

"Spec." *Line Etchings. A Trip from the Missouri River to the Rocky Mountains via the Kansas Pacific Railway.* St. Louis: Woodward, Tiernan & Hale, 1875.

Statement of the Condition and Resources of the Kansas Central Railway (Narrow Gauge) from Leavenworth, Kansas, to Denver, Colorado. Leavenworth: Office of the Kansas Farmer, 1871.

Tewksbury, G. E. *The Kansas Picture Book.* Topeka, Kans.: A. S. Johnson, 1883.

Tice, J. H. *Over the Plains, on the Mountains; or Kansas, Colorado and the Rocky Mountains; Agriculturally, Mineralogically and Aesthetically Described.* St. Louis: Industrial Age Printing Co., 1872.

Trego County, Kansas: Its Soil and Climate and the Advantages It Affords to the Farmer and Stock Grower. Chicago: Warren, Keeney & Co. [1878].

"A Trip to the End of the Union Pacific in 1868." *Kansas Historical Quarterly* 13 (1944): 196–203.

The Union Pacific Railway Eastern Division or Kansas Pacific Railway. Importance of Its Route to All Sections of the Country. Washington, D.C.: Joseph L. Pearson, 1868.

U.S. Census Office. *Abstract of the Thirteenth Census.* Washington, D.C.: Government Printing Office, 1913.

————. *Compendium of the Eleventh Census: 1890.* Part I: *Population.* Washington, D.C.: Government Printing Office, 1892.

————. *Compendium of the Ninth Census.* Prepared by Francis A. Walker. Washington, D.C.: Government Printing Office, 1872.

————. *Compendium of the Tenth Census.* Prepared by Francis A. Walker. Washington, D.C.: Government Printing Office, 1883.

————. *Report on Agriculture by Irrigation in the Western Part of the United States at the Eleventh Census: 1890.* Washington, D.C.: Government Printing Office, 1894.

————. *Report on the Productions of Agriculture.* Washington, D.C.: Government Printing Office, 1883.

————. *Report on the Statistics of Agriculture in the United States at the Eleventh Census: 1890.* Washington, D.C.: Government Printing Office, 1895.

————. *The Statistics of the Population of the United States.* Washington, D.C.: Government Printing Office, 1872.

U.S. Department of War. *Annual Reports of the Secretary of War.* Washington, D.C.: Government Printing Office, 1869–70.

U.S. General Land Office, *Annual Report of the Commissioner of the General Land Office.* Washington, D.C.: Government Printing Office, 1879–91.

Van Sickel, S. S. *A Story of Real Life on the Plains: A True Narrative of the Author's Experience.* [1890].

Webb, W. E. *Buffalo Land: An Authentic Account of the Discoveries, Adventures and Mishaps of a Scientific and Sporting Party in the Wild West.* Philadelphia: Hubbard Brothers, 1872.

The Western Kansas Agricultural Association, Chartered June 6, 1870. Quincy, Ill.: Whig Company, 1871.

Winsor, M., and James Scarborough. *History of Jewell County, Kansas, with a Full Account of its Early Settlements and the Indian Atrocities Committed within its Borders.* Jewell City, Kans.: "Diamond" Printing Office, 1878.

Yingling, W. A. *Westward or Central Western Kansas.* Ness City, Kans.: Star Printing Co., 1890.

Youngblood, Charles. *A Mighty Hunter: The Adventures of Charles L. Youngblood on the Plains and Mountains.* Chicago: Rand, McNally & Company, 1890.

Secondary Works

Anderson, George. "The Administration of Federal Land Laws in Western Kansas, 1880–1890: A Factor in Adjustment to a New Environment." *Kansas Historical Quarterly* 20 (1952): 233–51.

————. *Kansas West.* San Marino, Calif.: Golden West Books, 1963.

Andreas, A. T., *History of the State of Kansas.* Chicago: A. T. Andreas, 1883.

Argersinger, Peter. "Road to a Republican Waterloo: The Farmers' Alliance and the Election of 1890 in Kansas." *Kansas Historical Quarterly* 33 (1967): 443–69.

Arrington, Leonard. *Great Basin Kingdom: An Economic History of the Latter Day Saints.* Cambridge, Mass.: Harvard University Press, 1958.

Athearn, Robert. *In Search of Canaan: Black Migration to Kansas 1879-80.* Lawrence: Regents Press of Kansas, 1978.

Atherton, Lewis. *Main Street on the Middle Border.* Bloomington: Indiana University Press, 1954.

Bailes, Kendell. "The Mennonites Come to Kansas." *American Heritage* 10 (1959): 30-33, 102-5.

Barry, Louise. "A Kansas Cattle Ranch: The American Cattle Company's 23,000 Acres in Clark County." *Kansas Historical Quarterly* 35 (1969): 46-49.

Barth, Gunther. *Instant Cities: Urbanization and the Rise of Denver and San Francisco.* New York: Oxford University Press, 1975.

Battensberger, B. H. "Newspaper Images of the Central Great Plains in the Late Nineteenth Century." *Journal of the West* 19 (1980): 64-70.

Beckman, Peter. *Kansas Monks: A History of St. Benedict's Abbey.* Atchison, Kans.: Abbey Student, 1957.

Bell, Robert G. "James C. Malin and the Grasslands of North America." *Agricultural History* 46 (1972): 414-24.

Bergin, Alfred. "The Swedish Settlements in Central Kansas." *Kansas State Historical Society Collections* 2 (1909-10): 19-46.

Berkhofer, Robert. *A Behavioral Approach to Historical Analysis.* New York: Free Press, 1969.

————. "Space, Time, Culture and the New Frontier." *Agricultural History* 38 (1964): 21-30.

Berry, Wendell. *The Unsettling of America: Culture and Agriculture.* New York: Avon Books, 1977.

A Biographical History of Central Kansas. New York: Lewis Publishing Company, 1902.

Blackman, E. E. "Sherman County and the HUA." *Kansas State Historical Society Collections* 8 (1903-4): 50.

Blouet, Brian, and Lawson Merlin, eds. *Images of the Plains: The Role of Human Nature in Settlement.* Lincoln: University of Nebraska Press, 1975.

Blouet, Brian, and Frederick Luebke, eds. *The Great Plains: Environment and Culture.* Lincoln: University of Nebraska Press, 1979.

Bogue, Allan. "Farmer Debtors in Pioneer Kinsley." *Kansas Historical Quarterly* 20 (1952): 82-107.

————. "The Land Mortgage Company in the Early Plains States." *Agricultural History* 25 (1951): 20-33.

Boughn, Zacariah. "The Free Land Myth in the Disposal of the Public Domain in South Cedar County, Nebraska." *Nebraska History* 58 (1977): 359-69.

Briggs, Harold E. "Early Bonanza Farming in the Red River Valley of the North." *Agricultural History* 6 (1932): 26-37.

————. "Grasshopper Plagues and Early Dakota Agriculture, 1864-1876." *Agricultural History* 7 (1934): 51-63.

Britton, Davis, and Linda Wilcox. "Pestiferous Ironclads: The Grasshopper Problem in Pioneer Utah." *Utah Historical Quarterly* 46 (1978): 336-55.

Bryant, Keith. *History of the Atchison, Topeka and Santa Fe Railway.* New York: Macmillan, 1974.

Buscemi, Doreen. "The Grasshopper Years." *American History Illustrated* 12 (1978): 20-25.

Byers, O. P. "Early History of the El Paso Line of the Chicago, Rock Island & Pacific Railway." *Kansas State Historical Society Collections* 15 (1919-22): 573-78.

Caldwell, Margaret. "The Mudge Ranch." *Kansas Historical Quarterly* 24 (1958): 285-304.

Caughey, John. *The American West: Frontier and Region.* Los Angeles: Ward Ritchie Press, 1969.

Chapman, William. "The Wakefield Colony." *Kansas State Historical Society Collections* 10 (1907-8): 485-533.

Chase, Julia. "Mother Bickerdyke." *Kansas State Historical Society Collections* 7 (1901-2): 189-98.

Clark, John, ed. *The Frontier Challenge: Re-*

sponses to the Trans-Mississippi West. Lawrence: University Press of Kansas, 1971.

Clark, Olive A. "Early Days along the Solomon Valley." *Kansas State Historical Society Collections* 18 (1926–28): 719–29.

Clark County Historical Society. *Notes on Early Clark County, Kansas.* 6 vols. Ashland, Kans.: Clark Co. Historical Society, n.d.

Climate and Man: Yearbook of Agriculture. Washington, D.C.: U.S. Dept. of Agriculture, 1941.

Crawford, Samuel. *Kansas in the Sixties.* Chicago: A. C. McClurg & Co., 1911.

Cruise, John. "Early Days On the Union Pacific." *Kansas State Historical Society Collections* 2 (1909–10): 529–49.

Cunningham, Gary. "Gambling in the Kansas Cattle Towns: A Prominent and Somewhat Honorable Profession." *Kansas History* 5 (1982): 2–22.

Dale, Kittie. *Echoes and Etchings of Early Ellis.* N.p.: Big Mountain Press, 1964.

Davis, Rodney. "Before Barbed Wire: Herd Law Agitation in Early Kansas and Nebraska." *Journal of the West* 6 (1964): 41–52.

Decker, Leslie. *Railroads, Lands, and Politics: The Taxation of the Railroad Land Grants.* Providence, R.I.: Brown University Press, 1964.

Dick, Everett. *Conquering the Great American Desert: Nebraska.* Lincoln: Nebraska State Historical Society, 1975.

———. "The Great Nebraska Drouth of 1894: The Exodus." *Arizona and the West* 15 (1973): 333–44.

———. *The Sod House Frontier 1854–1890.* New York: Appleton-Century, 1937.

Droze, W. H. "Changing the Plains Environment: The Afforestation of the Trans-Mississippi West." *Agricultural History* 51 (1977): 6–22.

Dunbar, Robert. "Agricultural Adjustments in Eastern Colorado in the Eighteen Nineties." *Agricultural History* 18 (1944): 41–52.

Dykstra, Robert. *The Cattle Towns.* New York: Alfred A. Knopf, 1968.

———. "Ellsworth, 1869–1875: The Rise and Fall of a Kansas Cowtown." *Kansas Historical Quarterly* 27 (1961): 161–92.

Einsel, Mary. "Some Notes on the Commanche Cattle Pool." *Kansas Historical Quarterly* 26 (1960): 59–66.

Elkins, Stanley. *Slavery: A Problem in American Institutional and Intellectual Life.* Chicago: University of Chicago Press, 1959.

Emmons, David. *Garden in the Grasslands: Boomer Literature of the Central Great Plains.* Lincoln: University of Nebraska Press, 1971.

———. "Richard Smith Elliott, Kansas Promoter." *Kansas Historical Quarterly* 36 (1970): 390–401.

Epp, Todd. "The State of Kansas v. Wild Hog, et al." *Kansas History* 5 (1982): 139–46.

Erisman, Fred. "Western Regional Writers and the Uses of Place." *Journal of the West* 19 (1980): 36–44.

Fels, Rendig. *American Business Cycles 1865–1897.* Chapel Hill: University of North Carolina Press, 1959.

Finney County Historical Society. *History of Finney County, Kansas.* 2 vols. Garden City, Kans.: Finney County Historical Society, 1954.

Fite, Gilbert. "Daydreams and Nightmares: The Late Nineteenth-Century Agricultural Frontiers." *Agricultural History* 40 (1966): 285–94.

———. *The Farmers' Frontier 1865–1900.* New York: Holt, Rinehart and Winston, 1966.

———. "Great Plains Farming: A Century of Change and Adjustment." *Agricultural History* 51 (1977): 244–56.

———. "The United States Army and Relief to Pioneer Settlers." *Journal of the West* 6 (1967): 99–107.

Fletcher, Robert. "That Hard Winter in Montana." *Agricultural History* 4 (1930): 123–30.

Forsythe, James. "Environmental Considerations in the Settling of Ellis County, Kansas." *Agricultural History* 51 (1977): 38–50.

Friedberger, Mark, and Janice Webster. "Social Structure and State and Local History." *Western Historical Quarterly* 9 (1978): 297–314.

Fuson, Ben. "Prairie Dreamers of 1890: Three Kansas Utopian Novels and Novelists." *Kansas Quarterly* 5 (1973): 63–77.

Galenson, David. "The Profitability of the Long Drive." *Agricultural History* 51 (1977): 737–58.

Gambone, Joseph. "Economic Relief in Territorial Kansas, 1860–61." *Kansas Historical Quarterly* 36 (1970): 149–74.

Gardner, James, and George Adams, eds. *Ordinary People and Everyday Life: Perspectives on the New Social History.* Nashville, Tenn.: American Association for State and Local History, 1983.

Gates, Charles. "Boom Stages in American Expansion." *Business History Review* 33 (1959): 32–42.

Gates, Paul. *Fifty Million Acres: Struggles over Kansas Land Policy, 1854–1890.* Ithaca, N.Y.: Cornell University Press, 1954.

———. "Homesteading in the High Plains." *Agricultural History* 51 (1977): 109–33.

———. "The Homestead Law in an Incongruous Land System." *American Historical Review* 41 (1936): 652–81.

Gill, Helen. "The Establishment of Counties in Kansas." *Kansas State Historical Society Collections* 8 (1904): 449–72.

Girgus, Sam, ed. *The American Self: Myth, Ideology and Popular Culture.* Albuquerque: University of New Mexico Press, 1981.

Goble, Danney. "A New Kind of State: Settlement and State-Making in Oklahoma to 1907." Ph.D. diss., University of Missouri, Columbia, 1976.

Gressley, Gene. *Bankers and Cattlemen.* New York: Alfred A. Knopf, 1966.

Hadley, James A. "The Nineteenth Kansas Cavalry and the Conquest of the Plains Indians." *Kansas State Historical Society Collections* 10 (1907–8): 428–56.

Hamburg, James. "Railroads and the Settlement of South Dakota during the Great Dakota Boom, 1878–1887." *South Dakota History* 5 (1975): 165–78.

Hampsten, Elizabeth. *Read This Only to Yourself: The Private Writings of Midwestern Women, 1880–1910.* Bloomington: Indiana University Press, 1982.

Hayden, Ruth. *The Time That Was: The Courageous Acts and Accounts of Rawlins County Kansas 1875–1915.* Colby, Kans.: Colby Community College, 1973.

Hayter, Earl. "Barbed Wire Fencing—A Prairie Invention: Its Rise and Influence in the Western States." *Agricultural History* 13 (1939): 189–207.

Haywood, Robert. "Pearlette: A Mutual Aid Colony." *Kansas Historical Quarterly* 42 (1976): 263–76.

Higham, John. "The Cult of the Consensus: Homogenizing Our History." *Commentary* 17 (1959).

Hollen, Eugene. *The Great American Desert: Then and Now.* New York: Oxford University Press, 1966.

———. *The Southwest: Old and New.* New York: Alfred A. Knopf, 1961.

Hurt, Douglas. "Grasshopper Harvesters on the Great Plains." *Great Plains Journal* 16 (1977): 123–34.

Hutchinson, C. C. *Resources of Kansas.* Topeka, Kans.: By the author, 1872.

Ise, John. *Sod and Stubble.* Lincoln: University of Nebraska Press, 1966. First published in 1936.

Jackson, John. *The Necessity for Ruins and Other Topics.* Amherst: University of Massachusetts Press, 1980.

Jeffrey, Julie. *Frontier Women: The Trans-Mississippi West 1840–1880.* New York: Hill and Wang, 1979.

Johannes, Sister Mary. *A Study of the Russian-German Settlements in Ellis County, Kansas.* Washington, D.C.: Catholic University of America Press, 1946.

Ketchum, Mrs. Charles. *The Morton County Pioneer.* Elkhart, Kans.: Elkhart Lions Club, 1961.

King, Walter. "The County Seat Dispute of Sherman County, Kansas 1885–1888." Master's thesis, Wichita State University, 1970.

Kings and Queens of the Range: A Pictorial Record of Early Day Cattlemen of Clark County, Kansas from 1884 to 1904. Ashland, Kans.: Clark County Historical Society, n.d.

Knight, Oliver. "Toward an Understanding of the Western Town." *Western Historical Quarterly* 4 (1973): 27–42.

Kolodny, Annette. *The Land Before Her: Fantasy and Experience of the American Frontiers, 1630–1860.* Chapel Hill: University of North Carolina Press, 1984.

Kraenzel, Carl. *The Great Plains in Transition.* Norman: University of Oklahoma Press, 1955.

Laing, Francis. "German-Russian Settlements in Ellis County, Kansas." *Kansas State Historical Society Collections* 11 (1909–10): 489–528.

Lamar, Howard. *Dakota Territory 1861–1889: A Study of Frontier Politics.* New Haven: Yale University Press, 1956.

————. *The Far Southwest 1846–1912: A Territorial History.* New Haven, Conn.: Yale University Press, 1966.

————. "Public Values and Private Dreams: South Dakota's Search for Identity 1850–1900." *South Dakota History* 8 (1978): 117–42.

Lawson, Merlin, and Maurice Baker, eds. *The Great Plains: Perspectives and Prospects.* Lincoln: University of Nebraska Press, 1981.

Leonard, Carol, and Isidor Wallimann. "Prostitution and Changing Morality in the Frontier Cattle Towns of Kansas." *Kansas History* 2 (1979): 34–53.

Leonard, Carol, Isidor Wallimann, and Wayne Rohrer. "Groups and Social Organizations in Frontier Cattle Towns in Kansas." *Kansas Quarterly* 12 (1980): 59–64.

Lewis, G. M. "Changing Emphases in the Description of the Natural Environment of the American Great Plains Area." *Transactions and Papers of the Institute of British Geographers* 30 (1962): 75–90.

Lochtin, Roger. *San Francisco 1846–1856: From Hamlet to City.* New York: Oxford University Press, 1974.

Luebke, Frederick. "Regionalism and the Great Plains: Problems of Concept and Method." *Western Historical Quarterly* 15 (1984): 19–38.

Luebke, Frederick, ed. *Ethnicity on the Great Plains.* Lincoln: University of Nebraska Press, 1980.

Madden, John. "An Emerging Agricultural Economy: Kansas 1860–1880." *Kansas Historical Quarterly* 39 (1973): 101–14.

Madson, John. *Where the Sky Began: Land of the Tallgrass Prairie.* Boston: Houghton Mifflin, 1982.

Malin, James. "The Agricultural Regionalism of the Trans-Mississippi West as Delineated by Cyrus Thomas." *Agricultural History* 21 (1947): 208–16.

————. "Dodge City Varieties—A Summer Interlude of Entertainment 1878." *Kansas Historical Quarterly* 22 (1956): 347–53.

————. "Dust Storms: Part Two, 1861–80." *Kansas Historical Quarterly* 14 (1946): 265–96.

————. *The Grassland of North America: Prolegomena to Its History.* Lawrence, Kans.: For the Author, 1956.

————. "The Kinsley Boom in the Late Eighties." *Kansas Historical Quarterly* 4 (1935): 23–49, 164–87.

————. "The Turnover of Farm Population in Kansas." *Kansas Historical Quarterly* 4 (1935): 339–72.

————. *Winter Wheat in the Golden Belt of Kansas: A Study in Adaption to a Subhumid Geographical Environment.* Lawrence: University of Kansas Press, 1944.

Malin, James, ed. "J. A. Walker's Early History of Edwards County." *Kansas Historical Quarterly* 9 (1940): 259–84.

Manley, Robert. "In the Wake of the Grasshoppers: Public Relief in Nebraska 1874–75." *Nebraska History* 44 (1963): 255–76.

Martin, C. J. "A Pioneer Picnic." *Kansas Magazine* 2 (1909): 60–62.

Mason, Henry. "County Seat Controversies in Southwest Kansas." *Kansas Historical Quarterly* 2 (1933): 45–65.

McCarter, Margaret. *Winning the Wilderness.* Chicago: A. C. McClurg & Co., 1914.

McMath, Robert. "Preface to Populism: The Origin and Economic Development of the

'Southern Farmers' Alliance in Kansas." *Kansas Historical Quarterly* 42 (1976): 55–65.

McNeal, T. A. *When Kansas Was Young*. Topeka, Kans.: Capper Publications, 1934.

Meinig, Donald. *The Great Columbia Plain: A Historical Geography 1805–1910*. Seattle: University of Washington Press, 1968.

———. *Imperial Texas: An Interpretive Essay in Cultural Geography*. Austin: University of Texas Press, 1969.

Mercer, Lloyd. *Railroads and Land Grant Policy: A Study in Government Intervention*. New York: Academic Press, 1982.

Millbrook, Minnie. "Dr. Samuel Grant Rodgers, Gentleman from Ness." *Kansas Historical Quarterly* 20 (1953): 305–49.

———. "The Jordan Massacre." *Kansas History* 2 (1979): 219–30.

———. *Ness: Western County Kansas*. Detroit: Millbrook Publishing Co., 1955.

———. "North from Dodge: Troubles along the Trail." *Kansas Quarterly* 6 (1974): 5–14.

Miller, Kenneth. "Danish Socialism on the Kansas Prairie." *Kansas Historical Quarterly* 38 (1972): 156–68.

Miller, Nyle, ed. "An English Runneymede in Kansas." *Kansas Historical Quarterly* 41 (1975): 22–62, 183–224.

Miller, Nyle, and Robert Richmond. "Sheridan, A Fabled End-of-Track Town of the Union Pacific Railroad, E.D., 1868–69." *Kansas Historical Quarterly* 34 (1968): 427–42.

Miner, Craig. *Wichita: The Early Years, 1865–1880*. Lincoln: University of Nebraska Press, 1982.

Montgomery, Mrs. Frank. "Fort Wallace and Its Relation to the Frontier." *Kansas State Historical Society Collections* 7 (1926–28): 189–282.

———. "United States Surveyors Massacred by Indians." *Kansas Historical Quarterly* 1 (1932): 266–272.

Muir, Leonard. "Elam Bartholomew: Farmer Extraordinary." *Agricultural History* 34 (1960): 189–93.

Mullhall, Michael. *The Dictionary of Statistics*. 4th ed. London: George Rutledge & Sons, 1899.

Myres, Sandra. *Westering Women and the Frontier Experience, 1800–1915*. Albuquerque: University of New Mexico Press, 1982.

Myres, Sandra, et al. *Essays on the American West*. Austin: University of Texas Press, 1969.

Oliva, Leo. *Ash Rock and the Stone Church: The History of a Kansas Rural Community*. Ellsworth, Kans.: Ellsworth Printing Company, 1983.

———. *Fort Hays*. Topeka: Kansas State Historical Society, 1980.

———. *Fort Larned*. Topeka: Kansas State Historical Society, 1982.

Olson, Gary, ed. "Relief for Nebraska Grasshopper Victims: The Official Journal of Lieutenant Theodore E. True." *Nebraska History* 48 (1967): 19–40.

Osgood, Ernest. "The Cattleman in the Agricultural History of the Northwest." *Agricultural History* 3 (1929): 117–30.

Painter, Nell. *Exodusters: Black Migration to Kansas after Reconstruction*. New York: Alfred A. Knopf, 1977.

Peterson, Albert. "The German-Russian Settlement Pattern in Ellis County Kansas." *Rocky Mountain Social Science Journal* 5 (1968): 52–62.

Petrowski, William. "Kansas City to Denver to Cheyenne: Pacific Railroad Construction Costs and Profits." *Business History Review* 48 (1974): 206–24.

———. "The Kansas Pacific Railroad in the Southwest." *Arizona and the West* 11 (1969): 129–46.

Pickens, Donald. "Westward Expansion and the End of American Exceptionalism: Sumner, Turner and Webb." *Western Historical Quarterly* 12 (1981): 409–32.

Pioneer Plows & Steel Rails; Outriders of Civilization in the Valley of the Solomon. Downs, Kans.: Downs News & Times, 1961.

Pomeroy, Earl. *The Pacific Slope: A History*. New York: Alfred A. Knopf, 1965.

———. "Rediscovering the West." *American Quarterly* 12 (1960): 20–30.

Putnam, Jackson. "The Turner Thesis and the

Westward Movement: A Reappraisal." *Western Historical Quarterly* 7 (1976): 377–404.

Rightmore, W. F. "The Alliance Movement in Kansas—Origin of the People's Party." *Kansas State Historical Society Collections* 9 (1905–6): 1–7.

Riley, Glenda. "The Specter of a Savage: Rumors and Alarmism on the Overland Trail." *Western Historical Quarterly* 15 (1984): 427–43.

Robbins, Roy. "The Public Domain in the Era of Exploitation, 1862–1901." *Agricultural History* 13 (1939): 97–108.

Robinson, Elwyn. "An Interpretation of the History of the Great Plains." *North Dakota History* 41 (1974): 5–19.

Rölvaag, Ole. *Giants in the Earth: A Saga of the Prairie.* New York: Harper and Brothers, 1927.

Rooney, John, Wilbur Zelinsky, Dean Louder, and John Vitek, eds. *This Remarkable Continent: An Atlas of United States and Canadian Society and Cultures.* College Station: Texas A&M University Press, 1982.

Root, George. "Ferries in Kansas: Part VII Saline River." *Kansas Historical Quarterly* 4 (1935): 149–54.

Rudin, James. "Beersheba, Kan.: God's Pure Air on Government Land." *Kansas Historical Quarterly* 34 (1968): 282–90.

Ruppenthal, Jacob. "The German Element in Central Kansas." *Kansas State Historical Society Collections* 13 (1913–14): 513–33.

Rydjord, John. *Kansas Place-Names.* Norman: University of Oklahoma Press, 1972.

Saarinen, Thomas. *Perception of the Drought Hazard on the Great Plains.* Chicago: University of Chicago Press, 1966.

Sagaser, A. Bower. "Building the Main Line of the Missouri Pacific Through Kansas." *Kansas Historical Quarterly* 21 (1955): 326–30.

———. "Editor Bristow and the Great Plains Irrigation Revival of the 1890s." *Journal of the West* 3 (1964): 75–89.

———. "The Rails Go Westward." In *Kansas: The First Century,* edited by John Bright. Vol. 1. New York: Lewis Historical Publishing Company, 1956.

Salutos, Theodore. "The Agricultural Problem and Nineteenth-Century Industrialism." *Agricultural History* 22 (1948): 156–74.

Sandoz, Mari. *Cheyenne Autumn.* New York: McGraw-Hill Book Company, 1953.

Saul, Norman. "The Migration of the Russian-Germans to Kansas." *Kansas Historical Quarterly* 40 (1974): 38–62.

Schell, Herbert. "Droughts and Agriculture in Eastern South Dakota During the Eighteen Nineties." *Agricultural History* 5 (1931): 162–80.

———. "The Grange and the Credit Problem in Dakota Territory." *Agricultural History* 10 (1936): 59–83.

Schlebecker, John. "Grasshoppers in American Agricultural History." *Agricultural History* 27 (1953): 85–93.

Schwartzkopf, Calvin. "The Rush County-Seat War." *Kansas Historical Quarterly* 36 (1970): 40–61.

Schwendemann, Glenn. "Nicodemus: Negro Haven on the Solomon." *Kansas Historical Quarterly* 34 (1968): 10–31.

Seiler, William. "Magazine Writers Look at Kansas, 1854–1904." *Kansas Historical Quarterly* 38 (1972): 1–42.

Self, Huber, *Environment and Man in Kansas: A Geographical Analysis.* Lawrence: Regents Press of Kansas, 1978.

Sherow, James. "Rural Town Origins in Southwest Reno County." *Kansas History* 3 (1980): 99–112.

Shimmick, Lillian. *Early Pioneer Families in Decatur County, Kansas.* Hays, Kans.: Fort Hays State University, 1979.

Shumpeter, Joseph. *Business Cycles: A Theoretical, Historical and Statistical Analysis of the Capitalist Process.* 2 vols. New York: McGraw-Hill, 1939.

Smith, Duane. "The Land unto Itself: The Western Slope." *Colorado Magazine* 55 (1978): 181–204.

Smith, Henry. *Virgin Land: The American West as Symbol and Myth.* Cambridge, Mass.: Harvard University Press, 1950.

————. "The West as an Image of the American Past." *University of Kansas City Review* 18 (1951): 29–35.

Smith, Page. *As a City upon a Hill: The Town in American History.* New York: Alfred A. Knopf, 1966.

Snell, Joseph. "The Stevens County Seat Controversy." Master's thesis, University of Kansas, 1962.

Snell, Joseph, and Robert Richmond. "When the Union and Kansas Pacific Built through Kansas." *Kansas Historical Quarterly* 32 (1966): 161–86, 334–52.

Snell, Joseph, and Don Wilson. "The Birth of the Atchison, Topeka & Santa Fe Railroad." *Kansas Historical Quarterly* 34 (1968): 113–42, 325–56.

"Some Lost Towns of Kansas." *Kansas State Historical Society Collections* 12 (1911–12): 426–471.

Sorenson, Conner. "Federal Reclamation on the High Plains: The Garden City Project." *Great Plains Journal* 15 (1976): 114–33.

————. "A History of Irrigation in the Arkansas River Valley in Western Kansas, 1880–1910." Master's thesis, University of Kansas, 1968.

Steffen, Jerome, ed. *The American West: New Perspectives, New Dimensions.* Norman: University of Oklahoma Press, 1979.

Steinhardt, Peter. "Fear of Snakes." *Audubon* 86 (1984): 6–9.

Stilgoe, John. *Common Landscape of America, 1580–1845.* New Haven, Conn.: Yale University Press, 1982.

————. *Metropolitan Corridor: Railroads and the American Scene.* New Haven, Conn.: Yale University Press, 1983.

Storey, Brit. "The Kansas Pacific Seeks the Pacific." *Journal of the West* 8 (1969): 402–13.

Stratton, Joanna. *Pioneer Women: Voices from the Kansas Frontier.* New York: Simon and Schuster, 1981.

Swehla, F. J. "Bohemians in Central Kansas." *Kansas State Historical Society Collections* 13 (1913–14): 469–512.

Taylor, Paul. "Reclamation: The Rise and Fall of

an American Idea." *American West* 7 (1970): 27–33.

Terbouich, John. "Religious Folklore among the German Russians in Ellis County, Kansas." *Western Folklore* 22 (1962): 79–88.

Thernstrom, Stephen. "Reflections on the New Urban History." *Daedalus* 100 (1971): 359–75.

Thompson, W. F. "Peter Robidoux: A Real Kansas Pioneer." *Kansas State Historical Society Collections* 17 (1926–28): 283–90.

Thorne, Mildred. "Suggested Research on Railroad Aid to the Farmer with Particular Reference to Iowa and Kansas." *Agricultural History* 31 (1957): 50–56.

Tomayko, James. "The Ditch Irrigation Boom in Southwest Kansas: Changing an Environment." *Journal of the West* 22 (1983): 20–25.

Travis, Paul. "Changing Climate in Kansas: A Late 19th-Century Myth." *Kansas History* 1 (1978): 48–58.

Turner, Frederick. *The Significance of Sections in American History.* New York: Henry Holt & Co., 1932.

Unsere Leute. Hays, Kans.: Volga-German Centennial Association, 1976.

Veysey, Laurence. "Myth and Reality in Approaching American Regionalism." *American Quarterly* 12 (1960): 31–43.

Waldron, Nell. "Colonization in Kansas from 1861 to 1890." Ph.D. diss., Northwestern University, 1923.

Washington, Mrs. M. V. "The Grasshopper Raid." *Magazine of Western History* 13 (1891): 531–33.

Webb, Bernice. "First Homesteaders and the Battle of Sappa Creek." *Kansas Quarterly* 10 (1978): 52–58.

Webb, Walter. *The Great Plains.* Boston: Ginn & Co., 1931.

Welty, Raymond. "Supplying the Frontier Military Posts." *Kansas Historical Quarterly* 7 (1938): 154–69.

Wessel, Thomas, ed. *Agriculture in the Great Plains, 1876–1936.* Washington, D.C.: Agricultural History Society, 1977.

White, Lonnie. "The Cheyenne Barrier on the

Kansas Frontier, 1868–69.'' *Arizona and the West* 4 (1962): 51–64.

———. ''White Women Captives of Southern Plains Indians, 1866–1875.'' *Journal of the West* 8 (1969): 327–54.

Wilder, D. W. *The Annals of Kansas.* Topeka: T. Dwight Thacher, Kansas Publishing House, 1886.

———. ''Where Kansans Were Born.'' *Kansas State Historical Society Collections* 9 (1905): 506–8.

Williams, John. ''A New Look at an Old Field.'' *Western Historical Quarterly* 9 (1978): 281–96.

Wilson, Hill. *A Biographical History of Eminent Men of the State of Kansas with Portraits Engraved Expressly for This Work.* Topeka, Kans.: Hal Lithographing Co., 1901.

———. ''Black Kettle's Last Raid—1868.'' *Kansas State Historical Society Collections* 8 (1904): 110–17.

Wilson, Paul. ''Reflections of Mike Sutton.'' *Journal of Kansas Bar Association* 45 (1976): 277.

Wise, Gene. *American Historical Explanations: A Strategy For Grounded Inquiry.* Homewood, Ill.: Dorsey Press, 1973.

Wood, Charles. ''C. D. Perry: Clark County Farmer and Rancher, 1884–1908.'' *Kansas Historical Quarterly* 39 (1973): 449–77.

———. ''Upbreeding Western Range Cattle: Notes on Kansas, 1880–1920.'' *Journal of the West* 16 (1977): 16–28.

Young, James. *The Washington Community, 1800–1828.* New York: Columbia University Press, 1966.

Young, Mary. ''The West and American Cultural Identity.'' *Western Historical Quarterly* 1 (1970): 137–61.

Index